REVISITING STAR STUDIES

REVISITING STAR STUDIES

Cultures, Themes and Methods

Edited by
Sabrina Qiong Yu and Guy Austin

Edinburgh University Press is one of the leading university presses in the UK. We publish academic books and journals in our selected subject areas across the humanities and social sciences, combining cutting-edge scholarship with high editorial and production values to produce academic works of lasting importance. For more information visit our website: edinburghuniversitypress.com

Edinburgh University Press Ltd
The Tun – Holyrood Road
12 (2f) Jackson's Entry
Edinburgh EH8 8PJ

First published in hardback by Edinburgh University Press 2017

Typeset in 10/12.5 pt Sabon by
Servis Filmsetting Ltd, Stockport, Cheshire
and printed and bound by CPI Group (UK) Ltd
Croydon, CR0 4YY

A CIP record for this book is available from the British Library

ISBN 978 1 4744 0431 0 (hardback)
ISBN 978 1 4744 4097 4 (paperback)
ISBN 978 1 4744 0432 7 (webready PDF)
ISBN 978 1 4744 0433 4 (epub)

CONTENTS

PART 3 STARS AND ETHNICITY

PART 4 STARS AND AGEING

PART 5 STARS AND AUDIENCES

PART 6 ABERRANT STARDOM

PART 7 AT THE MARGINS OF FILM STARDOM

FIGURES

ACKNOWLEDGEMENTS

Firstly, we would like to thank all our contributors for their commitment and patience. We would also like to thank the following for their very welcome help with the original *Revisiting Star Studies* conference in 2013, out of which many of these chapters emerged: Melanie Bell, Pam Cook, Ann Davies, Stephanie Dennison, Sheila Heppel, Sarah Leahy, Neepa Majumdar, Andrew Shail, Martin Shingler, Susan Smith, Ginette Vincendeau, Rosie White, Lydia Dan Wu, Yingjin Zhang, and all the other conference participants. Finally, our sincere gratitude goes to Edinburgh University Press, and in particular our editors Gillian Leslie and Richard Strachan for their persistent support.

INTRODUCTION
PERFORMING STARDOM: STAR STUDIES IN TRANSFORMATION AND EXPANSION

Sabrina Qiong Yu

Star studies, as a vibrant and elastic field, has been in constant revision and expansion since the 1990s, and this revision and expansion will undoubtedly continue. The current collection intends to contribute to this process and open up more discussions, mainly outside of the conventional scholarship of star studies. By revisiting, we mean testing boundaries, offering alternatives and challenging clichés. This opening chapter aims to address two key features of stardom – performativity and locality/translocality – in relation to existing research and also to the chapters in this collection.

Performativity of Stardom

Since the star became a subject of scholarly inquiry, critics have never stopped the attempt to define stars and stardom, whether it is 'the combination of myth and capital, of goddess and merchandise' (Morin 1960: 71), a 'powerless elite' (Alberoni 1962), an ideological site of reconciliation and resistance (Dyer 1979), the object of desire and identification (Gledhill 1991), a category of labour and a form of capital (McDonald 2000) or a cultural institution that 'justifies high reward' (King 2015). Among numerous words used to describe stars, what we come across most frequently are probably glamour, charisma and desire. Being glamorous and desirable has long been seen as the essential step into stardom.

Many stars discussed in the current volume, however, are neither glamorous nor desirable. Can they be seen as stars? To be more specific, when one is from an infamous genre such as pornography and morally stigmatised, is one a star? When one is a child who does not project sexual desirability, is one a star? When one comes from a socially and ethnically disadvantaged position and struggles to get mainstream recognition, is one a star? When one comes from a non-Hollywood cinema and is largely unknown to a global audience, is one a star? When one is not actually a human being but a creature who is deemed not expressive and self-aware, is one a star? Moreover, will a previous star continue to be a star when s/he no longer fits in with general definitions of the star? For example, when a star gets older and becomes less glamorous, is s/he still a star? When a star's face gets injured and loses her/his acclaimed beauty, is s/he still a star? When a star from a past era is unscrupulously appropriated and reconfigured by social media users, is s/he still a star?

To answer these questions, attention should firstly be paid to the fact that there has never been a clear set of criteria about what it means to be glamorous, charismatic or desirable apart from those defined by Hollywood stars. As Corey (2013: 27) points out, though, these are not universal concepts, and are viewed differently in different contexts, so cultural specificity should be taken into consideration. Indeed, in the past few decades, many works on stars around the world have clearly demonstrated that how a star is understood in Hollywood is not necessarily how they are understood in other cultures. In her influential book *Stars: Industry of Desire*, Gledhill defines stardom as 'a product of capitalism and the ideology of individualism' (1991, xiii). This definition not only assumes a homogenous origin of stardom in different cultural contexts, but also potentially excludes the exploration of the stars and the formation of stardom in non-capitalist (or previously non-capitalist) societies. For example, Hollywood stardom, with its emphasis on 'conspicuous consumption, material culture, consumer products, and visible lifestyles' (2009: 6), was antithetical to the project of nationalism in India in the first half of the twentieth century, according to Majumdar's study of Indian female stardom between the 1930s and the 1950s. Even within capitalist society, 'a certain incompatibility between the concept of stardom and a European sensibility' (Hedling 2009: 260) has been suggested, and the star was commented on by the French film director Jean-Pierre Melville as an 'American definition' (Melville 1971: 133, quoted in Hedling 2009).

Furthermore, is there only one definition of star/stardom within Hollywood? While mainstream Hollywood stars are marked by their glamour, charisma and desirability, how about those stars from independent films and cult films? In their recent anthology on cult film stardom, Egan and Thomas (2013) suggest that unconventionality and offbeat attraction are key to understanding cult stardom, whether a cult star makes his/her name in cult films or mainstream films. Cult stars and niche stars are often discussed in terms of their distance from mainstream or conventional stars, which perpetuates the dominance of mainstream stardom but nonetheless functions as a way to legitimate rather than to disqualify such stars and a different type of stardom. In a slight departure from Dyer's classic statement of the star as a combination of the ordinary and the extraordinary, Susan Hayward (2006), in her concise introduction to the key concepts in star studies, claims that the star is representative of both normality and 'acceptable' excess. As Hayward rightly points out, when a star transgresses normality, excess is quickly translated into deviancy and the star becomes a deviant. It is important to point out, however, that deviancy is not necessarily a denial of star status but part of star image. Instead of conforming to the conventional association of the star with glamour and success, and reinforcing the binary of the mainstream and the marginalised, this volume collectively seeks to expand the notion of stardom to include less glamorous, more troubling elements such as the ageing star, the 'crip' star, the porn star, and so on. We argue that disturbing aspects also construct part of star attraction and are sometimes in resonance with the audience's secretive or illegitimate desire. In short, we reject a fixed and Hollywood-centred definition of the star, and highlight performativity as a central notion of stardom that can be observed in multiple dimensions.

By performativity of stardom, we mean that stardom is like a masquerade, easily put on, changed and manipulated by the industry, but also by stars and audiences. Masquerade is defined as 'an action or appearance that is mere disguise or show' (Merriam-Webster online dictionary 2010). To put on a deceptive appearance and pretend to be someone you are not is fundamental to stars' performance both onscreen and offscreen, and to star image as a whole. As Kathleen Woodward observes, the notion of masquerade can involve 'submission to dominant social codes' and also 'resistance to them' (1989: 125). So does the notion of stardom. The star is regarded as a product predominantly made by the industry and media, so studies often describe stars as someone voluntarily or forcedly compliant with the manufacture of the industry or powerlessly submitting to media manipulation. This perception holds more truth probably to stars in the Hollywood studios era when most of them were bound with fix-term contracts with studios but takes little consideration of different cultural and industrial contexts, as well as the changing Hollywood environment. Contemporary Hollywood stars, according to King (2010: 15), 'have become producers and entrepreneurs' and therefore have more control over their own image. Outside Hollywood, some other factors, such as politics and morality, play a more important role in star-making (Majumdar 2009; Yu 2012b) than film industry and media. In compiling this collection, we would like to foreground the idea that stardom has always functioned as a masquerade, and stars have been actively participating in the making of their own image from the beginning, albeit to various extents, even for those stars from the studio era, exemplified by two case studies here on Anna May Wong and Montgomery Clift.

Ethnicity as masquerade

Yiman Wang's chapter explores early American-Chinese star Anna May Wong's self-reflexive enactment of the 'Oriental' (or other exotic roles) through her multi-faceted vocal performance (English with British accent, French, German and Taishan dialect) in a transnational context from Hollywood to Europe, as a way to ridicule the stereotypical roles imposed on her. By suggesting Wong's linguistic virtuosity as a form of satiric masquerade and a challenge to white supremacy, the chapter reveals an important notion of ethnicity as a masquerade and its importance in constructing the image of ethnic minority stars. Alongside language and accent, skin colour is another notable racial marker. Jaap Kooijman's chapter on Beyoncé and Diana Ross focuses on how 'blackface' and 'whitewashing' help shape the star image of two African-American superstars from two different eras. As Kooijman demonstrates, the practice of 'whitewashing' reveals how ethnicity has been used strategically by the industry to please mainstream 'white' audiences, but the stars themselves also skilfully play with skin colour – the symbol of their ethnicity – and reduce it to a pure masquerade, thereby challenging the crude dichotomy of the association of whiteness with artificiality and blackness with authenticity.

When Richardson discusses the treatment of the exotic and the representation of other cultures in Hollywood films, he points out that stereotyping and caricature (whether negative or positive) are legitimate and essential elements of cultural representation due to the reductive nature of representation that 'emphasizes certain characteristics at the expense of others' (2010: 10). Indeed, ethnic minority stars will have to endure distortions and stereotypes in their Hollywood adventure, but their ethnic identity can also be mobilised as a means of empowerment. For example, Phillips and Vincendeau recognise that European actors' accent is their greatest handicap in Hollywood stardom but also point out it was their 'major job asset and cultural capital' to provide 'colour' and 'tone' (2006: 12). In my examination of Chinese action star Jet Li's Hollywood career, I notice that by conforming to racial stereotypes, that is, taking up roles such as villain, killer and child-like man, Li's heroism is compromised, but his newly gained screen identities 'not only enriched his star persona and brought him new global fans, but opened up a broader range of roles for Li' (2012a: 125), which led to his later breakthrough to become one of the three kung fu stars to win Best Actor in the history of the prestigious Hong Kong Film Awards. In sum, while racial features such as accent, skin colour and body shape often function as an effective tool to perpetuate racial stereotypes and ethnic minority stars' marginalised position, many stars are fully aware of such pitfalls and have tried to engage with ethnicity as a masquerade and appropriate it in constructing their complex star persona.

Ageing as masquerade

Ageing is another type of masquerade relevant to stars, and its impact on stars has gained growing critical attention in recent years. The ageing star body is probably not the favourite of the industry, but it does not necessarily mark the end of one's stardom, as demonstrated by many case studies on ageing stars, including those in this collection. As Basting claims, ageing and old age are 'performative acts, both on- and offstage' (1998: 9). Ageing stars can survive and in fewer cases thrive if ageing is appropriated to their advantage. Bette Davis probably best embodies the notion of ageing as a masquerade. Martin Shingler argues that the longevity of Davis' film career was partly 'determined by her ability to perform age as well as to reinvent herself as she aged' (2015: 54). Davis took up unglamorous and old characters when she was still young, in Shingler's words, using 'a grotesquely aged mask to highlight her own youthfulness' (2015: 52), while later on in her career, instead of disguising her age on or off the screen, Davis displayed her old age in a darkly comic and unsympathetic way. Linda Berkvens' chapter on Barbara Stanwyck in this collection discloses a similar strategy. Just as Bette Davis made a generic shift from romantic drama to horror/thriller/exploitation, subsequently reinventing her star image, the ageing Stanwyck, as Berkvens argues, 'stripped off her petticoats' and extended her film career until well into the 1960s by performing wise-cracking, tough and unfeminine roles in B Westerns and establishing herself as a role model for mature women. Not unlike Davis' defiant attitude towards Hollywood stereotypes of ageing female stars, Berkvens delineates Stanwyck as a star who refused to dye her prematurely grey hair but turned it into part of her star image; who did not hesitate to play her age onscreen, including women older than herself; who never hid her real age from the public and instead advocated the advantages of getting older. As Berkvens emphasises, as a freelance star Stanwyck had more control of her own image. Through her on- and offscreen performance of ageing, Stanwyck was able to age successfully.

There is a common perception that ageing is less an issue for male stars than female stars, since appearance weighs much more in a female star's career. This explains why researchers focus heavily on ageing and female stars (Swinnen and Stotesbury 2012; Jermyn and Holmes 2015). But some recent works attest that despite the existence of gender inequality, male stars have to confront the challenges of ageing and old age as much as female stars. As Gates claims, 'the assumption – on the part of stars and society in general – is that aging lessens a man's masculinity' (2010: 279). It is probably harder for male stars to face an ageing and vulnerable body, especially for those stars who bank on their physical ability, action stars in particular whose performance requires fitness which is in decline when one gets older. But even for versatile male stars with acclaimed acting skills, ageing has proved a big challenge, as revealed by Sue Harris (2015) in her recent article in which she relates Gérard Depardieu's struggle with ageing-related issues such as obesity to the plight of an ageing, undereducated and politically frustrated element in French society. Lisa Purse's chapter on Tom Cruise adds one more important case study to the current interest in ageing male action stars, in addition to such works as Holmlund's examination of Jackie Chan's middle-aged Asian action body (2010) and Gates' study of the 1980s American action heroes, now ageing male stars such as Clint Eastwood, Sylvester Stallone, Bruce Willis and Harrison Ford, and different models of ageing (2010). By examining the physical performance of a range of ageing male action stars in post-2000 action films, Purse suggests an intense cultural negotiation over the ageing male body but makes the differentiation between Cruise, who defies the age-related decline narrative, and other stars who do not. Interestingly, all these three studies of ageing male stars reveal that by not acting their age and continuing to look physically capable and invincible, male action stars stay popular, which seems opposite to what Shingler and Berkvens observe in ageing female stars who actually act their age both onscreen and offscreen in order to maintain their star presence. This once again attests to the notion of ageing as a masquerade that can be skilfully employed to shape one's star persona.

Appearance as masquerade

The flexible and sometimes playful employment of ethnicity and ageing as masquerade exhibits the performativity of stardom. Another related and probably more visible masquerade of stardom is the star's appearance. Face and (to a lesser extent) body are the most important and identifiable property possessed by any film star. Although not every star builds his or her stardom on good looks, as Martin Shingler notices, 'the loss of such qualities as looks, voice and glamour [. . .] may account for a decline in popularity' (2012: 91). Successful ageing female stars, however, as discussed above, have proved this might not always be the case. Other chapters in this collection further demonstrate that a thoughtful alteration of facial and body features could be used as an effective strategy to reinvent one's star image. In her chapter on Montgomery Clift, Elisabetta Girelli examines Clift's bold decision to change his already battered looks for the worse and to present a highly disturbing and alienated image in *The Young Lions* (1958) after his car accident. Girelli analyses Clift's deliberate self-distortion as an act of subversive intervention in his own image and an explicit declaration of deviancy from the requirements and expectations of the Hollywood star system. The chapter thus questions what stardom is, and challenges the established norms of male stardom – which are represented by Clift's earlier star image and also his co-stars in *The Young*

Lions such as Marlon Brando and Dean Martin. Girelli's chapter provides a case study that a star's image can go against the pleasure of the spectator and be disturbing rather than pleasurable. After all, the quality of being glamorous, attractive and desirable that has been seen essential to stardom is merely a masquerade, albeit a more popularly adopted one, compared to masquerades associated with painful, aberrant or 'crip' (disabled) identity. This point is also taken up by Leon Hunt in his chapter on the Italian female star Silvana Mangano.

Arguing that Mangano was a reluctant diva, Hunt discusses her publicly expressed antipathy towards filmmaking, a radical reshaping of her previous voluptuous body that made her famous and desirable, and her later roles in arthouse films in which her glamour is stripped away and replaced with an almost grotesque appearance. In Hunt's view, the auteurs' cynical and playful attitude towards cinema's diva-making and the muting of stardom that often accompanies arthouse cinema result in this de-glamorising, but Mangano's own ambition of turning into a character actress is also commented on. Not unlike Clift's reconstruction of his own face as Noah in *The Young Lions*, Mangano transformed her once-sensuous body into a slender, elegant one, in order to make the transition to more serious arthouse films. Marginalised and underrated, largely due to her label as a *maggiorate*-type female star, seen as bankable only for the showcase of their highly sexualised bodies, Mangano uses her mutable figure and changing appearances to perform and defy the notion of glamour associated with post-war Italian female stars.

Appearance is especially important to child stars, often expressed in terms of how 'cute' they are. In his chapter on Indian child star Safary, Michael Lawrence analyses the importance and brevity of child stars' physical attractiveness and points out the cuteness vanishes as the child increases in size and loses their original features, so jeopardising her or his popularity. Lawrence then goes on to analyse two of his latest films in which Safary alters his facial features (using braces to correct his signature buck teeth in one film and wearing a prosthetic nose in another), and suggests reading it as 'a strategic response to the inevitable disappearance of the child star's cuteness' and a way to stretch his acting skills and grow into a serious actor. Indeed, as Pam Cook notes in her discussion of Nicole Kidman, 'actors are more likely to achieve award nominations if they display dedication to their craft by making themselves almost unrecognizable in portraying character' (2012: 62). Self-transformation of one's appearance (often into worse-looking), whatever the reasons behind it, has proved a fruitful means of overcoming disadvantages and regenerating one's star image. As a highly de-naturalising and performative strategy, it defies the traditional notions of stardom as attractive and glamorous, and reveals the mutability of star appearance. Star appearance has thus proved to be a powerful mode of performance.

Acting as masquerade

Compared to ethnicity, age and appearance, acting is the most obvious masquerade at stars' disposal to construct their star image. From Charles Affron's early work *Star Acting: Gish, Garbo, Davis* (1977), later on Karen Hollinger's study of Hollywood acting and the female stars (2006), to more recent case studies of individual star performance (Cook 2012; Smith 2012; Rees-Roberts and Waldron 2015), the importance of screen acting has always been recognised by star studies scholars. However, compared to other areas in star studies, the analysis of acting and performance is less prolific. Some have attributed this to Richard Dyer's seminal works on stars (1979; 1986), which are seen to have made stardom primarily an ideological issue and consequently rendered insignificant the examination of their acting. In addition, the long-term difficulty in describing, analysing and evaluating screen acting is probably another reason, along with a common assumption that stars are not good actors. The existing works on star acting either adopt a semiotic reading of the elements of acting (gestures, eyes, facial expressions), or articulate different acting styles (the Method, for example), or examine the intertextuality of star performance (Barry 1985; Naremore 1990; Carnicke 2003; Drake 2006; Hjort 2010; Raeburn and Shingler 2013). These approaches have proved productive in exploring the role of acting in the construction of star persona but present a rather narrow definition of star acting. Acting, as a main asset and skill possessed by film stars, has been central to all kinds of star performance. In this collection we seek to discuss acting in a more comprehensive way. It includes both more conventional facial and vocal acting and less-valued physical acting (for example, the performance of action, singing or sex), both human acting and non-human acting, and both acting as the character onscreen and acting as a star offscreen.

Yingjin Zhang's chapter on acclaimed Chinese star Tony Leung uses repetition and dark play as two dominant tropes to discuss Leung's star performance in two award-winning films. According to Zhang, Leung employs a tactic of performance-as-repetition to enact a pensive and self-effacing star persona in *In the Mood for Love*, while in *Lust, Caution* he offers a rule-breaking and controversial performance as troubled and violent wartime collaborator Mr Yee. By engaging with dark play – which is characterised by subversion, deceit, excess and disruption – and highly explicit sex scenes, Leung not only subverts the deep-rooted male stereotype of the collaborator in Chinese cinema, but also reinvents himself as a sympathetic and vulnerable villain. Similarly examining star performance, but from another cultural context and another aspect of acting, Kiranmayi Indraganti presents a case study of musical stardom in Indian cinema. Indraganti argues that film song has become the face of many Indian film stars and a distinct vehicle to deploy stardom, and introduces star-song performative spaces as the site for star-making and star consumption. The chapter discusses film song as a mediated idiom deriving from global and local methods of performance, and singing and performing film songs as an ideal way to maintain Indian-ness while reaching out for a national and global audience. Indeed, performance for a song onscreen, just like performing martial arts onscreen (Yu 2012a), instead of being dismissed as a less-esteemed type of performance, should be seen as a culture-specific acting skill that has contributed to unique ways of star-making in a particular cultural context, warranting further exploration.

Apart from non-Western acting styles, non-human acting is another area that is rarely acknowledged and studied. While star studies have benefited enormously from the analysis of screen acting, this analysis has hardly been extended to children or non-human subjects. In his article on celebrity and acting, Quinn suggests 'animals and children, notoriously, seem never to be quite sure they're in a play, and that constitutes the largest part of their delightfulness' (1990: 155). Lawrence's chapter on Indian child star Safary has shown this perception is not always accurate, while Stella Hockenhull's study of the canine star Uggie further challenges this view. The chapter provides a detailed reading of Uggie's performance in *The Artist* that contributes to his loyal, heroic and endearing screen image, and an examination of the ways media and industry promote him to super-individual status. Hockenhull convincingly introduces the notion of animal as star and opens up a series of important questions related to animal stardom such as animal acting and ethical considerations on animal celebrity ownership and welfare.

While the star's offscreen existence has been given much critical attention and is seen as an indivisible part of star persona, little research has acknowledged the fact that the star also acts outside the film, on TV shows, commercials and other media forms, so offscreen performance is just as important as onscreen performance in constructing star image. Pam Cook's chapter looks at Nicole Kidman's enactment of commodity stardom and the acting techniques she deploys in her multimedia appearances, including talk shows, magazine fashion shoots, celebrity tabloid gossip, commercials and philanthropy. Cook contends that the study of acting and performance should go beyond the confines of the film text to examine 'the poses, gestures, costume, make-up, props, scripted dialogue and photographic *mise en scène* that constitute the star interview and photo shoot', for example. Cook's opening chapter foregrounds the importance of the performativity of stardom itself, a concept so fundamental to star phenomena, which is reiterated and elaborated in all the chapters of this collection.

In a similar vein, Smith and Taylor-Harman in their chapter examine James Deen's extra-cinematic performance as a way to redeem his reputation as a porn star. Pornography is regarded as 'the most culturally derided genre' (Wimmer

2013: 210). Unsurprisingly, the stars associated with this genre are marginal-ised and stigmatised, not being deemed 'real' stars and receiving little academic attention. For example, made famous by soft-core films but not a hard-core porn star, French/Dutch actress Sylvia Kristel nevertheless illustrates this cul-turally disparaged stardom, as Leila Wimmer's case study (2013) vividly shows (see also Austin 2003). Despite being the top-grossing female actress of all time in France and having a strong international presence, Kristel is a neglected figure in star studies due to her label as 'an excessively sexualized type of femi-ninity' and 'her association with the abject genre of soft-core' (Wimmer 2013: 209). The situation is worse for porn performers, especially male porn stars, as they are simply seen as stand-ins for the male viewers. However, Smith and Taylor-Harman draw attention to the previously unacknowledged physical and acting skills involved in doing sex for the camera, by analysing Deen's multi-layered performance style in his pornographic scenes. More importantly, they look at Deen's effort to expand his stardom outside his film performance which is little valued, by discussing his involvement in adult industry activism and various charity work, and his use of social media and engagement with his fans as a way to supplement or correct his onscreen persona. Deen, via a skilful performance both onscreen and offscreen, conforms to while sometimes undermining the conventions of (male) porn stardom and assumes a 'worrying' mainstream popularity.

Camp as masquerade

In their chapter, Smith and Taylor-Harman reveal how a network of female teenage bloggers trade Deen videos and post candid photographs to express their desire for Deen. By circulating and appropriating Deen's star image and allowing a marginalised porn star to cross over to the mainstream, fans' power in star-making is undeniable. The role that the audience (fans included) plays in constructing star images has received some scholarly attention (Stacey 1994; DeAngelis 2001; Mosley 2003) but has never been in the spotlight. For particular types of stardom, cult stardom for example, fans can play a more decisive role than the industry and media. According to Matt Hills, the birth of a cult star is often strongly linked to 'subcultural audience discernment, recognition and valorization rather than marketing-led or industry/PR-related constructions of stardom' (2013: 22). With the proliferation of electronic com-munication channels such as YouTube, Twitter, online forums and blogs, the amount of star discourse and more direct interaction between stars and fans has been significantly increased. The new media, as King (2015) notices, have vastly extended the public sphere and generated new forms of fan discourse and activities. As a result, the boundary between the private life and the public image of a star has been further broken down, and fans have assumed more power in star construction. The 'dispersal of authorship in star discourse' McDonald (2000: 115) observed more than fifteen years ago is certainly continuing and deepening.

Among different strategies deployed by fans in their participation in star-making, a popular one is camp. As Susan Sontag defines it, camp appreciates artifice in a playful, ironic and parodic way, therefore converting 'the serious into the frivolous' (1964, reprinted 1966: 276). Camp and parody are characterised by transgression, subversion and queerness, and often used to challenge 'the normalized boundaries of the social order' (Harries 1990: 14). It is therefore not surprising for both stars and fans to favour camp and parody as strategies to exploit or subvert stardom largely defined by glamour, charisma and extraordinariness. However, the relationship between camp and stardom has not been given much critical attention after a couple of early attempts. In his second book on stars, Dyer explores gay audiences' campy identification with Hollywood female star Judy Garland as a gay icon, and makes camp 'a characteristically gay way of handling the values, images and products of the dominant culture through irony, exaggeration, trivialisation, theatricalisation and an ambivalent making fun of and out of the serious and respectable' (1986: 176). Dan M. Harries (1990) applies Bakhtin's carnival theory and the theory of camp to his discussion of Divine, a Hollywood male actor playing female characters. Harries identifies the multi-levelled operation of parody – a parody of gender roles, a parody of Hollywood stardom and its notion of glamour, and a self-parody of his own established star persona – in the construction of Divine's star persona marked by the challenge to gender normality. Recently, 'certain ideas (camp, queerness, entertainment as irony) that relate to stardom and its media production and once were subversive have inhabited the mainstream' (Kallioniemi, Kärki et al. 2007), therefore demanding more critical attention. Two chapters included in this anthology eloquently demonstrate camp as a powerful tool and a masquerade to construct or deconstruct stardom, now more used by fans, gay and straight alike, across the world.

Anna Malinowska's chapter provides an overview of the history and forms of camp's engagement with Hollywood stardom, and examines exploitative fandom in the practice of the camp reuse (or 'abuse') of Hollywood star images in post-communist Poland, using the drag queens of a realist Polish novel and their relation to Alexis Carrington-Colby/Joan Collins of *Dynasty* as a case study. This chapter brings to light camp as an alternative form of star-making which, while full of admiration for traditional star images, makes a blasphemous incorporation and transposition of the Hollywood model. Malinowska argues that by 'taking stars' mainstream images to the margins of culture, camp exploits the glamorous and the sublime of a star and destabilises the idea of stardom itself'. The distance between Hollywood and Poland is not just cultural or geographical – in this case it is also political, since the two blocs (East/West) were ideologically opposed in the Cold War. Non-Western camp travesty of Western star images thus operates at many levels and adds a political relevance to camp engagement with stardom. Malinowska's compelling study shows that although Hollywood stars are produced under the North American star system, Hollywood stardom is not a fixed entity and not ultimately decided by Hollywood but by audiences around the world, who consume it within different local contexts. This practice has existed since the beginning of the history of stardom. For example, in his book on early Japanese stardom, Hideaki Fujiki argues Hollywood stars became pervasive in Japan in the 1910s, but 'images of American stars did not necessarily circulate, become popular, and gain meaning and value in Japan in the same way as they did in the United States' (2013: 7). Camp can therefore be seen as a masquerade of an alternative stardom, produced mainly by fan discourse and activities.

Similarly focusing on fans' authorship of star images, Niamh Thornton's chapter on YouTube fans' activities of creating the star text of three Mexican male stars from the 1930s to the 1950s suggests that fans are curators and amateur creators of the star discourse and have developed their own aesthetics in creating new meanings of stars who do not have an onscreen presence anymore. Social media, YouTube in particular in this case – described as a 'transient fan archive', in which original star texts are reconfigured – has empowered fans to exploit and reconstruct star images. Thornton's earlier work (2010) on the online stardom of two Mexican female stars from the same era provides an interesting reference point for the current chapter. In the former, by considering fan vids on YouTube from fans around the world, Thornton analyses the way fans manipulate and change the female star texts by reordering, restyling and appropriating them in highly individual ways. Thornton notices there is a clear gender difference in fans' treatment of star discourse, that is, male stars receive much less attention than their female contemporaries; fan curation of male star content is less creative and more respectful. Although the term 'camp' does not appear in Thornton's chapter, and although a less playful way of treating male stars than female stars among fans can be observed, camp is still characteristic of fans' engagement with, and online creation of, star texts.

As shown in this critical overview of the existing research in star studies and the works in this collection, the film star is a culturally and historically contingent notion, rejecting any homogenous or fixed definition. While the study of previously dismissed, marginalised or overlooked types of stardom, such as 'cripped' stardom, porn stardom, child stardom and animal stardom, can effectively expand the scope of star studies, it is equally important to constantly question the centrality of the notions of pleasure, glamour and attraction in star studies, a still largely Hollywood-oriented research field. By foregrounding the performativity of stardom, we contend that the orthodox definitions of stardom can be challenged, defied and expanded by stars and fans alike. Stars and fans have played a bigger role in star-making than previously acknowledged, because they have been actively engaging with different types of masquerade, probably more so now than before due to a fast-changing industry and communication landscape.

Diffusion or disappearance of star studies?

After the discussion of 'what is a star?', the next question naturally would be 'what is star studies?'. Star studies, as a booming field, has grown tremendously over the past three decades and demonstrated itself as one of the most effective critical tools to engage with the world of cinema and beyond. Meanwhile, the study of star phenomena has gone beyond film, and rapidly expanded into other media or non-media discourses, as evidenced by the rise of 'Celebrity Studies' (Marshall 1997; Holmes and Redmond 2006). While there is an arguably clear differentiation between star studies and celebrity studies, many subjects discussed in both fields combine the identity of film star and celebrity. The list is long, from Marilyn Monroe and Elizabeth Taylor to George Clooney and Angelina Jolie, to name a few. However, there seems to exist a danger that star studies could be incorporated into celebrity studies. It has been suggested that stars should be understood as a subcategory of the celebrity (Marshall 1997), and celebrity studies, as an expansion of star studies previously associated primarily with film stars, has not only widened the scope of analysis by including sport stardom, TV stardom, music stardom, etc., but also opened up more critical and methodological approaches (Holmes and Negra 2011).

While these claims are justified to various extents and in certain contexts, I would like to suggest that instead of being considered a subcategory of celebrity, film stardom is a distinct type of stardom, just as celebrity is another type of stardom. Barry King proposes a useful differentiation between stardom and celebrity by pointing out the former refers to renown, 'a condition of fame that rests on excellence in a particular field of human endeavour', and the latter means 'being widely known, without any necessary or demonstrable link to specific achievements' (2015: 5). However, King also argues that, instead of being seen as a degeneration, the celebrity is the 'fundamental category of stardom' (2015: 196). Film star and celebrity are not two mutually exclusive terms, but not always exchangeable either. A film star can be a celebrity and vice versa. But a film star does not have to be a celebrity, which is often the case outside of the Hollywood system. For example, in Maoist China the notions of stars associated with glamour, individualism and capitalism were firmly rejected. 'Red stars' of Socialist China were a product of communist ideology and could establish their stardom solely on their screen roles (Lu 2010; Yu 2012b). Lacking publicity and an offscreen existence, these stars can hardly have been considered as celebrities. If film star is seen as a distinctive category, paralleled with celebrity, film star studies should similarly not be considered as a subcategory of celebrity studies. The study of film stardom has its own sets of research questions and priorities, which might or might not apply to study of other types of stardom.

Egan and Thomas argue that the conventional boundaries of film stardom have a limited perspective, and consequently film stardom has become 'a comparative point with which to investigate other modes of fame and to examine key features of contemporary celebrity culture that seem to offer deviations and digressions from the conventionality of the "film star"' (2013: 5–6). All chapters in this collection are challenging such conventional boundaries of film stardom. Indeed, those boundaries have been constantly breached and expanded by new research in the field. More than merely being a comparative point for the study of other kinds of fame, the study of film stardom has the power to reinvigorate itself and redefine the concept of star and stardom. As Martin Shingler argues, 'since the 1970s, star studies has become an important branch of film studies precisely because of its capacity to reinvent itself and embrace new areas of investigation and methodology' (2012: 35). In addition to constantly bringing into light various types of previously under-researched star texts, the current star studies are also characterised by a visible interdisciplinary approach, which has effectively transformed and expanded the field in unexpected ways, as the chapters in this collection perfectly illustrate.

An increasing focus on performance studies in recent star studies is visible in many chapters, especially Zhang's chapter on Tony Leung, which shows that star studies can benefit from performance studies' approaches and concepts, enabling us to 'further explore a wider range of cinematic and performative tactics that challenge our entrenched habit of signification and interpretation and open up spaces for new alterations and alternatives'. Our chapters also demonstrate fruitful interaction between genre studies and star studies. The star has been associated with genre from the very beginning of the cinema, and the star's interaction with genre has been a productive field of inquiry. However, most works so far have focused on the study of mainstream Hollywood genres, such as melodrama and action cinema. In this collection, in addition to the continuing attention to such genres as action cinema (Purse) and the Western (Berkvens), we also see Hunt's examination of Mangano and the episode film, which was prevalent in French and Italian cinema in the 1960s and 1970s; Smith and Taylor-Harman's investigation into Deen and pornography; and Indraganti's discussion of Indian stars and Bollywood musicals. The exploration of genre's role in star-making has been extended to a wider cultural context as well as to marginalised genres. Furthermore, Girelli's chapter refreshingly applies crip theory to the analysis of Clift's star image in his post-accident film, hence signalling one of the first attempts to engage with disability studies in star studies. Hockenhull's chapter opens up debate concerning animal stardom within a framework of performance theory and critical animal studies. Thornton's chapter introduces 'online remediated star studies' by using social media (YouTube) as a digital archive and invaluable resource for researchers of stardom and fandom. The interdisciplinary method is also manifested in the chapters where stardom is studied in relation to fandom (Thornton, Malinowska), songs and sound (Kooijman, Wang, Indraganti), and multimediality (Cook, Lawrence). The current collection undoubtedly expands star studies to a wider range of critical disciplines, but star studies, as an elastic field and a powerful critical tool, has always drawn upon theories and methods from different disciplines, to reveal rich layers of meaning produced by stars, fans and film texts.

LOCALITY AND TRANSLOCALITY OF STARDOM

Writing this introductory chapter provides a good opportunity to look back at my journey of researching stars and stardom in the past ten years. Starting with a PhD thesis, later turned into a book (2012a, 2015), on transnational action star Jet Li, my interest naturally extends to Chinese stardom as a whole and other transnational Chinese stars. To address the former, I propose the notion of star vulnerability, manifested as culturally despised, morally suspicious and politically subordinated, as a main framework to understand Chinese stardom (2012b). In my discussions of transnational Chinese stardom and performance (2014, 2015), I suggest we should explore a transnational star's career in both Hollywood and his/her home country to reveal how these two aspects 'interact with, influence and determine one another, thereby mutually shaping the star status and star image of a transnational star' (2015: 105). In these past works I proposed to, on the one hand, define national stardom in a more distinctive and definitive way rather than treat it as merely a variation on the theme of Hollywood stardom; on the other hand, to examine transnational stardom in a truly transnational vein, not solely measured by one's Hollywood presence and success. While these arguments still stand, and star studies continues to produce inspiring works in the areas of national stardom and transnational stardom, in this chapter I would like to suggest a new way of looking at stardom beyond the existing national/transnational model.

In media and critical discourse, we hear about Hollywood stars, national stars, transnational stars, international stars, global stars, Western stars, East Asian stars, European stars, African stars, Latin American stars, Indian stars, Chinese stars, French stars, and so on. Among all these designations, the common patterns are 1) whether one is a Hollywood or non-Hollywood star, and 2) whether one is a national, regional or international/global star. The former attests to the dominance of Hollywood stars and the latter conforms to the geopolitical ways in which we discuss cultural products around the world. Firstly, I want to problematise Hollywood-centrism inherent in this conventional dichotomy of Hollywood stars and national stars (or world stars). Many critics have noted the tendency in anglophone film studies towards 'a hierarchical division between Hollywood as the universal standard and national cinemas as the alternative to this standard' (Fujiki 2013: 16). This observation indeed applies to the study of stars.

From Dyer onwards, stardom in essence is perceived as a Hollywood phenomenon and defined decisively by Hollywood stars. Stars from other cultures are seen as imitations of Hollywood stars. In the past two decades, numerous studies on stars from Asia, Europe and Latin America have provided a rich amendment to a homogenous Hollywood-dominated star world. Fisher and Landy, however, argue that even in these works, 'the specter of Hollywood looms large', and 'Hollywood has played a key role in shaping star images in numerous other cultures' (2004: 7). Their argument has not been outdated. In his latest work, King defines a film star as 'a species of the genus actor that is epitomized in the popular imagination by Hollywood' (2015: 6), while stars from other national cinemas such as Indian cinema make sense by being compared to Hollywood stardom. Although King claims that he only uses Hollywood stars as one critical case to explore the process of star-making and the nature of fame, the implication is still that Hollywood stardom represents the standard and something to be modelled, and therefore understanding Hollywood stardom is key to understanding stardom.

While the above perceptions hold much truth, I contend they also indicate a long-term ignorance of the fact that stardom is primarily formed in specific social, political and cultural contexts, and is not necessarily influenced by the Hollywood star system. Researchers on French stardom (Abel 1998; Vincendeau 2000) have challenged the idea that film stardom originated in America in 1910 by pointing out the formation of a star system in France at around the same time or even earlier. Chinese and Indian cinemas also produced their own stars from the early era of their cinema in the 1920s, with distinctive cultural characteristics, when there was not much interaction with the outside world (Majumdar 2009; Farquhar and Zhang 2010). It is not sufficient to assume all other stardoms are just mimicry or variants of Hollywood stardom, sometimes deviating from but ultimately conforming to the mechanisms of Hollywood stardom. In order to shake the seemingly unshakable Hollywood-centric approach to film stardom, we must cast off the deep-rooted habit of epistemologically privileging Hollywood stars and the Hollywood star system. To achieve that, I propose to replace the term national stardom with local stardom.

If the concept of nation as an imagined community is more ingrained in the West, it is less applicable in other regions such as Asia, Africa and the Middle

East, where the notion of nationhood is more slippery and complicated. As a result, the application of national stardom in these territories is more problematic than in their Western counterparts. For example, as a former British colony and now special administrative region of China, Hong Kong used to be famous for its production of film stars who were popular across the East Asian region. But can Hong Kong stardom be seen as a form of national stardom? Another good example is Ri Koran (Li Xianglan, 1920–2014), who was ethnically Japanese but raised in China, with her Japanese origins concealed for a long time. She commenced her film career and gained popularity at the end of the 1930s in Manchukuo, a Japanese colony in Northern China. As Fujiki suggests, her fame later 'extended beyond Manchukuo and Japan throughout the Japanese empire, which included Korea, Taiwan, and Shanghai' (2013: 2). Due to this complex ethnical and geopolitical background, it is very hard to decide whether Ri is a Chinese star or a Japanese star. National stardom has difficulty in explaining stardom built in territories that are not easily defined as nation-states, but also in the nations where several cinemas and stardoms coexist. For instance, under the umbrella of Indian stars, there are Hindi stars, Telugu stars and Tamil stars with distinctive characteristics attached to each of these categories. Even for European star images, Downing and Harris think a national stardom approach is insufficient, as European stars 'tend to float across a series of national cinemas', while 'bearing the weight of representing their own nationality' (2007: 7). Furthermore, the term national stardom easily lends itself to the construction of national stereotypes and the subsequent projection of such stereotypes onto the stars from that nation. As Soila argues, national stars either confirm the alleged national qualities in a positive or negative way or deviate from them by 'embodying the "other" of a presumed national stereotype' (2009: 9).

To deconstruct the binary of Hollywood stardom vs national stardom which perpetuates the divide of centre vs periphery, we support a polycentric approach, as advocated by Shohat and Stam, and agree that 'the world has many dynamic cultural locations, many vantage points' (Shohat and Stam 1994: 48). In other words, rather than positing a centre (in this case, Hollywood), against which, either explicitly or implicitly, the culture of other places is evaluated, a multiplicity of places, all treated as equal, should be borne in mind. With its impressive range of stars from sixteen different cultures, *Stars in World Cinemas* (Bandhauer and Royer 2015) foregrounds such a polycentric approach, 'with no privileged position being given to any one star or community' (2), and with a desire to shift the primary focus of star studies away from Hollywood and examine stardom from local perspectives. Bandhauer and Royer highlight the notion of the local by arguing that 'stars are firmly situated in the local' and constructed by 'local politics and ideologies, film industries, linguistic contexts' (3). I would like to expand this notion and propose to replace national stardom with local stardom. As Hayward argues, 'stars are signs of indigenous cultural codes' and 'gestures, words, intonations, attitudes, postures' are all culturally generated, 'affirming the plurality of the cultures' (2006: 376). By advocating the concept of local stardom, I hope to emphasise the locality of stardom, and encourage the discussion of culture-specific star phenomena as an independent category, rather than as a variation or supplement of Hollywood stardom. In this optic, locality is crucial but, with the proviso that we remain aware of geopolitical power differentials impacting on stardom, our conception is non-hierarchical (no one place or culture is set above another). And indeed, Hollywood stars are firstly local stars as well, produced by the powerful machine of the Hollywood film industry. The fact that they are more visible on the global stage does not mean that they are not located in a local film industry, culture and society.

To some extent, the notion of transnational stardom shares national stardom's privileging of Hollywood stardom. Although only recently has more academic attention been paid to transnational stardom, stars' transnational movement and the transnational circulation of star texts are century-old phenomena. Meeuf and Raphael (2013) argue that it is impossible to understand stardom within the singular scale of the nation, while Soila (2009) stresses stardom should always be studied in transnational contexts as there are many shared features across different cultures. However, as I argue elsewhere, transnational stardom is a predominantly Hollywood phenomenon (Yu 2014). In the preface to a section on European and Asian stars, Fischer and Landy claim that 'any discussion of the phenomenon of stardom in a transnational context must take into account the actual and spectral role of Hollywood' (2004: 57). Similarly, Bandhauer and Royer contend, Meeuf and Raphael's book on transnational stardom shows that the concept of the transnational is very useful in an understanding of stars' mobility and the cross-cultural dynamics of celebrity cultures, but that 'Hollywood is still considered to be at the centre of the transnational mobility of stars' (2). To overcome this Hollywood-centrism inherent to the exploration of transnational stardom and to correspond to my proposal of 'local stardom', I suggest using the notion of translocal stardom to scrutinise the travel of stars and star texts beyond the local context.

Although Freitag and Oppen think translocality as a descriptive tool is 'more adapted to the specific realities of Africa, Asia and the Middle East than related terms established with regard to the West' (2010: 4), I see no reason why 'translocal' or 'translocality' cannot be used to discuss Western realities. As Freitag and Oppen suggest, 'central to the notion of translocality is a holistic perspective on mobilities, movements and flows, and the way in which these dynamics produce connectedness between different scales' (8). Based on this perception, Greiner and Sakdapolrak (2013) argue that a translocal perspective can overcome the limitations of nationalist historiographies and facilitate a non-Eurocentric understanding of global history. The notion of translocality therefore particularly suits our aim to envision an equal and mutually beneficial relationship between different local stardoms (including Hollywood stardom), and to address those transgressions of boundaries beyond the scope of nation-states. Translocality of stardom is notably present across the chapters in this collection.

Indraganti's chapter explores the role of song in constructing 'post-millennium India stardom across Hindi, Telugu and other film industries with thriving businesses globally'. Focusing on Telugu stars in particular, she argues that Indian film song allows the star to be relocated across cultural spaces in a vast country like India. Malinowska's chapter discusses the translocal flow of iconography (from Hollywood to Poland) and analyses the use of camp in the post-communist Eastern bloc as a means of accessing 'Western' star iconography. Such imagery is repositioned in a form of everyday life which is geographically, culturally and politically far removed from the USA. Wang's chapter shows the complexity of translocal flows, in the USA/Europe/China itineraries of Anna May Wong's stardom and reception (her identity is perceived as variable depending on who the audience is). Thornton's case study of the local Mexican stars and the global platform YouTube is an exploration of flows between local and translocal spaces in the creation, re-creation and consumption of star images. The translocal flows examined in this collection include flows within the same nation, between different continents and countries, or between real and virtual worlds. To discuss star phenomena via a local/translocal dimension has proved a particularly productive approach in the current anthology and we are confident in its continuing potential to produce exciting work in star studies.

With almost half of the chapters in the collection on Hollywood stars, we acknowledge Hollywood as a particularly active place for star creation. But the organisation of the chapters aims to break the conventional dichotomies between Hollywood and non-Hollywood, the West and the East, the past and the present. Our chapters are categorised instead around themes, as indicated by the title of each section. By so doing, we want to emphasise that Hollywood stardom is also one type of local stardom and needs to be discussed around the same issues that are relevant to stars in other cultures, such as performance, pleasure/displeasure and transgression. In sum, I hope we have achieved the following in this chapter and this collection as a whole: first, a destabilising and deconstruction of the notion of stardom associated with glamour and desirability by highlighting the performativity of stardom; and second, a decentring and de-dichotomising of traditional star studies tailored for the study of Hollywood stars by introducing the new critical mode of local/translocal stardom.

BIBLIOGRAPHY

Abel, Richard (1998), *The Cine Goes to Town: French Cinema, 1986–1914*, Oakland: University of California Press.

Affron, Charles (1977), *Star Acting: Gish, Garbo, Davis*, New York: Dutton.

Alberoni, Francesco (1972), 'The Powerless "Elite": Theory and Sociological Research on the Phenomenon of the Stars', trans. Denis McQuail, in D. McQuail (ed.), *Sociology of Mass Communications*, London: Penguin, pp. 75–98.

Austin, Guy (2003), *Stars and Stardom in Modern French Cinema*, London: Edward Arnold.

Bandhauer, Andrea and Michelle Royer (eds) (2015), *Stars in World Cinema: Screen Icons and Star Systems Across Cultures*, London and New York: I. B. Tauris.

Basting, A. Davis (1998), *The Stages of Age: Performing Age in Contemporary American Culture*, Ann Arbor: The University of Michigan Press.

Carnicke, S. Marie (2003), 'From Acting Guru to Hollywood Star: Lee Strasberg as Actor', in Thomas Austin and Martin Barker (eds), *Contemporary Hollywood Stardom*, London: Hodder, pp. 118–34.

Cook, Pam (2012), *Nicole Kidman*, London: Palgrave Macmillan.

Corey Creekmur, quoted in 'A Panel Discussion on Transnational Stardom', in Meeuf, Russell and Raphael Raphael (2013), *Transnational Stardom: International Celebrity in Film and Popular Culture*, London: Palgrave Macmillan, pp. 19–28.

DeAngelis, Michael (2001), *Gay Fandom and Crossover Stardom: James Dean, Mel Gibson, and Keanu Reeves*, Durham, NC and London: Duke University Press.

Drake, Philip (2006), 'Reconceptualizing Screen Performance', *Journal of Film and Video* 58:1–2, 84–94.

Downing, Lisa and Sue Harris (2007), 'Introduction', in Downing and Harris (eds), *From Perversion to Purity: The Stardom of Catherine Deneuve*, Manchester: Manchester University Press, pp. 1–13.

Dyer, Richard (1979), *Stars*, London: British Film Institute.

— (1986), *Heavenly Bodies: Film Stars and Society*, London: British Film Institute.

Egan, Kate and Sarah Thomas (eds) (2013), *Cult Film Stardom: Offbeat Attractions and Processes of Cultification*, London: Palgrave Macmillan.

Fischer, Lucy and Marcia Landy (eds) (2004), *Stars: The Film Reader*, New York and London: Routledge.

Freitag, Ulrike and Achim von Oppen (2010), 'Introduction: "Translocality": An Approach to Connection and Transfer in Area Studies', in *Translocality: The Study of Globalising Processes from a Southern Perspective*, Leiden and Boston, MA: Brill, pp. 1–24.

Fujiki, Hideaki (2013), *Making Personas: Transnational Film Stardom in Modern Japan*, Cambridge, MA: Harvard University Press.

Gates, Philippa (2010), 'Acting His Age? The Resurrection of the '80s Action Heroes and Their Aging Stars', *Quarterly Review of Film and Video* 27:4, 276–89.

Gledhill, Christine (1991), *Stardom: Industry of Desire*, London: Routledge.

Greiner, Clemens and Patrick Sakdapolrak (2013), 'Translocality: Concepts, Applications and Emerging Research Perspectives', *Geography Compass* 7:5, 373–84.

Harries, Dan M. (1990), 'Camping with Lady Divine: Star Persona and Parody', *Quarterly Review of Film and Video* 12:1–2, 13–22.

Harris, Sue (2015), 'Gérard Depardieu and the abject star body', *Screen* 56:3, 319–34.

Hayward, Susan (2006), *Cinema Studies: The Key Concepts* (3rd edn), London and New York: Routledge.

Hedling, Olof (2009), 'Possibilities of Stardom in European Cinema Culture', in Tytti Soila (ed.), *Stellar Encounters: Stardom in Popular European Cinema*, New Barnet: John Libbey Publishing Ltd, pp. 254–64.

Hills, Matt (2013), 'Cult Movies With and Without Cult Stars: Differentiating Discourses of Stardom', in Kate Egan and Sarah Thomas (eds), *Cult Film Stardom*, London: Palgrave Macmillan.

Hjort, Mette (2010), 'Ruan Lingyu: Reflections on an Individual Performance Style', in Mary Farquhar and Yingjin Zhang (eds), *Chinese Film Stars*, New York and London: Routledge.

Hollinger, Karen (2006), *The Actress: Hollywood Acting and the Female Star*, New York and London: Routledge.

Holmes, Su and Sean Redmond (eds) (2006), *Framing Celebrity: New Directions in Celebrity Culture*, New York and London: Routledge.

Holmes, Su and Diane Negra (eds) (2011), *In the Limelight and Under the Microscope: Forms and Functions of Female Celebrity*, New York: Continuum.

Holmlund, Chris (2010), 'Celebrity, ageing and Jackie Chan: middle-aged Asian in Transnational action', *Celebrity Studies* 1:1, 96–112.

Jermyn, Deborah and Su Holmes (eds) (2015), *Women, Celebrity & Cultures of Ageing: Freeze Frame*, London: Palgrave Macmillan.

Kallioniemi, Kari, Kimi Kärki, Janne Mäkelä and Hannu Salmi (eds) (2007), *History of Stardom Reconsidered*, Turku: International Institute for Popular Culture. Available as an ebook at http://iipc.utu.fi/reconsidered/.

King, Barry (1985), 'Articulating Stardom', *Screen* 26:5, 27–51.

— (2015), *Taking Fame to Market: On the Pre-History and Post-History of Hollywood Stardom*, London: Palgrave Macmillan.

Lu, Xiaoning (2010), 'Zhang Riufang: Modelling the Socialist Red Star', in Mary Farquhar and Yingjin Zhang (eds), *Chinese Film Stars*, pp. 97–107.

McDonald, Paul (2000), *The Star System: Hollywood's Production of Popular Identities*, London and New York: Wallflower Press.

— (2013), *Hollywood Stardom*, Chichester: Wiley-Blackwell.

Majumdar, Neepa (2009), *Wanted Cultured Ladies Only! Female Stardom and Cinema in India 1930–1950*, Urbana and Chicago: University of Illinois Press.

Marshall, P. David (1997), *Celebrity and Power: Fame in Contemporary Culture*, Minneapolis and London: University of Minnesota Press.

Meeuf, Russell and Raphael Raphael (2013), *Transnational Stardom: International Celebrity in Film and Popular Culture*, London: Palgrave Macmillan.

Merriam-Webster's online dictionary, 'Masquerade', available at http://www.merriam-webster.com/dictionary/masquerade, last accessed 13 June 2016.

Morin, Edgar (1960), *The Stars: An Account of the Star System in the Motion Pictures*, New York: Evergreen Profile Book.

Moseley, Rachel (2003), *Growing Up with Audrey Hepburn: Text, Audience, Resonance*, Manchester: Manchester University Press.

Phillips, Alastair and Ginette Vincendeau (2006), 'Film Trade, Global Culture and Transnational Cinema: An Introduction', in Phillips and Vincendeau (eds), *Journeys of Desire: European Actors in Hollywood*, London: British Film Institute, pp. 3–18.

Quinn, Michael L. (1990), 'Celebrity and the Semiotics of Acting', *New Theatre Quarterly* 6:22, 154–61.

Rees-Roberts, Nick and Darren Waldron (eds) (2015), *Alain Delon: Style, Stardom and Masculinity*, New York and London: Bloomsbury Publishing.

Richardson, Michael (2010), *Otherness in Hollywood Cinema*, London: Continuum International Publishing.

Shingler, Martin (2012), *Star Studies: A Critical Guide*, London: Palgrave Macmillan.

— (2015), 'Bette Davis: Acting and Not Acting Her Age', in Jermyn, Deborah and Su Holmes (eds), *Women, Celebrity & Cultures of Ageing: Freeze Frame*, pp. 43–58.

Shohat, Ella and Robert Stam (1994), *Unthinking Eurocentrism*, London and New York: Routledge.

Smith, Susan (2012), *Elizabeth Taylor*, London: Palgrave Macmillan.

Soila, Tytti (2009), *Stellar Encounter: Stardom in Popular European Cinema*, Chichester: John Libbey Publishing Ltd.

Sontag, Susan (1964, reprinted 1966), 'Notes on Camp', in Sontag, *Against Interpretation*, New York: Farrar, Straus & Giroux, pp. 275–92.

Stacey, Jackie (1994), *Star Gazing: Hollywood Cinema and Female Spectatorship*, New York and London: Routledge.

Swinnen, A. and J. A. Stotesbury (eds) (2012), *Aging, Performance and Stardom: Doing Age on the Stage of Consumerist Culture*, Zurich and Berlin: LIT Verlag.

Thornton, Niamh (2010), 'YouTube: Transnational Fandom and Mexican Divas', *Transnational Cinemas* 1:1, 53–67.

Wang, Yiman (2005), 'The Art of "Screen Passing": Anna May Wong's "Yellow Yellowface Performance" in the Art Deco Era', *Camera Obscura* 20:3, 159–91.

Wimmer, Leila (2013), 'Forever Emmanuelle: Sylvia Kristel and Soft-Core Cult Stardom', in Kate Egan and Sarah Thomas (eds) (2013), *Cult Film Stardom: Offbeat Attractions and Processes of Cultification*, London: Palgrave Macmillan.

Vincendeau, Ginette (2000), *Stars and Stardom in French Cinema*, New York: Continuum. Woodward, Kathleen (1989), 'Youthfulness as a Masquerade', *Discourse* 11:1, 119–42.

Yu, Sabrina Q. (2012a), *Jet Li: Chinese Masculinity and Transnational Stardom*, Edinburgh: Edinburgh University Press.

— (2012b), 'Vulnerable Chinese Stars: From *Xizi* to Film Worker', in Yingjin Zhang (ed.), *A Companion to Chinese Cinema*, Chichester: Wiley-Blackwell, pp. 218–39.

— (2014), 'Film Acting as Cultural Practice and Transnational Vehicle: Tang Wei's Minimalist Performance in *Late Autumn* (2011)', *Transnational Cinema* 5:2, 141–55.

— (2015), 'Dancing with Hollywood: Re-defining Transnational Chinese Stardom', in Andrea Bandhauer and Michelle Royer (eds) (2015), *Stars in World Cinema: Screen Icons and Star Systems Across Cultures*, London and New York: I. B. Tauris, pp. 104–16.

PART I

STAR PERFORMANCE

1. REVISITING PERFORMANCE: NICOLE KIDMAN'S ENACTMENT OF STARDOM

Pam Cook

In recent years, star study has evolved from semiotic, sociological and ideological analysis to take in the significance of stars in the history of Hollywood as a business, conceived as the centre of global media industries. In this light, the history of stardom from the early picture personalities to today's personal star brands emerges as one of increasing commodification. While stars have always been commodities, the proliferation of cross-media marketing synergies has produced a form of commodity stardom in which the commercial aspects of their work are more visible, and more accessible, to consumers via new technologies. In investigating the phenomenon of star power, scholars focus on stars' value in selling films (and themselves) as part of the market-driven enterprises of global media conglomerates, looking at their promotional activities and their function in branding processes (Grainge 2008). A growing body of academic work focuses on the impact of celebrity culture on modern stardom, shifting attention towards extra-cinematic manifestations of star identities. As star discourse traverses an increasing number of channels and platforms, the challenge for star study is to unpick the intricate intertextual relationships between the arenas in which it appears. In this fluid situation, star personas are made and remade in consumer interactions with media outpourings that are not easy to apprehend. Nicole Kidman exemplifies this quandary; she epitomises the modern commodity star whose image is displayed across a bewildering array of media forms and commercial activities.

In spite of the acknowledgement that stardom encompasses multiple activities across diverse sites, there is relatively little detailed analysis of star acting outside their dramatic roles in film, or consideration of the different kinds of performance produced in specific media contexts. An actor's onscreen roles and their wider public persona both depend on performance and the adoption of a character. However, the skills deployed in acting for the cinema are more highly esteemed and have received more critical attention than those used in interactions with the media. Writing about acting in cinema, James Naremore draws on Erving Goffman's pioneering work to argue that professional acting is related to the role-playing that characterises everyday social behaviour and presentations of self (Naremore 1998: 3). In his study of self-presentation, Goffman outlines the performance techniques adopted by individuals and groups to control perceptions of themselves in social situations, relating these practices to theatre stagecraft, and pointing to the importance of setting, costume and props in creating characters and stories for individuals (Goffman 1990: 26–7). Goffman is concerned with person-to-person interactions, but his research opens up new areas for the study of performance beyond the confines of the film text. The poses, gestures, costume, make-up, props, scripted dialogue and photographic *mise en scène* that constitute the star interview and photo shoot are ripe for analysis and reveal much about the transactions of modern stardom.

A broad conception of acting that covers all the arenas in which stars practise their craft is particularly useful in approaching Kidman's multifarious performance activities. In what follows, I examine in detail some of her media appearances, focusing on her enactment of commodity stardom, the acting techniques she deploys in different situations and the particular aesthetic conventions and technologies of each media context. Such appearances promote her as a special individual and are often regarded as marketing hype. In his study of extra-cinematic marketing practices, Jonathan Gray points out the limits of such conceptions, arguing that although promotional materials belong to the realms of profit, and are regarded as disposable peripherals, they can be seen as textual entities in their own right. Developing the work of Gérard Genette on paratexts, Gray argues that far from being subsidiary to the 'main text' (the film), they are an intrinsic part of it, and play a constitutive role in textual production (Gray 2010: 5). Gray's call for a new approach to 'off-screen studies' in which paratexts are valued for their significance in the processes of making meanings informs my approach. However, I would contend that it is not always simply the film product (in Gray's terms, 'the show') that is being sold. In the examples I consider here, while the release of a film may be part of the motivation for the star's media appearances, it is arguable that the promotion and performance of stardom itself is uppermost. In some cases, this produces a knowing commentary on the construction of Kidman's star status for the benefit of consumers who are versed in the operations of star discourse.

Gray's account adds nuance to Barry King's focus on the profit motive in his approach to the star persona. For King, the persona brings together the so-called private person and the parts they play in films to create a type capable of satisfying market-led rather than artistic imperatives (King 2010: 7–19). King maintains that in the contemporary global industry with its multiplying commercial spin-offs, product sponsorship, promotion and advertising deals have as much significance as indicators of value as the star's critical reception and box-office success, while their performances extend into spheres such as music, theatre and television. In these circumstances the star's reputation rests on a portfolio of performance expertise rather than on their accomplishments in film, and skills of self-presentation, acquired through training, are equally if not more important than those of character acting (King 2010: 9). The modern star celebrity (as opposed to a character actor, though they may be both) operates between film and extra-cinematic appearances to achieve maximum publicity, becoming a personal brand. They may still privilege the cinematic execution of their craft as part of their self-presentation, which enables the persona to retain artistic credibility, or 'creative capital', that can be exchanged in the marketplace.[1] Nicole Kidman's commodity stardom epitomises the construction of a multi-faceted identity that is fundamental to the employment practices of today's entertainment industries, where visibility influences perceptions of market value. However, it also has symbolic and cultural aspects, presented through narrative, performance, and other forms of representation.

The star celebrity is projected as special via myriad channels. The press, leisure and lifestyle magazines, book publishing, photo shoots, radio and television appearances, award ceremonies, film festivals, philanthropic functions, advertising, online databases, websites, Wikipedia, YouTube, fan activity and the Internet contribute to the circulation of information and meaning by relaying and replaying highly conventionalised stories and visual representations. Performances in film and television cameos, music videos, commercials and DVD extra materials also play a part in establishing star identity. Although star discourse has always been distributed across different media, the proliferation of electronic communication channels and the networks that connect them has both increased the amount of information that is generated and opened up more direct forms of access. Opportunities for unauthorised interaction with the process of constructing celebrity stardom have mushroomed, making the gossip circuit a more powerful conduit for speculation and alternative versions of official star narratives. Conversations formerly confined to private enclaves are now made public via online discussion boards. In this situation, control of the circulation of star images exercised by studios, publicity agents and stars themselves has dissipated and personas have fragmented. As contradictory views vie with one another, the sense of a 'real', unique and coherent self behind the star persona has given way to a more fluid and contested notion of identity. King argues that this decentred, labile construction of fame exists because it is commercially efficacious (King 2010: 9). However, it has other dimensions. The input of diverse agencies with different kinds and degrees of investment creates a culture of dispute and dialogue in which, although hierarchies are in operation, power relations are less settled and predictable than King's analysis allows.

TELEVISION TALK SHOWS

Public appearances on television are a key site in which play with notions of star power takes place. P. David Marshall sets out the different ways in which film and television position their celebrities, with film stardom defined by an aura of distinction and television personalities by familiarity (Marshall 1997: 121). Discussing the specific format and performance conventions of talk shows, he outlines the role of the host in bringing film stars from the rarified ambience of their movie roles into the realm of the everyday, and the use of humour in getting the star to reveal private details about their life, a process that plays on the tension between ordinariness and special qualities in star personas. For Marshall, television talk-show hosts participate in the construction of stardom by aiding the creation of a character or persona for the star. While the host has an identity, she or he gains celebrity status through proximity to other celebrities (Marshall 1997: 125–6).

In 2004 Kidman appeared on *The Ellen DeGeneres Show* as part of the promotion drive for *Birth* (Jonathan Glazer, 2004) (Thomson 2006: 234–6). The live interview was preceded by a teaser in which host DeGeneres is in the middle of a frantic telephone call trying to find a big star guest for the show when Kidman knocks on her dressing room door (see Figure 1.1), wanting to hang out because her car has broken down.[2] The distracted DeGeneres tries to get rid of her, then, realising her mistake, persuades the hesitant Kidman to appear as one of her guests, offering to lend her some of her own clothes. The teaser plays on the exceptional nature of Kidman's star glamour in contrast to the dressed-down DeGeneres' informal presentation style. The elegance of Kidman's clothing, jewellery, make-up and glossy, long blonde hair give her a look of carefully designed casual chic that appears exotic against DeGeneres' ordinariness, which seems natural. Her sultry voice and Australian accent also mark her as special, while Degeneres' vocal style is familiar from her comic persona. Both celebrities are acting, but each uses different conventions deriving from their professional contexts to project a distinctive persona. This produces an ironic commentary on the relationship between film stardom and television celebrity that the interview reinforces.

In the teaser, DeGeneres acts as the conduit for Kidman's journey from the rarified world of movie glamour to television's staging of the everyday. During the interview that follows, the contrast in their visual styles and body

Figure 1.1   Nicole Kidman and Ellen DeGeneres enact stardom: teaser for Kidman's interview on *The Ellen DeGeneres Show* (2004: A Very Good Production Inc.).

language remains marked: Kidman sits upright with her knees together while DeGeneres' stance is more relaxed, as she rests her hand on her right leg, which is balanced on her left knee.[3] The set, which has a fire in the background, resembles a living room (see Figure 1.2). Kidman appears at ease and laughs a lot, responding to the studio audience as well as the host, which increases the atmosphere of intimacy and accessibility. DeGeneres begins with questions about the actress' film career and moves on to more personal territory with her predilection for extreme sports. When DeGeneres asks about her children, Kidman hesitates and appears resistant to saying too much. In a comic reference to the contrived familiarity of the setting and to invasion of privacy, DeGeneres pretends to pick up the phone to call Isabella (Kidman and Tom Cruise's adopted daughter). When Kidman's hair falling on her lapel microphone causes a sound blip, DeGeneres uses the occurrence to make fun of the star's super-glamorous locks, highlighting the fact that her style is out of place in the homely surroundings.

Kidman regains the ground of ordinariness by referring to her habit of

Figure 1.2   At home: Kidman on *The Ellen DeGeneres Show* (2004: A Very Good Production Inc.).

honking when she laughs, whereupon DeGeneres suggests car bumper stickers bearing the legend 'Honk if you love Nicole', reducing her star aura to the level of the banal. Kidman appears to enjoy the joke, but when DeGeneres returns to the subject of her children, she forcefully reasserts her authority by making it clear that she will not answer any more questions about them. Later, DeGeneres refers to Kidman's skill with different accents, joking about her own lack of acting ability. In this exchange, artifice is associated with film and non-acting with television. When the host displays a two-page magazine spread featuring the Chanel No. 5 advertising campaign and mentions the associated Baz Luhrmann commercial, Kidman professes to be embarrassed at being confronted with her professional persona in the personal context of the interview. DeGeneres underscores this when she again emphasises the difference between them by claiming that she is available to appear in perfume commercials herself, a joke that draws attention to Kidman's commodity star status.

The interview exemplifies the ambivalence and synergies that exist between the media and celebrity stardom. DeGeneres mocks Kidman's star persona and power at the same time as furthering it by appearing to reveal her more private side. She uses humour to put Kidman at a disadvantage; although the actress is skilful at recovery, she appears taken by surprise and therefore more human at times. DeGeneres adopts a contradictory attitude that is reverent towards Kidman's acting talent yet sets out to cut her movie-star aura down to size. Her own persona connotes lack of star quality, concealing her status as a powerful celebrity performer. In the exchanges between the two women, which pivot on a contrast between public persona and private self, the conventions of television realism are revealed. The set-up and performances are as staged as any in film or theatre; although parts of the conversation seem impromptu, there is clearly a rudimentary script and it is likely that Kidman and her 'people' met with the show's producers and host to discuss what would (and could) be covered. DeGeneres represents the audience's conflicting feelings towards powerful stars: the desire to get close to those who are worshipped from afar and expose them. These mixed emotions have a further dimension: in playing off Kidman's artificiality against DeGeneres' naturalism, an opposition is created between the star's noticeably styled heterosexual image, designed to be looked at, and the rumpled refusal of fashion characteristic of DeGeneres' gay identity. In the context of the show, this contrast of styles both hints at the rumours surrounding Kidman's (hetero)sexuality and confirms DeGeneres' sexuality as more authentic. The visual aspects of the performance and setting contribute an allusive subtext to the interview that plays on elements of Kidman's public persona without directly referring to them. Whether she is aware of this is not entirely clear.

Magazine fashion shoots

Kidman's appearance on *The Ellen DeGeneres Show* manifests a degree of awareness in the format and in the participants' performances of the mechanisms through which stardom is produced and sustained. The star, who emerges as fabricated rather than authentic, is revealed as a product of those conventions, and her control of the situation appears circumscribed. In magazine photo shoots, where the projection of Kidman's star power may seem to be more secure, there are also indications that her persona is a highly mediated construct. The fashion photo shoot sets the stage for a character that personifies her commodity stardom and her personal brand. Kidman's elegance and status as a fashion icon are central to her brand. Although this aspect circulates across media outlets, the strongest focus on her star glamour occurs in high-end fashion and lifestyle magazines such as *Vanity Fair*, *Vogue* and *Harper's Bazaar*, which are directed at consumers interested in culture and style.

Kidman's exposure in these magazines is extensive, even excessive. Her tall, slim physique is eminently suited to displaying designer clothing, while her investment in beauty makes her supremely photogenic. In addition, fashion's predilection for performance, masquerade and mutable identities is the ideal theatre for presenting her adaptable persona and acting ability. The coverage is conventionalised; it consists of photo-shoot images supported by a feature article, generally containing interview material with the star and those who know her, that recycles well-known details from Kidman's biography combined with updated information about her current and future film work. The style and tone of the feature articles are complimentary, even when touching on difficult or controversial personal issues. Almost without exception they present the star in a positive light, although in some cases the persona projected by the photo shoot contrasts with that offered by the article. The feature articles set out a familiar story focused on life events while the photo-shoot images are often removed from the everyday, depicting her as an idealised figure. Although there are elements of fantasy in both articles and photo shoots, it is more strongly marked in the images, where she adopts an assortment of guises around which readers may weave their own daydreams.

The fashion shoots feature a cover picture of Kidman, linked to the images inside the magazine, in which she appears in a frontal pose directed at the viewer. The cover shot and byline entice consumers to buy the magazine in order to enjoy looking at the star and to possess her image. The illusion of access to inside knowledge and possession of Kidman's image promised by such coverage sells magazines and is a primary mechanism for acquiring maximum public attention for the star. Some of the covers are racy, implying intimacy with the viewer and playing on their sexual fantasies.[4] As with Kidman's movie appearances, her performance in fashion shoots is directed by the photographer and involves the input of teams of creative, business and technical personnel, some of whom are credited on the photographs. Just as the promotion of a film often features the name of an auteur, the quality fashion shoot gives prominence to renowned photographers, designers and brand names. Despite their commercial motivations, a high level of artistry, craft and theatrical display is apparent in the shoots. Although the photographs are not scripted in the conventional sense, they depict Kidman as characters in stories consumers can develop for themselves. The characters and style of the photos vary with the photographer in the same way that the director influences the look of a film and the actors' performances.

The photo shoots are tied in to and draw on the star's film work. In September 2003, when Kidman's success was at a peak following her best actress Academy Award for *The Hours*, *Vogue* magazine featured a lavish twenty-page spread of portraits of her by top photographers Irving Penn, Annie Leibovitz, Helmut Newton and Craig McDean, supported by a short feature article (Singer 2003: 642–62). The magazine cover displays a Leibovitz shot of a divaesque Kidman standing on a gleaming stage, lit from behind by theatre spotlights, looking directly at the camera with a steady, almost challenging gaze. Her height is emphasised by her hairstyle, which is swept upwards, and by her revealing dress, which is transparent and skin-tight with a voluminous train. Her head and shoulders break into the *Vogue* masthead and a headline proclaims: 'Fashion's brightest star: Nicole Kidman on life as an icon'. On the contents page a box entitled 'Cover look: Venus rising' lists credits for the dress (Atelier Versace mermaid gown), jewellery, make-up, hair, photographer and fashion editor.

Leibovitz's cover shot, in which Kidman's body is clearly photographically enhanced, is artistic at the same time as projecting an eroticised vision of the star that emphasises her physical allure and elegance as sources of power. The spread opens with a double-page monochrome head-and-shoulders shot by Irving Penn in which she appears pensive and a little melancholy, gazing off-camera with her head tilted to the side and her hand held up to her chin and mouth. The lighting and Kidman's dress and hairstyle give the photo an arty retro look, also evident in Penn's other monochrome shot of the star in a Rochas tiered brocade gown, where she sports a parasol. A box with credits for the dress, jewellery, hair and make-up features a quote from the designer Olivier Theyskens: 'Nicole is always Nicole, no matter who made the dress', confirming Kidman's star status in the fashion world. These sentiments are echoed in the feature article, which is littered with quotations from the likes of John Galliano, Valentino and Tom Ford extolling her beauty and sense of style. A distinction is made between her red-carpet appearances, where she is always herself, and her performances in film, where she becomes someone else. In upcoming films such as *The Human Stain* (Robert Benton, 2003), *Cold Mountain* (Anthony Minghella, 2003) and *Birth* she is 'arguably the most versatile and consistently surprising actress of her generation [. . .] and she is fearless in pursuit of her craft' (Singer 2003: 658). 'Being herself' does not mean revealing the 'real' Nicole Kidman. Rather, as Tom Ford puts it, 'She's developed a character for the red carpet, a public persona that is very groomed, very sleek, very controlled [. . .] very much the star [. . .]'. According to Emanuel Ungaro, 'Nobody seems to really know Nicole Kidman because she has pulled off the miracle of being recognized in her art without unveiling herself', while Craig McDean is quoted as saying, 'I don't think she likes looking natural'. The article goes on to claim that Kidman has achieved iconicity by adopting a variety of looks and masks. Baz Luhrmann acknowledges that the red carpet is part of her job, 'and, boy, is it a lot of work' (Singer 2003: 644). This comment highlights the labour involved in the enactment of stardom (McDonald 2000: 8–10).

The article foregrounds the connections between Kidman's fashion and film performance, seeing them both as the result of artistic endeavour, hard work and professionalism. In between the accolades, it offers astute commentary on the nature of Kidman's stardom and the construction of her persona. Kidman is presented as a lead character, supported by a cohort of top creative talent, in the story of her own success. The extent of her achievement can be measured by the amount of space devoted to her, the tributes paid by so many leading fashion names, and the high production values of the photo shoot. The article's affirmation of Kidman's persona as a collection of different guises is supported by the photo shoot, which, in addition to the Irving Penn shots, depicts her in tomboy mode, androgynous in fashionable menswear and displaying attitude (Craig McDean); as the height of exclusive glamour in haute couture (Annie Leibovitz); and as sultry sex goddess in revealing underwear (Helmut Newton). Kidman's performances on the red carpet and in fashion shoots are not regarded as subsidiary. They are given equivalent status with her film work, and both are considered equally important to her persona. The *Vogue* feature constructs her star identity and defines the source of her power, illuminating the extent of her investment in the image and its significance for modern commodity stardom.

CELEBRITY TABLOID GOSSIP

Whereas the quality lifestyle magazines focus respectfully on positive aspects of Kidman's life and work, devising a heroic character, the celebrity press does the obverse. Concentrating on secrets, scandal and speculation, the celebrity tabloids set out to expose what lies beneath the surface of the star image. In the case of female celebrities, the attention paid to their bodies, appearance, dress, family and emotional tribulations is relentless. The coverage is ephemeral and has the immediacy of gossip, returning constantly to the same themes. In Kidman's case these revolve around rumours about her sex life and sexuality, marriage, children, fertility and plastic surgery, and commentary on her image, finances, work and sartorial style. Because of the emphasis on exposé, invasion of privacy is a major issue and Kidman has on occasion asserted her rights in this respect.[5] The circulation of star discourse in the tabloid press may seem to be less top-down than in quality magazines and television talk shows, outside the control of the star and her publicity agencies. The activity of constructing and deconstructing the star image and persona via gossip mills appears to be the province of consumers. Coverage is defined by to-and-fro between rumour and denial, all of which contributes to building character and story. Such exchanges are part and parcel of the interdependent relationship between famous personalities and the media in the pursuit of public interest.

As a powerful star celebrity Kidman is on show all the time. Even seemingly private moments are captured by candid photographs that apparently catch her unawares (Driver 2009). These off-the-record glimpses give the illusion that the consumer is privy to inside information that the star would prefer not to make public. In contrast to her appearances on the red carpet, in fashion magazines and on television, where her awareness of the camera is part of the performance, in candid shots Kidman often acts as though she is off-camera even when she knows that photographers are present. She colludes with the processes of celebrity exposure up to a point, while resisting intrusion into her privacy in certain areas. After the birth of her first daughter, when she was forty-one, Kidman nurtured rumours that she may be pregnant again by stating in interviews that she would like another child with husband Keith Urban. In 2010 stories circulated that the couple were undergoing fertility treatment, with Kidman's age a key issue, and she was reported to be on 'celebrity bump watch'. Her body was subjected to a frenzy of inspection; candid photographs of her exposed stomach appeared in the tabloid press, fuelling speculation, while Kidman's denials only intensified the rumours.[6] In January 2011 she and Urban announced the birth of their second daughter via 'gestational carrier', a controversial term that generated debate in the press, already fired up over the couple's decision to use surrogacy and their success at keeping the birth secret.[7] The story was not a scandal – the use of surrogates by celebrities has become more common in recent years – but the assertion of the right to secrecy by Kidman was a challenge to the power of the media and set limits on the public's right to know. The revelation had the effect of precipitating a spate of media comment, further boosting Kidman's profile.

Kidman is adept at playing the rumour, denial and disclosure game. When celebrities issue denials they are generally assumed to be hiding something, which exacerbates speculation. Revelations then acquire additional impact. Kidman's commodity stardom depends on the photogenic appeal of her face and body, and the time and effort she invests in her looks can be regarded as star labour (McDonald 2000: 9–10). Just as her appearance in films is crafted using cosmetics and prosthetics, her public image is designed and created by teams of stylists and hair and make-up technicians. However, while disguise is regarded as laudable in the execution of her art, it is deemed deceitful when it comes to her offscreen image. Her assumed use of skin and body enhancement techniques such as Botox and plastic surgery are presented as revealing her beauty as fake, with a consequent loss of authenticity and esteem (Hurtz 2009). It is accepted by the tabloid press that celebrities work on their image as part of their job; considerable space is devoted to discussion of stars' fitness regimes, weight loss and gain and other physical changes. But the obsessive appraisal and critique of female celebrities' appearance betray complex emotions, including fascination with and distrust of images; an impossible desire for intimate contact with famous personalities; and the impulse to demean the rich and powerful. Personalities and tabloids alike exploit these feelings to keep consumer interest alive. Attempts to fend off the effects of ageing are a particular preoccupation, providing material for dramas of personal and professional success and failure through before-and-after and surgical disaster scenarios.

Kidman's reputed fondness for Botox, which she consistently denied despite visible evidence of lip enhancement and other procedures, led to reports that her acting had suffered and a spate of jokes at the expense of her forehead (Paskin 2010). Botox is controversial for health and other reasons; it works by freezing the face muscles (Cooke 2008: 25–7). As its widespread use as an anti-ageing treatment by A-list stars became a discussion topic, the stigma attached to it developed into a debate about the pressures on stars to remain looking young (Triggs 2008). Comments from casting agents and directors such as Baz Luhrmann and Martin Scorsese about the difficulty of finding actresses with expressive features contributed to a growing antipathy towards the use of Botox and admissions by female stars that they used it emerged (Hill 2003). The fact that digital and HD technologies reveal fine details of the face and body, so that the evidence of augmentation is discernible, was a contributing factor. This context led to Kidman's confession in 2010 that she had used Botox but had now stopped.[8] She claimed to have retrieved her demonstrative forehead. Kidman's revelation went against her previous disclaimers; this was clearly less important than drawing attention to her renewed acting prowess or achieving publicity. It also served the purpose of explaining why her face had become perceptibly Botox-free, probably for health reasons connected to her first pregnancy and fertility treatment. The arguments around and backlash against Botox in the industry resulted in a cultural shift in which leading actresses, including Kidman, proclaimed their intention to remain 'natural' and renounce cosmetic procedures (Holson 2010). A characteristic scepticism about such claims was evident in parts of the celebrity press.[9]

Botox and other measures are part of Kidman's effort to create a proprietary image that caters to preconceptions of beauty and can be exchanged in the marketplace. When the use of Botox became detrimental to her brand she overhauled her public image, adopting a curly red hairstyle reminiscent of her youth. Just as Botox eradicates the marks of time on the human face, Kidman's 'natural' rebrand, by returning to her younger incarnation, symbolised her determination to defy the ageing process and remained consistent with the tenets of the glamour industry.[10] Botox's creation of frozen faces free from the signs of lived experience generates masks that expunge the existence of the individual human being and personal history assumed to lie behind the image. This chimes with Goffman's argument, noted earlier, that self-presentation depends on the individual's adoption of masks that project a preferred persona rather than a true identity (Goffman 1990: 30). Kidman's use and rejection of Botox, and her assumption of a natural guise, epitomise the performance of her star persona as pure façade. In its drive to strip away the masquerade, the celebrity tabloid press contributes to the exposure and deconstruction of the processes of commodity stardom even as it shores them up.

COMMERCIALS

In addition to selling films, the commodity star undertakes a range of marketing activities including sponsorship, advertising and product endorsements. While this has always been the case, the increased emphasis on branding and expansion of cross-media networks in the contemporary entertainment industries has resulted in the growth and realignment of publicity operations. A star's involvement in an advertising campaign now extends across multiple outlets such as the press, magazines, film, television, the Internet and live appearances (Wyatt 1994: 81–93). By associating their identity with a product, the star links their personal brand with another in a mutual self-promotional exchange through which both expect to gain increased visibility and financial rewards. While some celebrities participate regularly in selling products, A-list stars are judicious in choosing brands with which to affiliate, and many do not take part in advertising at all. The chosen brand generally conforms to the values represented by the star persona. Kidman's engagement with marketing campaigns is confined to luxury and quality labels such as Omega, Nintendo, Schweppes, Chanel and Jimmy Choo, for whom she has appeared in commercials and related promotional work.[11] Like the activities of the modern commodity star, commercials cross over between different media and entail creative input from people in fashion, film and music.[12]

Her most high-profile appearance to date is in Baz Luhrmann's *No. 5 The Film* (2004), for which she was reputed to have earned the highest fee ever paid to an actress for a commercial.[13] Perfume commercials, which have become a genre in their own right, are often directed by auteurs and feature major stars.[14] They are devised and produced in the same way as feature-length movies, bear the unmistakable imprint of the director and are listed in their canon of works. Because they are edited for showing in different media, a full-length master copy, or director's cut, often exists. For example, *No. 5 The Film*, envisaged by Luhrmann as a trailer for a film that might have been, was made in a definitive three-minute version for theatrical release that was cut for screening on television. The full version includes one minute of end-credits (Cook 2010: 32–3, 110–15). Like all Luhrmann's work, the mini-film was treated as a special event designed to attract maximum media coverage. As the face of the Chanel No. 5 label, Kidman took part in an extensive campaign spanning print and audiovisual media that drew on the visual design and imagery of the short film, which was in the mode of Luhrmann's celebrated Red Curtain Trilogy. *No. 5 The Film* brought together several iconic brands: Chanel No. 5, the world's top-selling perfume, which is associated with glamorous female personalities such as Catherine Deneuve, Jacqueline Kennedy Onassis and Marilyn Monroe; Karl Lagerfeld, controversial head designer for Chanel, who designed Kidman's couture gowns for the commercial; Baz Luhrmann and Catherine Martin, who together were responsible for the style of the Red Curtain films; and Kidman, one of the world's most powerful and bankable stars. This was a potent creative and commercial alliance that promised to consolidate the positions of all concerned. The script echoed the story and romantic themes of *Moulin Rouge!* (2001) and, as with Kidman's performance as Satine, her image consisted of a pastiche of famous women linked with the fragrance.

The action is set in an imaginary locale, a hybrid of Paris and New York created through special visual effects. Kidman plays 'the most famous woman in the world', who disappears from the glare of the cameras to have a brief affair with a penniless bohemian writer (Rodrigo Santoro) before returning to her former life. In the time spent in the writer's garret, she discards her expensive gown for her lover's shirt, shorts and black jacket, switching from ultra-feminine glamour to dishevelled tomboy. For the final 'red carpet' moment she wears an elegant, backless, fitted black dress, her blonde hair scraped back into a smooth bun, apparently once again in control of her star image. The diamond necklace that emblazons 'No. 5' on her back is the only emblem of the product that appears in the film, whose relationship to a commercial is equivocal. The role of the perfume in Kidman's journey is obscure, while the ubiquitous Chanel signage that confines her in the city streets is also there on the rooftop garret, with the result that her escape is presented as illusory. *No. 5 The Film* might be seen as an ironic reflection on the branding process and on Kidman's commodity stardom.[15] The dazzling necklace displays the No. 5 insignia inside a circle so that it resembles the marque used to brand cattle. It hangs from her neck rather like a rein, suggesting restraint. It is as though Kidman is an object stamped by the image-saturated commercial environment she inhabits and entirely defined by it. The artifice of her performance underlines her entrapment in an unreal world of surfaces. Luhrmann's mini-film uses Kidman's star persona to question the superficial glamour of the very brand it sets out to promote.

PHILANTHROPY

Philanthropic activities and charitable donations play a significant part in the construction of star personas. Indeed, humanitarian causes and awards feature prominently in the operations of the entertainment industries. The website *Look to the Stars*, dedicated to 'the world of celebrity giving', lists over two thousand charities and more than three thousand celebrities, posting 'charity biographies' for celebrities. Nicole Kidman's entry records her work for UNICEF and UNIFEM, her charity donations and fundraising activities. A roll call of charities and foundations she has supported includes Artists for Peace and Justice, Global Green Plan and Breast Cancer Care. She is quoted as saying: 'I find trying to solve problems and save lives is far more important than my film career.'[16] Kidman's sponsorship and humanitarian work is both Australian and international: from 1993 to 2002 she was ambassador for the Australian Theatre for Young People (atyp), becoming its patron in 2002. In the 1990s she was appointed a national Goodwill Ambassador for UNICEF in Australia and in 2006 she became a Goodwill Ambassador for UNIFEM, which supports women's rights and gender equality around the world. In 2009 she lent her voice to the 'Say NO – UNiTE' initiative to end violence against women, speaking in front of the US House Subcommittee on Human Rights.[17] As part of her advocacy for women's rights she travelled to the Democratic Republic of the Congo and Kosovo to talk to victims of violence. In 2006 Kidman was awarded Australia's highest civilian honour, the Companion of the Order of Australia, for her services to the performing arts, youth sponsorship, health care issues and humanitarian causes.[18] In 2010 she and Keith Urban announced plans to fund a school in Haiti and Kidman made a goodwill visit there to meet earthquake survivors and women's rights activists.[19] Together with other celebrities, she participated in a fundraising telethon to help homeless victims of the Nashville floods, helping to raise $1.7 million.[20]

All these activities involve live and other kinds of performances by Kidman for which she and the various causes (many of which are themselves major brands) receive substantial media coverage. It is unclear whether she receives financial remuneration in some cases. Ostensibly she plays herself, portraying a character who prioritises humanitarian issues over career or money. There is a redemptive aspect to stars' philanthropy whereby the rich and famous can be seen to use their power and influence to help those less fortunate. In Kidman's case, human rights advocacy contributes to building a 'good' character who is aware of her own luck and wants to give something back. It also strengthens her Australian identity; she frequently traces her commitment to fighting injustice to her parents' social conscience and her work in cancer research to her mother's breast cancer, both of which turn up regularly in her biographical details. Philanthropy forms part of the portfolio of skills to which King refers (King 2010: 9), and in the context of Kidman's commodity stardom it is difficult not to regard her philanthropic activity as a bid for publicity and as a product for exchange in the market. Although she may not profit directly in financial terms in every case, she gains what might be termed 'altruistic capital', akin to the cultural capital defined by Pierre Bourdieu (Swartz 1997), that enhances her star power by bolstering her authenticity. Her stardom depends on her status as a special individual; benevolent enterprises bring her out of her exclusive, elite world, forge a connection with a wider society of deserving human beings and attempt to build an affective relationship with consumers.

Her performance in these areas contributes to the sense that there is a unified, knowable person behind the vagaries of her star image and her film roles. The fact that her compassion may be motivated in part by career interests generates scepticism in some quarters. In response to Kidman's role as advocate for Say NO, Janet Street Porter wrote a scathing piece in the *Independent*, heaping scorn on the idea of stars as goodwill ambassadors and claiming that Kidman's participation in a misogynist entertainment industry was a betrayal of real women (Street Porter 2009). This was followed by a more sympathetic article in the *Guardian* by Samantha Morton praising Kidman's stand against Hollywood's demeaning portrayal of women and her bravery in speaking out against studio interests (Morton 2009). Both columnists viewed Kidman's philanthropy as performance: Street Porter saw it as hypocrisy, inveighing against the star's collusion with the degrading fictions perpetrated by Hollywood and their part in encouraging actual sexual violence against women; Morton, on the other hand, argued that Kidman's advocacy performance demonstrated that actresses are real women who can make responsible choices about the roles they play. The controversy highlights the conundrums surrounding commodity stars; the fragmented nature of Kidman's image could encourage the perception that her philanthropic identity is yet another character in her portfolio rather than an authentic expression of her real self. The suspicion that she may be having it both ways is one of the consequences of her success in creating a multi-faceted persona. As with the conjunction of commerce and art in her career, an unease exists around the commodification of human kindness as part of the promotion of her brand.

Conclusion

In the current media landscape, star discourse has expanded across many different sites, some of which are interconnected networks, while others are less official. The star persona, previously seen as a contradictory entity that circulates in subsidiary media, has taken on a life of its own and is no longer secondary to the cinematic performance, as John Ellis claims in his account of stars as a cinematic phenomenon (Ellis 1992: 93). Now more protean, it has dispersed into areas that do not so much offer an invitation to the cinematic performance, rather, they provide opportunities for direct access to star images and narratives, and exploration of consumer fantasies and emotions. The experience of 'cinema' has become one of immersion in and interaction with a plethora of commercial and cultural activities, not all of which satisfy corporate interests. The images and micro-narratives that construct, dissect and deconstruct the star persona are part of an unstable environment in which economic and cultural power does not entirely rest with global corporations, despite their massive investment in marketing (Gray 2010: 7). In this situation of intense intertextual productivity, paratextual materials of various kinds have increased importance in the circulation of star discourse.

My analysis has highlighted elements of performance and aesthetic conventions in order to draw attention to the synergies between extra-cinematic media forms and the wider commercial networks in which they participate. However, my case studies also demonstrate that these media operations have a certain autonomy. As well as satisfying market demands, they create narratives that comment on the processes of stardom, engaging with audiences skilled in navigating the complexities of media protocols and accustomed to producing their own meanings. Nicole Kidman's fragmented persona and self-referential enactment of celebrity emerge from this unpredictable context. Through skills of self-presentation she projects a chameleon identity available for reworking into configurations capable of serving diverse interests. Paying detailed attention to Kidman's appearances in extra-cinematic media events not only sheds light on the transformation of stardom, it also opens the way to a broad understanding of performance that extends beyond acting in film. This approach requires a shift of focus from the conception of close analysis of film that has preoccupied moving image studies, to the textual status of so-called ancillary incidences of star discourse, and their potential to produce narratives and amplify or change the meanings of other texts. The revaluation and repositioning of material often considered peripheral, or marketing hype, challenges textual boundaries as well as highlighting the intimate connections between art and commerce. It has the potential to transform established critical and analytical methods, and illuminate the complex, mediated relationships and interactions that constitute consumer experience of contemporary stardom.

Acknowledgement

This is a substantially revised, re-edited and updated version of material that appears in Pam Cook (2012), *Nicole Kidman*, London: Palgrave Macmillan/ British Film Institute. Extracts reproduced with permission of Palgrave Macmillan.

Notes

1. I discuss the strategic acquisition of 'creative capital' in *Baz Luhrmann* (Cook 2010: 26, 157).
2. Teaser available at http://www.youtube.com/watch?v=ZENjHwlrG98, last accessed 11 August 2015.
3. Second part of interview available at http://www.youtube.com/watch?v=KlsLZ7J LhUQ, last accessed 11 August 2015.
4. For example, *Vanity Fair* 566, October 2007 has a cover image of Kidman looking into the camera with lips parted, sporting a sailor's cap and exposing her upper torso to the waist to reveal her plunge bra. The byline reads 'Nicole Kidman bares all'. See also Thomson's discussion of Kidman's risqué glamour shoot for the December 2004 issue of Italian *GQ* (Thomson 2006: 240).
5. In 2003 Kidman won substantial undisclosed damages in the UK courts against the *Daily Mail* and *Sun* newspapers, who reported that she had had an affair with her *Cold Mountain* co-star Jude Law (Cook 2012: 76).

6. See 'Another kid for Kidman? Nicole reveals glimpse of bump sparking baby rumours', *Daily Mail*, 18 June 2010, available at http://www.dailymail.co.uk/tvshowbiz/article-1287420/Nicole-Kidman-reveals-glimpse-bump-sparking-baby-rumours.html, last accessed 11 August 2015.
7. See 'Kidman, Urban have 2nd child through surrogate', *Washington Times*, 18 January 2011, available at http://www.washingtontimes.com/news/2011/jan/18/kidman-urban-have-2nd-child-through-surrogate/, last accessed 11 August 2015.
8. See 'Kidman admits to botox face freeze', *Herald Sun*, 13 January 2011, available at http://www.heraldsun.com.au/ipad/kidman-admits-to-botox-face-freeze/story-fn6bn80a-1225986555083, last accessed 11 August 2015.
9. See 'Back to the botox? Nicole Kidman displays suspiciously frozen features at the CMAs', *Daily Mail*, 4 April 2011, available at http://www.dailymail.co.uk/tvshowbiz/article-1373123/ACM-Awards-Nicole-Kidman-displays-suspiciously-frozen-featu res.html, last accessed 11 August 2015.
10. See fashion shoot photographed by Alexi Lubomirski, *Harper's Bazaar* (US), February 2011, available at http://www.harpersbazaar.com/fashion/photography/g1384/nicole-kidman-style-pictures-0211/, last accessed 11 August 2015.
11. Kidman's commercials for these brands are available on YouTube.
12. For example, Kidman's Bollywood-style Schweppes commercial, which featured Indian star Arjun Rampal and child actress Rubina Ali, who appeared in *Slumdog Millionaire* (Danny Boyle, 2008), was produced by Ridley Scott and directed by Shekhar Kapur (*Elizabeth*, 1998).
13. See IMDb News for Baz Luhrmann page: 'Kidman Lands in Guinness Book of Records', 29 November 2004, available at http://www.imdb.com/name/nm0525303/news?year=2004, last accessed 11 August 2015.
14. For example: Martin Scorsese's *Bleu de Chanel* (2010) with Gaspard Ulliel; Sofia Coppola's *Miss Dior Chérie* (2011) with Natalie Portman; Frank Miller's *Gucci Guilty* (2010) with Evan Rachel Wood.
15. Grainge (2008), pp. 38–42, discusses the branding operations in *No. 5 The Film*.
16. See *Look to the stars: the world of celebrity giving*, http://www.looktothestars.org/celebrity/185-nicole-kidman, last accessed 11 August 2015.
17. See 'Testimony of Nicole Kidman', *US House Subcommittee on International Organizations, Human Rights and Oversight*, 21 October 2009, available at http://archives.foreignaffairs.house.gov/111/kid102109.pdf, last accessed 11 August 2015.
18. See Nicole Kidman entry, *It's an Honour* website, http://www.itsanhonour.gov.au/honours/honour_roll/search.cfm?aus_award_id=1131287&search_type=simple&showInd=true, last accessed 11 August 2015.
19. See 'Nicole and Keith Make Huge Pledge to Haiti', *PopSugar Australia*, 19 February 2010, http://www.popsugar.com.au/celebrity/Keith-Urban-Nicole-Kidman-make-huge-donation-Haiti-fund-school-port-au-prince-7460031, last accessed 11 August 2015.
20. See 'Nicole Kidman Raises $1.7 Mil for Nashville Flood Relief', *Us Weekly*, 17 May 2010, http://www.usmagazine.com/celebritynews/news/nicole-kidman-brad-paisley-raise-17-million-for-nashville-flood-relief-2010175, last accessed 11 August 2015.

BIBLIOGRAPHY

'Another kid for Kidman? Nicole reveals glimpse of bump sparking baby rumours' (2010), *Daily Mail*, 18 June, http://www.dailymail.co.uk/tvshowbiz/article-1287420/Nicole-Kidman-reveals-glimpse-bump-sparking-baby-rumours.html, last accessed 18 June 2015.

'Back to the botox? Nicole Kidman displays suspiciously frozen features at the CMAs' (2011), *Daily Mail*, 4 April, http://www.dailymail.co.uk/tvshowbiz/article-1373123/ACM-Awards-Nicole-Kidman-displays-suspiciously-frozen-features.html, last accessed 18 June 2015.

Cook, Pam (2010), *Baz Luhrmann*, London: BFI/Palgrave.

Cooke, Grayson (2008), 'Effacing the face: Botox and the anarchivic archive', *Body & Society* 14:2.

Driver, Carol (2009), 'Nicole Kidman's fitness regime to lose baby curves for next film role-playing a transsexual', *Daily Mail*, 30 November, http://www.dailymail.co.uk/tvshowbiz/article-1232055/Nicole-Kidmans-fitness-regime-lose-baby-curves-latest-film-role-playing-transsexual.html, last accessed 18 June 2015.

Ellis, John (1992), *Visible Fictions: Cinema, Television, Video*, London and New York: Routledge.

Goffman, Erving (1990), *The Presentation of Self in Everyday Life*, London: Penguin Books.

Grainge, Paul (2008), *Brand Hollywood: Selling Entertainment in a Global Media Age*, Oxford and New York: Routledge.

Gray, Jonathan (2010), *Show Sold Separately: Promos, Spoilers, and Other Media Paratexts*, New York: New York University Press.

Hill, Amelia (2003), 'Actors warned to keep off the Botox', *Observer*, 9 February, http://www.guardian.co.uk/uk/2003/feb/09/film.filmnews, last accessed 18 June 2015.

Holson, Laura M. (2010), 'A little too ready for her close-up?', *New York Times*, 23 April, http://www.nytimes.com/2010/04/25/fashion/25natural.html?ref=style&pagewanted=all, last accessed 18 June 2015.

Hurtz, Erica (2009), 'Nine plastic surgery procedures that Nicole Kidman had', *Make {me} Heal*, 21 December, http://news.makemeheal.com/celebrity-plastic-surgery/nicole-kidman-nine-plastic-surgery-2/, last accessed 18 June 2015.

'Kidman admits to botox face freeze' (2011), *Herald Sun*, 13 January, http://www.heraldsun.com.au/ipad/kidman-admits-to-botox-face-freeze/story-fn6bn80a-1225986555083, last accessed 18 June 2015.

'Kidman lands in Guinness Book of Records', IMDb, 29 November 2004, http://www.imdb.com/name/nm0525303/news?year=2004, last accessed 18 June 2015.

'Kidman, Urban have 2nd child through surrogate' (2011), *Washington Times*, 18 January, http://www.washingtontimes.com/news/2011/jan/18/kidman-urban-have-2nd-child-through-surrogate/, last accessed 18 June 2015.

King, Barry (2010), 'Stardom, celebrity, and the money form', *Velvet Light Trap* 65, Spring.

Look to the stars: the world of celebrity giving, http://www.looktothestars.org/celebrity/185-nicole-kidman, last accessed 19 June 2015.

Marshall, P. David (1997), *Celebrity and Power: Fame in Contemporary Culture*, Minneapolis: University of Minnesota Press.

Morton, Samantha (2009), 'Why Nicole Kidman was brave to speak out', *Guardian*, 26 October, http://www.guardian.co.uk/film/2009/oct/26/nicole-kidman, last accessed 22 June 2015.

Naremore, James (1998), *Acting in the Cinema*, Berkeley: University of California Press.

'Nicole and Keith Make Huge Pledge to Haiti' (2010), *PopSugar Australia*, 19 February, http://www.popsugar.com.au/celebrity/Keith-Urban-Nicole-Kidman-make-huge-donation-Haiti-fund-school-port-au-prince-7460031, last accessed 22 June 2015.

Nicole Kidman fashion shoot (2011), *Harper's Bazaar* (US), February, http://www.harpersbazaar.com/fashion/photography/g1384/nicole-kidman-style-pictures-0211/, last accessed 22 June 2015.

'Nicole Kidman Raises $1.7 Mil for Nashville Flood Relief' (2010), *Us Weekly*, 17 May, http://www.usmagazine.com/celebritynews/news/nicole-kidman-brad-paisley-raise-17-million-for-nashville-flood-relief-2010175, last accessed 11 August 2015.

'Nicole Mary Kidman', *It's an Honour* website, http://www.itsanhonour.gov.au/honours/honour_roll/search.cfm?aus_award_id=1131287&search_type=simple&showInd=true, last accessed 19 June 2015.

Paskin, Willa (2010), 'Nicole Kidman's forehead is back!: an animated retrospective', *Vulture*, 15 December, http://www.vulture.com/2010/12/we_warmly_welcome_back_nicole.html, last accessed 18 June 2015.

Singer, Sally (2003), 'Master class', *Vogue*, September.

Street Porter, Janet (2009), 'Editor-At-Large: Nicole's Sex Roles Betray Women in the Real World', *Independent*, 25 October, http://www.independent.co.uk/opinion/columnists/janet-street-porter/editoratlarge-nicoles-sex-roles--betray-women-in-the-real-world-1808989.html, last accessed 22 June 2015.

'Testimony of Nicole Kidman'(2009), *US House Subcommittee on International Organizations, Human Rights and Oversight*, 21 October, http://www.democrats.foreignaffairs.house.gov/111/kid102109.pdf, last accessed 19 June 2015.

Thomson, David (2006), *Nicole Kidman*, London: Bloomsbury.

Triggs, Charlotte with Maureen Harrington (2008), 'Botox confessions', *People* 70:21, 24 November, http://www.people.com/people/archive/article/0,,20245470,00.html, last accessed 18 June 2015.

Vanity Fair, 566, October 2007.

Wyatt, Justin (1994), 'Uncertainty in the marketplace: the development of the contemporary industry structure', in *High Concept: Movies and Marketing in Hollywood*, Austin: University of Texas Press.

2. FILM STARS IN THE PERSPECTIVE OF PERFORMANCE STUDIES: PLAY, LIMINALITY AND ALTERATION IN CHINESE CINEMA

Yingjin Zhang

Star studies, performance studies

Richard Dyer, whose work helped launch star studies as a legitimate subfield in cinema studies, observes: 'From the perspective of ideology, analyses of stars, as images existing in films and other media texts, stress their structured polysemy, that is, the finite multiplicity of meanings and affects they embody and the attempt so to structure them that some meanings and affects are foregrounded and others are masked or displaced' (1979: 3). By combining semiotics and sociology, Dyer's approach 'analyzes the star image as an inter-textual construct produced across a range of media and cultural practices . . . [and] study of stars becomes an issue in the social production and circulation of meaning, linking industry and text, films and society' (Gledhill 1991: xiv).

Dyer's approach has directed attention away from issues of truth and authenticity surrounding star images and refocused on ideological functions of star texts in cultural, historical and geopolitical contexts. Since the early 1990s, stardom as an 'industry of desire' (Gledhill 1991) in Hollywood and Europe has been examined by a growing number of scholars. A veritable bloom of scholarship in the new century demonstrates that this growing field has benefited from its foundational socio-semiotic approach and has inves-tigated other aspects of stardom and star texts hitherto neglected, especially those outside or on the margins of Western cinemas.

This chapter explores a productive connection between star studies and performance studies, two interdisciplinary areas that have developed quickly since the 1990s. As suggested earlier (Farquhar and Zhang 2010: 6), in the perspective of performance studies, Dyer's 'structured polysemy' of star texts may be reconceptualised as an assemblage of polysemy not so much structured as conjunctural, for the simple reason that star performance, like performance in general, 'isn't "in" anything, but "between"' (Schechner 2002: 24), that is, between various acts of embodiment rather than one singular act. In this sense, performance studies' emphasis on actions, interactions and relationships dovetails with star studies' focus on contextuality and intertextuality, but the former's conjunctural vision focuses less on an apparently stable structure of embodied meaning than on glaring cracks and fissures opened up by repeated performances.

A distinct feature of performance studies is its approach to texts not as mere objects but as practices, events and behaviours (Schechner 2002: 2). For Richard Schechner, 'the uniqueness of an event is not in its materiality but in its interactivity', for 'the context of every reception makes each instance different' (2002: 23). This emphasis on the liveness of contingency rather than the structured essence of any meaning or affect associated with a star text foregrounds its fundamental instability and variability, thereby opening up a new space for envisioning alternatives and alterations.

This chapter links two evolving disciplines and explores the ways star studies may benefit from performance studies' emphasis on liveness, interactivity and alteration. What interests me in particular is how key concepts in performance studies such as play and liminality can help address an apparent lack of attention to romantic male roles in Chinese films. While the popularity of martial arts and action genres have pushed Chinese actors like Jackie Chan (Cheng Long, b. 1954), Chow Yun-fat (Zhou Runfa, b. 1955) and Jet Li (Li Lianjie, b. 1963) to the forefront of star studies recently, equally successful actors like Tony Leung Chiu Wai (Liang Chaowei, b. 1962) have been largely kept out of sight. With references to Leung's performances in *In the Mood for Love* (Wong Kar-wai, 2000), which won him the Best Actor Award at the Cannes International Film Festival, and *Lust, Caution* (Ang Lee, 2007), which won the Golden Lion at the 2007 Venice Film Festival, this chapter analyses acts of repetition, dark play and alteration in the perspective of performance studies and suggests that these concepts enhance a conjunctural view of polysemy in star studies.

THEORY OF PLAY AND LIMINALITY

Johan Huizinga traces the etymology of *play* to the Old English *plegan* and German *pflegen* – both meaning 'to vouch', 'to take a risk, to expose oneself to danger', 'to pledge' – and comments: 'Play and danger, risk, chance, feat – it is all a single field of action where something is at stake' (1970: 38–40). The etymological link of play to danger has also inspired Victor Turner (1983: 233–4) to speculate:

> Playfulness is a volatile, sometimes dangerously explosive essence, which cultural institutions seek to bottle or contain [. . .] Play can be everywhere and nowhere, imitate anything, yet be identified with nothing [. . .] Its metamessages are composed of a potpourri of apparently incongruous elements [. . .] Yet [. . .] the wheel of play reveals to us [. . .] the possibility of changing our goals and, therefore, the restructuring of what our culture states to be reality.

While its inherent transient, incongruous and unpredictable elements highlight the disruptive and destructive power of play, Turner's speculation also reveals the possibility of restructuring our reality through play and hence the constructive and productive potential of play. This duality of play is likewise emphasised by Friedrich Nietzsche (1962: 62): 'as children and artists play, so plays the ever-living fire. It constructs and destroys [. . .] Not hubris but the ever self-renewing impulse to play calls new worlds into being.'

There is insufficient space here to expound on play as a compelling concept in the history of Western aesthetics, but I would like to summarise my recent argument regarding play (Y. Zhang 2012: 353). Play promises the possibility of undoing historical violence in a textual world and of imagining not just what was irretrievably lost but also what might have been emergent at a given time. Play presupposes the alterity and alterability of both self and other, and it refuses to accept any permanent demarcation or solution and opts instead for reimagined alternatives and alterations. Play foregrounds the repeatability of acts and the reversibility of roles, and its predication on incompleteness demands a continual reconfiguration of scenarios across spatial, temporal, sexual, racial, conceptual and other divides. Play constitutes a broad spectrum of tactics deployed by filmmakers and performers to 'put in play' various forces of history, in an imaginary but imaginative game defined not so much by linearity or oppositionality as by contingency and liminality.

A key notion of performance studies, liminality is defined by Turner as 'an interval, however brief, of *margin* or *limen*, when the past is momentarily negated, suspended or abrogated, and the future has not yet begun, an instant of pure potentiality when everything, as it were, trembles in the balance' (1982: 44). Rituals provide abundant examples of such liminality, as Schechner (2002: 57–8) enumerates:

> The work of the liminal phase is twofold: first, to reduce those undergoing the ritual to a state of vulnerability so that they are open to change. Persons are stripped of their former identities [. . .]; they enter a

time-place where they are not-this-not-that, neither here nor there, in the midst of a journey from one social self to another. For the time being, they are literally powerless and often identityless. Second, during the liminal phase, persons are inscribed with their new identities and initiated into their new powers.

Liminality is therefore a state of transition that involves risk and vulnerability but promises rewards of new identities and new powers.

Not surprisingly, film stars frequently play with risk and vulnerability on- and offscreen, and their performances generate moments of liminality that complicate their images and identities, challenge conventional rules of the game, command the audience's fascination, and provoke media responses. In the next two sections, I will develop repetition and dark play as two dominant tropes to discuss Tony Leung's star performances in *In the Mood for Love* and *Lust, Caution*, so as to evaluate the implications of play and liminality for star studies.

IN THE MOOD FOR LOVE: ROLE-PLAYING AS REPETITION FOR VARIATION

Two definitions of performance foreground repetition and interaction as crucial to my re-examination of star texts in this section. First, Schechner's conception of all performances of art, rituals and ordinary life as 'twice-behaved behavior' or 'restored behaviors' reveals the indispensability of repetition, although repetition does not necessarily result in a reproduction of the same because '[n]ot only the behavior itself – nuances of mood, tone of voice, body language, and so on, but also the specific occasion and context make each instance unique' (Schechner 2002: 22–3). Performance, in other words, involves repetition with subtle variation or alteration. Second, Erving Goffman's definition of performance as 'all the activity of a given participant on a given occasion which serves to influence in any way any of the other participants' (1959: 15–16) points to the dynamics of interaction through which performance engages itself with the other and builds relationships. Performance is never exclusively an end in itself; rather, it is always a means of interactivity that links the self to the other, here to elsewhere, and now to elsewhen.

Critics have concurred that repetition is integral to the aesthetics of Wong Kar-wai (Wang Jiawei, b. 1956) and *In the Mood for Love* is a masterpiece of repetition. Based on 'Intersection/Duidao' (also translated as *Tête-bêche*), a story by Hong Kong writer Liu Yichang (b. 1918), Wong's film features Maggie Cheung (Zhang Manyu, b. 1964) as Su Li-zhen and Tony Leung as Chow Mo-wan, and repetition occurs on the film's various registers. In terms of narrative, the film weaves 'repetitive patterns of story action' and its 'obsessive reenactment justifies much of *In the Mood for Love*'s motivic action'

(Bettinson 2009: 172). In terms of intertextuality, Cheung and Leung both appeared in Wong's early piece, *Days of Being Wild/A Fei zhengzhuan* (1990), and '2046' refers to a room number in both *In the Mood for Love* and its sequel *2046* (2004), as well as to a fictional place where people retrieve their lost memory in *2046* and to the year before the end of the fifty-year deadline within which the current system of Hong Kong, according to Beijing's promise, would not change after the transfer of sovereignty from Britain to China on 1 July 1997 (Yue 2008: 145). In terms of cinematography, the frame composition of Li-zhen and Mo-wan's taxi ride in the film resembles that of a taxi ride of Lai Yiu-fai (Tony Leung) and Ho Po-wing (Leslie Cheung/Zhang Guorong, 1956–2003) in Wong's *Happy Together/Chunguang zhaxie* (1997), both scenes punctuated by emotional fidelity or infidelity (Brunette 2005: 78, 102). In terms of costume and art design, a repetition of floral motifs in her dress and her surroundings draws Li-zhen's interior to the surface: as she 'drifts away into a reflective state of mind, the floral pattern of her dress blends into the flowery folds of the curtain, the vase of flowers, and the lampshade, equally decorated with floral motifs' (Bruno 2011: 97). In terms of music and songs, the rhythm of Nat King Cole's 'Quizas Quizas Quizas' ('Perhaps, Perhaps, Perhaps') expresses Li-zhen's ambivalent feelings after Mo-wan asks her to accompany him to Singapore; even in moments when nothing happens, music still 'serves as a sound bridge to link the two characters thematically and psychologically, as for example when we cut from Mo-wan smoking forlornly in his office to Li-zhen, alone in her office, spotted through the filtering, distorting curtains, as she always is' (Brunette 2005: 97).

Yet, above all it is star performance that best exemplifies Wong's aesthetics of repetition, and attention is repeatedly directed to Maggie Cheung's exhibition of more than twenty gorgeous dresses. Male critics are delighted at Wong's sartorial symbolism of female sexuality. Peter Brunette comments on Cheung's dresses: 'Form-fitting and tightly wound, even around her neck, they are thus at the same time highly sexual and highly repressed' (2005: 91). Stephen Teo is more enthusiastic: '*In the Mood for Love* is a virtual *cheongsam* show [. . .] and who among the Chinese of the baby-boom generation could fail to be moved by the allusive and sensual properties of the body-hugging *cheongsam* (or *qipao* in Mandarin)?' (2001: n.p.). Nonetheless, there may be a gender difference here, as female scholar Yuh-yi Tan delves beneath Li-zhen's fashion surface and suggests that 'her high-neck style and blue-and-red spiral pattern [. . .] imply her split psyche torn between the conformist and mysterious qualities' (2010: 158). By pursuing a feminist psychoanalytic reading of fetishism in relation to Li-zhen's *qipao*, slippers, high-heel shoes, lipstick and cigarettes, Tan contends that the 'function of the woman-as-fetish occurs through the sublimation and regulation of her libidinal energy into performative pleasure' (2010: 163); rather than being objectified in male fantasy, such female performance articulates 'a yearning for the maternal embrace and empowerment' (2010: 177), as seen in the scene of Li-zhen with her son near the end.

I find it quite extraordinary that, in most scholarship on Wong Kar-wai and *In the Mood for Love*, male performance is largely absent, and Tony Leung is virtually invisible despite the fact that he won the Best Actor at Cannes for his lead role as Chow Mo-wan. How are we going to account for this conspicuous oversight? We may recall Leung's long list of pensive, inarticulate characters, for instance the mute brother Lin Wen-ching in *City of Sadness/Beiqing cheng-shi* (Hou Hsiao-hsien, 1989) or the enigmatic poet in *Cyclo* (Tran Anh Hung, 1995). Sure, Leung is an internationally known star and has played in action and martial arts films, but his stardom has a peculiar charm: 'Leung's manner is reserved and enigmatic. His characters reflect his public persona – shy, intro-verted, and self-effacing' (Nochimson 2005: 16).

A challenge to star studies arises here: How do we theorise a 'self-effacing' star performance? Here, I suggest that we conceptualise repetition as a type of performativity that naturalises itself to the point of invisibility. For Judith Butler, 'stylised repetition of acts' repeats itself into invisibility and makes performance seem natural and therefore unlike a performance (1990: 140). To modify Della Pollock's description of Butler's performance theory (2006: 4), 'the ultimate trick of performance-as-repetition is to make itself disappear into the appearance of history as "given"', we may hypothesise that Tony Leung's star performance is a peculiar kind of performance-as-repetition that makes itself disappear into the intricate design of a given film and thus represents a visual trick of invisibility in direct contrast to the performance of high visibility as embodied by Maggie Cheung and her male counterparts like Jackie Chan. In Leung's performance, what 'self-effacing' means is not that the self is actually invisible – for his fans around the world never fail to appreciate his charms onscreen – but that the self is always already in transition into something else precisely due to the trick of performance-as-repetition.

In the perspective of performance studies, we have realised by now that all those 'role-playing games' (Tan 2010: 155) in which Tony Leung actively engages Maggie Cheung in *In the Mood for Love* are not meant to assert any fixed identity but rather to explore emotional uncertainty in a slowly developing relationship. Play has enabled them to imagine what it feels to be their respective cheating spouses when they ask each other to order dishes for them – or their absent spouses – in a restaurant. Similarly, 'this play of substitution' in what seems to be 'Wong's most mischievous moment in the film' (Brunette 2005: 96) leads to an intimate scene in which Li-zhen twice rehearses her planned confrontation with her unfaithful husband. In these two rehearsals, Leung appears invisible not only because he turns his back to us most of the time but also because he disappears into his role as Li-zhen's

Figure 2.1   Tony Leung's role-playing as a cheating husband in *In the Mood for Love* (Wong Kar-wai, 2000).

otherwise invisible husband when he faces the camera (see Figure 2.1). In this particular performance-as-repetition, Leung skilfully plays with absence and presence, encouraging himself simultaneously to act on a moral high ground – as captured by Li-zhen's announcement, 'We will never be like them' (that is, their cheating spouses) – and to experience what transgressive desire tastes like. When Mo-wan and Li-zhen start rehearsing their upcoming separation in a subsequent scene, it is obvious that 'virtually all of the emotions in this film are prerehearsed' (Brunette 2005: 96), and it is thus impossible to obtain what Wong Kar-wai has expected as 'primary emotions' from the two stars (Rayns 2000: 36).

Leung's style of self-effacing performance-as-repetition represents a special type of performativity that questions aggression and fixation in representation. Peggy Phelan (1993: 3) distinguishes representation and performance this way: 'Representation reproduces the Other as the Same. Performance, insofar as it can be defined as representation without reproduction, can be seen as a model for another representational economy, one in which the reproduction of the Other as the Same is not assured.' Similarly, performance-as-repetition entertains both sides of self and other, and rehearses approaching the other without fixing it as the same, as a reproduced self-image. Such performance may result in a degree of invisibility as the self always appears together with and sometimes even as the other, but it opens up the space for imagining unrecognised or unforeseeable alternatives.

Teo judges *In the Mood for Love* (2001) to be 'conservative' and 'didactic' in its main protagonists' 'unambiguous' moral constraint and ethical propriety (2001: n.p.). Yet my reading demonstrates that the dynamics of repetition with variation – for Teo also agrees that 'repetition as a signifier of changes becomes a motif throughout the film' (2005b: 127) – makes the film's moral message ambiguous. After all, Li-zhen cares for her son near the end of the film, and one of Wong Kar-wai's deleted scenes, 'The Secret of Room 2046', as offered on the Criterion Collection special edition DVD of *In the Mood for Love*, actually features Mo-wan and Li-zhen consummate their love, although Wong deliberately keeps the identity of the child's father ambiguous (Ciment and Niogret 2000: 78).

Obviously, role-playing never reproduces the same but always involves repetition with variation, which can be carried to a surprising extreme. For *2046*, Wong Kar-wai preserves the role Chow Mo-wan for Tony Leung but reverses the character's traits. This unusual repetition has occasioned not only variations – Leung insists on wearing a moustache to mark a difference in the new Chow Mo-wan in *2046* – but even new discoveries as well. Leung recalls (Nochimson 2005: 16): 'He [Wong] explores some qualities inside me that I don't even know I have, which is frightening, but also very interesting. He always surprises me.' By surprising variations and reversals through repetition, Wong Kar-wai has emerged not just a mere star director but a director as star (Austin and Barker 2003: 7).

LUST, CAUTION: DARK PLAY AS SUBVERSION THROUGH LIMINALITY

Schechner reminds us of two kinds of playing: rule-bound (as in sport competitions) and rule-breaking (as in the Nietzschean fire play), and Tony Leung's star performance covers both. If Chow Mo-wan in *In the Mood for Love* belongs to the 'sympathetic wimp and loser: the archetypal weak male here in the tradition of Chinese romantic melodramas' (Teo 2005b: 122), then in *2046* he reappears as its reversal, a playboy romantically dallying with gorgeous women played by leading Chinese female stars, including Gong Li (b. 1965) and Zhang Ziyi (b. 1979). As in *In the Mood for Love*, however, Leung's Mo-wan still suffers from lost love, and as Wong Kar-wai's loose adaptation of Liu Yichang's novel *The Drunkard/Jiutu* (1963), *2046* remains 'a film about mood and character, elegiac in tone, pervaded by a sense of sadness, fatalism and resignation' (Teo 2005a: n.p.). When it comes to *Lust, Caution*, Leung 'seems to be playing some darker version of Chow Mo-wan' (Marchetti 2012: 148), but this time his astoundingly rule-breaking performance as Mr Yee – especially in three notorious sex scenes, which earned the film NC-17 rating in the US – foregrounds his tortuous body and its controversial embodiment, rendering them impossible to be dismissed as invisible or self-effacing.

In many ways Mr Yee is engaged in deep play, 'the kind of play in which the risks to the player outweigh the potential rewards' (Schechner 2002: 82) and which 'draws the whole person into what amounts to a life-and-death struggle expressing not only individual commitment (even to the irrational), but cultural values' (Schechner 2002: 106). As Clifford Geertz (1973: 433) observes of gambling in Bali, in deep play, 'where the amounts of money are great, much more is at stake than material gain: namely, esteem, honor, dignity, respect.' From Geertz's deep play, Schechner develops a concept of dark play, which 'involves fantasy, risk, luck, daring, invention, and deception' (2002: 106). As Schechner explains (2002: 107),

> Dark play subverts order, dissolves frames, and breaks its own rules – so much so that the playing itself is in danger of being destroyed, as in spying, double-agentry, con games, and stings [. . .] [D]ark play is truly subversive, its agendas always hidden. Dark play's goals are deceit, disruption, excess, and gratification.

The relevance of dark play to *Lust, Caution* is obvious. Replete with 'deceit, disruption, excess, and gratification', the film involves wartime double-agentry in a clandestine affair between Wang Chia-chih (played by Tang Wei, b. 1979), an innocent college student recruited by the Nationalist underground resistance to play seductress Mai Tai-tai (or Mrs Mak), and Mr Yee, a pro-Japanese police chief who knowingly risks his 'esteem, honor, dignity, respect' by playing the life-and-death game of seduction and who in the end orders the execution of Chia-chih and her fellow student patriots. Adapted from a story of the same title by Eileen Chang (Zhang Ailing, b. 1920) (E. Chang 2007: 1–57; A. Zhang 1991), herself a controversial writer briefly married to Hu Lancheng (1906–81), an infamous wartime collaborator and womaniser (Lee 2008: 231–2) – inspired by a real-life wartime espionage case involving Zheng Pingru (1918–40), a half-Japanese, half-Chinese female Nationalist agent, and Ding Mocun (1901–47), a pro-Japanese intelligence chief who might be a double agent himself (Marchetti 2012: 133) – the film has proven to be transgressive and subversive both on- and offscreen due to its intricate layers of dark play.

The dark play in *Lust, Caution* foregrounds the vulnerability of the players in a game of high risks and uncertain rewards. Interestingly, several critics have used the word 'vulnerable' to depict Tony Leung's performance in this film. Leo Ou-fan Lee notices the different characterisation of Mr Yee, who appears cautious, manipulative and even cold-blooded in Eileen Chang's original story, and concludes that Ang 'Lee has made him [Leung] more vulnerable – a victim of his own excessive repression' (2008: 237). By exposing vulnerability onscreen, Leung has successfully portrayed a sympathetic character whose repression of feelings requires comprehension in a larger historical context, as Leo Lee suggests (2008: 233):

> The by now notorious love scenes between the heroine and the villain, with their torsos twisted in pain and pleasure, and progressing from a scene of sadistic rape to that of anguished ecstasy, serve to convey the intertwining of the two characters' sexual act and the repressive political environment in which they live. But this provides merely the veneer of a historical crisis in which both the traitor-predator and the patriot-victim are trapped – they are doomed by circumstances beyond their individual control.

Whereas Leo Lee resorts to a historical understanding of 'the repressive political environment' as a factor for the largely positive reception of the film in Taiwan, Stephanie Hemelryk Donald points to the foregrounding of visible body images onscreen beyond mere ideological or moral coding as a source for the overwhelmingly negative reception in mainland China: 'The film's transgression lies in its visual commitment to the entanglement of the female sexual body, with a violent but vulnerable male body' (2010: 51). For Donald, Lee's film is transgressive in that, as in *Last Tango in Paris* (Bernardo Bertolucci, 1972; starring Marlon Brando), 'the tactile and quivering quality' of the star performance 'blurs the reality principle, so that we are seduced by his strength on screen to assume that somehow we are indeed watching the unmediated unfolding of a human being' (2010: 59). Because star power is able to command audiences' affective identification beyond entrenched ideological positions, Donald argues that 'Leung's portrayal of a key type in mainland Chinese cinema as not merely ruthless, but also vulnerable, and – I think this is crucial to negative reactions – sexually more potent than any other man in the film, represents a profound shift in characterisation' (2010: 61).

The key type referenced above is the screen portrayal of the Chinese collaborator (*hanjian*) as always scheming, subservient and thus despicable, not only throughout mainland Chinese film history, as Donald mentions, but also – I would add – in Hong Kong's patriotic films of the 1940s and Taiwan's Mandarin productions of the 1960s and '70s. Given this long cinematic tradition, it is an exploit for Leung's complex persona of Mr Yee – at once risk-taking and cautious, vulnerable and aggressive, courteous and abusive, tender-hearted and cold-blooded – to subvert the deep-rooted stereotype, solicit sympathy, and create a liminal space for imagining unforeseen or unforeseeable alternatives.

However, what is ironic in the negative reception of *Lust, Caution* in mainland China is perhaps not so much that audiences were angered by the onscreen exhibition of the male traitor-predator's rape of the female patriot-victim and the latter's apparently voluntary submission to his power, wealth and charm, as that they are mostly unaware of a subtle clue in the film narrative that Mr Yee may have covertly worked for the Communists by arranging the shipment of ammunition to them (Wang 2010: 584–5). Mr Yee's real-life prototype, Ding Mocun, had switched his loyalty from the Communists to the Nationalists in the late 1920s and then to the Japanese in the late 1930s, and eventually he was put on trial and executed as a traitor by the Nationalists after the war (Peng and Dilley 2014: 114–15). Rather than the stereotypical 'villain' or 'traitor-predator' (Leo Lee's phrases), Sebastian Liao (2010: 181) allegorically reinterprets Mr Yee as the representative of the state, nationalism and modernity, with Wang Chia-chih representing the people who are repeatedly deceived in their willing supply of unrequited love and self-sacrifice.

The possibility of Mr Yee as double agent complicates the space of liminality opened up by the dark play in *Lust, Caution*. Paradoxically, it is because he is daring enough to expose himself to vulnerability that Mr Yee may feel 'safe in the Freudian "darkness" of a female sexual embrace, his one "dark space"' (Donald 2010: 56) available only in the liminality of performance. Similarly, the dark play of her sadomasochistic sexual ordeals/orgasms with Mr Yee pushes Wang Chia-chih to the brink of being 'identityless', temporarily losing track of her multiple roles as assassin, seductress and lover. As Schechner sees it, the function of liminality is to place those undergoing a ritual in a state of vulnerability so that they are ready to transition to a new identity or – I would add – back and forth between identities. By insisting on filming three prolonged graphic sex scenes, which are based on passing references in Eileen Chang's story, Ang Lee has added the liminality of fluid identities to an otherwise typical black-and-white narrative of wartime espionage, and such liminality poses a serious challenge to conventional representation and interpretation based on nationalism and patriotism.

To a certain extent, the unusual Chinese film title 'Se | jie' – Ang Lee's repetition with variation on Eileen Chang's title, 'Se, jie', which carries a comma between the Chinese characters (Zhang 1991) – embodies the ideas of liminality and performativity. Chang Hsiao-hung (2008: 33) interprets the rare perpendicular line between the two Chinese characters in the film's title as both 'a line of blockage that separates the right from the left' and 'a line of bloc that conjoins the right with the left', and suggests that '[t]his double mechanism of separation and assemblage makes "|" simultaneously and paradoxically a border-division and a border-proximity'. Following Gilles Deleuze, Chang Hsiao-hung contends (2008: 47),

> The affective line of bloc as initially suggested by the '|' in the Chinese title of *Lust, Caution* can thus successfully oppose the *line-system* (or

bloc-system) of becoming to the *point-system* of representation, origin, coordinates and memory that has long been dominating the traditional 'historical' approach. Instead of excluding before from after, there from here, now from then, it superimposes them to make them collide, connect and become.

The perpendicular line 'l' therefore functions as a sign of liminality, tactically conjoining what is otherwise considered to be the opposite and forcing them to play in a new game of imbricating and becoming.

Actually, the film *Lust, Caution* itself has been engaged in a larger stage of performance offscreen. Leo Lee (2008) traces the film's contrastive receptions in the US and the Chinese-speaking world, and Chang Hsiao-hung (2008: 34) starts her meditation on transnational affect with a discussion of 'two peculiar *affective* discharges, anger in the mainland and tears in Taiwan', the latter reportedly from Ang Lee himself and from President Ma Ying-jeou. Robert Chi (2009) elaborates the exhibition of different versions of the film in different territories – the favourite story being that many mainland tourists visited Hong Kong to see the uncut version – and the circulation of the film's DVD editions of varied cuts and lengths. More recently, several critics (Donald 2010; Peng and Dilley 2014) have analysed Beijing's controversial censure of the rising star Tang Wei for her compelling performance of a patriotic young woman who, in a crucial moment of the assassination scheme, urges Mr Yee to leave quickly, perhaps because Wang Chia-chih believes Mr Yee really loves her when he is buying her a huge six-carat diamond ring, or perhaps because she realises that they are but two vulnerable victims in a precarious historical environment.

A CONJUNCTURAL VIEW OF STAR PERFORMANCE

The amazing variety of offscreen performances of *Lust, Caution* once again highlights the dynamics of interactivity engendered by star performance onscreen. On the one hand, Vivian Shen (2011: 318) defends Tang's Wang Chia-chih on the basis of individual desire: 'While it is noble to fight for the collective and for one's nation, a person's individual needs may surpass his or her social and moral obligations to country.' On the other hand, Wang Xiaoping blames Chia-chih's unexpected act of saving Mr Yee on her confusing performative roles: 'When she is unable to distinguish her real self from the fictional one, she has misplaced her body and her psyche in a class that she does not belong to, and her true nature is distorted by the role she is assigned' (2010: 579). However, from the perspective of performance studies, it is precisely this conviction on anyone's 'true nature' and 'real self' that the liminality of play intentionally challenges and successfully subverts.

James Schamus, one of the film's scriptwriters and Ang Lee's long-time collaborator, thus revisits the key moment in *Lust, Caution* (2007: 63–4):

> What act, exactly, does Wang Chia-chih perform at that fateful moment in the jeweler's shop when she decides whether or not to go through with the murder of her lover?
>
> And here, two words – *act* and *perform* – indicate the troubling question Zhang Ailing (Eileen Chang) asks us: for at the crucial moment when we *choose*, when we *decide*, when we *exercise our free will*, are we not also *performing*?
>
> One could say that *Lust, Caution* depicts a heroine who 'becomes herself' only when she takes on the identity of another, for only behind the mask of the character Mai Tai-tai can Chia-chih truly desire, and thus truly live – playacting allows her to discover her one real love. But this is too reductive. For the performer always, by definition, performs *for* someone. And that audience, no matter how entranced, is always complicit: it knows deep down that the performance isn't real, but it also knows the cathartic truth the performer strives for is attainable only when that truth is, indeed, *performed*. Yee doesn't simply desire Mai Tai-tai while suspecting she is not who she says she is; it is precisely *because* he suspects her that he desires her.

For Schamus, desire and love are performative acts, and so are nationalism and espionage, as *Lust, Caution* has repeatedly staged them as such, from Chia-chih's drama performance in Hong Kong through her disguise as Mai Tai-tai to her enigmatic final look before the group execution. Yet what remains unsettling is that the audience is fully complicit in the unfolding game of sexual seduction and gratification the stars are performing onscreen, because inevitably the stars perform for us and deliver what is attainable only in and through the liminality of performance.

The unsettling power of star performance is evident in the contrastive receptions of *Lust, Caution* in various regions of the world. As Schamus admits (2007: 65): 'I think one of the things that drew Ang Lee, and the rest of us with him, toward Zhang Ailing's work was a feeling that her writing itself is just this kind of "act" – a profound cry of protest against the warring structures of domination that so cataclysmically shaped midcentury China.' Although this view contradicts Leo Lee's evaluation of Ang Lee's 'loser mentality', which 'can be seen in his films as a subtle and indirect form of articulation – not contestation, protest, or revolt' (Lee 2008: 226), Leo Lee nonetheless concedes that Ang Lee has chosen *to* protest on Eileen Chang's behalf.

The idea of performance as protest is likewise taken up by Stephanie Donald. Taking 'visual conjecture' to reference a tactic of critique assumed by contemporary Chinese independent documentary, Donald (2010: 58) contends that the three explicit sexual scenes in *Lust, Caution* are a cumulative refusal to engage, quoting Paola Voci (2004: 65), in 'an antagonistic dialogue with an assumed dominant ideology, but rather [to] display an exhibitionist form of resistance'. Sure, this kind of thinking on corporeal and visual performance as resistance, subversion and protest dovetails with the theory of performance studies in general. Dwight Conquerwood conceives performance as 'a tactics of intervention, an alterative space of struggle' (2002: 152), and he adds activism and critique to the agenda of performance studies (Madison and Hamera 2006: xii).

Conquerwood's term 'alterative' reminds us of an array of tactics available to performance beyond resistance or subversion, as the alterative may very well be another effective tactic of performance in producing liminality and change. For Turner, liminality opens the possibility of 'standing aside not only from one's own social position but from all social positions and of formulating a potentially unlimited series of alternative social arrangements' (1974: 14). This alternative – and I would add 'alterative' – formulation occurs for both the performer and the audience, and it is the unforeseen potential of such alterations that makes performance unsettling to the dominant and the conventional.

Not surprisingly, Tony Leung's performance covers the spectrum from radical subversion (as in *Lust, Caution*) to subtle alteration (as in *In the Mood for Love*). He has performed repetitions with variations in Wong Kar-wai's films, and the radicalness of his performance in *Lust, Caution* is unsettling in that not only has he subverted the stereotype of the collaborator through a series of dark plays but he has altered, in an uncanny way, the very ground for justifying the film as a protest Ang Lee has courageously made on Eileen Chang's behalf. After all, by secreting working for the Communists as a double agent and therefore becoming 'apparently a stauncher-than-usual nationalist' (Liao 2010: 181), which is the exact opposite of a traitor, Mr Yee may have worked in part for the power to come, the very power that constitutes a major part of 'the warring structures of domination' in Schamus' interpretation. Mr Yee's enigmatic identities bring us to Schechner's cautious remark (2002: 79): 'Playing is double-edged, ambiguous, moving in several directions simultaneously [. . .] Play can subvert the powers-that-be, as in parody or carnival, or it can be cruel, absolute power.'

At the end of the film *Lust, Caution*, instead of congratulating himself, as in the original story, in a male-chauvinistic manner – 'And now he possessed her utterly, primitively – as a hunter does his quarry, a tiger his kill. Alive, her body belonged to him; dead, she was his ghost' (E. Chang 2007: 54; A. Zhang 1991: 34) – Tony Leung's Mr Yee sits on Wang Chia-chih's empty bed, his fingers touching the satin sheet, and his look melancholy (see Figure 2.2).

Figure 2.2 Tony Leung's dark play with vulnerability in *Lust, Caution* (Ang Lee, 2007).

He stands up and leaves slowly, his dark shadow cast on the bed. This scene reminds us of Paul Arthur's description of *In the Mood for Love*: 'The figures up on the screen are at once immediate and absent' (2001: 41). Leung is there on the screen, but he seems absent, and so are Mr Yee's multiple contradictory roles (killer/lover, villain/hero, traitor/patriot) and the audience's identification. Despite such contradiction and confusion, what is unmistakably projected there is vulnerability, a quality characteristic of the majority of Chinese stars in film history (Yu 2012).

All stardom is performative in nature, but Tony Leung's self-effacing performance directs attention to a special type of 'spectral aesthetics' (Khoo 2006: 239) that plays with absence/presence, vanishing/returning, and thrives on the space of play and liminality. Rather than 'structured polysemy' that presumes a bounded system of meaning for decoding and differentiation, I propose that a conjunctural vision of star studies informed by performance studies enables us to re-envision meaning as not so much structured as conjunctural – as coincidental, concurrent, improvisational and juxtapositional – and to further explore a wider range of cinematic and performative tactics that challenge our entrenched habit of signification and interpretation, and open up spaces for new alterations and alternatives.

Bibliography

Arthur, P. (2001), 'Review of *In the Mood for Love*', *Cineaste* 26:3, 40–1.
Austin, T. and M. Barker (eds) (2003), *Contemporary Hollywood Stardom*, London: Arnold.
Bettinson, G. (2009), 'Happy together?: Generic Hybridity in *2046* and *In the Mood for Love*', in W. Buckland (ed.), *Puzzle Films: Complex Storytelling in Contemporary Cinema*, Malden: Wiley-Blackwell, pp. 167–86.
Brunette, P. (2005), *Wong Kar-wai*, Urbana: University of Illinois Press.
Bruno, G. (2011), 'Surface, Fabric, Weave: the Fashioned World of Wong Kar-wai', in A. Munich (ed.), *Fashion in Film*, Bloomington: Indiana University Press, pp. 83–105.
Butler, J. (1990), *Gender Trouble*, New York: Routledge.
Chang, E. (2007), *Lust, Caution: The Story*, trans. J. Lovell, New York: Anchor Books.
Chang, H. (2008), 'Transnational Affect: Cold Anger, Hot Tears and *Lust, Caution*', *Concentric: Literary and Cultural Studies* 35.1, 31–50.
Chi, R. (2009), 'Exhibitionism: *Lust, Caution*', *Journal of Chinese Cinemas* 3.2, 177–87.
Ciment, M. and H. Niogret (2000), 'Entretien avec Wong Kar-Wai', *Positif* 477, 76–80.
Conquerwood, D. (2002), 'Performance Studies: Intervention and Radical Research', *The Drama Review* 20, 325–41.
Donald, S. H. (2010), 'Tang Wei: Sex, the City and the Scapegoat in *Lust, Caution*', *Theory, Culture & Society* 27, 46–68.
Dyer, R. (1979), *Stars*, London: British Film Institute.
Farquhar, M. and Y. Zhang (eds) (2010), *Chinese Film Stars*, London: Routledge.
Geertz, C. (1973), *The Interpretation of Cultures*, New York: Basic Books.
Gledhill, C. (ed.) (1991), *Stardom: Industry of Desire*, London: Routledge.
Goffman, E. (1959), *The Presentation of Self in Everyday Life*, Garden City: Doubleday.
Huizinga, J. (1970), *Homo Ludens: A Study of the Play Element in Culture*, New York: Harper.
Khoo, O. (2006), 'Love in Ruins: Spectral Bodies in Wong Kar-wai's *In the Mood for Love*', in F. Martin and L. Heinrich (eds), *Embodied Modernities: Corporeality, Representation, and Chinese Cultures*, Honolulu: University of Hawaii Press, pp. 235–52.
Lee, L. (2008), 'Ang Lee's *Lust, Caution* and Its Reception', *boundary 2* 35:3, 223–38.
Liao, H. S. (2010), 'Becoming Modernized or Simply "Modern": Sex, Chineseness, and Diasporic Consciousness in *Lust and Caution*', *Concentric: Literary and Cultural Studies* 36:2 (2010), 181–211.
Madison, D. S. and J. Hamera (eds) (2006), *The Sage Handbook of Performance Studies*, Thousand Oaks: Sage.
Marchetti, G. (2012), 'Eileen Chang and Ang Lee at the Movies: The Cinematic Politics of *Lust, Caution*', in Kam Louie (ed.), *Eileen Chang: Romancing Languages, Cultures and Genres*, Hong Kong: Hong Kong University Press, pp, 131–54.
Nietzsche, F. W. (1962), *Philosophy in the Tragic Age of the Greeks*, South Bend: Gateway Editions.
Nochimson, M. P. (2005), 'Lies and Loneliness: An Interview with Tony Leung Chiu Wai', *Cinéaste* 30:4, 16–17.
Peng, H. and W. C. Dilley (eds) (2014), *From Eileen Chang to Ang Lee: Lust, Caution*, London: Routledge.
Phelan, P. (1993), *Unmarked: The Politics of Performance*, London: Routledge.
Pollock, D. (2006), 'Performance Trouble', in D. S. Madison and J. Hamera (eds), *The Sage Handbook of Performance Studies*, Thousand Oaks: Sage, pp. 1–8.
Rayns, T. (2000), 'Charisma Express', *Sight and Sound* 10:1, 34–6.

Schechner, R. (2002), *Performance Studies: An Introduction*, London: Routledge.

Schamus, J. (2007), 'Why Did She Do It?', in E. Chang, *Lust, Caution: The Story*, New York: Anchor Books, pp. 63–8.

Shen, V. (2012), 'History, Fiction, and Film *Lust, Caution* Revisited', *Asian Cinema* 22:2, 305–21.

Tan, Y. (2010), 'Resisting the Lure of the Fetish: Between Abjection and Fetishism in Kar Wai Wong's *In the Mood for Love*', *Concentric: Literary and Cultural Studies* 36:2, 149–79.

Teo, S. (2001), 'Wong Kar-wai's *In the Mood for Love*: Like a Ritual in Transfigured Time', *Senses of Cinema* 13, http://sensesofcinema.com/2001/13/wong-kar-wai/mood/, last accessed 18 December 2014.

— (2005a), '*2046*: A Matter of Time, a Labour of Love', *Sense of Cinema* 35, http://sensesofcinema.com/2005/35/2046/, last accessed 18 December 2014.

— (2005b), *Wong Kar-wai*, London: British Film Institute.

Turner, V. (1974), *Dramas, Fields, and Metaphors: Symbolic Action in Human Society*, Ithaca: Cornell University Press.

— (1982), *From Ritual to Theatre: The Human Seriousness of Play*, New York: Performing Arts Journal Publications.

— (1983), 'Body, Brain, and Culture', *Zygon* 18:3, 221–45.

Wang, X. (2010), 'Making a Historical Fable: The Narrative Strategy of *Lust, Caution* and Its Social Repercussions', *Journal of Contemporary China* 19:65, 573–90.

Yu, S. Q. (2012), 'Vulnerable Chinese Stars: From Xizi to Film Worker', in Y. Zhang (ed.), *A Companion to Chinese Cinema*, Malden: Wiley-Blackwell, pp. 218–38.

Yue, A. (2008), '*In the Mood for Love*: Intersections of Hong Kong's Modernity', in C. Berry (ed.), *Chinese Films in Focus II*, New York: Palgrave Macmillan, pp. 144–52.

Zhang, A. (1991), 'Se, jie' (Lust, caution), in *Wangran ji* (Tales of bewilderment), *Zhang Ailing quanji* (Complete works of Eileen Chang), vol. 12, Taipei: Huangguan, pp. 9–36.

Zhang, Y. (2013), 'Witness outside History: Play for Alteration in Modern Chinese Culture', *Modernism/Modernity* 20:2, 349–69.

PART 2

STAR VOICES

3. 'SPEAKING IN A FORKED TONGUE': ANNA MAY WONG'S LINGUISTIC COSMOPOLITANISM*

Yiman Wang

Anna May Wong (1905–61), the iconic early twentieth-century Chinese-American stage and screen performer, ventured into film acting at the age of fourteen in Hollywood as an extra in an Alla Nazimova vehicle, *Red Lantern* (Albert Capellini, 1919). Submerged in the large number of uncredited ethnic extras recruited for the film, Wong silently contributed to the so-called 'Chinese atmosphere' (designed for the Hollywood Orientalist fantasy about turn-of-the-twentieth-century China), while Nazimova, the leading star, portrayed the mixed-race Chinese protagonist as well as her white half-sister. Wong's screen debut, inconspicuous as it was, led to more appearances as an extra in a string of films until 1921, when she obtained her first credited role as the abused Chinese wife of Lon Chaney's character in *Bits of Life* (Marshall Neilan, 1921).

Her tenacity during Hollywood's silent era eventually won mainstream public recognition, especially with her portrayal of the tragic Chinese Madame Butterfly in *The Toll of the Sea* (Chester M. Franklin, 1922), Hollywood's first two-colour Technicolor feature, and of the scantily costumed Mongol slave in Douglas Fairbanks's spectacular exotic fantasy, *The Thief of Bagdad* (Raoul Walsh, 1924). Nonetheless, acutely aware of her limited career prospects due to Hollywood's racist practices, Wong sailed for Germany on 29 March 1928, armed with a one-film contract with the German film studio, Universum Film AG (UFA). Written by Karl Vollmoeller as her vehicle, Wong's European screen debut, *Show Life* (aka *Song*) (Richard Eichberg, 1928), quickly snowballed into a multitude of film and theatre performances in Germany, France, Britain and Austria, catapulting her into unprecedented stardom. In June 1928, barely three months after her arrival in Europe, *Show Life* was finished; and Wong was pronounced a 'decided hit' in a US report. Later reports were to reinforce her unique stellar status, touting her Oriental mystique combined with cosmopolitanism.

How did Wong attain such leading lady hyper-visibility in interwar Europe, a fame that eluded her in the US, her home country? What strategies did she develop to mobilise her itinerant and interstitial position for greater star and celebrity value? The key to these questions is her successful bid for cosmopolitanism, which, I argue, hinged upon her versatile linguistic performance, or the ability to speak in a 'forked tongue' with a subversive effect that inverted Homi Bhabha's use of the same term. If Bhabha's post-Enlightenment English colonial discourses speak in a forked tongue to mandate colonial mimicry, that is, to demand 'a reformed, recognizable Other, as a subject of a difference that is almost the same, but not quite' (Bhabha 1994: 85), then Wong's ability to speak in a forked tongue represented a tactical rejoinder to this colonial demand by performing a form of mimicry that completely reshuffled the order of sameness and differences, throwing into disarray the colonial hierarchy and the correlated racist Orientalism.[1]

Wong's contention for cosmopolitanism through linguistic versatility, therefore, 'expose[d] those slippages and contradictions' in the 'Eurocentric ideological assumptions of cosmopolitanism', as Shirley Lim argues (2012: 9). Mediated through her alien body, Wong's international mobility suggested 'a simultaneous incommensurability yet hyper-compatibility between the terms Asian American and cosmopolitanism' – incommensurable due to Asian-Americans' ethnic particularity in opposition to cosmopolitanism's desire for universality, yet hyper-compatible insofar that the 'alien origins' of Asian-Americans rendered their nation-state subjectivity ambivalent, therefore more amenable to extra-national affiliation including cosmopolitanism (Lim 2012: 9–10). The other side of the story, however, is that Wong's cosmopolitanism was inherently paradoxical. She was simultaneously forced into border-crossing movements due to her limited work opportunities in any single place, *and* therefore excluded from cosmopolitanism's freedoms (Lim 2012: 13).

Lim's analysis calls into question the celebratory discourses on Eurocentric cosmopolitanism while foregrounding the material conditions that necessitated Wong's mobility without guaranteeing the liberal sense of freedom. What remains unanswered is the question of *exactly what strategies* Wong developed and deployed in negotiating the variegated local and global constrictions in the domains of politics, economy and cultural commerce. Lim does summarise Wong's performance in terms of 'Orientalist performance'; that is, Wong performed the female racial minority body, and thereby participated in constructing her image as an 'authentic' Chinese subject (Lim 2012: 10). This statement naturalises the notion of 'authenticity', and therefore risks reifying authentic Chinese femininity. Underscoring the ambivalence of Wong's 'authenticating' performance, I proposed the concept of 'yellow yellowface' performance in a 2005 article, arguing that Wong strategically played into Western Orientalist expectations to simultaneously appeal to and subvert such expectations. As a result, her performance exposed the ideological premise and constructedness of the Orientalist imaginary of Chinese femininity (Wang 2005).

To adopt a different focus in this analysis of Wong's identity performance, this chapter specifically studies her linguistic strategy, encapsulated in her ability to speak in a forked tongue, as a form of satiric masquerade, echoing yet reshuffling what Bhabha calls colonial mimicry. Going further than her visually based yellow yellowface performance, Wong's linguistic virtuosity not only parodied and debunked the image of the Orient (especially Oriental femininity), but more importantly, showed that the very image of the Orient itself did not exist in the first place. Through this focused study, I argue that Wong simultaneously engineered her new-found stardom and appropriated cosmopolitanism from a marginalised, non-white stance. She injected linguistic and racial/ethnic politics into cosmopolitanism, leading to what I call her lingua-ethno cosmopolitanism, which effectively challenged the conventional assumption of white supremacy and Euro-American-centrism. By focusing on Wong's linguistically oriented performative strategies and the resulting lingua-ethno cosmopolitanism, I foreground the active role racialised performers played by strategising their marginalised positioning, thereby carving out a space for non-mainstream stardom.

I begin by revisiting Mary Anna Doane's essay, 'The Voice in the Cinema: The Articulation of Body and Space', with the goal of laying out the fundamental elements in building an integrated audiovisual illusion centred on a fictional character. I then analyse the Euro-American media discourses that registered Western commentators and critics' bafflement at Wong's perceived vocal-visual mismatching that ruptured their Orientalist fantasy. Finally, I delineate Wong's performative strategy of deploying precisely the vocal-visual mismatch to tease and mock her Orientalist audience with the result of challenging them (and us) to think beyond the stereotypes so as to envision a composite and multi-faceted racial/ethnic identity. I understand the composite identity as different from hybridity and a hyphenated identity. While hybridity and hyphenation ultimately aim at a degree of reconciliation or synthesis of different components, the composite figure relishes in and strategises the perceived vocal-visual conflict and frictions as the very raison d'être of their interstitial identity. In this process, what started out as Orientalist and colonialist constraints, which blocked full recognition of Wong's interstitial racial/ethnic identity, were transformed into the very conditions necessitating such an identity. By scrutinising the perceived vocal-visual split in the composite identity, we can critique the ideological constraints and create a space for building and understanding uncategorisable identities and the correlated non-mainstream stardom.

The 'phantasmatic body'

The key to understanding the value of Wong's composite (and potentially split) identity is to recognise how her linguistic performance was considered alienating in relation to her visual presentation, and in what ways the perceived alienation effect breached illusions presented by racial, national and cultural stereotyping. To understand the origin of the alienation effect, I refer to Mary Ann Doane's analysis of the illusion of an integral space surrounding verisimilar characters in cinema. In her essay, 'The Voice in the Cinema: The Articulation of Body and Space', Doane argues that the illusion of a three-dimensional 'phantasmatic body' prized in classic Hollywood films is constructed through the coordination of three spaces: the space of the diegesis, the space of the screen made visible through synchronised sound, and the quasi-realist auditory ambience in theatre that 'envelops the audience' in sound (Doane 1980, in Rosen 1986: 377). This 'phantasmatic body' in turn supports the illusion of an imaginary subject and agency (Doane 1980, in Rosen 1986: 380–2). Conversely, when a character's speech is separated or alienated from the image of his/her body, an 'uncanny' effect results, rupturing the illusion of audiovisual unity and spatial integrity.

Doane's analysis pinpoints not only the articulation of the character's body and the diegetic space, but more importantly, the ways in which a spectator is sutured into the audiovisual space that is anchored in the phantasmatic body of a film's fictional character. This suturing process is predicated upon two crucial factors: 1) the fictional character must overshadow the actor to become a quasi-real-life individual; and 2) the theatre space must augment the appropriate audiovisual effects to generate and maintain psychological realism of the fictional character. These two factors hinge upon the apparatus of filmmaking and projection, the actor's acting method, and the audience's participation in illusion-making. All of these are problematic and require in-depth re-examination once we take into account Anna May Wong's ambivalent relationship with her assigned roles, and with the audiences as well as the media form (be it film or theatre).

The conundrum of Wong

Euro-American race discourses are dominated by ocular-centrism that gives rise to epidermal determinism. That is, racial identities are predominantly defined in terms of visual perception of the skin tone, which is in turn mobilised to justify the hierarchy of racialisation. Such epidermal determinism led to Wong's inescapable pigeonholing as 'Chinese', eliding the gap between her ethnicity and her linguistic and cultural upbringing as well as her transnational experiences. Contrary to the ocular-centric race discourses, Wong's vocal performance summarily confounded reductive colour coding. Instead of presenting herself as an integral 'phantasmatic body' that would offer a reassuring match between her Chinese looks and her supposed Chinese accent, Wong's American English and, later, European languages invalidated and challenged the illusion of the 'phantasmatic body' and the associated ideology that privileged white subjectivity.

Before analysing the Euro-American discourses that registered Western bafflement with Wong's conundrum, it is important to note that such a composite persona was initially fostered and encouraged by the interwar European film industry and theatre critics. Her multilingual performance was catalysed by the coincidence between her first European tour and the inception of sound in filmmaking. At the cusp of the silent-to-sound transition, European film studios worked together across national boundaries to create a 'film Europe' to stave off Hollywood's onslaught (Bergfelder 1999). For this purpose, the studios needed to cultivate stars that commanded border-crossing appeal. They also invested in producing multiple language versions of the same narrative, using crews and casts of different national and linguistic backgrounds. The arrival of Anna May Wong proved a godsend opportunity to facilitate the project of 'film Europe'. Promoted as an ethnic Chinese with the flair of an American flapper, Wong felicitously yoked together the traditional and the modern, the exotic and the familiar, the East and the West, emerging as a polysemous icon of versatile appeal. This advantage was further enhanced by her active acquisition of European languages, which was conducive to her linguistic cosmopolitanism.

Ironically, the cosmopolitan persona fostered for broad-spectrum appeal necessarily violated racial/ethnic legibility, therefore confusing her commentators and critics who, governed by ocular-centric racial discourses, could not help but trip over Wong's perceived vocal-visual inconsistency. The conundrum of Wong was frequently noted by white Euro-American writers, ranging from the German cultural critic Walter Benjamin to a reporter for *Atlantic City Gazette*. In his 1928 article on meeting with Wong in Berlin, Benjamin opened with a laboriously hyperbolic sentence striving to pin down Wong's 'Orientalness': 'May Wong – the name sounds colorfully edged, vital and light like the petite sticks are, which develop into an unscented blossom within a tea bowl' (Benjamin 1928: 1).[2] He went on to detail Wong's outfit: 'Her dress wouldn't be ill fitted for such a garden play: dark blue coat and skirt, light blue blouse, a yellow tie in addition – one would like to know a Chinese verse for it. She always wore this attire, because she wasn't born in China, but in Chinatown in Los Angeles' (Benjamin 1928: 1). As Lim notes, Benjamin's struggle for words reveals his epistemological crisis in the face of the conundrum posed by the uncategorisable Wong, with 'her Chinese face and American colloquialisms' (Lim 2012: 7).

While the German cultural critic struggled (in vain) to find words and metaphors that could adequately resolve the epistemological conundrum posed by Wong, an American reporter for *Atlantic City Gazette* summarised Wong's perceived incoherence in one pithy catchphrase, 'an American girl with a Chinese epidermis', with her Chinese epidermis being manifested in 'slim ivory grace', eyes that 'are brown bamboo butterflies, glinting oriental mysteries', while her American-ness is epitomised in her 'glib American speech, mannerisms and smart attire' (Jungmeyer 1929).

Wong's American accent further emerged as a major scandal following her debut stage performance in *The Circle of Chalk*.[3] While the London reviewers mostly affirmed her physical acting (including her lotus dance), they criticised her shockingly Americanised or, more specifically, Californian accent that 'falls from Celestial lips'. Furthermore, her voice was described as 'an undistinguished one, clipping words leaving many of them almost inaudible. She got no variety into the long speeches.' The same reviewer concluded that Wong 'was at her most effective when silent', and that he would return to her dance 'as a real experience' (Hubert Griffith in Leibfried and Lane 2003: 149).

Descriptions and reviews such as these consistently highlighted Wong's vocal-visual incoherence and the ways it breached the illusion of an integrated 'phantasmatic body'. In disrupting absorption-oriented spectatorship, it specifically challenged the colonialist, Orientalist epistemology that was predicated on segregating the Other from the Self, rendering the Other a mere homogenous object of fetishisation or disavowal. The last critic cited above bespoke precisely such a colonialist desire in symptomatically privileging Wong's silent physical performance over her vocal performance. Interestingly, however, whereas he deemed Wong's California accent too mundane (even crass) for her silent Oriental performance, he did not require that Wong speak a Sinitic language to match her Chinese image. In other words, a seamlessly performed 'celestial' did not indicate a realistic Chinese, but rather an ideal fetish figure that was simultaneously different and exotic enough to reconfirm the colonialist superiority, and legible enough to be digestible. The reason that Wong confounded Euro-American racial discourses and aesthetic sensibility was precisely that her apparent split identity defied simplistic ethnic and national legibility. Yet, that her composite vocal-visual persona was *perceived* as incoherent had everything to do with the ocular-centric racial discourses that created the homogenising expectation that certain racialised looks must be matched with certainly racialised speech. By the same logic, Wong's perceived vocal-visual incoherence proved to be baffling to the Chinese as well. Subscribing to the same lingua-ethno isomorphism, the Chinese she encountered during her 1936 China trip experienced the discomfort of being led to see her as a Chinese woman, only to become befuddled by her American speech and style of dress. Her limited Taishan dialect (her ancestral language) did not help in confirming her 'Chineseness', since it was unintelligible to people outside the Taishan area in southern China. Consequently, with her trademark wry humour, Wong commented on her 'strange experience of talking to my own people through an interpreter' (Wong 1936: 6).

In the next section, I analyse the ways in which Wong's conundrum called attention to and disrupted such reductive racial discourses. On this basis, I posit Wong's paradoxical agency in negotiating the constraints creatively through ironic vocal-visual mismatch, which in turn led to her composite identity and lingua-ethno-cosmopolitanism.

COMPOSITE IDENTITY AND LINGUA-ETHNO-COSMOPOLITANISM

In theorising Wong's composite identity performance, I do not see Wong as a liberal agent with absolute self-determination. Rather, my emphasis on the *perceived* vocal-visual conflict indicates that her composite identity must be understood in relation to the homogenising ideological constraints during the era of colonial Orientalism. More specifically, given her oftentimes marginalised minority status within the predominantly white Euro-American film and stage systems, her performance was overdetermined by industrial practices, mainstream ideologies, audience expectations, film and stage acting conventions, and star discourses. Her participation within mainstream entertainment industries challenges us to re-recognise her agency as situated consciousness (as opposed to self-determination). Furthermore, her agency is immanent in what Anne Cheng calls an 'ethics of immersion' and 'contaminated desires'.[4]

Thus, instead of seeing Wong's paradoxical agency and 'contaminated desires' as somewhat compromised and inadequate, it is more productive to think, along with Stuart Hall, that her composite identity and agency derived from 'using the resources of history, language and culture in the process of becoming rather than being' (Hall 1996: 4). Her identity performance can be summarised as continuous, eclectic and strategic utilisation and ambivalent appropriation of available resources. Since her embodied differences tended to be marked as exotic – a quality that was simultaneously deemed desirable and subjected to scrutiny, even disavowal – the crucial question, then, was how she might marshal all available resources to package her differences as an asset for her international audiences and critics. Importantly, Wong's strategic composite identity performance benefited not simply one actress's individualist trajectory. Rather, it experimented with strategies of rupturing systemic constraints and transforming them into the very conditions of identity innovation (or what Stuart Hall calls 'becoming'). As such, Wong's strategic self-empowerment intersected with and emblematised all marginalised performers' collective negotiation with the inequity of power. This approach to Wong's non-mainstream stardom recasts star studies, bringing to the fore the political ramifications and potential of star image formation.

To understand the working of Wong's eclectic appropriation of available resources and paradoxical agency, let us return to the 'uncanny' scene where her American English destroyed her 'celestial' 'phantasmatic body' in *The Circle of Chalk*. As argued previously, the critic's privileging of her silent physical Oriental performance over her vocal performance indicated an attempt to preserve the colonialist fantasy of the Oriental other, instead of a genuine concern for the realistic portrayal of a Chinese character. Realising that realism was not the requirement here, Wong decided to acquire the British accent at the cost of 200 guineas, instead of performing in her ancestral Taishan dialect, which, arguably, would have served the principle of realism given her putative Chinese role. Wong's response indicated not simple compliance with the Orientalist fantasy, but rather an irony-tinged strategic appropriation of the available resources for cosmopolitan self-reinvention. In her 1931 interview with the *Los Angeles Evening Herald Express*, shortly after her return to the US, Wong recalled, 'since the play [*The Circle of Chalk*] was Chinese, even an English accent would have been out of place. But I explained [to the British audience] I was sorry I had offended their ears and would try not to do it again. My next move was to get a coach. And that was how I happened to learn 200 guineas' worth of English' (Carroll 1931: 9). For the rest of her career, Wong retained the British accent for, as she explained it, it was an 'investment' she was determined to 'protect' (Carroll 1931: 9).

Wong's remarks are noteworthy on two accounts. Firstly, instead of resorting to her ancestral Taishan dialect or adopting broken English (as invented by the mainstream film studio and theatre for yellowface actors, i.e. Caucasian actors dressed up to play Asian roles), Wong replaced one 'uncanny' performance with another (from American English to British English). Thus, she refused to cave in to an easy 'phantasmatic body' based on lingua-ethno isomorphism (or matching her Chinese face with some kind of Chinese accent). Meanwhile, she also exposed and mocked even while taking advantage of the British critics' Euro-centric bias.

Secondly, she played British and American lingua-cultural pride against each other, while positioning herself as a transnational cultural citizen who could more flexibly latch onto and mix and match the most desirable cultural capital. She manifested and channelled British-American mutual contempt, letting herself be seen from the British perspective as a self-deprecating supporter of British superiority, then humorously describing her British accent as a two hundred guineas investment so that American readers (of her interview) could have the opportunity of laughing off the old empire's imperial pride. Meanwhile, since Wong had already successfully ascended to stardom in

Europe thanks to her King's English as well as German and French, which she acquired to play in her first talkie in Germany and France, her deliberately flippant tone did not discount the importance of her linguistic cosmopolitanism. Rather, her proven popularity in Europe enhanced her value upon her return to the US. Thus, Wong strategically played her American and European cards so as to create a flexible and composite persona. As Shirley Lim (2012: 9–10) argues, due to Asian-Americans' ambivalent national subjectivity, Wong was able to actively cultivate her extra-national affiliation, including cosmopolitanism.

By adopting the British accent for her character and for her own career, Wong metaphorically dubbed her own voice. That is, she self-consciously performed a vocal-visual split between her racialised looks and her vocal abilities with the result of defying reductive racialisation. This strategy allowed Wong to stave off the broken English that was routinely required of ethnic Asian actors and yellowface actors. In addition to the two hundred guineas' worth of British accent, Wong also studied German and French, which not only enabled her to play the lead role in stage plays and multi-language films co-produced by Britain, France and Germany, but also to give interviews in different languages. Furthermore, as she toured northern Europe in 1935, giving revue performances in various countries, she strategically retitled a song as 'A Danish Girl' or 'A Norwegian Girl' depending on the country she was performing in. She phonetically memorised the Danish and Norwegian lyrics, and enacted the corresponding persona.

Splicing her Chinese looks with these European languages defied what may be called the illusion of the 'phantasmatic racial body'. In so doing, Wong performed a composite identity on and off the stage and screen. This composite persona allowed her to play with, appropriate, even cater to, variant Euro-American mainstream expectations while simultaneously staging her strategic distanciation from these expectations. This flexible self-positioning derived from her situated, relational consciousness that did not directly go against the systems, but was rather immersed in the latter, turning them into the very conditions of her self-reinvention and promotion.

Armed with European languages and newly found cosmopolitanism, Wong undermined the 1920s US media description of her as 'an American girl with a Chinese epidermis', a label that cast her as a wannabe flapper who could never be completely American due to her racial mark. Her linguistic cosmopolitanism gave her a status superior to that of her less cosmopolitan American colleagues. Turning her persevering work ethic, affective labour and financial investment into unique cultural capital, she appropriated and reinvented her otherwise stereotypical roles, effectively problematising the image of the inscrutable Oriental and the hybrid, yet ultimately inadequately assimilated, alien.

Wong's cosmopolitan stardom, centred on her linguistic versatility, was duly acknowledged in American media upon her return to the US in 1930. One report commented, 'She has a wonderful gift of languages. Her English sounds as if acquired at Harvard, with its broad "a" and precise enunciation'; 'She can read and even translate Chinese classic poetry. She speaks German and French fluently' (in Hamann 2002: 20). The rave reviews went on, 'She left Hollywood a Chinese girl reared as an American. She returns an almost legendary figure – a strange, cultured woman, the sole living Chinese actress of importance on the screen or stage' (Oliver 1931 in Hamann 2002: 14). Whereas her screen roles in Hollywood remained confined to the legible 'Chinese' type, and the reviews continued to harp on her visual attraction – a slender figure wrapped in exotic Chinese costumes, the insertion of her multilingual abilities offered an opportunity for witty and ironic disruption.

In *Daughter of Shanghai*, a 1937 B movie produced by Paramount as an 'Anna May Wong Story', the script dated 9 September 1937 describes her character as 'beautiful, posed, gracious, with the briskness of her American training overlying like a sparkle the dignity and charm of her Chinese nature. Capable of quick decisions and bravery in the face of deadly danger.'[5] Whereas this characterisation remains fixated on her 'Chinese nature', Wong's character's capability of 'quick decisions and bravery in the face of deadly danger' is demonstrated in the actress' speech as well as bodily performance. In the sequence where she ventures into the club on a Caribbean island in order to track down the ringleader in charge of illegal labourer trafficking, she encounters a dancer who takes a look at her and snobbishly says, 'I don't speak Chinese.' In response, Wong's character retorts with good humour, 'But I speak English', which instantly thwarts the colonialist and ocular-centric assumption that a racialised body must go with a voice that is equally racialised.

Furthermore, her dignified British accent enables her to beat her white competitor at the latter's own game. Her ability to speak not only English, but also the King's English (that commands higher cultural capital), problematises the discourse of assimilation (that assumes a homogenous American identity to which a person of colour must surrender him/herself with no guaranteed success). The perceived vocal-visual mismatch that surprised the white characters and the audience, and that was mobilised by Wong and her character to their own advantage, created a dubbing effect that was alienating and ironic. By flaunting the metaphorical dubbing effect, Wong and her character usurped the high-class status of King's English, de-proprietarised the language, and thereby challenged her contemporary audience and us to imagine beyond the binary of reified alien Oriental on the one hand, and slavish assimilation on the other.

If Wong deployed British English with aplomb as a means of self-branding, rendering herself *positively* different (with elevated class and cultural status) from mainstream America, then one must ask whether her manoeuvre reinforced the linguistic hierarchy, with British English signalling high culture and refinement, American English embodying commerce and popular culture, and Chinese (including her ancestral Taishan dialect) once again negatively marked as the exotic, incomprehensible gibberish. Again, Wong's vocal performance offered a nuanced response to this question.

In 1932, Paramount released *Shanghai Express* (dir. Josef von Sternberg), featuring Wong speaking her ancestral Taishan dialect. In this film she plays Hui Fei, a Chinese courtesan, sharing a first-class train cabin with Marlene Dietrich's Shanghai Lily, another high-class courtesan. When the train is hijacked by Chang, the mixed-race revolutionary leader played by Warner Oland (most famous for his Charlie Chan image), the first-class passengers are held hostage. The crisis is resolved when Hui Fei takes it upon herself to kill Chang. This dagger-in-the-back is a clichéd plot device in films featuring Wong as a dragon lady, even though this time her violence is directed against the bad guy, which makes her a heroine. What *is* unconventional in Hui Fei's characterisation, however, is that prior to her summary disposal of Chang, she practically serves as an interpreter, translating Chang and his soldiers' orders into English for the Western hostages. In parallel, Dietrich's Shanghai Lily briefly serves as an interpreter for an ex-French military man, translating English into French and vice versa.

A significant difference lies in Wong's translation and Dietrich's translation, however. Dietrich's translation is justified by the plot (that is, a French man who has very limited understanding of English) and the casting (the actor, Emile Chautard, who played the French man was originally from France, and spoke real-life French as his native language). Wong's translation, however, is contrived for the sheer purpose of demonstrating Wong's exoticism. Warner Oland, who played Chang, was one of Hollywood's best-known yellowface actors originally from Sweden. His nonsensical 'Cantonese', as part of the yellowface masquerade, was not real-life Cantonese, just as his face was not Chinese. The syncing of Oland's yellowface make-up with yellowface 'Cantonese' served to construct a phantasmatic racial body of an Oriental Other. This yellowface character was the polar opposite to Wong's composite vocal-visual performance that accentuated the incongruity and discord in order to undermine the essentialist, ocular-centric conception of race. Since Oland's phantasmatic vocal-visual yellowface displaced and disavowed the real-life referent (that is, a historically and culturally situated Chinese character), it was incompatible with the idea of translation, which theoretically is supposed to bridge differences by establishing equivalence between referents or real-life languages. If it does not make sense to equate Oland's yellowface visage with a Chinese face, then, similarly, to treat his faux 'Cantonese' as any real-life Sinitic language that needs translation into English constitutes no more than a *staging* of the Oriental linguistic eccentricity. To put it simply, Oland's yellow-face 'Cantonese' does not require translation because it was part of the yellow-face masquerade with no (or banished) referent, rather than a communicative linguistic vehicle.

As the faux yellowface 'Cantonese' renders Wong's translation gratuitous in the film, we must ask what, then, justifies her shuttling between English and her Taishan dialect; what purpose does it serve? One easy answer is that Wong's use of Taishan dialect (along with her costuming and hairstyle) authenticated the 'Chinese' identity of herself and the film. This would mean that she was rehearsing the illusory phantasmatic Oriental role with a straight face.

This reading fails to account for a crucial element, namely, the element of ironic play and performance, in Wong's act of translation. The notion of play invites us to pay closer attention to Wong's interactions with her assigned, oftentimes stereotypical, Oriental roles. Rather than authenticating her role, Wong performed (not simply spoke) the Taishan dialect just as she performed all other languages. Performing her ancestral dialect presented a dramatic persona that offered her one more channel for addressing her transnational audiences. We may elucidate the significance of Wong's linguistic play in three instances of Wong playing herself in a vaudeville show and two short films, produced by Paramount and MGM respectively.

In the 1932 vaudeville show that prefigured what she would do in Italy and northern Europe in 1935, Wong gave a multilingual performance. She opened with a Chinese folk song, then performed a song entitled 'The American Girl', followed by a novelty song called 'Any Minute Now'. In the finale, she thanked the audience in English, French, Chinese, German and Hebrew (H. P. in Hamann 2002: 27).[6] This vaudeville show epitomised Wong's vocal perfor-mance par excellence. The reviewer complimented her as an especially clever Chinese, an acclamation that rehashed racial discourse, but at least deviated from the exclusive ocular-centric focus on her decorative visual value. For Wong, the multilingual performance enabled playful self-dubbing, flaunting her perceived vocal-visual incoherence. It not only recalled her acting in multi-lingual European films, but also reasserted her cosmopolitan ability to address multilingual and international audiences. Among the array of languages she performed, Taishan dialect was one ingredient, which she performed just like other languages. Thus, she projected a flexible and improvisational cul-tural (if not political) citizenship that exceeded any mono-lingual identity. By defying the ocular-centric illusion that a phantasmatic Oriental body should be matched with some quaint Oriental accent, Wong's linguistic virtuosity emphasised a composite figure that indulged in ostensible inconsistencies and multiple channels of addressing (and confusing) audiences.

That Wong's use of the Taishan dialect was no less performative and playful than her use of other languages was also illustrated in Paramount's short

Figure 3.1 Wong recites a Chinese poem in Taishan dialect to a confused MC.

musical comedy, *Hollywood on Parade* (5 June 1932). In this short musical, Wong plays herself as one of Paramount's contracted actors to be paraded on the stage. When asked what she is going to perform, she recites a Chinese poem in Taishan dialect. Her complete absorption in the act of reciting (as indicated in her turning away from her own reflection in the dressing mirror) contrasts comically with the clueless MC, the stand-in for the equally mystified white audience. Making funny faces as if he were trying (albeit unsuccessfully) to understand Wong's quaint Oriental elocution, the MC lamely comments that it sounds lovely, but he dislikes one word. When Wong asks eagerly, 'Which word?', he self-dismissively says, 'Never mind. They wouldn't know the difference anyway' (see Figure 3.1). Indeed, 'they' refers to the white audience including himself, who would enjoy Wong's Oriental (dis)play as nothing but an exotic and quaint performance. Wong's highly performative Taishan dialect rendition of the poem, therefore, serves two purposes. One is to cater to the Western audience's Orientalist desire. The other is to confound the same audience, and potentially to force them to encounter their own ignorance and problematic consumption of the Other.

The performative nature of Wong's Taishanese persona becomes more apparent if we take into consideration that her Taishan dialect was too corrupted by her American accent to be 'authentic' (according to her account of her father's discontent). Thus, Wong's act of playing (into) the role of the inscrutable Oriental Other does not so much endorse a racialised identity as present a dubbed persona, a vocal-visual camouflage that enabled slippery points of identification and dis-identification. If the non-Chinese-speaking mainstream white audience was simultaneously entertained and confused by such slippery performance, then a viewer sharing Wong's flexible positioning could appreciate her performance as witty and ironic because it displayed Chineseness to the hilt, only to expose its constructed nature.

Wong's Sinophone performance took on a further twist after her 1936 China trip. In 1937, the same year that saw Wong playing the courageous, English-speaking heroine in *Daughter of Shanghai*, MGM's *Hollywood Party in Technicolor* staged an entire show centred on the Oriental theme. In the short film, the entire Caucasian cast act in yellowface, construing a mélange of Oriental exotica and Hollywood glitz. In this context, Wong again is conveniently cast as the only 'authentic Chinese' who has just returned from her China trip and now plays herself modelling various fashions she has procured in China. Her costume show is framed behind bamboo blinds that a purple-clad Chinese woman pulls open only upon the gong signal sent by a green-dressed Chinese woman. Thus, Wong is presented to us as a tantalising, shifting image that is revealed only briefly when the blinds are open; and each revelation shows her in a new dress. Through the opened blinds, we first see her standing in a long shot, back to us, in front of a faux-temple structure, clad in a long blue dress. Then she turns around and walks towards the camera, opening her blue fan. The camera then cuts to a medium close-up shot of her, with the blinds removed, as she bows to greet the audience, introducing her 'Peking blue' afternoon dress, a signal of her 'completely going Chinese' in her wardrobe, as she jokingly puts it. After another round of blinds closing and opening, she dons and introduces a yellow dragon dress and a silver cape that combines the old and the new.

In this show, Wong assumes the task of introducing and promoting modern Chinese female fashions to the West. In showing off her first-hand experience in modern China and making her Western audience privy to what she has learned (such as the symbolic meanings of the colours and fabric of the dresses), she performs and embodies her new-found authentic Chineseness. Linguistically, however, she performs a forked identity. On the one hand, she addresses her American audience in British English, using the broad 'a' and rolling 'r' in words like 'smart' and 'imperial' to assert her cosmopolitan sophistication. Her accurate rendition of the upper-class sociolect sets the Fu Manchu-esque MC's fake Chinese accent (or what I call the yellowface Chinese) into comic relief. Yet, in the mid-flow of King's English, she abruptly turns to the green-clad Chinese woman and asks a question in Chinese (see Figure 3.2). The woman answers in idiomatic American English: 'I'm sorry, but I only understand Cantonese.' Wong turns to the audience with a wink and a smile, saying, 'Oh, I thought I could brush up my Mandarin.' With barely a pause, she resumes her description of the dragon dress in King's English.

Figure 3.2   Wong speaking Chinese to the green-clad Chinese woman during her Chinese costume party.

The 'Chinese interlude' shifts the vocal register with complex implications that require careful unpacking. In this interlude, Wong acts as if she tries to instantly shed her cosmopolitan voice projected to the white public, and switch to a more 'encrypted' Oriental voice addressed exclusively to her perceived compatriots. The ostensible purpose is twofold: 1) to demonstrate her multilingual skills; and 2) to gratify the Orientalist desire for an inscrutable (or unintelligible) Other, even when the Other is simultaneously shown as more cosmopolitan than the Self. However, this dual purpose does not exhaust the complexity of the 'Chinese interlude', for Wong's claim to have spoken one line of Mandarin that is unintelligible to her Cantonese-speaking compatriot must be understood as subtle commentary on and leverage of her new Chinese image. In laying claim to Mandarin Chinese, she articulated identification with the new China and its governing Nationalist government that was vigorously promoting Mandarin Chinese, while banning Cantonese in filmmaking. To align herself with the new China (by demonstrating her Mandarin) was also to distance herself from Cantonese (and her ancestral Taishan dialect), relegating it to the old China. The green-clad Chinese woman's professed inability to understand Wong thus ostensibly substantiated Wong's claim to an updated and upgraded identity – from the old to the new, from the local to the national. And yet the privileging of the new nation-state, which the Nationalist government strived to project and the US media had learned to support,[7] was also a tongue-in-cheek hoax and inside joke. For her Mandarin line was not really

Mandarin, but something closer to her Taishan dialect – a distinction lost on her white audience. Her professed desire to acquire Mandarin, therefore, could be barely more than a lip service to the 'new' Chinese image. Her 'Chinese interlude', then, became a make-believe performance amenable to multiple, potentially contradictory, interpretations.

A further spin of Wong's performance of the officially sanctioned 'new' Chineseness in MGM's *The Hollywood Parade* is that it allowed her to stage covert competition with MGM's recently released mega-production, *The Good Earth*. Having lobbied unsuccessfully for the female lead role in *The Good Earth*, Wong embarked on her first and only journey to China in 1936. Wong's failure to get the role has been commonly attributed to the US anti-miscegenation law. When Paul Muni was selected as the male lead, the female lead could not be a woman of colour. Another reason had to do with Wong's controversial reputation in China, simultaneously adored as an icon of fashion and modernity, and chastised for playing China-humiliating roles in Western films. Moreover, her working-class background (born to a laundryman's family) was considered inglorious and incapable of representing modern China. Her lack of Mandarin was increasingly deemed indicative of her inadequacy as a modern Chinese.

To confront the ironic dilemma that she was barred from representing modern China while the American studio MGM was allowed to do so in filming *The Good Earth*, with all main roles played by Caucasian actors, Wong turned the MGM Technicolor short into a stage to assert her legitimacy as a China spokesperson. This implicit competition was already unfolding during Wong's China trip, which paralleled MGM cameramen George Hill and Charles Clarke's tour in China, where they conducted extensive location shooting for *The Good Earth*. For both the MGM cameramen and Wong, going to China and to be on location constituted the necessary step towards understanding the real contemporary China. If MGM sought to inject realism into the film with location footage, Wong adopted the strategy of sartorial and linguistic acquisition, that is, 'going completely Chinese in my wardrobe' (in her words) and studying Mandarin Chinese and traditional art in Beijing.

Yet, just as MGM's location footage barely made its way into the finished film, Wong's plan to 'go Chinese' remained largely a discursive claim. MGM ended up building a life-size replica Chinese farm in San Fernando Valley, which was reputedly so authentic that the Chinese consular official tasked to monitor the film production was unable to tell the on-location footage from the ersatz farm scenes.[8] Analogously, Wong's 'Chinese' show in MGM's *Hollywood Party in Technicolor* projected an imaginary about China through her claim to speak one line of Mandarin and her display of knowledge of modern Chinese fashions. Importantly, this imaginary about China was emphatically composite and a-essentialist. It was framed by the imperial aura that Wong appropriated from King's English. As such, this imaginary embodied Wong's strategy of speaking in a forked tongue (literally switching between her acquired British accent and the proclaimed Mandarin Chinese). It simultaneously titillated and confounded a Western audience's Orientalist fantasy.

CONCLUSION

In all the instances of linguistic as well as visual performance analysed in this chapter, Wong addressed her audiences in a forked tongue, simultaneously saying two or more ostensibly incompatible things that led to a composite identity with intractable incoherence and self-contradictions. Wong's perfor- mance demonstrated what the British poet, John Keats, famously calls the 'negative capability', that is, the ability to entertain two radically opposing thoughts at the same time, thus to inhabit uncertainty.[9] Understood in the colo- nial context, Wong's negative capability both accommodated and frustrated the colonial desire for 'a reformed, recognizable Other, as a subject of differ- ence that is almost the same, but not quite' (Bhabha 1994: 85). In catering to and confounding this desire, Wong became her own dubber, speaking in a forked tongue (inverting Bhabha's use of this tem), challenging race discourses' ocular-centrism, thereby throwing racial legibility, stability and self-assured white supremacy into crisis.[10] If, as Dorinne Kondo (2000: 83) has argued, cross-racial performance can 'cast into relief the ways our essentialist notions of race and other social forces are in part enacted through intonation, gesture, movement and accent', then Wong's linguistic masquerade and lingua-ethno- cosmopolitanism demonstrated that the unified racial image predicated on re-enactment was always already on the brink of being de-acted and exploded into incongruous composites.

NOTES

*   I would like to thank the editors for their constructive comments. Any remaining errors are my responsibility entirely.
1. Here I follow Edward Said's canonical diagnostic definition of Orientalism as 'a system of representations framed by political forces that brought the Orient into Western learning, Western consciousness, and Western empire' (Said 1978: 202–3).
2. I thank Sabine Crawford for her help with translating this article into English.
3. Wong was selected to play the female protagonist in the play when her photo in the press release for *Piccadilly*, Wong's last silent film, was being filmed in London.
4. Anne Cheng describes the 'ethics of immersion' as a hermeneutics necessary for recognising racial injury without naturalising it, but rather understanding it in the face of 'contaminated desires' (Cheng 2010: 195–6, note 16).
5. See the script file on *Daughter of Shanghai* held in Margaret Herrick Library special collection.

6. The song entitled 'The American Girl' could be the template that would become 'The Danish Girl' and 'The Norwegian Girl' performed in corresponding languages in her 1935 northern European tour.
7. The US attitude towards China took a positive turn around the mid-1930s partially due to the popularisation of Pearl S. Buck's award-winning novel, *The Good Earth*. This was reinforced when MGM released the film adaptation in January 1937, just three months before the studio's short film, *The Hollywood Party*, featuring Wong's fashion show.
8. For a detailed analysis of MGM's construction of an 'authentic' China in Los Angeles, see Roan 2010: 113–55.
9. Keats' original description of 'Negative Capability' is 'the ability to contemplate the world without the desire to try and reconcile contradictory aspects or fit it into closed and rational systems'. This also means the capability of 'being in uncertainties. Mysteries, doubts . . .' See Keats' letter to his brothers in 1817, in Rollins 1958: 193–4.
10. A parallel case may be found in Lee Tung Foo, a turn-of-the-twentieth-century Chinese-American vaudeville artist who performed in English, German and Latin on the stage, and later played minor roles in film. According to Krystyn Moon (2005), Lee presented an 'incongruity between fixed preconceptions of race and his capacity to impersonate non-Asian characters, speak English without an accent, and sing American and European popular songs'. Lee's linguistic versatility, unfortunately, was not carried into his film acting. In all the minor roles he played, he had to speak English with a fake Chinese accent. This linguistic racialisation was precisely what Wong resisted in all media domains.

BIBLIOGRAPHY

Benjamin, Walter (1928), 'Gespräch mit Anne May Wong' ('Speaking with Anna May Wong: A Chinoiserie from the Old West'), *Die Literarische Welt* (*The Literary World*), 6 July, p. 1.
Bergfelder, Tim (1999), 'Negotiating Exoticism: Hollywood, Film Europe and Cultural Reception of Anna May Wong', in Andrew Higson and Richard Maltby (eds), *"Film Europe" and "Film America": Cinema, Commerce and Cultural Exchange 1920–1939*, Exeter: University of Exeter Press, pp. 302–24.
Bhabha, Homi (1994), 'Of mimicry and man: The ambivalence of colonial discourse', in Bhabha, *The Location of Culture*, New York: Routledge, pp. 85–92.
Carroll, Harrison (1931), 'Oriental Girl Crashes Gates Via Footlights', *Los Angeles Evening Herald Express* (6 June), reprinted in G. D. Hamann (ed.) (2002), *Anna May Wong in the 1930s*, Hollywood, CA: Film Today Press, p. 9.
Cheng, Anne Anling (2010), *Second Skin: Josephine Baker & the Modern Surface*, Oxford: Oxford University Press, pp. 195–6, note 16.
Doane, Mary Ann (1980), 'The Voice in the Cinema: The Articulation of Body and Space', in Philip Rosen (ed.) (1986), *Narrative, Apparatus, Ideology: A Film Theory Reader*, New York: Columbia University Press, pp. 335–48.
Hall, Stuart (1996), 'Introduction: Who Needs "Identity"?', in Stuart Hall and Paul du Gay (eds), *Questions of Cultural Identity*, SAGE Publications, pp. 1–17.
Hamann, G. D. (ed.) (2002), *Anna May Wong in the 1930s*, Hollywood, CA: Film Today Press.
H. P. (1932), 'Stage Attractions', *Motion Picture Herald* (23 July), reprinted in G. D. Hamann (ed.) (2002), *Anna May Wong in the 1930s*, Hollywood, CA: Film Today Press.
Jungmeyer, Jack (1929), 'Anna May Wong Seeks to Recapture Her Recial [sic]

Mannerisms and Modes', *Atlantic City Gazette* (2 December), held in Margaret Herrick Library core collection.

Kondo, Dorinne (2000), '(Re)Visions of Race: Contemporary Race Theory and the Cultural Politics of Racial Crossover in Documentary Theatre', *Theatre Journal* 52:1, 81–107.

Leibfried, Philip and Chei Mi Lane (2003), *Anna May Wong: A Complete Guide to Her Film, Stage, Radio and Television Work*, McFarland & Company.

Lim, Shirley Jennifer (2012), '"Speaking German Like Nobody's Business": Anna May Wong, Walter Benjamin, and the Possibilities of Asian American Cosmopolitanism', *Journal of Transnational American Studies* 4:1, 1–17.

'Miss Wong Played Hookey and Won Her First Movie Part', *Los Angeles Record* (12 September 1931), reprinted in G. D. Hamann (ed.) (2002), *Anna May Wong in the 1930s*, Hollywood, CA: Film Today Press, p. 20.

Moon, Krystyn (2005), 'Lee Tung Foo and the Making of a Chinese American Vaudevillian, 1900s–1920s', *Journal of Asian American Studies* 8:1, 23–48.

Oliver, W. E. (1931), 'Anna May Wong is a Real Person', *Los Angeles Evening Herald Express* (22 August), reprinted in G. D. Hamann (ed.) (2002), *Anna May Wong in the 1930s*, Hollywood, CA: Film Today Press, p. 14.

Roan, Jeanette (2010), 'Knowing China: Accuracy, Authenticity, and the Good Earth', in Roan, *Envisioning Asia: On Location, Travel, and the Cinematic Geography of US Orientalism*, Ann Arbor, MI: University of Michigan Press, pp. 113–55.

Rollins, H. E. (ed.) (1958), *The Letters of John Keats*, 2 vols, Cambridge: Cambridge University Press, i, pp. 193–4.

Said, Edward (1978), *Orientalism: Western Representations of the Orient*, London: Routledge & Kegan Paul, pp. 202–3.

Wang, Yiman (2005), 'The Art of "Screen Passing" – Anna May Wong's "Yellow Yellowface" Performance in the Art Deco Era', *Camera Obscura* 20:3, 159–91.

Wong, Anna May (1936), 'Anna May Wong Tells of Voyage on 1st Trip to China', *New York Herald-Tribune*, 17 May, p. 6.

4. SONG TAXONOMIES: INDIAN POPULAR CINEMA'S TERRITORIES OF STARDOM

Kiranmayi Indraganti

Film song has permeated the socio-cultural life of modern India in deep and impactful ways. The collective and individual consumption of film song, which is a critical component of the larger popular culture, has come to signify the bridging of an otherwise polarised society and its tradition of the appreciation of fine arts along the lines of class, caste, geopolitical and gender divide. How does the film song stay afloat? A quick and simple reckoning can be: it is a major force that *packages star energies* in it effectively. Film song has become *a* defining experience of film viewing and its attendant issues relating to the 'star persona', singing or miming the song onscreen. It is no exaggeration to say that film song has become *the face* of many Indian film stars such as Dilip Kumar, Meena Kumari, Amitabh Bachchan, NT Rama Rao, Savitri, Uttam Kumar, Sivaji Ganesan and several others from various linguistic and exhibition circuits of Mumbai, Chennai and other industries. The expansion of the audio industry (alongside film) has benefited stars since the 1940s, each era befittingly with a technology that sustained and extended their influence beyond the movie theatre, and in relocating them across cultural spaces. If one were to understand Indian film stars' engagement with film songs as an indication of stardom inflected with musicality, then it might prompt one to investigate the layers that this 'musical stardom' portends to forms of music and the uniqueness of stars. More particularly, it allows one to understand musical stardom beyond the traditional understanding of aural material and the materiality of song.

This chapter traces the historical formation of Indian film industries' masterful use of song as a distinct vehicle to deploy stardom, and argues that film song since 2000 has begun to fulfil specific functions of entertainment in mapping masculinities and femininities through the visual realisation of song ('picturisation').

So why is this investigation important? The way film performative stardom is mapped onto the form of song and has established critical links between the production of the visual (face) and aural (voice) is a unique phenomenon peculiar to Indian cinema, and its investigation can explain ways in which the diffusion of this stardom happens. In the more recent times of new digital platforms, this stardom has diversified into various channels of entertainment. Analyses of star-song performative spaces can point to reconfigurations of economy and entertainment apparatus and the way audiences are engaged. Neepa Majumdar's scholarly work introduces us to Indian cinema's use of song and its embodiment onscreen, its peculiarity of two sets of 'stardom' through the practice of playback singing – the visual and the aural – where the actor has a corresponding singer (Majumdar 2010). The two stars are available for public consumption in unique ways. The performance *for a* song, regardless of who sings it behind the screen, has been of tremendous consequence for actors, as it is through the 'applied art'[1] of song-making that stars have historically forayed into narrative discourses on authenticity, youth, righteousness, virtue (or its lack), power, honour, and so on. What a character in a filmic narrative stands for, feels, goes through and faces, has been articulated in a song, its location within the narrative coming to signify the star value. Stardom and song have long fostered a filial love that has come to determine entertainment in a certain way in India and define its *success*. While historically this convergence has channelled into different markets, in more recent years it has splintered across different economies (Anant 2008: 6).

This chapter maps out the role of song in the Indian cinema, particularly the Telugu cinema in the Internet era, and its function as a star vehicle across digital forums. Historically, the import of Hollywood apparatus to India, as Neepa Majumdar points out, included not only Hollywood films starring popular actors and actresses, film equipment, genres and narrative forms, 'but perhaps more important, the paraphernalia of publicity such as photography and film magazines, and the ideologies underlying stardom' (Majumdar 2010: 3). But it is a complex process, she further argues, to consider the stardom of non-Hollywood industries where it is active because of/in reference to Hollywood. In multiple national contexts, the local debates reflected anxieties around cinema and stardom not only in relation to their encounter with Hollywood but also about 'older contexts of performance predating Hollywood and often drawing on similarly vernacularized idioms of negotiated global and local performative modes' (Majumdar 2010: 5). Indian film song is one such highly mediated idiom deriving from global and local methods of performance using specific apparatus. The chapter engages with this encounter and examines the way post-millennium Indian stardom across Hindi, Telugu and other film industries with thriving businesses globally, straddles the 'vernacularized idiom' of performative mode and the Hollywood model of star consumption where the form of song is used as a star vehicle towards the film-viewing experience in theatres and private spaces. It consciously shifts focus to a specific narrative mode: the song and its new spaces, the specific cinematic formal elements evidenced in Indian cinema as the site of a new positioning of stardom and star consumption. In realising this objective, the chapter draws on Hugo Munsterberg's observations on cinematic apparatus, narrative art and his insight that the object is the context. Munsterberg's idea of film proposes that the 'object' for experience requires us to relate it to the seat of experience, which is the mind. It follows the neo-Kantian principle that each perfectly designed part works towards a magnificent whole and that one can do nothing with it except experience it: 'Both the mind and the object are free-floating during this experience [. . .]. We don't look at it to see how it can aid us, nor to find out its place in the larger scheme of things. During the aesthetic experience, that object becomes for us the whole context, an end in itself, a *terminal value*' (Andrew 1976: 23). In a Kantian sense, for Munsterberg, film's claim to aesthetic validity lies in its transforming of a reality into an object of imagination; it exists not on celluloid but in the mind, actualised through the mind's conferring of movement, attention, memory, imagination and emotion. Arguably, film song serves the 'whole context' and is an end in itself as a free-floating entity/phenomenon. This nature of song and its availability as a floating *object* functions as a delicacy, a familiar, tasteful component, in Indian cinematic art, available for consumption across digital platforms.

Historically, the very form of film song (generally, a refrain and two stanzas set to a tune and orchestral support, lasting three to four minutes) has emerged out of curious alliances in the pre-independent India (Indraganti 2016: 54). The gramophone industry in the 1920s and '30s shaped the 'audio' production of stage drama material on 'plates' alongside classical and semi-classical music by eminent singers, until film songs began to be seen as bankable products from 1933, the year in which gramophone companies started to release film soundtracks as a way to promote a film and its music. They needed to be re-recorded for better acoustic quality (Booth 2008: 36). Thus emerged an approximate three-and-a-half-minute duration of film song (Ranade 2006: 110), which allowed a certain number to be printed on both sides of a plate. HMV and other companies carried out the re-recording in separate studios with different sets of orchestra members, who made minor changes in the original soundtrack to fit the song in the stipulated duration of the lacquer record. Just as a starlet was groomed into becoming a star with a new name, style, look and manner, a song too was tailored and decked to be released into the Indian gramophone economy in the 1940s. An entire playback system by the end of the same decade also separated the two industries of image and sound, producing two sets of stars. The implication here was to secure and sustain the gramophone industry's local market with non-Western musical forms, already a tested ground. Subsequently, the system by the 1950s guaranteed a secure positioning of songs to promote both visual and aural stars on the one hand and the cinemas and gramophone records on the other. A well-oiled system such as this facilitated songs to slither into every narrative context, embody and disembody the performative persona, masquerade as plot-related poem yet float around unbound: the film song has, more often than not, risen above ludicrous censorship rules, reflected dexterous beat structures and lyrics, gone along rigid classical music norms and courted Western musical modes, stayed ambivalent over genre definitions and above all stayed put in all technological eras – gramophone, radio, cassette, digital. This 'musicality', at the heart of Indian stardom, has constantly striven to adapt to new demands of the *capital* that is the star.

The song culture, having started as an embedded feature of traditional theatrical performance, turned into a 'taste-making' culture during the gramophone era and expanded tremendously during the cassette boom in the 1980s, stakes in the audio business growing with the rise of television industries in the 1990s. The indispensability of film song can be reckoned as a discursive formation of cinematic performance's larger purpose in society for its players: the stars. In realising their various political, social, economic agendas, stars relied on songs and film dialogues. For example, the political life of south Indian Tamil film star M. G. Ramachandran (1917–87) cannot be dissociated from the songs his films showcased expressing his political aspirations. Similarly, Telugu actors NT Rama Rao (1923–96) and A. Nageswara Rao (1924–2014), among others, became household names in the Telugu-speaking regions for a variety of songs which bestowed upon them formidable visual and aural mileage (even though their songs were sung by professional playback singers). These songs were used either in their original form or as recycled numbers with new lyrics to create specific clout for stars in their political and social endeavours. For example, NT Rama Rao rose to prominence relaying his songs, dialogue, specific portrayals of characters onscreen and his own matinee idol image to 'salvage' Telugu pride. The result of this effort was that he became the Chief Minister of the state of erstwhile Andhra Pradesh. Akkineni Nageswara Rao (ANR) came to represent the Telugu cultural 'ethos' at social and cultural gatherings in the Telugu-speaking regions, although his credentials did not include literature and music. 'Big' stars and their songs brought in presuppositions about tastes, markets, investments and song aesthetics constitutive of sets, locations, costumes, colours and 'get-ups' in song performances. In addition, playback singing, multi-string orchestras, stereo recording, the use of chorus, and rehearsal and recording dynamics went with the capital that was the star-actor. All of this added more complexity to the production of songs that matched the stars and, vice versa, carried specific agendas.

The song-making culture has not stayed consistent across the years but the urgency of neoliberal markets and their salient technologies arguably brought new dimensions to song-star mobility in terms of value and mileage. While the star's mobility has always been guaranteed through the travels of songs, the nature of these travels has changed fascinatingly in the post-2000 era. For example, in the gramophone (or pre-cassette) era of film music, the circulation of songs tapped into the socially and culturally inquisitive natures of the audiences rather than pure commercial enterprise through the release of gramophone records, as Anna Morcom explains:

> Though film songs were a social and cultural phenomenon of enormous proportion, in commercial terms, they were insignificant compared to the film. [. . .] the role of audience taste had greater relative importance than in the cassette and television era, where economic reform and techno-logical development presented immense potential for growth. (Morcom 2008: 68)

In the cassette era from the 1980s to 2000, film songs amounted to about 70 per cent of HMV (now Saregama)'s total sales. By 2000 the cassettes were still selling more than CDs at the rate of 210 million cassettes to 13 million CDs.[2] However, towards the end of the decade, with the Internet taking over a major portion of the entertainment world, downloading has become the chief method of distribution for music. In their materiality, while the early songs were bound by the cassette players, now, in the post-2000 era, they became simultaneous visual and aural carriers in the porous Internet networks which the Indian film stars have actively been using to promote their multimillion projects.

What is at stake for the Indian stars is the fact that the positioning of the audience has become more complex, and their own (star) 'performances' have become decentralised. On the one hand, the task is to maintain the 'Indianness' of their feat, and on the other, to ensure that their negotiation of the song culture is open enough to co-opt new global song styles. I shall discuss this more elaborately in the following sections.

MUNSTERBERG TO JENKINS: CONVERGENCE OF SONG AND STAR

Of the two major positions in film theory, the realist and the formalist, the realist position distinguished cinema from other artistic enterprises such as painting and literature and the formalists tried to redeem cinema from mere endeavour of reproduction. In both these positions, film theorists, by looking at raw material, techniques, forms and the purpose and value of cinema, had tried to envisage ways and methods of understanding the magic of cinema: processes involved, whether deliberate, whether at the individual or collective level, and so on (Andrew 1976: 11–13). One of the most fascinating theorists of the formalist tradition, Hugo Munsterberg, offers useful guidance in this chapter's endeavour to look into the star–song relationship. The materiality, meaning and convergence of formal elements of song in the post-millennium Internet age can be analysed in the light of Munsterberg's argument about photo-play and the mind as the seat of experience (Munsterberg 1916). All cinematic properties are mental, and camera angles and special cinematic features such as close-ups work because of the *attention* of the human mind. Machinery reproduces images for the raw material of the mind, which sets the picture in motion. By virtue of its capacity of attention, the mind is a great organiser of the moving world. Therefore, a motion picture is not a mere record of motion but an organised record of the way the mind creates a meaningful reality out of distinct stimuli (Andrew 1976: 21). Technology provides the body to the phenomenon of cinema and society animates it, according to Munsterberg. In making song an abiding priority of its storytelling, Indian cinema of the Internet era has de-territorialised the star from narrative context and organised narrative stimuli for the mind with new technologies. The technology *re-creates* distinct stimuli to stage *emotion* (which Munsterberg calls 'complete mental events') and grasp *attention* through the specific use of machineries which characterise the 'access for all' culture (Elsaesser 2011). One can view or re-view narrative art any number of times in a space enshrined in distinct intimacy, which was not entirely the way cinema or cinematic 'elements' operated in the pre-Internet era. This has definitely facilitated stardom to replay in households strewn around the world by neoliberal markets, pursuits and traditional ideas of entertainment. The way song accommodates star energies has lent itself to evoking specific 'emotions' in narrative art and also its consumption in unhinged spaces.

The industry and its stars availed themselves of this opportunity and used media platforms to ensure multiple communications with audiences. There are new ways, more 'migratory' ways in Henry Jenkins' words, of appreciating film songs where the mind and the object remain free-floating, where one is cut off from the normal continuity of self-interest and 'purposiveness' (Jenkins 2006: 2). One can argue that a song is teleologically ordered to bring in additional 'good' by being within and without the narrative, by being ordained by the purpose of the narrative yet maintaining its independence. Whether this *good* is, or can be, an *objective good* is a separate investigation, but the goal of song in the 'grand narrative' of Indian cinema has been to forge a relation with the narrative context and also to liberate itself of narrative limitations through the use of technologies such as gramophone, radio, cassettes and now the Internet, prompting curious diversification of markets, agendas and reach. The years between 2000 and 2015 witnessed an explosion of choice-making by viewers to consume stardom on dimension-changing televisions, laptops, the Internet and phones, which reaffirmed their participation in its making and accessing. Indian star performances and global journeys, for this reason, contrast significantly with any other kind of star encounters in the entertainment business of the world because their performances are often closely linked to their *song performances* from films. An example of this phenomenon is the global tours of the Indian film stars to perform for a 'live' diasporic audience in metropolises around the world, picking songs from whichever language they represented – Hindi, Telugu, Tamil, and so on. They have utilised the media culture in *centre-staging* the 'star' in many ways. In this new scenario, Bollywood superstars Shah Rukh Khan and Salman Khan's (or a Tamil or Telugu superstar's) live show is seen and touted as a global *event*. The mammoth local publicity pales into insignificance compared to the way the Internet explodes with details of ticket sales and countdowns. Corresponding to this frenzy will be ideas of 'live streaming' and telecasts of the show, with a promise of repeats, while the Internet will be agog with amateur uploads of their presence. On the other hand, playback singers too have been enormously popular with their shows, where their songs, filmed on superstars such as Shah Rukh Khan, Salman Khan and Rajnikant, have received massive box-office returns and support. As an enduring narrative phenomenon of Indian cinema (one would scarcely see it in other cinemas of the world in the same format), song has been a forte to promote stardom. What has been an alliance since the 1940s of the star and the song is also a calibration of multimedia convergence which functions 'as a flow of content across multiple media platforms . . . across different media systems, competing media economies and national borders – depend[ing] heavily on consumers' active participation' (Jenkins 2006: 2).

BOX WITHIN A BOX: INDIAN CINEMA AND THE TELUGU CINEMA

After synchronicity of discretely recorded elements of image and sound was accomplished by the late 1930s, song production for films went through various negotiations of voice recording. In some instances, star actors recorded songs prior to acting, and in some others, professional singers replaced unmusical actor-voices and made decent careers. Indian popular cinema, in all languages including Hindi and Telugu, postulated songs as both indispensable and nationalistic cultural symbols in a bid to integrate them into the ethos of many things 'Indian'. By 1945 there was, however, criticism about the propensity of songs and the multitude of problems they brought, thematically and structurally: 'Our film industry produces over 160 pictures a year and calculating an average of nine songs per picture, our producers impose on our long-suffering public about 1440 songs – which are all different permutations and combinations of about a dozen basic tunes which were discovered in the early talkies', lamented a 1945 write-up.[3] The formal exploration of song distorted a 'realistic' mode of storytelling for the pre-independence Indian public, which had already been negotiating the charismatic apparatus of Hollywood and the vociferous protection of *Swadesh* (self-rule) interests. Songs captured this impulse and irony, and continued nevertheless in films across genres and variations of Natya-Shastra (Indian treatise on dance-music)-bound dramatic forms. The point is: where other oppositions rose and fell, the songs sustained narratives, box-office returns and the so-called early Indian identity.

As a business model similar to the Hindi cinema, the Telugu cinema in its early stages recycled for celluloid the ready-made mythological drama scripts of companies touring the Telugu-speaking regions across south India. By the late 1930s, while this borrowing of 'drama' texts continued, the Telugu cinema also saw greater scope beyond the prevalent theatrical practices in terms of engagement with the audience. 'Social films' such as *Malapilla* (Gudavalli Ramabrahmam, 1938) and *Raitu Bidda* (Gudavalli Ramabrahmam, 1939) proved that non-mythological thematic content was possible, as was the use of language within the narrative, from versification to simple prose (Srinivas 2013: 52–5). These impactful attempts seized the moment to induce new cinematic performances and languages even as the mythological and folkloristic narratives continued in the 1940s, '50s and later. Across the decades and changing linguistic scopes, songs have been integrated into cinematic plot in many ways: from the celebration of birth and a child growing up over a montage to the separation of lovers – hero and heroine conveying their love through moonlight, clouds, rain, boat and horse rides and motor travel to the events of family separation and reunion. A star's look, grooming and remuneration were not determined by clothes, accessories and glossy photos alone, but also by his/her songs in specific narrative situations. A multitude of them being available in public space, there came the specificity of a star's good and bad songs and films (complex tunes, orchestrated and rendered efficiently in badly plotted and acted films holding no narrative interest, and so on). For example, Dev Anand, the Hindi film star of the 1950s through to the 1970s, was remembered for many songs that were filmed on him sung by playback singers. His own production house, Nav Ketan, became a distinguished banner for 'quality' film songs, often composed by music director S. D. Burman. However, Dev

Anand also registered several box-office flops, which showcased popular songs. *Jaali Note* (*Counterfeit Money*, Shakti Samanta, 1960) can be cited as one of the many examples where the songs composed by O. P. Nayyar super-seded the popularity of the film at the theatres. More than as a Dev Anand film, *Jaali Note* is remembered for its songs sung by Asha Bhonsle, the female playback singer, and Mohammed Rafi, the male playback singer. Similarly, the Telugu film *Jayabheri* (*The Clarion of Victory*, P. Pulliah, 1959), featuring the male superstar of the time ANR (Akkineni Nageswara Rao) and female star Anjali Devi, failed at the box office, but its songs became major hits on radio and other circuits. Films such as *Jayabheri* feature in special encomiums of the actor's body of work as a tribute to *his* stardom. It is not uncommon to see fluctuating success between film's aural and visual impact on audiences, and stars optimising their value through both the networks, even if they themselves have never sung the songs. This hierarchy within the songs of stars has had tremendous impact on building simultaneously the 'culture' of appreciation as well as the career of a star. The 'taste' of film music changing with each decade became more a normative occurrence than peculiar where stars flourished as actors showcasing songs sung by playback singers in 'good' and 'bad' films. It also saw the continuous rise of playback singers, male and female, as did the songs and their circulation favouring growth-oriented business and specific monetary gains.

Major shifts: the story of 'idlebrain'

In 1999, a Telugu-speaking engineering graduate from the prestigious Birla Institute of Technology and Science or BITS, Pilani, living in Mumbai, launched a website with the help of a friend in Sunnyvale, California. The website was meant to provide small, interesting and immediate information about the Telugu-language films being produced, released and talked about in India. The website, known as 'idlebrain.com', is one of the most successful websites catering to Telugu-film-viewing people across the globe. The BITS graduate, G. V. Ramana, left his job in 2001 and made 'idlebrain' his work-shop for spreading his understanding of the changing face of cinema, stars in it, his grades for stories, stars and stardom, technology used to capture them and the entertainment, and a point of their interface. By 2010, there came a score of such websites and the verdict of these forums on stars, films, songs and their production and distribution began to influence the way Telugu films were being received. As mainstream films reach the public in a much more diffused manner now than earlier through the print media, home video, televi-sion, cable television, Direct to Home (DTH) networks, radio, music industry and the Internet, besides the cinemas, the audience is engaged in choice-making over the various elements of film entertainment involving their favourite stars.

As one of the prolific industries, the Telugu film industry, situated in the city of Hyderabad (currently the combined capital of the bifurcated Telugu-language states of Telangana and Andhra Pradesh), is considered the second-largest in India with the production of nearly two hundred films a year. While the media and entertainment market (which includes films, television, print and radio) of south India is estimated at 190 billion rupees,[4] the south Indian film industry alone is put at over 20 billion, to which Tamil and Telugu industries contribute 45 per cent each. The Telugu industry is the more prolific of the two, although both industries invest in big-budget films, where a film costs over 70 million rupees, often not recovering the costs. A significant number of the films often do not make it to theatrical release either. Ironically, the major source of revenue, 75 per cent, comes from the domestic market.[5] Tamil and Telugu films enjoy releases in the neighbouring states within the country, besides releases abroad, which is where websites like 'idlebrain.com' influence viewers' choices.

Songs and films became a staple on services like DTH, among others, which came into operation in 2000, enabling the rapid growth in digital distribution platforms. The rise in FM radio stations in 2007 from twenty-five to two-hundred accounts for the great demand for film music. Music companies earn substantial revenues from licensing music to radio stations and television channels. For an airing channel, the cost of acquisition of a song could vary between 1,000 rupees and 200,000 rupees. And per annum, the income on songs ranges between 800 million and a billion rupees.[6] Although there has been a decline in the sales of recorded music across retail counters, there is a growth of 70 to 80 per cent in digital revenues through mobile download purchases. According to a report, about 600,000 to 800,000 ringtones were downloaded daily in India between 2006 and 2007, providing a revenue of 1.8 billion rupees.[7] While ringtones (of film songs, predominantly) formed a major portion of these downloads, star images/posters too were high in demand. Shah Rukh Khan and Katrina Kaif were 'the most downloaded movie stars to mobile', while the others included Salman Khan, Hrithik Roshan, Akshay Kumar and Sanjay Dutt from the Mumbai industry. The top five actresses, apart from Katrina Kaif, included Deepika Padukone, Priyanka Chopra, Lara Dutta and Aishwarya Rai.[8]

CARVING STARDOM THROUGH SONG

Amid such an expanding and digitally vibrant scenario, male Telugu film stars such as Pawan Kalyan, Allu Arjun, Mahesh Babu and Balakrishna, among others, found their audiences on the Internet beyond the cinema theatres. In the new context of unsure returns on theatrical releases, songs have become independent investment entities encapsulating global and local experiences quite remote to the logic of the narrative. The unrelated music, scenic location and deliberately choreographed frontal movements test not only the star's ability at dance, or 'steps' as they are more popularly known, but also the audience's knowledge of a star's style of dancing. The effort is expressly aimed at distancing the audience from the world of the narrative, emphasising the star persona in a way that contrasts with the earlier integration of songs in film narratives. Originally seen as having a sense of belonging and motivation in the narrative, songs were structuring devices to show progress, development and transformation of character by supplementing the story with motifs, metaphors, thematic parallels and synthesis, and, from the 1950s to the 1980s, served formulaic requirements connected by the logic of cause and effect.

Eventually, however, songs have carved an extrapolative value for the stars since the 1990s to emphasise their power, the address of the film, and its commercial potential, for example, as spicy mass entertainer showcasing fantastic locales, and as a *forthcoming* blockbuster. The collateral of these elements received major emotional investment from the fan clubs, which worked at village, town and city levels worshipping billboards of the stars. There is scholarly work on the phenomenon of fan activities of the south Indian cinema, including the Telugu cinema (Srinivas 2009). The fan is a loyal being and 'can do anything to "promote the star," from hoisting flags to celebrating religious festivals. The choice of fan-based activity is contextually determined and evolves in the competitive environment of the fan domain' (Srinivas 2009: 53). While their theatre-based activity on the release of their star's film might involve anywhere between the fans screaming, whistling and throwing coins, festoons and flower petals at the screen upon the first sighting of the star ('the entry' point in the film), it might not stop there but extend to the social sphere of writing letters, seeking photographs and mobilising support for philanthropic causes (Srinivas 2009: 50–3). In a narrative context, the presence of the fan or his performance can especially be located when songs play out and when a song marks the entry of the star at an early point in the film (Srinivas 2009: 94–6). The 'hero's entry', sometimes accompanied by a song, carries a set of characteristics such as low camera angles looking up at the hero's step towards the audience, a dramatic turn of the face towards the camera in slow-motion with blazing fire in the background or even the roar of an animal (preferably, a lion or tiger). Heroism of the male star is clearly marked in the teasers and trailers too (*Lion*, Satyadev, 2015 and *Panja*, Vishnu Vardhan, 2011 exemplify this), often deploying techniques of histrionic exaggeration, dramatic fights and emphatic dialogue. The loud orchestra, whether as a song or background piece of music, presents a combination of rousing strings, beats and choral support. This kind of introduction allows the audience to anticipate specific sequences of power that the star carries within a 'mass film' narrative. What is broadly known and promoted as a 'mass film' is spicy, overtly emphasising the pure entertainment value of it. 'Mass film' is a term used to indicate the film's address to the masses, where the main star is cast as the representative of the masses. However, in this implicit structure of oppositions, each song carries a separate function. The star hero represents the masses *but/and* wears expensive clothes and watches, and sings duets against the Alps or some picturesque location, distinctly *foreign*. It may be useful here to point out that the terms 'class' and 'mass' signify elements a particular film potentially has and the kind of theatrical run it could have or fit into. A mass film orients audiences towards specific expectations of the male star and his actions in the film, often serving the masses. S. V. Srinivas offers a valuable analysis to suggest that the mass film's hero is a commoner (Srinivas 2009: 77). Here, songs are carved out of a need to legitimise the star power, and thereby the mass power. The big stars cannot afford to register flops because their success portends phenomenal growth to the industry and its prestige. They are also perceived as 'embodiments of the problem–solution of Telugu cinema' (Srinivas 2009: xxvii), because it is their presence that allows the industry to come back after a flop. Also, a political career is seen as the 'next' step by some film stars, and instances of south Indian film stars turning to politics are common. They have won mandates either as candidates of an established political party or have started parties of their own. Male stars NTR and Chiranjeevi are two examples from the Telugu film industry, their stardom becoming a convertible vehicle on a road of varying degrees of success and waning youth. In addition to politics, bringing one's own children into the film industry is also recognised as a familiar trajectory, a way to extend their own stardom and to nurture the next generation of stars, and thereby fans. The manufacture of new star material from the family receives exciting coverage from the media about new sets of songs and dances devised for the new star to please the *generations of fans* that await a film from 'the family'. In the larger scheme of relations between the star and the song lies the abiding feature of anticipation of a film featuring the father-son, uncle-nephew, brother-brother, grandfather-grandson relations appearing in the same frame, or in the same song, to serve not the narrative need but as a source of pleasure of knowingness of extraneous factors that allow the songs to be there in the first place. A recent example was the Telugu film *Manam* (Vikram Kumar, 2014), which featured ANR (his last film, as he died before the release), his star-son Nagarjuna and grandson, a rising star, Naga Chaitanya, where the narrative presents them in the reverse order of the grandson in real life (Naga Chaitanya) playing the grandfather in the film and the grandfather in real life (ANR) playing the onscreen grandson, while the film operates on a series of flashbacks. Similarly, Chiranjeevi, a Telugu superstar of the 1980s and '90s, and his son Ram Charan Teja, a star now, have appeared in the latter's film (*Magadhira*, S. S. Rajamouli, 2009) to dance together briefly for an old number from one of Chiranjeevi's blockbusters.

There are many such examples and these generational crossover energies are especially packaged in songs, as they allow innovations in techniques and can reach through independent circuits.

A distinct feature that illuminates the star–song relation is the 'item song' where a young woman's cabaret number becomes *a* way in which a male (star) protagonist's presence or dancing represents his judicious 'authority' and 'charm'. The item song emphasises female agency in a dubiously unrepressed way, during which she dances to a hinterland crowd using transgressive lyrics in specific dialects, often narrating an event of desire and fulfilment. The male protagonist's presence may be suggested only towards the end or maybe staged throughout the song. There is a way in which an item song is staged: it *brings* an unrelated *female* star – someone who has no role in the film except to appear in the said dance number – and marks the extraneous element of the presence of that star and the film's unique ability to afford such disjuncture as noteworthy. Now, 'item song' is a category which would have been called a cabaret dance number in the 1960s or '70s. To call something an 'item' is a way of emphasising its usefulness in terms of value, in terms of money. As a voucher of additional promise attached to the price of the ticket, an 'item song' is not unique to Telugu films alone. They have controversially been nurtured in other language film industries too, most certainly the Mumbai industry.

The Telugu film *Arya 2* (Sukumar, 2009) has an item song in which the 'hero' (played by Allu Arjun, reputed for his dancing skills) dances with a fair-skinned, non-Indian girl (Erina Andrea), a major success in 2009–10 (see Figure 4.1). A girl who dances in an 'item song' is termed an 'item' girl; major Bollywood stars have keenly done an item number or two in Hindi, Telugu and Tamil films, to prove their talents at dancing and a *kind of dancing*. When *Ringa ringa* in *Arya 2* became a particularly big hit with its provocatively transgressive lyrics, the song was much in demand as a ringtone, and was played on various audiovisual networks. Starting with a much- praised dance move by Arjun, the song presents the amorous escapades of a young 'fair-skinned' woman travelling from Washington to India (to the specific Telugu-speaking region of Rayalaseema in Andhra Pradesh) looking for 'real men'. In what can be seen as a great irony, the song, de-territorialised and floating around through downloads and the Internet, celebrates marked territories of masculinity – Rayalaseema holds a dubious reputation for a machismo-driven culture of political gang wars and factional feuds. The 'men' of Rayalaseema (similar to the legendary men of the southern Italian region) portend frolic for the 'item girl' in the song, who coquettishly courts them and the hero as authentic subjects of the 'local' culture. While the lyrics raised debates about censorship, the song freely circulated in public and private spaces. It should be noted that item songs work as subgenres within the narrative: unrelated to the main plot, the general theme is that of a young woman failing to have enough

Figure 4.1 Telugu star Allu Arjun is often seen dancing and lipsynching to a variety of cross-cultural musical numbers.

fun or find the right partner. This theme runs consistently across stories, where the use of English words, urban or global cities and experiences recur while praising the 'local' men, culture, festivals and food, and expressing fascination with the flavour of the local. Films such as *Narasimha Naidu* (B. Gopal, 2001), *Pokiri* (Puri Jagannath, 2006), *Arya* (Sukumar, 2004) and *Gabbar Singh* (Harish Shankar, 2012), among several others, had enormously popular songs, of which 'item songs', despite their lyrics (or because of them), carved out stars' value and promise in offering pleasure and identification.

Curiously, this theme is common across all languages: Hindi, Telugu, and so on. The song about female desire is devised through the objectification of the female body, which the star hero pays heed to or is amused to encounter. The 'item song' is often staged in a villain's den or a place where corruption and dubious morals thrive: the star hero joins the party (or pretends to) either to get vital information about the bad guys or to really dance with the girl. Item songs are freewheeling adaptations of star power and sensuality for cinema. From the 1960s to the '80s, these songs were filmed on 'club dancers' or dancers who only did cabaret numbers and had only limited careers as 'actresses' or leading ladies. However, in more recent times these carefully choreographed dance numbers have been taken up by top female stars of Bollywood, who have done an item 'number' either in Hindi or in south Indian films of the Telugu and Tamil languages, where they are said to be paid legendary remunerations. In Bollywood, doing an 'item song' is seen as a skill and as a way to showcase a certain glamour of the top-billing actresses. There are many examples of Bollywood female stars dancing to these numbers in Hindi and Telugu among other language films. Examples from Hindi cinema: Aishwarya Rai (*Bunty aur Babli*, Shaad Ali, 2005), Shilpa Shetty (*Shool*, E. Niwas, 1999), Katrina Kaif (*Tees Maar Khan*, Farah Khan, 2010), Vidya Balan (*Ferrari ki Sawari*, Rajesh Mapuskar, 2012), Rani Mukherjee (*Aiyaa*, Sachin Kundalkar, 2012) and Malaika Arora (*Dil Se*, Mani Ratnam, 1998). In the Telugu films too, flagrantly enough, Bollywood stars did become popular for their item numbers. Examples include: Mallika Sherawat (*Guru*, Mani Ratnam, 2007), Malaika Arora (*Gabbar Singh*, Harish Shankar, 2012) and Deepika Padukone (*Kantri Mogudu*, Indrajit Lankesh, 2010), among others.

Item songs affirmed notions of femininity and masculinity, giving rise to publicity of controversies and debates around traditional values being disrupted by cinema. On the other hand, romantic songs presented a different scope for stars. They are often shot outside India against picturesque settings, except when the hero's virtues are to be extolled. In such a case, the song is filmed on a distinctly local, holy, important site within India to assert his patriarchal authority. In other words, the physical space within which a song is filmed determines how it is intended to be associated with the audience rather than its exact location within the narrative. For example, the 2001 blockbuster *Narasimha Naidu* (B. Gopal) and the 2002 hit *Indra* (B. Gopal) starring Chiranjeevi, one of the biggest stars of south India, clearly executed

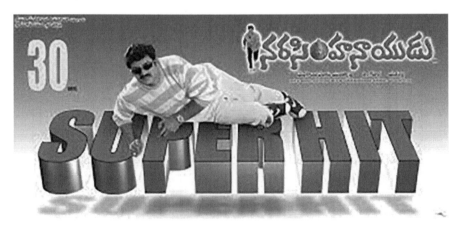

Figure 4.2   Telugu star Nandamuri Balakrishna celebrates *Narasimha Naidu* (B. Gopal, 2001).

this spatial distinction. In *Narasimha Naidu*, the lead actor Balakrishna (see Figure 4.2) plays a teacher of Indian classical dance who leads a peaceful life in a distinctly designed Indian cottage by a rivulet, where no one knows about his past of family feuds and gang wars and his heroics as a man of his word. Now, when he meets the heroine, all the imaginary songs take place on the streets of Canada. While the 'romantic' songs are filmed on the male and female protagonists (the star hero and heroine) and are pitched as musical numbers on *romantic love*, the item song, on the other hand, purposely strays away from this mode and proffers other possibilities for the star hero (and the audience) to mark out their desire outside of the *norm* of romantic love. This hint, or visually rather a wink, becomes the foundation for an item song and its logic of disconnect from the classical paradigm of *cause and effect*. The hero's aspirations and deeds are cast in terms of what a hero *should be*, extolling his virtues, showing him as a man of the masses who fulfils his promise to them. In *Indra*, Chiranjeevi dances to a classically inclined song on the banks of the Ganges, on the ghats of Banaras, whereas his dream sequences unfold against the backdrop of European cities. The item song is always rendered by a female singer for a female dancer, who appears onscreen only to perform that song. The female singing voice tends to be nasal and bold, *different* from the one used in romantic songs, often rendering the words in a mannered style, provoking and beckoning. There is predictability to the situations created in the narrative, thematically and structurally, and to the way they are staged. The dancers are different from film to film, as are the star protagonists, but the stock (visual and aural) conventions bestow upon the songs a *genre* or *subgenre* status. The new scenario enables stars to become transcultural capital, travelling across national boundaries while contrastingly inhabiting intimate individual spaces. Allu Arjun (star actor of the *Arya* duo) is as reachable to his fans in America as is Brad Pitt or Johnny Depp in India (for those interested in the two different cinemas). Although limited in their artistic reach and mode of performance, Telugu and other Indian actors have distinguished themselves from their Hollywood counterparts in terms of their song performances. Whatever may be the limitations of these stars in the post-1990s scenario in terms of the roles they play, their 'star' value has remained strong in song and dance, and their availability on the Internet. Songs thus fit into what Munsterberg calls the object becoming the context, an end in itself, thereby creating independent value for stardom to thrive.

What this has achieved in the transnational scenario is that film songs have acted as active agents to dismember the experience of wholeness by deliberately drawing one's attention to new experiences outside everyday life. If the main story deals with more immediate concerns of family disputes over property, mistrust, revenge and killing, the songs deliberately show a world outside these disputes. The idea of the 'international' is absent or less frequently invoked in the narrative, except in the visual promise of the song. Because it is not linked to the narrative logic, it seems to offer a greater scope for the audience to admire the locales, as if watching a series of picture postcards strung together to a tune with two people dancing at a pleasant location. The idea of believability here does not come from the idea of realism but from the detachment from it, where one believes in something for its independent value, for its authentic dislocation. Visually, then, the songs become small capsules of pure pleasure or fun. This element, coming from the detachment of the song from the narrative, perfectly lends itself to the larger logic of digital convergence of the media across radio, television, CDs, DVDs and the Internet. As Sangita Gopal and Sujata Moorti suggest, 'film music and the production of the song-dance sequence remain autonomous' (Gopal and Moorti 2008: 6), enabling the possibility to influence audiences with the choice of musical genres, location, sets and their potential 'impact'. The two Telugu films *Arya* and *Arya 2* exemplify the lead star Arjun's interest in Western pop music and adapting it to his films. There are two songs ('You rock my world' and 'Feel my love') in *Arya* (Sukumar, 2004) that have English and Hindi lines aimed at a young, college-going demographic. The same film also has an 'item' (cabaret) number, 'Aa ante amalapuram', and a set of romantic numbers. Similarly, in *Arya 2*, 'My love is gone' and 'Mr Perfect' are laced not only with English and Hindi lines but also a heavy influence of the hip hop. Again, the same film also has an item song, 'Ringa ringa', which celebrates specific vocal tones, native colloquialisms and folk refrains. In a way, the *Arya* duo stick to the stock variety of songs, romantic songs, pop tunes and a folk, 'item' number. Arjun's stardom often recurs through the combination of these sonic conventions. The combining, manipulating and sharing of films, music, photos and text through digital formats have made the already autonomous process of film-song production more disaggregated to afford energies from diverse sources and contexts.

Conclusion

Between 2000 and 2010, commercially successful films like *Narasimha Naidu*, *Idiot*, *Indra*, *Okkadu*, *Pokiri* and *Arya 1 & 2*, among several others, have actively invited the public to learn about the content of songs, their production process and other details, revealing the stars' working style. An 'audio launch' programme is a common practice in this sense, where songs are released prior to film release, organised on a grand scale with the involvement of the media industry. The event is telecast and is covered by the print media in its exclusive entertainment sections. The songs are subsequently promoted through ringtones, CDs, downloads, and so on. In other words, the audience is invited to actively choose, not in the old sense of one song over the other, or one type of film over the other, but the same song or same film across different media platforms, which, in Henry Jenkins' words, would be tapping into 'the migratory behavior of media audiences who will go almost anywhere in search of the kinds of entertainment experiences they want' (Jenkins 2006: 2). The films of Arjun, especially *Arya*, have been dubbed into Malayalam (and Hindi), making him a star in that market. *Arya* was remade in Odiya, Bengali and Tamil, while inspiring other language versions. Much of his stardom rests on his dancing and acting abilities, and his interest in pop-inflected music allows him to go for distinctively choreographed numbers, which are seen as having 'complicated moves'. As an icon representing the youth and its global encounters with various types of entertainment, Allu Arjun reinvests his success and stardom in sustaining his fascination with specific stories and taxonomies of songs. His father Allu Aravind's production house, Geetha Arts, benefits too from this success. As is its wont, the star-making process reiterates close links with familial investments and proximity to the industry, while at an individual level each star has to prove his ability at dancing, fights and acting to attract different producers and audiences.

The changing function of film songs has therefore affected the construction of star image and its consumption. It has relocated stars across villages, towns, national and global cities to multiplexes, small theatres, television channels, political campaigns, familial ventures, audio launches and live stage shows, and as downloadable commodities on mobile phones and MP3 players. The song has expanded the functions of Indian stardom as never before. It is no longer 'aural material' alone – it is star material, attached to several malleable notions of stardom, mediated by technology, changing conventions of the narrative and a willing audience to receive this material. The post-2000 Indian film star, singing and performing to film song, shares not many similarities with the 1940s gramophone-era stars or 1980s cassette-era stardom, but stands on its unique ground characterised by various taxonomies of Indian musical and cinematic legacies.

NOTES

1. Theodore Baskaran, in an email communication with the author. Baskaran says, 'Film song does not exist by itself. It is created for a context in the film and is received with the visuals. The visuals are often an important factor in the success of a particular song; the context I think is important and to remember that film song is an applied art.' Email dated 7 April 2016.
2. Morcom quoting Mukesh Desai, chief executive of the music company T-Series from an interview (Morcom 2008: 69).
3. 'Wanted ghost singers', *filmindia*, October 1945, p. 17.
4. 'Movie Industry: Much drama in tinsel town', *Business Line*, 8 December 2011, http://www.thehindubusinessline.com/features/article2698058.ece
5. 'Movie Industry: Much drama in tinsel town', *Business Line*, 8 December 2011, http://www.thehindubusinessline.com/features/article2698058.ece

6. 'Channels hum a new tune to beat song blues', *Business Standard*, 24 January 2008, p. 24.
7. 'Entertainment at your fingertips', *The Financial Express*, 8 January 2008, p. 8.
8. 'SRK is new *baadshah* of mobile screen', *Business Standard*, 13 March 2008, p. 12.

BIBLIOGRAPHY

Anant, S. (2008), *Business of Culture, Project Commissioned by Culture: Industries and Diversity in Asia (CIDASIA) Research Programme*, Project Report, Bangalore: CIDASIA and Centre for the Study of Culture and Society.

Andrew, Dudley J. (1976), *The Major Film Theories: An Introduction*, New York: Oxford University Press.

Booth, Gregory (2008), *Behind the Curtain: Making Music in Mumbai Film Studios*, New Delhi: Oxford University Press.

Elsaesser, Thomas (2011), 'James Cameron's *Avatar*: access for all', *New Review of Film and Television Studies* 9:3 (2011), 247–64.

Gopal, S. and S. Moorti (eds) (2008), *Global Bollywood: Travels of Hindi Song and Dance*, Minneapolis: University of Minnesota Press.

Indraganti, Kiranmayi (2016), *Her Majestic Voice*, Oxford: Oxford University Press.

Jenkins, Henry (2006), *Convergence Culture: Where Old and New Media Collide*, New York: NYU Press.

Majumdar, Neepa (2010), *Wanted Cultured Ladies Only!*, New Delhi: Oxford University Press.

Morcom, Anna (2008), 'Tapping the Mass Market: The Commercial Life of Hindi Film Songs', in S. Gopal and S. Moorti (eds) (2008), *Global Bollywood: Travels of Hindi Song and Dance*, Minneapolis: University of Minnesota Press.

Munsterberg, Hugo (1916), 'The Photoplay: A Psychological Study', *Gutenberg,* D. Appleton & Company. Available at: http://www.gutenberg.org/files/15383/15383-h/15383-h.htm, accessed 25 July 2016.

Ranade, Ashok (2006), *Hindi Film Song: Music Beyond Boundaries*, New Delhi: Promilla Co.

Srinivas, S. V. (2009), *Megastar: Chiranjeevi and Telugu Cinema after N T Rama Rao*, New Delhi: Oxford University Press.

Srinivas, S. V. (2013), *Politics as Performance*, New Delhi: Permanent Black.

PART 3

STARS AND ETHNICITY

5. WHITEWASHING THE DREAMGIRLS: BEYONCÉ, DIANA ROSS AND THE COMMODIFICATION OF BLACKNESS

Jaap Kooijman

'Is Beyoncé the Diana Ross of our generation?' a television reporter asked Oprah Winfrey on the red carpet at the premiere of the 2013 documentary *Beyoncé: Life Is But a Dream*. Her response was clear: 'No, she is the Beyoncé of our generation. You cannot compare her to Diana Ross. Diana Ross was Diana Ross, and Beyoncé is Beyoncé' (Graham 2013). Winfrey is right, of course, as the careers of these two African-American female superstars are more than three decades apart, during which the media landscape has changed drastically. Much more than Ross ever was, Beyoncé is 'an ambulant brand, an advertisement for a new gilded age when commodities overpower everything – including race' (Cashmore 2010: 138). Back in the post-civil rights era of the 1970s, when Diana Ross became a solo superstar, no one could have envisioned an African-American female pop star featured on the cover of the 'The 100 Most Influential People' issue of *Time* magazine, as Beyoncé was in May 2014. As with many of her achievements, Beyoncé's appearance on the *Time* cover has been perceived as a sign of a 'post-racial' era in which race is no longer a barrier to superstardom. However, as Farah Jasmine Griffin argues, although Beyoncé does 'occupy a space unimagined by earlier generations', this does not signify a 'post-racial' time, but 'a historical moment in which race and racism operate differently than in the past' (Griffin 2011: 132–3). To perceive the shift from the 'post-civil rights' Ross to the allegedly 'post-racial' Beyoncé as sheer progress fails to recognise how race and racism still function in society and media today.

Beyoncé might not be the Diana Ross of our generation, yet the similarities between the two superstars cannot be ignored. Both Ross and Beyoncé started as out as lead singer of a very popular African-American 'girl group', the Supremes and Destiny's Child; both were managed by a strong male father figure from whom they had to distance themselves publicly to claim their independence; and both became global superstars, not just as bestselling pop singers performing in grand stadiums around the world, but also as movie actresses and fashion icons featured on the covers of glossy magazines. Significantly, both Diana Ross and Beyoncé publicly announced that they transcended 'race', that they were 'universal' and 'colour blind' in response to continuous scrutiny by the media, music critics and fans questioning their 'blackness'. 'I don't think in terms of race [. . .] it's people – not this race or that race', Diana Ross told *Ebony* magazine in 1981 (Massaquoi 1981: 44–6). Beyoncé, in turn, told *Vogue* in 2009: 'I'm universal [. . .] no one's paying attention to what race I am. I've kind of proven myself. I'm past that' (Cashmore 2010: 144).

However, as Alice Echols has pointed out, contrary to white artists who 'are hailed for their brave transgressions' when crossing the racially defined categories of the entertainment industry, black pop artists 'who defy the tests of "blackness" [. . .] may achieve superstardom, but they often find their racial crossings leave them open to charges of self-loathing and selling-out' (Echols 2002: 197). Debates about Diana Ross tend to centre on 'questions of racial authenticity' (Brooks 2014: 206), labelling her as 'an honorary white girl' (Kempton 2005: 265) who was 'out-whiting whitey' (Cardwell 1997: 118). In a 1976 *Village Voice* article, Jamaica Kincaid described Ross as the 'last of the black white girls [. . .] who had mastered without the slightest bit of self-consciousness or embarrassment, being white' (Kincaid 1976: 152). In stark contrast, four decades later, Judy Rosen of *The New Yorker* described Beyoncé as 'by far the "blackest" – musically and aesthetically – of all the post-Madonna pop divas; she represents African-American women's anger and power like no one in popular culture since Aretha Franklin' (Rosen 2013). Times indeed seem to have changed, but Beyoncé's 'blackness', musically and aesthetically, continues to be scrutinised and debated. The release of her 2011 solo album *4* prompted the question why Beyoncé's skin colour seemed lighter than on the covers of her previous albums, similar to the rumours about Ross 'airbrush[ing] herself into Doris Day oblivion' on her album covers (Taraborrelli 1989: 394). Discussing the issue of 'whitewashing' is important to reveal how race is strategically used by the industry, as became clear when Beyoncé was featured in a 2008 L'Oréal advertisement for hair colour products; Beyoncé's skin colour was significantly lighter in the advertisement printed in *Elle* magazine than the very same one in *Essence*, a glossy targeted at African-American women (Cashmore 2010: 145). However, too often the debate is reduced to the question of whether or not the artist is 'still black enough' or instead has 'become white'. In his seminal essay 'What is This

"Black" in Black Popular Culture?', Stuart Hall argues that 'black popular culture is a contradictory space' that 'can never be simplified or explained in terms of the simple binary oppositions that are still habitually used to map it out' (Hall 1992: 26). Arguments of 'whitewashing' or 'being not black enough' tend to fall back upon a crude black–white dichotomy to make value judgements about the artist's (lack of) 'authenticity', rather than to examine the roles that race and gender continue to play in the entertainment industry, and specifically in African-American female superstardom.

This chapter neither questions the 'blackness' of Beyoncé or Diana Ross, nor defends them against the accusations of being 'whitewashed'. Instead, I examine how 'blackness' and 'whiteness' function in the construction of their star images (Dyer 1998), shaped not only by their performances on record and film, but also by their offscreen appearances in promotional material and interviews, as well as critical reception and tabloid press stories (see Kooijman 2014). Following Richard Dyer, without denying their individual agency, I perceive these two African-American female superstars as 'embodiments of the social categories in which people are placed and through which they have to make sense of their lives, and indeed through which we make our lives' (Dyer 2004: 16). Rather than focusing on one star in one specific era, I emphasise the historical link between Beyoncé and Ross in an attempt to show how their star texts are interconnected and continue to inform each other over time. Beyoncé's performance as the Ross-inspired character Deena Jones in the film version of the 1981 Broadway musical *Dreamgirls* (Bill Condon, 2006) most explicitly merges the star images of Beyoncé and Ross, connecting them both to the question of 'whitewashing' and the betrayal of authentic 'black' culture.

The chapter's starting point is the revisionist narrative of the original 1981 Broadway musical *Dreamgirls*, in which the story of Diana Ross and the Supremes is reduced to a tale of the group's record company Motown betraying authentic 'black' culture in its aim to become economically successful in mainstream 'white' culture. This simple binary opposition is most apparent in the replacement of the group's 'original lead singer' Effie White (!), embodying 'blackness', by the more commercial Deena Jones, embodying 'whiteness'. Subsequently, I will discuss how the casting of Beyoncé as Deena in the 2006 film version not only added star power to the Broadway original, but also used the already existing connection between Beyoncé and Diana Ross to give form to the Deena character. Moreover, much of Beyoncé's performance of Deena is clearly modelled after the fictional character Mahogany that Ross plays in *Mahogany* (Berry Gordy, 1975), thereby blurring the lines between 'real' and fictional personas even more. Finally, I will compare the song 'Listen', performed by Deena/Beyoncé, to 'It's My Turn', the final solo hit single by Ross before leaving Motown in 1981, the year when *Dreamgirls* first appeared on Broadway. Connecting the 'post-civil rights' Diana Ross to the allegedly 'post-racial' Beyoncé foregrounds the historical continuity in African-American female superstardom, as well as showing how star images can travel over time, informing each other through 'real' and fictional personas.

BLACKNESS AS AUTHENTICITY

Set in 1960s Chicago, the musical *Dreamgirls* tells the story of the African-American girl group the Dreamettes, who become the Dreams after their manager Curtis Taylor replaces the group's soulful lead singer Effie White with the less talented yet better-looking and more commercial-sounding Deena Jones in an attempt to reach a mainstream (read white) audience. With Deena as the group's focal point, Effie is pushed into the background and is eventually forced to leave the Dreams, by then renamed Deena Jones and the Dreams. As a single mother on welfare (her daughter fathered by Curtis), Effie attempts a comeback with the ballad 'One Night Only', but soon finds out that Curtis is paying radio stations to boycott her single in favour of a disco version sung by Deena (by now married to Curtis). When the scheme is exposed, Deena leaves Curtis and reconciles with Effie, whose ballad version becomes a number-one hit song. As a grand finale, Effie joins Deena for the final performance of the Dreams. Starring Jennifer Holliday as Effie and Sheryl Lee Ralph as Deena, *Dreamgirls* opened on Broadway in December 1981 and received rave reviews, including from *The New York Times*, which named Holliday's solo 'And I'm Telling You I'm Not Going' as 'one of the most powerful theatrical coups to be found in a Broadway musical since Ethel Merman sang "Everything's Coming Up Roses" at the end of Act I of *Gypsy*' (Rich 1981: C11).

Dreamgirls is a thinly veiled retelling of the story of the Supremes, in which Deena Jones stands for Diana Ross, Effie White for Florence 'Flo' Ballard, Lorrell Robinson for Mary Wilson, and Curtis Taylor, Jr for Berry Gordy, Jr, founder and president of Motown. A *Dreamgirls* cover story in *Ebony* magazine (May 1982) made the connection explicit:

> Although enough names and details have been changed to avoid legal problems, *Dreamgirls* is remarkably similar [. . .] to the story of the Supremes – three girls from Detroit who were the Primettes, then the Supremes, then Diana Ross and the Supremes. While, in the story of the Supremes, singer Florence Ballard was dropped from the group for reasons which many Supremes fans still consider 'unexplained', in *Dreamgirls*, Effie is dropped because she is overweight, not very glamorous, thought of as a troublemaker, and has a voice that is a bit 'too black' for 'crossover' appeal to White audiences in, say, Las Vegas. (Bailey 1982: 92)

The article leaves out one significant difference between the two stories. Whereas the fictional Effie has a successful comeback and reconciles with Deena and the Dreams, the real Florence did not succeed as a solo singer and died in poverty at the age of thirty-two from cardiac arrest, eight years after she had left the Supremes. In earlier drafts of the musical, Effie was supposed to die before the intermission, much to the protest of Jennifer Holliday, who had been promised a starring role on Broadway and did not 'see how [she would] accomplish this being in a secondary role' (Lawson 1981: C5). By refusing to be pushed into the background, Holliday mirrored her onstage Effie character, eventually resulting in a fictional happy end that imagined how Florence Ballard's solo career could have been a success.

The credibility of *Dreamgirls* as telling the story of the Supremes was reaffirmed by the responses of the two remaining original Supremes. Diana Ross refused to see the show, sending her good friend Michael Jackson instead (Hirshey 1984: 164); Mary Wilson went to see it several times, knowing 'in [her] heart that this story rang far truer than the producers could have imagined' and prompting her to title her bestselling autobiography *Dreamgirl: My Life as a Supreme* (Wilson 1986: xii). In her book on girl groups, Jacqueline Warwick correctly points out that 'since the success of the Broadway musical *Dreamgirls*, it has become customary to lament Ballard as the truly gifted singer in the Supremes, unjustly ousted from the position of lead singer for purely political reasons when Berry Gordy [. . .] groomed the conniving and untalented Diana Ross for stardom' (Warwick 2007: 159–60). Nevertheless, by identifying their second Motown single 'Buttered Popcorn' (1961) – the only one on which Ballard sings lead – as the group's first single, Warwick repeats the suggestion that Ballard was the original lead singer of the Supremes. In reality, Ross sang lead on almost all of the songs from the start, including on their first and only pre-Motown single 'Tears Of Sorrow' (1960), during their audition at Motown, and on their first Motown single 'I Want A Guy' (1961). As Berry Gordy remembers the audition in his autobiography, it was the 'whiny voice of the girl singing lead', meaning Ross, that caught his attention and made him sign the group (Gordy 1994: 146). Pointing out this historical inaccuracy does not undermine the musical's main point that Curtis/Berry favoured Deena/Diana over Effie/Florence because of her commercial potential, but does raise the question why Ballard has to be perceived as the 'original lead singer' to make the *Dreamgirls* narrative work.

The answer lies in a simplistic black–white dichotomy on which the musical is based: the full-figured, darker-skinned Effie White with a powerful soul voice embodies 'blackness', whereas the skinny, light-skinned Deena Jones with a pop voice embodies 'whiteness'. Labelling Ballard the 'original lead singer' not only emphasises the authenticity of Effie/Florence in opposition to the artificiality of Deena/Diana, but also makes the choice for the latter an unfair one, a betrayal of 'blackness'. In his biography *The Lost Supreme: The Life of Dreamgirl Florence Ballard* (note the *Dreamgirls* reference), Peter Benjaminson uses this black–white dichotomy to explain why Gordy chose Ross over Ballard:

> His decision to back Diana totally over Flo also demonstrated how little Gordy cared about race and how much he cared about success and money. Diana epitomized style over substance and strove to look like Twiggy and Jacky Kennedy, two of the whitest women there ever were. Flo was just the opposite. She carried the essence of soul – a deep sadness – inside her and in her voice. Gordy believed correctly that whites preferred style to soul, and because whites were the major record buyers, he saw Ross as commercial success personified. (Benjaminson 2008: 77–8)

By equating 'whiteness' to artificiality ('style') and 'blackness' to authenticity ('substance' and 'essence'), Benjaminson uses the 'simple binary oppositions' that Stuart Hall recognised as simplifying the debate. Such a perspective fits the widely accepted perception of Florence Ballard as the 'antidote' to Diana Ross, placing the latter's 'alleged lack of black female authenticity' in juxtaposition to the former's 'quintessential, if not stereotypical, black femininity' (Lüthe 2011: 188).

Although using the same dichotomy, Craig Werner presents a far more nuanced interpretation in his discussion of Ross – whose pop voice 'lacked the earthy power that had made Flo the original lead singer' – by opposing her individual objective to a communal one: 'Unlike the gospel singers who dedicated their voices to uplifting their communities, Ross used her voice to escape' (Werner 1999: 98). Yet Werner too uses Ballard as an authentic counterpoint to the artificiality of Ross:

> Moving on up assumed a distinctly individual meaning when Diane changed her name, took top billing for the commercially reconstituted Diana Ross and the Supremes, and finally embarked on a solo career that led her through the silver screen to the disco inferno. Flo Ballard descended into the somewhat more literal hell of welfare and died of heart disease at age thirty-two. The wrong Supreme had the lead in *Lady Sings the Blues*. (Werner 1999: 99)

Werner's reference to the 1972 biopic starring Diana Ross as Billie Holiday says nothing about the acting abilities of either Ross or Ballard. Instead, like *Dreamgirls*, he uses the two Supremes as opposing poles in a black–white dichotomy to describe the crossover into 'white' commercial mainstream culture, in which the individual success of Ross is achieved at the expense of Ballard, who stands for the 'black' community that is left behind.

Returning to *Dreamgirls*, however, the artificial escapism that Diana Ross embodies is much closer to the musical genre than the authentic 'black' culture embodied by Florence Ballard. Nelson George has called this the 'irony' of *Dreamgirls*, as the musical, in its staging and musical styles, is in itself an example of its main premise, namely of how 'gritty soul music [is] being discarded in favour of insubstantial musical styles' (George 2004: 44). This irony becomes most apparent in the musical's signature song 'And I Am Telling You I'm Not Going'. In interviews, Jennifer Holliday revealed that she was asked 'to tone it down' and to 'make [the song] more pop', which she refused as that would have meant she 'sold out' (White and Branson 1993: 304), again mirroring her fictional character Effie. However, 'And I Am Telling You I'm Not Going' is far from 'gritty soul music' but a typical Broadway torch song, a bombastic and melodramatic showstopper, befitting a camp style that celebrates artificiality and theatricality. *Dreamgirls* as a whole 'reflects the camp, surreal view of black divas that is a significant part of the gay aesthetic' (George 2004: 44). Not surprisingly then, the three main men responsible for *Dreamgirls* were gay/bisexual white men born in the early 1940s: author and lyricist Tom Eyen, composer Henry Krieger and director Michael Bennett. Also Bill Condon, the director of the 2006 film version, is an openly gay white man.

Without suggesting that *Dreamgirls* is a 'gay [white] man's fantasy', as several reviewers commented about the film (Laurie 2012: 549), the musical fits within a camp tradition of 'diva worship' that in its search for 'utopian ideals' finds expression in excess and flamboyance (Jennex 2013: 344). The musical genre in general is one of the most prominent forms of entertainment that 'offers the image of "something better" to escape into, [. . .] the sense that things could be better, that something other than what is can be imagined and maybe realized' (Dyer 2002: 20). Effie's story of how authentic 'black' culture is betrayed might be the main premise of *Dreamgirls*, yet ends up functioning merely as a dramatising backstory to the spectacle offered by the musical performances, including Effie's own showstopping 'And I'm Telling You I'm Not Going'. Through its celebration of excessive glamour and fabulousness as embodied by Deena and the Dreams, *Dreamgirls* literally presents the utopian vision that dreams can come true, thereby challenging its own simplistic black–white dichotomy of the 'authentic' versus the 'artificial'.

THE COMMODIFICATION OF BLACKNESS

When Jennifer Hudson won both an Academy Award and a Golden Globe in the category of best supporting (!) actress for her role as Effie White in the film version of *Dreamgirls*, she gave a shout-out to Jennifer Holliday and dedicated her win to 'a lady who never really got a fair chance [. . .] Florence Ballard, you'll never be forgotten'. The casting of Hudson as Effie was fitting, as her experience on the television talent show *American Idol* in 2004 echoed the *Dreamgirls* narrative. In spite of her vocal mastery, Hudson was voted off early on, an event that many (including pop star Elton John) believed was based predominantly on her being full-figured and black (Meizel 2011: 179–80). Starring in *Dreamgirls* was a triumphant revenge similar to Effie's comeback, as was Hudson's posing on the cover of the American *Vogue* (March 2007). However, like Jennifer Holliday before her, Hudson could not repeat her acting success, suggesting that Effie in *Dreamgirls* is the only starring role available to 'larger' African-American actresses. Mirroring the choice for Deena over Effie, Hudson's co-star Beyoncé subsequently starred as Etta James in *Cadillac Records* (2008), even though to some critics Hudson seemed the more obvious choice (Laurie 2013: 519).

The presence of Beyoncé added a star power to the film missing from the musical, thereby increasing the importance of Deena Jones as a main character and enhancing the idea that *Dreamgirls* was really about Diana Ross after all. While Sheryl Lee Ralph, who played Deena in the Broadway version, always insisted that she 'was not playing Diana Ross' (Ralph 2011: 124), Beyoncé told reporters that during the filming she felt as if she 'was channelling Diana Ross' and that she had a 'shrine' of Ross photographs in her dressing room (Ulmer 2006). The film also stayed closer to the story of the Supremes by changing the setting from Chicago (back) to Detroit and by imitating the group's style through close copies of their album covers and television performances. Moreover, *Dreamgirls* tapped into the connection that already existed between Diana Ross and Beyoncé. From the start of her career with Destiny's Child, Beyoncé had been compared to Ross, including by herself. In interviews, Beyoncé named the Supremes as the group's main inspiration 'because they were glamorous [and] that's what Destiny's Child tries to do' (Farley 2001). Most tellingly, Destiny's Child mimicked an iconic 1968 publicity picture of the Supremes on the cover of *Vibe* magazine (February 2001), with Beyoncé posing as Ross in the middle. Beyoncé recognised that the comparison to Ross made her look like 'a diva [who goes] around kicking people out of the group', leaving the media and fans to wonder when she would 'do a Diana Ross' and go solo, which Beyoncé eventually did in 2003 (Bogle 2007: 361–2; Pointer 2014: 59). The Deena Jones character resembled both Ross and Beyoncé to such an extent that Beyoncé feared 'that audiences would think [*Dreamgirls*] is my life story' (Ulmer 2006).

While during the first half of the movie, the Deena character is modelled after Diana Ross of the 1960s, during the second half Beyoncé's performance seems inspired mainly by the fictional character that Ross performed in the movie *Mahogany* (1975), directed by Berry Gordy after he fired the white British director Tony Richardson (Gordy 1994: 335–9). In *Mahogany*, Ross plays Tracy Chambers, a young woman from the Chicago South Side who dreams of escaping the ghetto and becoming a successful fashion designer. The white fashion photographer Sean McAvoy (Anthony Perkins) discovers Tracy, takes her to Rome, and turns her into the top model named Mahogany. After becoming a successful fashion designer, Tracy realises that a life of glamour and richness does not bring her happiness and she returns to her black boyfriend Brian (Billy Dee Williams) in Chicago. Gerald Early has called *Mahogany* 'a brilliant film', not for its cinematic qualities but because the film succeeds 'to mythify Ross herself as dramatizing the dilemma of crossover success' (Early 2004: 121–2). Similar to *Dreamgirls*, the movie seems based on a simplistic black–white dichotomy: 'blackness' embodied by Brian in Chicago stands for authenticity, whereas 'whiteness' embodied by Sean in Rome stands for artificiality. However, again similar to *Dreamgirls*, the film undermines this dichotomy with its camp flamboyance. Miriam Thaggert has suggested that by having Tracy return to Chicago, 'the film cannot envision "Diana Ross's dream come true" – of being successful' (Thaggert 2012: 734), but that is exactly what the film does: not Tracy who returns to authentic 'black' culture, but Mahogany who is a success in the artificial 'white' world of fashion shapes the Diana Ross star image, turning 'a child of black, working-class Detroit [. . .] into a *Mahogany* pop-culture goddess' (Brooks 2014: 209). As Richard Dyer has argued, *Mahogany* tries to reconcile discourses of race that are irreconcilable (the black–white dichotomy and the dilemma of crossover success) by depending on the appeal of the star's performance (in this case, through the use of montage sequences) as 'the magical resolution of the irresolvable'; whether or not the movie succeeds 'depends a lot on how much you go for Diana Ross and sensuous montage' (Dyer 1986: 136–7).

The almost four-minutes-long montage sequence depicting how photographer Sean turns Tracy into the 'inanimate object' Mahogany is the most significant and spectacular part of *Mahogany* (see Figure 5.1). With the instrumental 'Theme From Mahogany (Do You Know Where You're Going To?)' as soundtrack, the sequence opens with close-ups of make-up being applied to Tracy's mouth and eyes, followed by her being photographed in different settings, outfits and poses. In *Dreamgirls*, the montage sequence of Deena's photo shoot for *Vogue*, with 'When I First Saw You' sung by Curtis (Jamie Foxx) as soundtrack, closely follows the *Mahogany* one, showing how Curtis 'made' the star Deena, like Sean 'made' supermodel Mahogany (and by extension, *Mahogany*'s director Berry Gordy 'made' Diana) (see Figure 5.2). Jane Gaines has argued that the *Mahogany* montage sequence is not only a clear example of 'woman-as-spectacle' but also presents a makeover from 'black' to 'white':

> Effected with wigs and make-up colours, the transformations are a play on and against 'darkness'; Diana Ross is a high-tech Egyptian Queen, a pale medieval princess, a turbaned Asiatic, a body-painted blue nymph.

Figure 5.1   Diana Ross as Mahogany in montage sequence from *Mahogany* (Berry Gordy, 1975).

Figure 5.2   Beyoncé Knowles as Deena Jones in montage sequence from *Dreamgirls* (Bill Condon, 2006).

> As her body colour is powdered over or washed out in bright light, and as her long-haired wigs blow around her face, she becomes suddenly 'white'. (Gaines 1988: 18)

This creation of Mahogany echoes the familiar narrative of Josephine Baker, who, in the 1920s, left the racially segregated America for Europe, where she became a celebrated icon of 'the black woman as something of a super-sexy noble savage' (Bogle 2007: 92). Similarly, while enabling her to escape the American reality of racial discrimination, the 'white' fashion world of Europe reduces Mahogany to a spectacle of the exotic Other, turning her into an inanimate object to be desired because of her/its darkness. Tracy/Ross is not literally becoming 'white', but her skin colour is disconnected from 'black' culture, only to be consumed as a fashionable accessory by 'white' culture: 'Losing her black community identity, Tracy becomes Mahogany, acquiring the darkness, richness and value the name connotes; that is, her blackness becomes commodified' (Gaines 1988: 19).

Here a connection can be made to the 'real' Diana Ross and Beyoncé, whose images, similar to their fictional counterparts Mahogany and Deena, are also shaped within the context of fashion and glamour photography. For example, both Ross and Beyoncé made the cover of *Vanity Fair* (March 1989 and November 2005, respectively), an event that can be seen as an indication of superstardom, 'particularly for African-American stars who rarely saw their faces on the full cover of *Vanity Fair*' (Bogle 2007: 362). Only two other African-American female stars have been featured on a *Vanity Fair* single-person cover: Tina Turner (May 1993) and, most recently, *Scandal* actress Kerry Washington (August 2013). The two covers are remarkably alike, as Ross and Beyoncé are both photographed with their bare back turned to the viewer, while looking over their left bare shoulder. The Ross cover, shot by Annie Leibovitz, shows a nude Diana wrapped in a white sheet, a childlike pose that is reinforced by the title 'Diana Ross: A Star Is Reborn'. With her black skin literally wrapped in whiteness, the Ross portrait 'contrasts whiteness and blackness', as bell hooks has argued: 'Whiteness dominates the page, obscuring and erasing the possibility of any assertion of black power. The longing that is most visible in this cover is that of the black woman to embody and be encircled by whiteness' (hooks 1992: 71). Whiteness also dominates the Beyoncé cover, shot by Patrick Demarchelier, as the 'beylightful, beylicious, beylovely [. . .] Beyoncé' is positioned against and engulfed by an ultra-bright white background. The commodification of blackness is emphasised by the word 'HIP-HOP' printed in bright orange letters across Beyoncé's body. While initially the cover raised the question of whether or not *Vanity Fair* had 'whitened' Beyoncé's skin colour (which assumes that an 'authentic' shade of skin colour exists), the real significant issue is the way whiteness and blackness are contrasted. Similar to the *Mahogany* montage sequence, the two covers are (using the words of the above-quoted Jane Gaines) a play on and against 'darkness' in which both Diana Ross and Beyoncé become suddenly 'white' – they have been commodified.

That 'becoming white' is more about commodification than actual skin colour is made clear by the portrait of Diana Ross that Andy Warhol made for her 1982 *Silk Electric* album. When designing the portrait, Warhol wondered 'what colour I should make her – I wonder if she wants to be black or white' (Warhol 1989: 400). The final portrait (a close-up of her face looking over her left bare shoulder, similar to the *Vanity Fair* cover) had Ross 'looking as white as [Ronald] Reagan himself', as Sue Steward and Sheryl Garratt argue, concluding that 'once black artists do, against all odds, "cross over" to a bigger audience, their fight becomes one of remaining black' (Steward and Garratt 1984: 50). By taking the whiteness of the Andy Warhol portrait literally rather than recognising its overt symbolism of commodified culture, Steward and Garratt fall back upon the black–white dichotomy in which 'remaining black' signifies authenticity and 'becoming white' signifies artificiality. In her discussion of the Warhol portrait, Nicole Fleetwood does not mention the colour of Diana Ross at all (with the exception of noting her 'shiny red' lips), but instead places the image in a longer tradition of Ross publicity photographs that can be viewed as 'a disruption of iconic whiteness', arguing that 'Ross is noted for the cultivation of her iconic face and for producing a cross-racial and gender-varied desirability' (Fleetwood 2015: 63). Instead of either 'remaining black' or 'becoming white', the Ross image challenges such a rigid black–white dichotomy.

The artificiality of commodified culture enables photographers of both Diana Ross and Beyoncé to use their skin colour as a matter of 'artistic choice' in which 'black' and 'white' are perceived as merely expressions of fashion, seemingly free from politics. Not surprisingly then, in the Mahogany-style photo shoot called 'African Queen' by Mark Pillai for the French fashion magazine *L'Officiel Paris* (February 2011), Beyoncé is pictured in a wide range of colours, from an extremely light-skinned portrait to a controversial 'black-face' one. Although in *Dreamgirls* Deena/Beyoncé is also shown in a dark-painted full-body shot as part of the fictional *Vogue* photo shoot, this time Beyoncé's donning blackface understandably sparked controversy. However, like Mahogany in Rome, Beyoncé in Paris moves in an artificial and commodified 'white' world of fashion, disconnected from explicit 'black' politics and history. The *L'Officiel Paris* photo shoot functions in a similar way to the *Mahogany* montage sequence and the *Vogue* photo shoot in *Dreamgirls*, suggesting that Mahogany and Deena as well as Diana Ross and Beyoncé occupy an ahistorical and utopian space in which 'black' or 'white' no longer seem to matter – but obviously still do. These images of Mahogany, Deena, Diana Ross and Beyoncé may challenge the black–white dichotomy; they are produced within an entertainment industry that continues to reduce black female artists to icons of the exotic other, while maintaining iconic whiteness as the ideal standard of beauty.

Beyoncé's 'Listen' is one of the four new songs added to the film version of *Dreamgirls*, which made the film eligible for the Academy Awards. More importantly, the song plays a key role in the film's narrative, appearing immediately after the scene in which Curtis reveals to Deena why he chose her as the lead singer of the Dreams: 'Your voice has no personality, no depth, except for what I put in it.' The bombastic pop ballad is a direct response to Curtis, enabling Deena to proclaim her independence from him: 'I'm more than what you've made of me/I followed the voice you think you gave to me/but now I've got to find my own.' The song showcases the vocal prowess of Deena, and by extension of Beyoncé, thereby refuting the film's main premise that Deena has a weak yet commercial voice, as well as assuring the audience that Beyoncé is vocally as powerful as her co-star Jennifer Hudson. Nevertheless, the proclaimed independence is limited, revealing the patriarchal control that Curtis maintains over Deena. Although she eventually does leave Curtis, Deena sings the song under his guidance in his recording booth at his studio (Laurie 2012: 547).

The notion that Deena's voice has 'no personality' and 'no depth' is reminiscent of comments made about the 'artificial' voice of Diana Ross, the main instrument of Berry Gordy's crossover strategy: 'Among Motown's singers, only Diana Ross had a truly "pop" voice, that is, an absolutely depthless, completely synthetic voice' (Early 2004: 58–9). Also the patriarchal relationship of Curtis and Deena resembles the one of Gordy and Ross, as becomes clear in the way the latter two describe each other. To Ross, Gordy was 'at times my surrogate father, at other times my controller and slave driver' (Ross 1993: 108), while Gordy recalled how Ross captivated him: 'I saw the butterfly emerge from the cocoon and I was dazzled. She was magic and *she was mine*' (Gordy 1994: 195, my emphasis). *Dreamgirls* is all about patriarchal control, telling the story of a black company trying to succeed in a white-dominated entertainment industry, a tale in which the black male entrepreneur Curtis ends up playing the villain. Timothy Laurie has pointed out the irony that this 'critique of black macho leadership' is expressed in a film made by white male producers claiming to tell a 'universal' story (Laurie 2012: 541–4). Moreover, *Dreamgirls* suggests that, while Curtis/Berry keeps Deena/Diana under patriarchal control, the white-dominated entertainment industry can offer black female artists the opportunity to find independence and economic success. And indeed, as Mark Anthony Neal shows in his discussion of Motown's 1970s crossover attempt into Hollywood, like Deena, Diana Ross was 'caught between the patriarchal struggles of two opposing corporate entities: the diversified [yet white-dominated] corporate conglomerate and the independently owned black business' (Neal 1999: 91). In reality, Hollywood had (and has) only a few opportunities for African-American female stars like Ross, while the actual impact of Motown in Hollywood remained relatively small. As Neal concludes, 'Ross's image as an independent black woman was as saccharine as her singing voice, while Gordy parlayed this imagery into a limited victory for black capitalist patriarchy' (Neal 1999: 90).

Eventually, in 1981, Diana Ross left Motown for a multimillion contract with RCA, the same year that the musical *Dreamgirls* premiered on Broadway. Her final Motown solo hit single was 'It's My Turn', a pop ballad that, similar to 'Listen', is a self-affirmative proclamation of independence. In her autobiography, Ross discusses how the song expressed her need 'to step up and take my share of chances' after feeling 'completely disempowered' at Motown: 'All of these people [including Berry Gordy] were making decisions for me, and I had no voice' (Ross 1993: 203). Both 'It's My Turn' and 'Listen' enunciate the symbolic shift from a weak, powerless voice to a strong, empowered one. However, whereas the enhanced vocal prowess of the performance by Deena/Beyoncé physically embodies this shift, Ross' voice on 'It's My Turn' does not sound distinctively different from her previous hit songs, just as 'depthless', 'synthetic' and 'saccharine' as before. Rather than judging Ross' voice in such harsh terms, Richard Dyer and Daphne Brooks have recognised its escapist and utopian character. As Dyer argues, Ross has 'an almost unreal voice' that has 'the vocal "purity" of white song, but is also capable of all the "dirty" notes as well' (Dyer 1982: 36). According to Brooks, its 'hyper-femme "womanly" and yet "childlike" delicacy' makes Diana Ross' voice 'its own kind of powerful statement of extremes, a queer gateway and an invitation to [. . .] never stop imagining that we might travel to other places – kinder, gentler, freer' (Brooks 2014: 206–7). Imagining these 'other places' is what makes up the 'dream' of *Dreamgirls* (and *Mahogany* as well), embodied by both Diana Ross and Beyoncé. Whether or not the dream can actually be fulfilled is less relevant than the pleasure the escapist fantasy provides, as Richard Dyer wrote about Ross in 1982, but which also seems to apply to Beyoncé three decades later: 'Ross epitomizes a success that is still out of reach of most black people or women (or indeed of working class white men). But isn't that part of her act, too? The sheer ecstasy of the whole Diana Ross thing is an outrageous revelling in what success could feel like, but not how to achieve it' (Dyer 1982: 37; see also Kooijman 2016).

'Listen' reappears early on in the 2013 HBO autobiographical documentary *Beyoncé: Life Is But a Dream*. The film's second scene, entitled 'Independence' on the DVD edition, shows how Beyoncé fires her manager and father Mathew Knowles, followed by her singing 'Listen' to herself in the back of her limousine on her way to *The Oprah Winfrey Show*. In this way, another layer of meaning is added to the song, now not just expressing how Deena/Diana breaks with Curtis/Berry, but also how Beyoncé only can become fully independent by breaking with her father. Independence from patriarchal control is the documentary's starting point and remains its main theme throughout the film. The documentary is presented as 'A film by Beyoncé Knowles' (note the use of her last name) and Beyoncé is not only its main topic and star, but also its co-director, co-writer, executive producer and narrator. The narrative follows her individual growth as artist, wife and eventually mother, all in addition to being a superstar. However, the documentary reveals little about how Beyoncé actually achieves and maintains her independence within the entertainment industry. Moreover, her growth is presented as predominantly female empowerment, leaving race unmentioned. In the documentary, Beyoncé compares herself to Nina Simone, the singer and civil rights activist who is known for her political engagement and race-conscious repertoire, which is surprising, as a comparison to pop divas such as Diana Ross, Madonna or Whitney Houston would seem to make more sense (Stanley 2013). Yet, instead of mentioning her political activism, Beyoncé emphasises Simone's artistry, using her as an example to point out that the contemporary entertainment industry relies too much on the glamorous façade of stardom rather than the star's artistic merits. In this way, and similar to the fictional Effie, Nina Simone functions as a sign of authenticity in a documentary that most of all celebrates the flamboyant success of Beyoncé, the Deena/Diana of her own *Dreamgirls*.

LIFE IS BUT A DREAMGIRL

On 26 June 2007, Viacom's BET (Black Entertainment Television) network broadcast the annual BET Awards. The show opened with Jennifer Hudson performing 'And I'm Telling You I'm Not Going'. One minute into the song, Hudson invited 'my Dreamgirl, the original Dreamgirl, miss Jennifer Holliday' to join her on stage. Performed as a duet, the song became a battle of the divas, with both Effies showing off their acrobatic vocal prowess. Throughout the performance, the camera showed the ecstatic audience response in medium shots, but once the duet had ended, two specific persons were singled out in close-up: first Diana Ross then Beyoncé, both applauding enthusiastically. Beyoncé also performed, singing 'Get Me Bodied' from her *B'Day* album rather than a song from *Dreamgirls*. She entered the stage in a golden robotic armour suit, out of which she emerged merely dressed in a bikini, Mahogany-style. That evening, almost all 'Dreamgirls' were winners: Jennifer Hudson won the awards for Best Actress and Best Newcomer, Beyoncé for Best Female R&B/Pop Artist, and Diana Ross the Lifetime Achievement Award. In her acceptance speech, Ross thanked 'the brilliant and extraordinary Berry Gordy' (who was present in the audience and was shown in close-up) 'for getting me started in this industry and believing in me', as well as 'all of the Supremes, especially Mary Wilson' (who was not present). The Lifetime Achievement

Award really was 'honouring the Motown legacy', Ross said, using the opportunity to promote 'high standards' in black pop music: 'We do not have to say the F-word, we do not have to bump and grind [. . .] you can stand tall and be classy, be ladies and gents, and have a long career.' Ross' words fittingly emphasised that both the Motown legacy and her own superstardom were all about social mobility, moving on up from the stereotypical expressions of 'black' culture. When Ross jokingly called her advice a 'diva master class', the camera zoomed in on Beyoncé.

The 2007 BET Awards broadcast reveals not only how the star images of Beyoncé and Diana Ross are connected, but also repositions them as the main characters in the *Dreamgirls* narrative. Although both Effies – Jennifer Holliday and Jennifer Hudson – are recognised and applauded, the television show – as does the movie – ends up celebrating the success that the Deena/Mahogany/Diana/Beyoncé character embodies. Like Ross, Beyoncé can be perceived as 'dramatizing the dilemma of crossover success' (Early 2004: 122), as the performances by both African-American female superstars address questions about maintaining authenticity in a process of commodification, in which authenticity is equated with 'remaining black', while commodification is equated with 'becoming white'. These questions are explicitly expressed in both their portrayals of the fictional characters Mahogany and Deena, as well as through their own 'real' star images, often challenging the simplistic black–white dichotomy on which the dilemma of crossover success is based. Although in the current, allegedly 'post-racial' times, Beyoncé is less easily criticised for 'becoming white' than Ross was three decades earlier, there is a clear continuity in the way both African-American female superstars are expected to account for their 'blackness' and how their commodification is discussed in racial terms, based on a black–white dichotomy signifying 'authenticity' versus 'artificiality'. Such a black–white dichotomy might remain irresolvable, yet both *Dreamgirls* and *Mahogany* provide 'a magical resolution' (Dyer 1986: 136) by relying on the excess and flamboyance of the star's performance, presenting a utopian dream space where race no longer seems to matter. Whether or not the dream works, to echo the words of Richard Dyer, depends a lot on how much you go for Diana Ross and Beyoncé, and sensuous montage.

CODA: POST-FORMATION

This chapter was written before Beyoncé released the single and music video 'Formation' on 6 February 2016, and before she performed the song live during the Super Bowl halftime show the next day. As many commentators have pointed out, with her performance, which included explicit references to the Black Panthers and Malcolm X, as well as Michael Jackson, Beyoncé presented herself as 'unapologetically black', prompting the comedy television show *Saturday Night Live* to feature a sketch entitled 'The Day Beyoncé Turned Black' (13 February 2016). This is not to suggest that political 'blackness' was absent from Beyoncé's earlier work. As the analysis of Beyoncé's 2006 album *B'Day* (on which 'Listen' from *Dreamgirls* features as bonus track) by Daphne Brooks convincingly shows, the album 'articulates the questions and concerns of black women who are wary of having their movements controlled and policed in the public eye', particularly in the wake of Hurricane Katrina (Brooks 2008: 201). However, 'Formation' and the subsequent audiovisual album *Lemonade*, released on 23 April 2016, present these political concerns far more explicitly – and indeed unapologetically – to such an extent that they cannot be ignored or dismissed.

When comparing the 2016 Super Bowl performance to Beyoncé's performing 'At Last' as part of the festivities of President Barack Obama's first inauguration in 2009, this political change becomes apparent. Both performances were targeted at a general audience, larger than Beyoncé's own, and both explicitly referred to the civil rights movement of the 1960s, albeit in significantly different ways. As I have discussed in more detail elsewhere, Beyoncé's performance of 'At Last' – from the 1942 Hollywood musical *Orchestra Wives* but best known in the soulful 1961 rendition by Etta James – evoked Martin Luther King, Jr's 'I Have a Dream' speech, and as such the performance became a celebration of the progress that had been made; Beyoncé serenading the first African-American president reinforced the promise of the American Dream and the possibility of its fulfilment (Kooijman 2013: 147–8). Beyoncé's performance of 'Formation' at the Super Bowl, in stark contrast, emphasised what had not been achieved, that racial discrimination is still rampant and that black militancy (hence the Black Panthers and Malcolm X) is needed to render such injustice visible. The two performances do not contradict each other, but instead bring the complexities of race and gender to the foreground, thereby reinforcing Stuart Hall's earlier quoted reminder that 'black popular culture is a contradictory space', which cannot be reduced to such simple binary oppositions such as 'black' and 'white' or 'authentic' and 'artificial' (Hall 1992: 26).

Acknowledgements

I would like to thank Greg DeCuir, Alexander Dhoest, Richard Dyer, Martin Lüthe, Maarten Reesink, and the participants of the Revisiting Star Studies conference (Newcastle, 2013), the Research Colloquium of the John F. Kennedy Institute (Berlin, 2015) and the NEH Videographic Criticism workshop (Middlebury, 2015) for critically commenting on earlier drafts and presentations of this chapter.

BIBLIOGRAPHY

Bailey, Peter (1982), 'Dreams Come True on Broadway for Young Stars in *Dreamgirls*', *Ebony*, May 1982, pp. 90–96.

Benjaminson, Peter (2008), *The Lost Supreme: The Life of Dreamgirl Florence Ballard*, Chicago: Lawrence Hill Books.

Bogle, Donald (2007), *Brown Sugar: Over One Hundred Years of America's Black Female Superstars* (updated and expanded edition), New York and London: Continuum.

Brooks, Daphne A. (2008), '"All That You Can't Leave Behind": Black Female Soul Singing and the Politics of Surrogation in the Age of Catastrophe', *Meridians: feminism, race, transnationalism* 8:1, 180–240.

Brooks, Daphne A. (2014), 'Let's Talk About Diana Ross', in Carl Wilson, *Let's Talk About Love: Why Other People Have Such Bad Taste* (expanded edition), New York: Bloomsbury, pp. 205–20.

Cardwell, Diane (1997), 'Diana Ross', in Barbara O'Dair (ed.), *Trouble Girls: The Rolling Stone Book of Women in Rock*, New York: Random House.

Cashmore, Ellis (2010), 'Buying Beyoncé', *Celebrities Studies* 1:2, 135–50.

Dyer, Richard (1982), 'Diana Ross', *Marxism Today*, June 1982, 36–7.

Dyer, Richard (1986), '*Mahogany*', in Charlotte Brundson (ed.), *Films for Women*, London: BFI Publishing, pp. 131–7.

Dyer, Richard (1998), *Stars* (second edition), London: British Film Institute.

Dyer, Richard (2002), *Only Entertainment* (second edition), London and New York: Routledge.

Dyer, Richard (2004), *Heavenly Bodies: Film Stars and Society* (second edition), London and New York: Routledge.

Early, Gerald (2004), *One Nation Under a Groove: Motown and American Culture* (revised and expanded edition), Ann Arbor: University of Michigan Press.

Echols, Alice (2002), *Shaky Ground: The Sixties and Its Aftershocks*, New York: Columbia University Press.

Farley, Christopher John (2001), 'Call Of the Child', *Time* (7 January 2001): http://content.time.com/time/magazine/article/0,9171,94003,00.html.

Fleetwood, Nicole R. (2015), *On Racial Icons: Blackness and the Public Imagination*, New Brunswick, NJ: Rutgers University Press.

Gaines, Jane (1988), 'White Privilege and Looking Relations: Race and Gender in Feminist Film Theory', *Screen* 29:4, 12–27.

George, Nelson (2004), *Post-Soul Nation: The Explosive, Contradictory, Triumphant, and Tragic 1980s as Experienced by African Americans (Previously Known as Blacks and Before That Negroes)*, New York: Viking.

Gordy, Berry (1994), *To Be Loved: The Music, the Magic, the Memories of Motown*, New York: Warner Books.

Graham, Mark (2013), 'Does Oprah Feel That Beyoncé Is The Diana Ross Of Her Generation?', VH1.com (13 February 2013): http://www.vh1.com/celebrity/2013-02-13/does-oprah-feel-that-beyonce-is-the-diana-ross-of-her-generation/

Griffin, Farah Jasmine (2011), 'At Last . . .?: Michelle Obama, Beyoncé, Race & History', *Daedalus* 140:1, 131–41.

Hall, Stuart (1992), 'What is This "Black" in Black Popular Culture?', in Gina Dent (ed.), *Black Popular Culture*, Seattle: Bay Press, pp. 21–33.

Hirshey, Gerri (1984), 'Did the Dream (Girls) Come True?', *Esquire* 101:5, May 1984, 163–8.

hooks, bell (1992), *Black Looks: Race and Representation*, Boston: South End Press.

Jennex, Craig (2013), 'Diva Worship and the Sonic Search for Queer Utopia', *Popular Music and Society* 36:3, 343–59.

Kempton, Arthur (2005), *Boogaloo: The Quintessence of American Popular Music*, Ann Arbor: University of Michigan Press.

Kincaid, Jamaica (1976), 'Last of the Black White Girls', *Village Voice*, 28 June 1976, pp. 152, 155.

Kooijman, Jaap (2013), *Fabricating the Absolute Fake: America in Contemporary Pop Culture* (revised and extended edition), Amsterdam: Amsterdam University Press.

Kooijman, Jaap (2014), 'The True Voice of Whitney Houston: Commodification, Authenticity, and African American Superstardom', *Celebrity Studies* 5:3, 305–20.

Kooijman, Jaap (2016), 'Success: Richard Dyer on Diana Ross [and *Beyond*]', *[in] Transition: Journal of Videographic Film & Moving Image Studies* 2:4: http://media commons.futureofthebook.org/intransition/2015/12/29/success

Laurie, Timothy (2012), 'Come Get These Memories: Gender, History and Racial Uplift in Bill Condon's *Dreamgirls*', *Social Identities: Journal for the Study of Race, Nation and Culture* 18:5, 537–53.

Lawson, Carol (1981), '[Jennifer Holliday] Fought Michael Bennett and Became His Star', *The New York Times*, 22 December 1981, p. C5.

Lüthe, Martin (2011), *Color-Line and Crossing-Over: Motown and Performances of Blackness in 1960s American Culture*, Trier: Wissenschaftlicher Verlag Trier.

Massaquoi, Hans J. (1981), '*Ebony* Interview With Diana Ross', *Ebony* 37:1, November 1981, 38–50.

Meizel, Katherine L. (2011), *Idolized: Music, Media, and Identity in* American Idol, Bloomington and Indianapolis: Indiana University Press.

Neal, Mark Anthony (1999), *What the Music Said: Black Popular Music and Black Popular Culture*, London and New York: Routledge.

Pointer, Anna (2014), *Beyoncé: Running the World: The Biography*, London: Coronet.

Ralph, Sheryl Lee (2011), *Redefining Diva: Life Lessons from the Original Dreamgirl*, New York: Gallery Books.

Rich, Frank (1981), '*Dreamgirls*, Michael Bennett's New Musical, Opens', *The New York Times*, 21 December 1981, p. C11.

Rosen, Jody (2013), 'Her Highness', *The New Yorker*, 20 February 2013: http://www.newyorker.com/culture/culture-desk/her-highness

Ross, Diana (1993), *Secrets of a Sparrow: Memoirs*, New York: Villard Books.

Stanley, Alessandra (2013), 'Another Cog in the Machinery of Divahood: Beyoncé's Documentary, "Life Is but a Dream", on HBO', *The New York Times*, 14 February 2013: http://www.nytimes.com/2013/02/15/arts/television/beyonces-documentary-life-is-but-a-dream-on-hbo.html

Steward, Sue and Sheryl Garratt (1984), *Signed, Sealed, and Delivered: True Life Stories of Women in Pop*, London and Sydney: Pluto Press.

Taraborrelli, J. Randy (1989), *Call Her Miss Ross: The Unauthorized Biography of Diana Ross*, New York: Birch Lane Press.

Thaggert, Miriam (2012), 'Marriage, Moynihan, Mahogany: Success and the Post-Civil Rights Black Female Professional in Film', *American Quarterly* 64:4, 715–40.

Ulmer, James (2006), 'After Conquering "Chicago", It's On to Motown', *The New York Times*, 10 September 2006: http://www.nytimes.com/2006/09/10/movies/moviesspecial/10ulme.html?n=Top%2FReference%2FTimes%20Topics%2FSubjects%2FT%2FTheater&_r=0

Warhol, Andy (1989), *The Andy Warhol Diaries* (edited by Pat Hackett), New York: Warner Books.

Warwick, Jacqueline (2007), *Girl Groups, Girl Culture: Popular Music and Identity in the 1960s*, London and New York: Routledge.

Werner, Craig (1999), *A Change is Gonna Come: Music, Race & the Soul of America*, New York: Plume.

White, Adam and Fred Bronson (1993), *The Billboard Book of Number One Rhythm & Blues Hits*, New York: Billboard Books.

Wilson, Mary, with Patricia Romanowski and Ahrgus Juilliar (1986), *Dreamgirl: My Life as a Supreme*, New York: St Martin's Press.

6. DARSHEEL SAFARY: GLOBALISATION, LIBERALISATION AND THE CHANGING FACE OF THE BOLLYWOOD CHILD STAR

Michael Lawrence

Between 2007 and 2015 Darsheel Safary enjoyed an – inevitably – brief tenure as the most popular and successful child star working in Bollywood, the commercial entertainment industry based in Mumbai, India. By comparison with other contemporary Bollywood stars, Safary is perhaps relatively unknown in the West, yet he has endured the same degree of fame and attention in India as Macaulay Culkin did in the United States in the early 1990s. In popular Hindi cinema, children appear fairly frequently as the protagonists' younger relations or companions, and over the decades there have been many child actors who became popular stars, such as Raju Shreshtha in the 1970s, Jugal Hansraj in the 1980s, and Sana Saeed in the 1990s. But it has traditionally been very rare for children to have leading roles in films aimed at family audiences, and even rarer for children to feature in the kinds of vehicles associated with popular superstars. Yet Safary has managed to be the lead actor in all of his Bollywood films, even when appearing alongside established megastars such as Aamir Khan. This chapter will consider Safary's film career and popular image in order to examine the child star's significance for the Bollywood industry and Indian society in the context of recent transformations associated with globalisation. For a short spell, Safary, who was born in 1996, appeared to embody India's accelerated imbrication in global capitalism following the country's economic liberalisation in the early 1990s, and to personify an ideological projection into the present of a future India that had fully endorsed and embraced consumerism and commodity culture. I will be discussing the media's coverage of Safary's professional career and personal life, before focusing on the two most recently released of his films in order to address the relationship between his screen roles and his public image and to determine his position in a globalised and transnational Indian cultural economy.

Sumita S. Chakravarty notes that '[in] the expanding field of Indian film studies, stars are a taken-for-granted aspect of Bollywood, but compared with other aspects of the institution and its products, they have been given less attention' (2013: 180). This chapter seeks to contribute to Indian film studies by focusing on contemporary Bollywood *stardom*, but at the same time it intends to contribute to star studies more generally not only by considering a *non-Western* star but by attending to the material and ideological specificity of the *child* star, a topic which has been largely neglected in academic scholarship on stardom.[1]

For John Ellis, '[the] basic definition of a star is that of a performer in a particular medium whose figure enters into subsidiary forms of circulation, and then feeds back into future performances' (1999: 531). And, as Barry King has suggested, a star's screen performances are always 'already contextualised by the circulation of biographical and personal anecdotal materials that frame their appearances on and off-screen'; such 'extra-filmic' discourses precede and supersede the 'the image-making capacities of film' and condition the way a star is apprehended in a particular film (1985: 39–40). Recent scholarship on contemporary Bollywood stardom suggests that many such foundational approaches to film stars remain valid and valuable: Rajinder Dudrah, for example, has examined superstar Shah Rukh Khan '[as] an actual and textual signifier [. . .] part of Bollywood's historical formation and global dissemination', and considered 'how . . . a notion of global Bollywood [is] achieved in and through the on- and off-screen possibilities that circulate around the star figure of SRK' (2015: 5). This chapter will explore the feedback loops generated by the symbiotic connections between Safary's film performances and his popular image, with a particular focus on how the figure of the fantastic child hero that features in his last two films resonates with the image of the child star.

For some critics the child star should be understood as a product of a precise historical moment, while for others she is a manifestation of mythological archetypes. Charles Eckert, for example, proposes that the Hollywood child star Shirley Temple should be regarded as 'a kind of artefact thrown up by a unique concatenation of social and economic forces', despite our desire to see the child as 'innocent of history', and then assesses the effects of external influences, and specifically 'intense economically-determined ideological pressures', on 'the content of Shirley's films and her public persona' (1991: 185, 186).[2] Jane O'Connor, by contrast, is less interested in 'the dictates of the socioeconomic environment from which [. . .] young performers emanate' and argues that 'child stars belong to the universal symbolic category of the "wonder-child" who recur throughout the myths and legends of the world'. For O'Connor, 'the "star-like" qualities of certain children [. . .] reinforce their supernatural status', making them extraordinary figures akin to child-gods (such as Krishna) (2009: 223, 220).[3] Drawing on Eckert and O'Connor, this chapter will consider Safary and his screen characters' association with 'magical' 'wonder-children', while also attending to his (and their) relation to specific 'concatenations' of historical determinants. At the same time, I will consider the role played by fantasy and technology in Safary's embodiment and personification of the transformations and ideologies associated with globalisation and liberalisation in twenty-first-century India. Chakravarty has recently argued for 'a consideration of stardom in Bollywood that foregrounds the relationship between cinema history, technology and the star body', in which 'the materiality of the body' is incorporated by 'the materiality of historical and technological processes'; as 'products of particular historical formations', stars need to be understood in relation to 'the technologies that help to mediate their presence' (2013: 198, 200, 184). In what follows, I consider how the materiality of this particular star body is both apprehended *as* a historical process and mediated *by* specific technologies.

O'Connor notes that in Western society child stars are 'separated from "normal" children' because 'children are no longer expected to contribute to their family's income', 'are not encouraged or expected to start their careers when still receiving their formal education' and 'are not required to maintain and manage a professional persona' (2009: 214). However, in India, children *are* very often expected to contribute to their family's income, and *are* often expected to work before or after school (if they attend school), and this has significant implications for the cultural meaning of the Indian child star: it is the kind of work they do that separates them from other 'normal' children, rather than the fact that they work, and the kind of work the child star does may be unusual but is generally accepted in the West. Safary's cute personification of India's global aspirations is, paradoxically, dependent upon a spectacular mode of visible child (star) labour, but while the ordinary working child in India may be 'unchildlike' by Western standards (Aitken 2001), the child star is of course an extraordinary child, and so Safary is able to embody ideological fantasies about Indians' access to Western goods and lifestyles.

The child star must function on the screen and in their films in particular ways (as a popular public persona emerges, and a professional career proceeds, both while the child is growing up), and the appeal of such children is apprehended and experienced by audiences, and utilised and exploited by the industry, as a precious, because inevitably finite, property. The child star cannot remain a child for very long: as a material star body she is 'subject to the vicissitudes of time' in a particularly palpable sense (Chakravarty 2013: 185). The child star's appeal involves a popular apprehension of both their physical charm (their being cute) and their acting abilities (their being talented), and while their professional skills might develop over time, their physical attractiveness might very well disappear entirely. As Lori Merish has argued, cuteness is 'distinguishable both by its formal aesthetic features and the formalized emotional response it engenders': specific features and dimensions associated with children's bodies are integral to the aesthetic of cuteness, because 'the cute stages [. . .] a need for adult care' (1996: 187). The cuteness so central to the popular appeal of stars like Safary, however, often vanishes as the child increases in size, loses their original features, and becomes more physically capable (and professionally autonomous), but never disappears entirely, due to the media's fascination with remembering the star's earlier appearance. For example, a recent *Times of India* photo gallery of 'Bollywood's cutest child actors' (Kaushal) described Safary, who was then nineteen, as '[the] kid with the bunny-teeth in *Taare Zameen Par*', referring to his first and extremely successful film, released in 2007 when he was nine, and in which he played Ishaan, a dyslexic schoolboy with a desperate because undiagnosed 'need for adult care'. The image of Safary as a 'cute' nine-year-old 'kid with the bunny-teeth' remains active in 'subsidiary forms of circulation' (Ellis 1999: 521), despite it being a decade out of date; as Timothy Shary has suggested, one reason so few child stars 'maintain their success and visibility as they grow into adulthood' is that 'audiences have difficulty accepting child stars' physical and mental changes as they transform into adults' (2012: 7).

Taare Zameen Par was celebrated by critics for its willingness to explore 'the traumatic side of childhood': the *Indian Express* proclaimed: 'This has to be Hindi cinema's first attempt in recent times to get a child so right', before acknowledging the film's young star's contribution: 'Ishaan comes across as a real, breathing, living child . . . first-time actor Darsheel Safary, all buck teeth, expressive frowns, and wide smiles, lights up the screen' (Gupta 2007). Safary subsequently became the youngest-ever nominee for the Filmfare Best Actor award (he lost to Shah Rukh Khan); the film won the award for Best Film and was India's official entry for the 2009 Academy Awards Best Foreign Film. Following a 'sabbatical' in 2008, Safary worked on two film projects during 2009, first *Zokkomon* (Satyajit Bhaktal), and then *Bumm Bumm Bole* (Priyardashan), a remake of the award-winning Iranian film *Children of Heaven* (*Bacheha-Ye aseman*, Majid Majidi, 1997). *BBB* was the first to be released, in spring 2010, with *Zokkomon* released a year later in spring 2011. These leading roles were followed by the small but significant part in *Midnight's Children*, a Canadian-British co-production, Deepa Mehta's adaptation of Salman Rushdie's celebrated novel, released in winter 2012. Safary therefore appeared in both mainstream family-oriented films intended for multiplex audiences in India and the diaspora, as well as more prestigious fare destined for international film festivals and art-house circuits. Since completing work on *Midnight's Children*, Safary has made fairly regular appearances on Indian television: he was the youngest-ever contestant on the dance reality series *Jhalak Dikhla Jaa* when he competed in the fifth season (2012), and he featured in an episode of *Lage Raho Chachu*, a children's series that airs on Walt Disney's Indian Channel, in 2015.

Interviewed in December 2009, a few months before the release of his second film, Safary claimed, with surprising maturity: 'I am not scared of my performances being compared with what I did in *Taare* [. . .] because I am not the same anymore. I would like to think I have grown as an actor' (Jha 2009). For the child star, professional development 'as an actor' will always be apprehended in relation to (and may be presented as compensation for) their physical development, the transformation of their physical features during adolescence, which is the inescapable destiny of every 'real, breathing, living child'. For Safary, the development of his professional career and the transformation of his physical features are even more closely connected, for his last two screen performances are notable for their display of cosmetic technologies that alter his appearance, and contribute to the disappearance of that cuteness apprehended in his first screen appearance (see Figure 6.1). I will consider here the visibility in the family-adventure/superhero film *Zokkomon*, in which Safary plays a masked avenger, of the braces the actor had worn in 2009 to correct those 'signature buck teeth' (Desai 2010), and the prominence in the second film, *Midnight's Children*, of a prosthetic nose that, together with special contact lenses, made Safary almost unrecognisable as an actor. These two films, which were made when Safary was a young teenager, demonstrate his flexibility as a performer and suggest his potential as an adult star in Bollywood; the transformations of his features presented in these films, the masking or disguising of his familiar face, moreover, suggest a strategic response to the inevitable disappearance of the child star's cuteness.

Figure 6.1   Safary's buck teeth in *Taare Zameen Par* (Aamir Khan, 2007).

SUBWAYS AND *DOSAS*: SAFARY AND POST-LIBERALISATION INDIA

In Richard Dyer's well-known formulation, 'one of the major forms of relationship between a star and her/his social context' is 'the reconciliation of
contradiction': 'Stars frequently speak to dominant contradictions in social
life – experienced as conflicting demands, contrary expectations, irreconcilable
but equally held values – in such a way as to appear to reconcile them' (1991:
216). It is very easy to discover reconciliations of the kind Dyer describes in
media coverage of Safary; as an idealised personification of post-liberalisation
India, he reconciles contradictions related to the impact of global capitalism
and consumerism on children in India. Ritty A. Lukose has argued that youth
is 'a key site for popular cultural reconfigurations of the Indian nation in the
age of liberalization', because an 'intensification and expansion of commodity flows through the liberalization of the Indian economy have made consumption of goods and mass-mediated images a key site for producing youth
identities' (2009: 6, 9). However, as Jyotsna Kapur notes, despite Indian children's knowledge of global brands like Barbie, Reebok, Coke and Dominoes,
'only the upper middle-class child [. . .] is integrated into this globalized consumer culture' because 'for the most part the policy of economic liberalization initiated in 1991 has polarized further the standard of living between the
urban and the rural, as well as between the professional middle class and the
urban poor' (1998: 389, 395). Since media coverage of Safary often focuses
on his relationship (both personal and professional) with various luxury commodity goods, as well as his tastes as a young consumer *of* global media, he is
popularly associated with both middle-class consumerism and cosmopolitan
culture, which aspects are however easily reconciled with attributes and interests that are more traditional.

Perhaps the most straightforward of these reconciliations is evidenced by
the media's emphasis on Safary's ordinariness – in interview after interview,
the star lists his hobbies as 'swimming, cricket, football', 'listening to music,
dancing, swimming and reading books' (Kulkarni 2011; Anon. 2012) – but
also by reports of his dedication to and success at school: in most interviews he
talks about studying while on set and focusing on exams between projects. In
July 2012 the *Times of India* stated that 'the dance-reality show that Darsheel
has taken on has been done on condition that he would rehearse for it only
during breaks from his school studies'; Safary then explained: 'I even carry
my books to the [rehearsal] hall and study during dance breaks' (Jha 2012).
In June 2015 the *Times of India* reported that Safary was 'pleased with his
[Higher Secondary School Certificate] scores', noting that 'the *Taare Zameen
Par* child actor, now 18-years-old, cleared his Class XII board examinations
recently and scored 80%' (Vyavhare 2015). Ironically, however, all four of
Safary's films present children who are terrorised or traumatised by their

teachers. Meheli Sen notes that 'as India pursues its global economic policies aggressively, children come to be seen as baton bearers for the nation's changing future. This fervent ambition translates into brutal school curriculums and sadistically demanding institutions of higher education' (200). While Sen suggests Hindi cinema has 'remained indifferent to these predicaments', he acknowledges *Taare Zameen Par* as a notable exception. Safary, however, appears to have excelled at school despite his work in films and television and his star labour as a celebrity. This is in stark contrast, then, to the child stars of the social realist cinema of the post-independence period. Nandini Chandra has examined the depiction of children in these films and 'the life narratives of the child actors who played them', and shown that while in the films schools are idealised and presented as 'the only legitimate place for the child', 'the child actors themselves, who articulated this notion of childhood, whether from the working class or the bourgeoisie, never went to school and never accessed this model life' (2010: 124).

Safary's relation to globalisation and post-liberalisation culture is more clearly indicated in his comments about the food he eats and the films he watches. Asked what he likes most to eat, Safary answers 'pizzas, Subways, *dosas* and *chatpata* chats' (Anon. 2012). He has always referred to both Bollywood and Hollywood when asked about films: favourite actor – Hrithik Roshan; favourite actress – Kareena Kapoor; favourite film – *3 Idiots* (Rajkumar Hirani, 2009); favourite *child* actor – Jaden Smith ('I liked him in *Karate Kid*'); favourite superhero – Spiderman. Safary has often mentioned Hollywood films such as *Avatar* (James Cameron, 2009) and *Toy Story 3* (Lee Unkrich, 2010), and in recent interviews has discussed the relative merits of *Mad Max: Fury Road* (George Miller, 2015), *The Revenant* (Alejandro González Iñárritu, 2016) and *Deadpool* (Tim Miller, 2016) (Anon. 2010; Anon. 2012; Kulkani 2011; Prabhakar 2016).

Nita Mathur has suggested that 'economic liberalization facilitated a rise in conspicuous consumption and the concomitant emergence of a consumer culture coupled with increasing affluence and individualism'; for the younger generation, 'status gets attached to a pretentious show of new fashions and styles and ownership of luxury commodities' whereby 'an ostentatious way of life and possession of enviable goods emerge as [. . .] signifiers of personal identity' (2010: 217, 226). When the fourteen-year-old Safary was asked in 2010 to talk about his 'gizmos' he admitted to having 'recently' acquired 'an iPod, an Xbox 360, a Wii console, a PSP, two Nintendo SPs and a DS', a considerable collection of desirable gadgets (Desai 2010). His association with such luxury goods is also professional; in 2012 Safary was the obvious choice to launch Sony PlayStation's *Wonderbook: Book of Spells* (based on the *Harry Potter* books). In July 2015 Safary featured in an advert for iBall's HD6 mobile phone, 'gaming on the big screen', according to the jingle (he posted the ad on his Facebook page). In December, however, Safary was among the stars 'adding fun and spark' at a children's marathon in Mumbai, which, according to the *Indian Express*, 'was held to encourage children to abandon their addiction to gadgets and to embrace running and other physical activities' (Anon. 2015a); as Peter N. Stearns observes in his account of globalisation and childhood, an increase in middle-class childhood obesity was first noticed in India in the 2000s (2011: 150). Safary effortlessly and quite literally endorses both the *acquisition* of luxury goods *and* their abandonment; or rather, he embodies the 'conflicting demands' (Dyer 1991: 216) placed on India's middle-class children by appearing to be both addicted to his PlayStation while aware of the importance of other more traditional (and more healthy) kinds of play.

In his account of contemporary celebrity, Barry King has argued that star careers are shaped as much by 'the drive to maximize the media visibility of their names and the branding opportunities that come from the intensive marketing of their personae' as by specific performances in particular films (2010: 9). Sangita Gopal argues that post-liberalisation Bollywood is marked by the intensification of such processes as 'the diffusion of cinematic signification into brands, lifestyles, and celebrity culture', and suggests 'we witness today a complete integration of advertising, marketing, retailing, mobile communications, and many related sectors of the entertainment industry' (2011: 13). As Anne Ciecko has argued, '[the] images and idiom of multinational and multimedia consumerism and tried-and-tested corporate advertising strategies such as product placement and celebrity endorsements are used to sell the idea of the Bollywood film star, and in turn, Bollywood as a masculinized global player' (2001: 127). It is not then surprising that Safary has from the beginning of his career established professional associations with various global companies, and has worked as an official brand ambassador for, among others, Adidas, Horlicks, PlayStation and Vodafone. He has also appeared in numerous advertisements, several of which refer to his feature film work: in 2009, for example, he was 'reunited' with Aamir Khan to promote Parle-G, India's 'number one biscuit'. At the same time, his feature films feature product placement for the brands with which he is associated: his second film, *Bumm Bumm Bole*, includes extended sequences showcasing Adidas sportswear, and the story itself revolves around a pair of Adidas trainers.[4] Safary appears to have quickly understood his professional responsibilities as an endorser when talking to the media; one journalist in 2011 described the fourteen-year-old Safary as 'the perfect teen star – child-like enough to be loveable, yet savvy enough to not name a brand when asked what toothpaste he uses' (Vetticad 2011). In his account of Shah Rukh Khan's celebrity endorsement work, Julien Cayla suggests that he 'stands for [. . .] access to commodities and services that until now were reserved to Western elites': 'the shift from Amitabh Bachchan [iconic Bollywood 'angry man' of the 1970s and 1980s] to Shah

Rukh Khan signals a movement from the figure of the Indian man as citizen fighting for the nation, to the celebration of the Indian man as connected to global networks of consumption and production, the Indian man as consumer and manager' (2008: 5–6, 7). Safary would appear to represent the Indian *child* as consumer citizen and it is his cuteness (rather than eroticism) that activates what Purnima Mankekar has called 'commodity affect', in which desire 'pertains not just to the pleasure of acquiring a commodity but also the pleasures of gazing upon it and longing for it' (2015: 115). Safary thus embodies a distinctly non-threatening and endearing version of Bollywood as a 'masculinized global player' (Ciecko 2001: 127). To return to Lori Merish, cuteness 'activates an erotics of maternal longing' and 'mobilizes' 'a peculiarly "feminine" proprietary desire [. . .] to care for, cherish and protect'; the cute child 'is pure spectacle, pure display', and is therefore unthinkable except in relation to and as an instance of 'commodity aesthetics' (1996: 188). I shall now consider in more detail Safary's most recently released feature films in order to trace connections between the characters he plays and his status as a child star, and in particular the role played by magic and technology in his film's presentation of the child hero's relation with historical and cultural change.

ZOKKOMON AND *MIDNIGHT'S CHILDREN*: SAFARY'S SCREEN HEROICS

Peter Krämer has suggested that 'a convergence of the children's/family film and the action-adventure movie' has enjoyed market dominance in Hollywood since the late 1970s (1998: 304–5). He argues that 'many of today's action-adventure movies are, in fact, family films. At the same time, the traditional children's or family film has been upgraded with a heavy injection of spectacular adventure to appeal to teenagers and young adults as well as children and their parents' (1998: 294–5). Along with *Zokkomon*, recent Bollywood films such as *Chillar Party* (Nitesh Tiwari/Vikas Bahl, 2011), *Havai Dada* (Ajay Kathik, 2011), *Stanley Ka Dabba* (Amole Gupta, 2011) and *Hawaa Hawaai* (Amole Gupta, 2014) have been understood as the industry's attempts to develop family films in the tradition of *Home Alone* (Chris Columbus, 1990), which was itself the inspiration for an earlier example of the Bollywood family film, *Harri Puttar: A Comedy of Terrors* (Lucky Kohli/Rajesh Bajaj, 2008). The importance of the lead star for a film's box-office success is regarded as one of the reasons studios are hesitant to produce child-centred films, and so child stars are increasingly being 'positioned as family entertainers' so as to maximise the appeal of their films (Pereira 2011). This development is inextricable from Walt Disney's interests in India. Siddharth Roy Kapur, managing director of the Walt Disney Company India (established 2004), stated, '[in] the past, most of the content we produced at Disney has had kids as the entry point. However, we are now moving to define the brand as one that brings great entertainment to the entire family' (Anon. 2015b).

Zokkomon, which according to the report quoted above 'was initially called a superhero film [but subsequently] promoted as a family film' (Perieria 2011), was one of the first Bollywood films to be co-produced by the Walt Disney Company, and subsequently distributed under its Disney World Cinema banner; their release of the international DVD of *Taare Zameen Par* (renamed *Like Stars on Earth*) was the first time a global corporation had acquired distribution rights for an Indian film. The Disney World Cinema website explains that it 'delivers remarkable foreign language family entertainment that celebrates the unique stories, cultures and traditions that define our world'. On the Disney India website it is claimed '*Zokkomon* will soar into the hearts and lives of audiences everywhere, to take his place alongside the world's most beloved heroes'. In *Zokkomon* Safary plays Kunal, an orphan, who is sent to stay with his uncle, Deshraj (Anupam Kher), a school principal. Deshraj abandons Kunal at a funfair and pretends his nephew has died in order to access Kunal's inheritance. Kunal returns to the village, and is mistaken for a ghost. He befriends an old scientist, Dr Vivek Roy (also played by Kher), whom Kunal calls 'Magic Uncle', and together they develop a 'supernatural' superhero avatar called Zokkomon, using jetpacks and other gadgets built in their laboratory, to expose and avenge Deshraj, inspire the village children, and (paradoxically) convince the village to abandon their superstitious beliefs (and thus embrace a more 'rational' modernity).

Presenting a superhero adventure to family audiences, *Zokkomon* follows what Iain Robert Smith has described as 'a long history of attempts to engage with the superhero genre in Indian cinema from the 1960s onwards' (2015: 114). *Superman* in particular worked well as a model for Indian films in which 'superpowers are generally attributed to mythological sources rather than the quasi-scientific origins of most US superheroes', but *Mr India* (Shekhar Kapur, 1987) marked a shift, since the hero 'does not possess any intrinsic superpowers' and instead possesses "magical" gadgets (2015: 123). Anustup Basu (2011) suggests that Bollywood's recent 'speculation' on the superhero genre – films such as *Krrish* (Rakesh Roshan, 2006), *Drona* (Goldie Behl, 2008) and *Ra.One* (Anubhav Sinha, 2011) – 'seems to draw its energies from an overall horizon of a new "shining India" in a fast globalizing world' (2011: 558). While historically popular Hindi cinema has presented villains associated with 'science' and 'gadgets' being defeated by ordinary everymen, and thus offered 'a frontal encounter between restoring powers of mythic kinds and instruments/ inscriptions of a scientific and technological modernity', this was only because 'science and technology had to find a home in a developing India and yet a spiritual essence of the nation could not be at home with the profane possibilities of science and technology' (2011: 559, 560). Of the new superhero films, Basu states: 'In contrast to an earlier "protectionist" order, what is immediately significant about this Indian fairy-tale/superhero scene is that the stakes have been upgraded in line with a brave new India in an era of globalization' (2011: 566). Indeed, in *Zokkomon* the eponymous superhero's incredible powers are all very clearly grounded in the scientific wizardry and technological expertise of Kunal's 'magic' yet emphatically 'modern' Uncle, which resonates with the significance for Safary's star image of all those marvellous gadgets he both enjoys and advertises as the personification of an upgraded India. However, as Basu notes, 'the universe of the Hindi superhero always ends up looking "tacky" compared to that of his western counterpart' due to a 'techno-specular lag' that separates Bollywood from Hollywood (2011: 558). And indeed, the special effects in *Zokommon* were widely criticised: *Box Office India* called *Zokkomon* 'a botched attempt to make a children's superhero film', and lamented in particular the 'out-dated' special effects, while the *New Indian Express* found '[the] ineptness of the special effects . . . surprising considering the film comes from the reputed international producers Walt Disney' (Anon. 2011; Jha 2011). For the *Hindu* the film was 'a dull exercise', another attempt by 'a Hollywood biggie to get a foothold in the Hindi film industry'. And, furthermore, the film's emphasis on technologically enhanced superheroics appeared to compromise its cultural specificity: '*Zokkomon* draws from all the global superheroes and has very little that's local about him. He flies, he jumps, changes his voice, but everything through a scientific way.' The critic concluded that 'Darsheel is the best thing about the film' (Kumar 2011). Another critic regretted the failure of 'Walt Disney's first Hindi venture', given how '[for] too many years little tots have worshipped *Superman* and *Spiderman*', noting not only that 'the timing was right to create a *desi* superhero who would be worshipped by kids and adults' but that 'Darsheel Safary was the most perfect casting since he was considered Bollywood's superkid' (Arora 2011). If *Zokkomon* was criticised for grounding its fantastic heroics in modern technology rather than traditional Indian mythology, then at least the 'Bollywood superkid' Safary was able to personally save the film, with the charm and skills that compensated for its lacklustre special effects.[5]

As a Safary vehicle, his third film in more than three years, *Zokkomon* provided his fans with an uncanny flashback to the summer of 2009, due to its archiving of the transformation of his features that began after the star had turned twelve: as the *Indian Express* (26 April 2011) put it, 'the buck-toothed Darsheel Safary who stole our hearts in *Taare Zameen Par* is back with this sci-fi adventure', adding that as 'the first superhero to wear braces' Safary was 'endearing' (Gupta 2011). The braces are indeed clearly visible throughout the film, but are never mentioned, whereas his teeth are; a mean teacher (played, ironically, by the buck-toothed actor Tinnu Anand) in fact calls Kunal 'rabbit' and asks, 'Why are you showing your teeth?' when Kunal struggles to suppress a smile. Braces are of course a kind of bionic contraption, since bionic means 'having anatomical structures of physiological processes that are replaced or enhanced by electronic or mechanical components', as well as 'having extraordinary strength, powers, or capabilities' (TheFreeDictionary.com). In *Zokkomon* the braces that we so clearly see throughout the film are arguably to the young star Safary what the jetpack is to the character he here plays: one device to enhance the actor's smile, and one to allow his character to fly.

In the summer of 2009 there was a great deal of media coverage about the disappearance of Safary's distinctive teeth, so central to his fame as a 'cute' star, with headlines such as 'Darsheel's toothy smile might be history soon!' (Anon. 2009). Features asked whether the braces were necessary and questioned the decision to undergo treatment. One journalist covered the correcting of Safary's 'famous bunny rabbit smile' and declared that the star 'will soon have a set of teeth which he can proudly show off', before asking whether the braces were 'because [his parents] want Darsheel to pursue a career in films and take up lead roles in the future', to which his father Mitesh answered, 'Whether to take up a career in films or not will entirely be Darsheel's decision. As parents, we will continue to support him. Anyway, have you seen any hero with buck-teeth?' (Mitesh then remembers the aforementioned Tinnu Annad, but insists 'he is not a hero'.) Safary's father continues to answer questions with questions of his own: 'Isn't it normal for any parent whose child has buck teeth to take him to a dentist and have them corrected?' (Maniar 2009). The feature 'reveals' '[the] Safarys are taking utmost care that Darsheel's treatment does not hinder the continuity in his ads and films', and again quotes Mitesh who insists (incorrectly) 'the braces cannot be seen at all in the camera. In our contract with Walt Disney we have specifically mentioned Darsheel's teeth treatment so that no problems arise later' (Maniar 2009). Interviewed in December 2009, Safary discusses his treatment himself: 'I got my teeth fixed. And I think it makes me look better. Everyone keeps saying I looked better with my teeth protruding, but I don't agree with that' (Jha 2009). The following May, Safary admitted that 'many millions' of his fans had objected to his having his teeth corrected (Desai 2010). In April 2011, Safary is still asked about his teeth: referring to his original teeth, he recalled how 'at that time everyone said "very cute"' but insists 'it's better to change yourself' (Vetticad 2011).

Discussing his involvement in the production of *Midnight's Children*, Salman Rushdie stated: 'I saw that kid [. . .] Darsheel in *Taare Zameen Par* and was very interested in him immediately because I knew we needed a very exceptional child actor. And I think he was that. In *Taare* [. . .] he had his teeth all over the place, but fortunately the braces came off in time for him to do this film. Otherwise we probably couldn't have used him with those bad teeth' (Soofi 2013). In the film Safary plays the protagonist as a little boy, and appears in a twenty-five-minute section towards the beginning of the film. All of the 'Midnight's Children' possess miraculous abilities, described in the novel as 'wonderfully discrete and varied gifts' (Rushdie 1981: 229). At one of their conferences, the 581 children discuss the purpose and meaning of these diverse supernatural powers, and indulge in 'fantasies of power'; as one child explains: '"They can't stop us, man! We can bewitch, and fly, and read minds, and turn them into frogs, and make gold and fishes, and they will fall in love with u, and we can vanish through mirrors and change our sex . . . how will they be able to fight?"' (1981: 228). At the same time, however, as Saleem observes, 'there was nothing unusual about the children except their gifts; their heads were full of all the usual things, fathers mothers money food land possessions fame power God' (1981: 229). Saleem and the other children, who like child stars are simultaneously ordinary and extraordinary, thus combine Eckert's understanding of the child star's being produced by unique concatenations of historical forces (in this case, India's independence) and O'Connor's notion of the child star sharing with mythical 'wonder-children' a quasi-supernatural status (in this case, their 'varied gifts').

Media coverage of Safary's appearance in *Midnight's Children* routinely referred to his decision to participate in the production, the development of his range as an actor, and his actual appearance in the film. In *Midnight's Children* Safary wears a large prosthetic nose as well as contact lenses that, in addition to the disappearance of his 'signature buck teeth', render his features unrecognisable. When famous stars transform their appearance with prosthetic noses it is usually understood (and often criticised or ridiculed) as a bid to be taken seriously as an actor: well-known examples include Nicole Kidman's performance as Virginia Woolf in *The Hours* (Stephen Daldry, 2002) and, more recently, Steve Carrell in *Foxcatcher* (Bennett Miller, 2014). As Pam Cook has noted (discussing Kidman), 'Actors are more likely to achieve award nominations if they display dedication to their craft by making themselves almost unrecognizable in portraying character' (2012: 62). Indeed, for the *Times of India* the stretching of Safary's acting skills was of a piece with the reshaping of his features: it reported that Safary 'had taken up a role that is more challenging' and would be 'sporting a prosthetic nose', as if the nose itself was external evidence of the imaginative efforts required by the part (Anon. 2012) (see Figure 6.2).

Safary's participation in these two productions suggests deliberate diversification, a demonstration of his flexibility as an actor that matches in many ways Bollywood's own strategic experimentations with new genres and the forging of transnational alliances to appeal to new audiences in more territories. It is somewhat ironic that Safary, who has throughout his career personified the transformations of Indian culture and society associated with economic liberalisation, and reconciled the contradictions associated with those transformations, should be chosen to play Saleem. In the film's opening moments (a

Figure 6.2   Safary's face unrecognisable in *Midnight's Children* (Deepa Mehta, 2012).

voiceover by Rushdie), Saleem explains 'at the precise instant of India's arrival at independence, I tumbled forth into the world [. . .] I had been mysteriously handcuffed to history, my destinies indissolubly chained to those of my country' (Rushdie 1981: 9). Both Safary the media star and Saleem the fictional character are fantastic children conceived or constructed so as to personify a profoundly transformative moment or 'instant' in India's history. As Ritty A. Lukose has shown, journalists in India refer to 'Liberalisation's Children' in order to distinguish the current generation from those born in the period immediately following independence – the 'Midnight's Children' of Rushdie's novel – and to suggest that the opening of the Indian economy to global market forces, and the subsequent spread of consumerism, has led to an irrevocable 'eclipsing of the Nehruvian vision of the Indian nation' (2009: 5).

The characters played by Safary in both films are associated with (they are believed to have or actually have) magical or supernatural powers. In *Zokkomon* technology is used *in* the film to create the impression of his superpowers (and special effects technologies are used *by* the film for the same purpose). In *Midnight's Children* the magical gifts are a conceit that allows the narrative to symbolically represent the generation born at the moment of independence. Ironically, several critics compared the Midnight's Children to the superheroes familiar from Hollywood cinema: *Variety* described them as 'a sort of Indian *X-Men* squad united by Saleem's unique ability to telepathically connect them all'; the *Telegraph* observed that 'the children [. . .] seem a little like *X-Men* applicants rejected for not having cool enough skills' (Debruge 2012; Robey 2012).[6] As with *Zokkomon*, most reviews of *Midnight's Children* were negative, and as the earlier Bollywood film was criticised for not being Indian enough (not grounded in mythology, too scientific) and not sufficiently Hollywood (substandard special effects), the later non-Bollywood film is attacked for not being Indian enough (despite its 'magical realist' conceit): the *New York Times*, for example, lamented the lack of magic in the 'modest, respectful adaptation', and suggested 'the film needs an injection of Bollywood's unembarrassed, anything-goes, bigger-than-life spirit' (Saltz 2013).

The apparent or actual magical or super powers possessed by these two characters refer us to the question of whether the child star's appeal depends upon their own possession of unique, extraordinary or even mysterious gifts. At the same time, the two films suggest the child star's difference from, and relation with, other children. In *Zokkomon*, Kunal's apparent superhero skills make him an inspirational model for other children who follow his example, don duplicate costumes, and assert their rights as 'ordinary' children; the film presents a straightforward staging of Safary's own appeal to real children as an image of exceptional and aspirational childhood. The tagline for the film – 'He rose from the ordinary to achieve the extraordinary' – neatly evokes Dyer's well-known argument about the star's combining the exceptional and the everyday (Dyer 1979). In *Midnight's Children*, on the other hand, Saleem's actual magical abilities do not distinguish him from the other children, all of whom are equally gifted, and yet at the same time just like normal children, and so his assumption of leadership is fragile; he must contend in particular with the jealous and aggressive Shiva, a poor child whose middle-class upbringing fell to Saleem after they were switched at birth. In other words, the film, in keeping with Safary's being almost unrecognisable, cannot stage a fantasy of the child star's inspirational influence over other children. Whereas in the fiction of *Midnight's Children* Saleem's magical nose allows him to communicate with other children as if he were 'All-India-Radio', the presentation of a technologically enhanced child superhero in *Zokkomon* seems intended to reach children all over the world; but while the 'magic' of Bollywood was felt as a lack in the non-Bollywood *Midnight's Children*, the 'science' of technology was felt as a non-Bollywood element in the Bollywood-Hollywood *Zokkomon*.

Both the films present a strategic reshaping of Safary's facial features, the most important and inalienable property possessed by any film star. Of course, it was inevitable that as Safary grew up he would lose those physical features that were central to his status as a 'cute' child star. The remodelling of Safary's face in these films functions in tandem with his physical development as a teenager, but also suggest a successful negotiation of the pressures that shape the professional actor's career. The braces that are so prominent on Safary's teeth in *Zokkomon*, and which have no meaning for the character he plays, remind us that the child must adapt to and abide by industry standards of attractiveness in order to sustain a film career as an adult, even if this involves the loss of such a familiar and fondly regarded feature as his 'signature buck teeth'. The prosthetic nose that so dramatically alters Safary's face in *Midnight's Children*, required to accurately embody the character, reflects the expectation that stars must be prepared to transform their appearance and take on 'challenging roles' to secure recognition as serious actors, even as this involves modification that temporarily removes the star from those industry standards of physical attractiveness the acquisition of which the actor's braces had made possible. If these films suggest the diverse projects that might constitute Safary's career as an adult Indian actor in an increasingly globalised culture, and archive his own physical and professional development, they also allegorise on the one hand the child star's association with magical powers, and O'Connor's suggestion that the child star is 'a recent contribution to an ancient tradition of extraordinary children in myth and folklore' (2009: 216), and, on the other hand, the child star's relation to their historical and social context, and Eckert's claim that the child star is 'a kind of artefact thrown up by a unique concatenation of social and economic forces' (1991: 185).

As Safary approaches his twenties, his performances (in film, on television, in adverts, in the media, as 'himself' and as fictional characters) enter a transitional phase in which memory of the 'cuteness' of his earlier self (as well as its traces on his youthful face) will eventually give way to a more distinct adult persona. The media has often asked him about his girlfriend/s, but he has always refused to disclose such information (Jha 2009). In 2015 Safary featured in a Vodafone spot as a teenaged footballer sending a girlfriend photographs of his bruised knee, and in the spring of 2016 Safary starred as a love-struck teenager in the television film *Sun Yaar Try Maar*. His graduation to more adult roles received a great deal of attention in the press: the *Times of India*, for example, announced '"Child star" Darsheel to romance on TV' (Maheshwri 2016). The coterminous relationship between Safary's physical maturation and professional development in the decade since his career began was again collapsed, with one critic observing, 'There is only a hint of that adorable toothy grin. Instead, what we see is an actor at remarkable ease cracking improvised jokes' (Prabhakar 2016).

By focusing on the ways in which Safary's physical features have altered on- and offscreen, I have sought to anchor my analysis of 'the changing face of the Bollywood child star' to the particularities of this one unique body and the images and stories which established and then sustained an idea and a narrative of that body as public property and professional persona. Safary suggests a new model for child stardom in twenty-first-century Bollywood: his stardom has been defined by leading roles and star vehicles; box-office failures and exam success; appearances in popular entertainment (both films and television, including as 'himself') and roles in prestigious art-house films; professional associations with global brands, and numerous sponsorships and endorsements; a significant presence in emerging transnational industrial alliances; a precocious self-presentation as an 'actor' and a successful marketing of the self as an ordinary child.

NOTES

1. See O'Connor (2008, 2011) for an exploration of the shifting status of child stars during the twentieth century, from Shirley Temple and Jackie Coogan to Macaulay Culkin. See Shary (2012) for a historical survey of (mainly) Hollywood child stars. Karen Lury (2010: 145–91) considers screen performances by child actors, including several stars.
2. Shirley Temple has attracted more scholarly attention than any other Hollywood child star; see for example Studlar (2013), Kasson (2014) and Hatch (2015). For a critical survey of Hollywood child stars before Temple, see Addison (2015). For an earlier (and nostalgic) account of the 'golden era' of the Hollywood child star (1920s and '30s), see Zierold (1965). Julia Lee (2015) has recently examined African-American child stars of this period.
3. This has a particular value for thinking about Indian (child) stars, since, as Behroze Gandhy and Rosie Thomas have noted, 'the parallels between Indian stars and the gods of the Hindu pantheon are frequently remarked upon [. . .] stars accept, on the whole graciously, an adoration close to veneration' (1991: 107).
4. For a discussion of child labour and commodity culture in this film, see Lawrence 2017.
5. The absence of mythological elements in *Zokkomon* distinguishes it from the children's animations featuring superhero 'toon-gods' which have proliferated on Indian screens in recent years, in films such as *Hunuman* (Manit, 2004), *The Return of Hanuman* (Anurag Kashyap, 2007) and *My Friend Ganesha* (Rajiv S. Ruia, 2007), and television shows such as Nickelodeon's *Little Krishna* (2009). As one marketing manager explains: 'Hanuman is the original superhero. He is thousands of years older than Superman, Spider-Man and Batman. He is a brand to reckon with among Indian children today' (Lakshmi 2008).
6. The fifth film in the *X-Men* franchise, *X-Men: First Class* (Matthew Vaughn), set in the 1960s, was released in summer 2011.

BIBLIOGRAPHY

Addison, Heather (2015), '"Holding Our Heartstrings in Their Rosy Hands": Child Stars in Early Hollywood', *Journal of Popular Culture* 48:6, 1250–69.
Aitken, Stuart C. (2001), 'Global Crises of Childhood: Rights, Justice and the Unchildlike Child', *Area* 33:3, 119–27.
Anon. (2009), 'Darsheel's toothy smile might be history soon!', *Hindustan Times*, 21 June, http://www.hindustantimes.com/india/darsheel-s-toothy-smile-might-be-history-soon/story-uOzLu17iNEGdUy0EIOutyO.html, accessed 28 April 2016.
Anon. (2010), 'Hrithik Roshan is my superhero in Bollywood: Darsheel Safary', *DNA India*, 25 January, http://www.dnaindia.com/entertainment/report-hrithik-roshan-is-my-superhero-in-bollywood-darsheel-safary-1339147, accessed 28 April 2016.
Anon. (2011), '*Zokkomon*', *Box Office India*, 22 April, http://www.boxofficeindia.co.in/zokkomon-4/, accessed 28 April 2016.
Anon. (2012), 'Darsheel gets a nose job', *Times of India*, 13 June, http://timesofindia.indiatimes.com/entertainment/hindi/bollywood/news/Darsheel-gets-a-nose-job/articleshow/14084337.cms, accessed 28 April 2016.
Anon. (2015a), 'Disney banks on upcoming films to build brand in India', *Livemint*, 1 December, http://www.livemint.com/Consumer/fOwac5eX6ClsdxwqM3aEul/Disney-banks-on-upcoming-films-to-build-brand-in-India.html, accessed 28 April 2016.
Anon. (2015b), 'Harshaali Malhotra, Darsheel Safary, Avneet Kaur add spark to Mumbai Juniorthon', *Indian Express*, 6 December, http://indianexpress.com/article/

entertainment/entertainment-others/harshaali-malhotra-darsheel-safary-avneet-kaur-add-spark-to-mumbai-juniorthon/, accessed 28 April 2016.

Anon. (2016), 'Aamir Khan is my mentor: *Taare Zameen Par* star Darsheel Safary', *Indian Express*, 14 January, http://indianexpress.com/article/entertainment/bolly wood/aamir-khan-is-my-mentor-taare-zameen-par-star-darsheel-safary/, accessed 28 April 2016.

Arora, Preeti (2011), '*Zokkomon* is another dud for Darsheel', *Rediff.com*, 22 April, http://www.rediff.com/movies/review/review-zokkomon/20110422.htm, accessed 28 April 2016.

Basu, Anustup (2011) 'The Eternal Return and Overcoming "Cape Fear": Science, Sensation, Superman and Hindu Nationalism in Recent Hindi Cinema', *South Asian History and Culture* 2:4, 557–71.

Cayla, Julien (2008), 'Following the Endorser's Shadow: Shah Rukh Khan and the Creation of the Cosmopolitan Indian Male', *Advertising and Society Review* 9:2.

Chakravarty, Sumita S. (2013), 'Con-figurations: The Body as World in Bollywood Stardom', in Meheli Sen and Anustup Basu (eds), *Figurations in Indian Film*, New York: Palgrave Macmillan, pp. 179–201.

Chandra, Nandini (2010), 'Merit and Opportunity in the Child-Centric Nationalist Films of the 1950s', in Manju Jain (ed.), *Narratives of Indian Cinema*, New Delhi: Primus, pp. 123–44.

Ciecko, Anne (2001), 'Superhit Hunk Heroes for Sale: Globalization and Bollywood's Gender Politics', *Asian Journal of Communication* 11:2, 121–43.

Cook, Pam (2012), *Nicole Kidman*, London: Palgrave Macmillan/British Film Institute.

Debruge, Peter (2012), 'Review: *Midnight's Children*', *Variety*, 7 September, http://variety.com/2012/film/markets-festivals/midnight-s-children-1117948232/, accessed 28 April 2016.

Desai, Malay (2010), 'Small Talk with Darsheel Safary', *Pune Mirror*, 23 May, Sunday Read, p. 24.

Dudrah, Rajinder (2015), 'Unthinking SRK and Global Bollywood', in Rajinder Dudrah, Elke Mader and Bernhard Fuchs (eds), *SRK and Global Bollywood*, New Delhi: Oxford University Press, pp. 3–24.

Dyer, Richard (1979), *Stars*, London: British Film Institute.

Dyer, Richard (1991), 'Four Films of Lana Turner', in Jeremy G. Butler (ed.), *Star Texts: Image and Performance in Film and Television*, Detroit: Wayne State University Press, pp. 214–40; originally published in *Movie* 25 (1977–8), 30–52.

Eckert, Charles (1991), 'Shirley Temple and the House of Rockerfeller', in Jeremy G. Butler (ed.), *Star Texts: Image and Performance in Film and Television*, Detroit: Wayne State University Press, pp. 184–202; originally published in *Jump Cut: A Review of Contemporary Media* 2 (1974), 1, 17–20.

Ellis, John (1999), 'Stars as a Cinematic Phenomenon', in Leo Braudy and Marshall Cohen (eds), *Film Theory and Criticism*, 5th edn, New York: Oxford University Press, pp. 539–46.

Gandhy, Behroze and Rosie Thomas (1991), 'Three Indian Film Stars', in Christine Gledhill (ed.), *Stardom: Industry of Desire*, London and New York: Routledge, pp. 107–31.

Gopal, Sangita (2011), *Conjugations: Marriage and Form in New Bollywood Cinema*, Chicago and London: University of Chicago Press.

Gupta, Shubhra (2007), '*Taare Zameen Par*', *Indian Express*, 23 December, http://archive.indianexpress.com/news/taare-zameen-par/253364/, accessed 28 April 2016.

Gupta, Shubhra (2011), '*Zokkomon*', *Indian Express*, 26 April, http://archive.indian express.com/news/zokkomon/779978/, accessed 28 April 2016.

Hatch, Kristen (2015), *Shirley Temple and the Performance of Girlhood*, New Brunswick, NJ and London: Rutgers University Press.

Jha, Subhash K. (2009), 'Darsheel has a girlfriend', *Mumbai Mirror*, 22 December, http://timesofindia.indiatimes.com/entertainment/hindi/bollywood/news/Darsheel-has-a-girlfriend/articleshow/5364645.cms, accessed 28 April 2016.

Jha, Subhash K. (2011), '*Zokkomon*', *New Indian Express*, 24 April, http://www.newindianexpress.com/entertainment/reviews/article386717.ece, accessed 28 April 2016.

Jha, Subhash K (2012), 'No more films for Darsheel Safary', *Times of India*, 3 July, http://timesofindia.indiatimes.com/entertainment/hindi/bollywood/news/No-more-films-for-Darsheel-Safary/articleshow/14634976.cms, accessed 28 April 2016.

Kapur, Jyotsna (1998), 'A Small World After All: Globalization and the Transformation of Childhood in India', *Visual Anthropology* 11:4, 387–97.

Kasson, John F. (2014), *The Little Girl Who Fought the Depression: Shirley Temple and 1930s America*, New York: W. W. Norton & Co.

Kaushal, Ruchi, 'Bollywood's Cutest Child Actors', *Times of India*, no date, http://timesofindia.indiatimes.com/entertainment/hindi/bollywood/Bollywoods-cutest-child-actors/photostory/48267879.cms, accessed 28 April 2016.

King, Barry (1985), 'Articulating Stardom', *Screen* 26:5, 27–50.

King, Barry (2010), 'Stardom, Celebrity, and the Money Form', *The Velvet Light Trap* 65, 7–19.

Krämer, Peter (1998), 'Would You Take Your Child To See This Film? The Cultural and Social Work of the Family-Adventure Movie', in Steve Neale and Murray Smith (eds), *Contemporary Hollywood Cinema*, London and New York: Routledge, pp. 294–311.

Kulkarni, Onkar (2011), 'The Little Superhero Darsheel Safary', *Indian Express*, 16 April, http://indianexpress.com/article/entertainment/entertainment-others/the-little-superhero-darsheel-safary/, accessed 28 April 2016.

Kumar, Anuj (2011), '*Zokkomon* or Bore-mon?', *Hindu*, 23 April, http://www.thehindu.com/features/cinema/zokkomon-or-boremon/article1761295.ece, accessed 28 April 2016.

Lakshmi, Rama (2008), 'In India, Gods Rule the "Toon" Universe', *Washington Post*, 9 January, http://www.washingtonpost.com/wp-dyn/content/article/2008/01/08/AR2008010804004.html, accessed 28 April 2016.

Lawrence, Michael (2017), 'Terrorism and Trainers in a Transnational Remake: Child Labour and Commodity Culture in the Bollywood Adaptation of New Iranian Cinema's *Children of Heaven*', in Stephanie Hemelryk-Donald, Emma Wilson and Sarah Wright (eds), *Childhood and Nation in Contemporary World Cinema: Borders and Encounters*, London: Bloomsbury, pp. 181–99.

Lee, Julia (2015), *Our Gang: A Racial History of* The Little Rascals, Minneapolis and London: University of Minnesota Press.

Lukose, Ritty A. (2009), *Liberalization's Children: Gender, Youth and Consumer Citizenship in Globalizing India*, Durham, NC and London: Duke University Press.

Maheshwri, Neha (2016), '"Child star" Darsheel to romance on TV', *Times of India*, 12 January, http://timesofindia.indiatimes.com/tv/news/hindi/Child-star-Darsheel-to-romance-on-TV/articleshow/50534234.cms, accessed 28 April 2016.

Mankekar, Purnima (2015), *Unsettling India: Affect, Temporality, Transnationality*, Durham, NC and London: Duke University Press.

Mathur, Nita (2010), 'Shopping Malls, Credit Cards and Global Brands: Consumer Culture and Lifestyle of India's New Middle Class', *South Asia Research* 30:3, 211–31.

Merish, Lori (1996), 'Cuteness and Commodity Aesthetics: Tom Thumb and Shirley Temple', in Rosemarie Garland Thomson (ed.), *Freakery: Cultural Spectacles of the Extraordinary Body*, New York and London: New York University Press, pp. 185–203.

O'Connor, Jane (2008), *The Cultural Significance of the Child Star*, New York: Routledge.

O'Connor, Jane (2009), 'Beyond Social Constructionism: A Structural Analysis of the Cultural Significance of the Child Star', *Children & Society* 23, 214–25.

O'Connor, Jane (2011), 'From Jackie Coogan to Michael Jackson: What Child Stars Can Tell Us About Ideologies of Childhood', *Journal of Children and Media* 5:3, 284–97.

Pereira, Priyanka (2011), 'The Little Biggies', *Indian Express*, 15 April, http://indianexpress.com/article/cities/chandigarh/the-little-biggies-2/, accessed 28 April 2016.

Prabhakar, Anu (2016), 'Small Talk: Star Grows Up, Stays Grounded', *Mumbai Mirror*, 13 March, http://www.mumbaimirror.com/others/sunday-read/Small-talk-Star-grows-up-stays-grounded/articleshow/51377252.cms, accessed 28 April 2016.

Robey, Tim (2012), 'Toronto Film Festival 2012: *Midnight's Children*, review', *Telegraph*, 7 September, http://www.telegraph.co.uk/culture/film/filmreviews/9529171/Toronto-Film-Festival-2012-Midnights-Children-review.html, accessed 28 April 2016.

Saltz, Rachel (2013), '*Midnight's Children*', *New York Times*, 25 April, http://www.nytimes.com/2013/04/26/movies/midnights-children-adaptation-of-salman-rushdies-novel.html?_r=0, accessed 28 April 2016.

Sen, Meheli (2011), 'Terrifying Tots and Hapless Homes: Undoing Modernity in Recent Bollywood Cinema', *Lit: Literature Interpretation Theory* 22:2, 197–217.

Shary, Timothy (2012), 'Oppositions of Aging: Stories About Children in Movies', *Interdisciplinary Humanities* 29:1, 7–20.

Smith, Iain Robert (2015), '*Tu Mera Superman*: Globalization, Cultural Exchange and the Indian Superhero', in Rayna Denison and Rachel Mizsei-Ward (eds), *Superheroes on World Screens*, Jackson: University Press of Mississippi, pp. 113–31.

Soofi, Mayan Austen (2013), 'I always place *Pather Panchali* above *Citizen Kane*: Rushdie', 24 January, *Livemint*, http://www.livemint.com/Consumer/dFAiv5aRsrXtOTtI4OAXyM/I-always-place-Pather-Panchali-above-Citizen-Kane-Rushd.html, accessed 27 April 2026.

Stearns, Peter N. (2011), *Childhood in World History*, 2nd edn, London and New York: Routledge.

Studlar, Gaylyn (2013), 'Cossetting the Nation; or, How to Conquer Fear Itself with Shirley Temple', *Precocious Charms: Stars Performing Girlhood in Classical Hollywood Cinema*, Berkeley, Los Angeles and London: University of California Press, pp. 51–90.

Vetticad, Anna (2011), 'Darsheel Safary, the teen-star', *New Indian Express*, 24 April, http://www.newindianexpress.com/entertainment/interviews/article386812.ece, accessed 28 April 2016.

Vyavhare, Renuka (2015), 'Darsheel Safary pleased with his HSC scores', *Times of India*, 1 June, http://timesofindia.indiatimes.com/entertainment/hindi/bollywood/news/Darsheel-Safary-pleased-with-his-HSC-scores/articleshow/47490122.cms, accessed 28 April 2016.

Zierold, Norman J. (1965), *The Child Stars*, London: Macdonald & Co.

PART 4

STARS AND AGEING

7. 'WHEN BARBARA STRIPS OFF HER PETTICOATS AND STRAPS ON HER GUNS': BARBARA STANWYCK, MATURITY AND STARDOM IN THE 1950s AND 1960s

Linda Berkvens

'When Barbara strips off her petticoats and straps on her guns' is the tag line from an advertisement for Barbara Stanwyck's film *Cattle Queen of Montana* (Allan Dwan, 1954), and it indicates one of the major shifts that took place in Stanwyck's career and image in the 1950s and 1960s. Unlike many of the female stars of her generation, who were over forty by this time, Stanwyck 'stripped off her petticoats' and extended her film career by performing in numerous 'B' Westerns where strong, female roles were uncommon until the post-war era. It is for these Western roles that Stanwyck is mostly remembered today.

In the late 1940s, the Hollywood film industry faced a series of crises such as a dramatic fall in attendances, escalating costs of production, the Paramount decrees, the popularity of television, and the development of drive-ins. This marked the beginning of the end for the studio era, and of the power the major studios wielded during this period (Anderson 1994: 6). Film attendance not only decreased, but audience composition and taste changed as well. The film industry attempted to lure audiences back to the cinemas through intensively publicised films that relied on spectacle, for example through the use of wide-screen or the production of large-scale epics or multi-star films (Belton 1990: 185). The industry's rapid decline led many studios to lay off staff, including stars, directors and writers, who were either forced into early retirement or freelancing. Many stars freelanced to have more creative and financial control over their images and films. Powerful talent agencies would offer package deals of stars, writers and directors to Hollywood producers. Because of these shifts in the Hollywood film industry, many mature female stars were forced to end their careers in the 1950s because there were insufficient parts for mature women. Film production changed and teenage audiences, especially, increased, so there was less demand for veteran female film stars. Stanwyck's maturity, emphasised by her rapidly greying hair, affected the roles she played but also turned her into a role model for mature women. In this chapter I examine the models of womanhood Stanwyck offered during this period. I will take a different look at star studies as it is conventionally approached within the field of film studies, by using a historical approach that examines Stanwyck to provide a better understanding of how she remained popular. I will use original archival material which unveils how gender and ageing were used as an advantage rather than a handicap in Stanwyck's image and career.

This chapter will particularly examine Stanwyck's position as a leading lady in Westerns, and how her maturity was used in her films in the 1950s and 1960s. Although Stanwyck was visibly ageing at this time, she became a role model for mature women. This is contradictory to the general notion that feminine ideals are 'youthful and thus vulnerable to deterioration with age' (Stacey 1994: 226). Susan Sontag notes that we (still) live in a culture where youth is dominant, and ageing – particularly the ageing of women – is widely feared. However, Stanwyck is a rare example of a mature film star whose career did not end when she aged (Sontag 1972: 29). The place of the ageing process in celebrity and film studies has been absent for a long time, although it has become a more popular research topic in the past few years (Jermyn 2012: 1). Most of the work on ageing and celebrities or film stars focuses on individual cases studies such as Elizabeth Taylor or Meryl Streep. Ageing and its consequences are more often studied within the social sciences, however – see for example Biggs (2004) and Lincoln and Allen (2004), who also examine ageing and female film stars from a sociological point of view.

Older women were usually not visible in classical Hollywood. Recently, this trend has started to change somewhat with very successful films featuring older women stars such as *Mamma Mia!* (Phyllida Lloyd, 2008) and *The Best Exotic Marigold Hotel* (John Madden, 2011). When Hollywood depicted mature women in the 1950s and 1960s, this usually took the form of films such as *Sunset Boulevard* (Billy Wilder, 1950) and *What Ever Happened to Baby Jane?* (Robert Aldrich, 1962), part of a Grand Guignol gothic horror cycle built around ageing female stars such as Bette Davis, Joan Crawford and Olivia de Havilland giving exaggerated and grotesque performances of female ageing. The films showed ageing itself as a horrific process of decline, and have been termed 'horror of personality' films (McCarthy 1994: 107). Stanwyck played in one such film, *The Night Walker* (William Castle, 1964).

Her character as a neurotic, ageing woman was completely opposite to the ageing women Stanwyck had played before, for example in *So Big* (William A. Wellman, 1932) and *The Great Man's Lady* (William A. Wellman, 1942), who were signifiers of wisdom and beauty.

Since the power balance in Hollywood shifted in the 1950s, the female stars from the 1930s (and 1940s) did not make as much money as their male counterparts, nor were they offered as many romantic leads (Carman 2012: 21). Because of the shift in audience demographic from a largely female audience in the 1930s and 1940s to a youth-oriented male audience, younger female stars such as Marilyn Monroe and Audrey Hepburn starred in the post-war box-office hits (Stokes 1999: 44; Unauthored 1956: 3). Both Emily Carman and Linda Berkvens have demonstrated that Stanwyck was one of the very few female stars (others include Irene Dunne and Miriam Hopkins) who was freelancing by the time she started to age (Carman 2012, Berkvens 2011). This freelancing 'challenges the familiar patriarchal, ageist pattern of female celebrity . . . in which women stars can expect to find less work and receive less compensation as they age' (Carman 2012: 14). Through freelancing and by

Figure 7.1   In the film *The Cattle Queen of Montana* (1954, RKO Radio Pictures), Stanwyck 'strips off her petticoats and straps on her guns' in order to continue her film career for another decade.

taking control of her career, Stanwyck prolonged it beyond what is generally expected of the career of a female film star (see Figure 7.1).

STANWYCK AS A MATURE ROLE MODEL

By the 1950s, the 1930s cohort of female stars (for example Stanwyck, Bette Davis, Joan Crawford and Ginger Rogers) was replaced by a new generation, including Elizabeth Taylor, Doris Day and Audrey Hepburn. The first group consisted of actresses who had become stars with the coming of sound, and when these stars were old they were slowly replaced by the latter group. To illustrate: of the top stars in 1946 only one of the four women (Greer Carson) was over forty, whereas four of the six male stars were (Weaver 1946: 13). And of the top stars of 1946–9, six of the eight male stars were over forty (Schatz 1999: 358). Because of broader industrial shifts, the careers of mature female stars diminished, but the careers of many male stars of similar age, such as James Stewart, Gary Cooper and Cary Grant, however, flourished (Schatz 1999: 470–1). There were more roles available for older, male stars and fewer opportunities for ageing actresses. Stanwyck referred to this fact in an article in the *Philadelphia Sun-Bulletin*, noting that there were 'no good screen roles for attractive but mature women'. She also mentioned the double standard that occurs between mature male and female stars: 'Male stars go on and on. The only parts [for mature female stars] are harridans in horror pictures' (Graham 1966). The fact that Stanwyck managed to continue her career while many of her female contemporaries were forced to retire is worth investigating to explain Stanwyck's fashionability in this period.

Make-up artists ran into various problems with the older female stars, most notably wrinkles and greying hair. Grey hair was especially a problem for Stanwyck, as she went prematurely grey in the 1940s. Studios touched up pictures and stills, but Stanwyck refused to dye her hair.[1] Similarly, an article about Stanwyck's film *Clash by Night* (Fritz Lang, 1952) noted that she 'never dyed her hair to look younger since it started to gray [sic] 15 years ago' (Parsons and Parsons). Stanwyck's standard biography even noted in the late 1940s that she was turning grey, 'which she makes no attempt to hide'.[2] Grey hair thus became part of Stanwyck's image. As hostess of *The Barbara Stanwyck Show* in 1961, Stanwyck drew attention to her hair in the closing sequence for the episode 'Frightened Doll': 'Some of my friends say I should go back to [my natural hair colour]. Why should I? It's just prematurely grey, that's all.' When Stanwyck signed with glamour studio MGM in 1948, MGM's head designer Irene supposedly decreed that the long greying hair had to go because 'no actress can have white hair. No one wants to make love to a gray-haired [sic] lady. To be over forty isn't possible [in Hollywood]' (Holland 1948: 78). Although Stanwyck's grey hair looked blonde in black-and-white films, for her colour films she was supplied with red or blonde wigs. Apparently (male) film producers and make-up designers agreed with Irene, and Stanwyck's grey hair was covered up. However, in her offscreen image, Stanwyck's grey hair was a point of focus.

According to Paramount publicity stories, Stanwyck never hesitated to play her age on film, including women older than herself.[3] In various articles she readily admitted to her real age. An article about Stanwyck from 1949 entitled 'Frankly 42!' immediately drew attention to her age and according to journalist Adela Rogers St Johns, Stanwyck was 'the only star in Hollywood whose routine biography carries the year of her birth' (Block; Rogers St Johns).[4] Promoting Stanwyck as mature differentiated her from the other female stars of her generation, who tended to hide their age to receive work, which meant that it was likely for studios to approach Stanwyck when they required a mature female star. Because Stanwyck did not hide her age, she was apparently considered a suitable model to represent female maturity. The model of womanhood Stanwyck offered was easy to imitate for female fans: it was cheap and did not take up much time to copy Stanwyck's looks and advice. There is a notable increase in articles detailing Stanwyck's advice for mature women in the 1950s. In various articles Stanwyck commented on the pros of getting older, and gave beauty and dietary advice. To illustrate, in an article in *Photoplay*, Stanwyck said that she 'never understood why women want to be forever "young"' and that her indifference to having her birth year published in her biography 'confounded some people'. At the age of forty-four, Stanwyck was quoted as saying that the '40s are a wonderful, challenging decade' when a woman could 'really appreciate life'. Stanwyck also explained how she 'stayed so slim' at her age: 'I watch my food and I don't diet.' She advised women to eat 'vegetables and meat' and 'avoid rich desserts and bread and butter' (Stanwyck). Journalist Lydia Lane published a series of articles for the *Los Angeles Times* in which she used Stanwyck as a mature role model. One of the articles argued that Stanwyck could 'get away with gray [sic] hair because she has such a young face and little girl sheen to her skin', suggesting that Stanwyck's wholesome, natural look fitted with her naturally grey hair (Lane 1951). Her naturalness was not only emphasised by Stanwyck's refusal to dye her hair and her way of life: she also noted that she did not 'give too much about beauty aids', which also alluded to her naturalness. Throughout her career, Stanwyck was known for her naturalness, both in her appearance and in her acting style. This attitude and style was contrary to, for example, Joan Crawford's image, which was based on glamour and artificiality (Berkvens 2011: 114). Hence, naturalness and maturity complemented each other as Stanwyck's unique selling points.

STANWYCK'S MATURITY AND HER FILM ROLES

The careers of many mature female stars suffered because they were no longer tied to studios that would develop roles for them. Because Stanwyck had not been a contract star, this change did not influence her career as much. As a freelance star, she could maintain control over her image and over the roles she played. By acting in different types of films, Stanwyck maintained a stable career. Her versatile, mature image was used in a positive way in different production trends (Berkvens 2011: 101). Stanwyck's performances in popular film cycles gave her better exposure than less popular (pre-war) genres and cycles did. As a freelance star Stanwyck could choose the roles she wanted and was not limited to specific vehicles, as contract stars were. Stanwyck and her agents managed to continue Stanwyck's earlier image in the 1950s and 1960s and even build upon it, as the following discussion of some of her roles and films demonstrates.

During the 1950s, Stanwyck's performances in what I term mature woman-centred dramas increased noticeably. These films include: *All I Desire* (Douglas Sirk, 1953), *The Lady Gambles* (Michael Gordon, 1949) and *There's Always Tomorrow* (Douglas Sirk, 1956). The mature woman dramas focus on the problems and insecurities of an older woman. The age of the woman is key here: she is mature, usually married (or divorced), and often returning to a place (frequently home) after a period of absence. The woman's return draws attention to her past and to the way her absence has influenced her subsequent behaviour: this turned her into an outsider. Hence, the mature woman is often unable to submit to domestic life, either because she finds domestic life suffocating or because she is too career-oriented. Another key element that can be found in most of the films is the appearance of a younger woman – either as competition, for example in *East Side, West Side* (Mervyn LeRoy, 1950), or as a companion who could be a younger version of the mature woman, for example in *Clash by Night*. For many veteran female stars, mature woman dramas were the only films that provided meaty roles, even if the films drew attention to the stars' age – for example, *The Star* (Stuart Heisler, 1952), *Pocketful of Miracles* (Frank Capra, 1961) and *Lady in a Cage* (Walter Grauman, 1964). For Stanwyck, it meant that many of her characters in these dramas were mature versions of her 1930s characters and therefore provided a continuance of her previous onscreen image. Many of Stanwyck's previous characters had struggled with domesticity – for example, in *Illicit* (Archie Mayo, 1931), *The Purchase Price* (William A. Wellman, 1932), *The Bride Walks Out* (Leigh Jason, 1936) and *Christmas in Connecticut* (Peter Godfrey, 1945) – and this aspect had been present in her image since the early 1930s, both onscreen and off.[5] Stanwyck's first marriage ended because career choices drove the couple apart. This was also, allegedly, the reason for the divorce between Stanwyck and matinee idol Robert Taylor. The foregrounding of her career rather than her family life in Stanwyck's image, as well as her divorces, suggested her struggles with domesticity. The inability to submit to domesticity is also the main topic in *Clash by Night*.

In this film, Stanwyck plays Mae Doyle, a sophisticated but bitter, restless woman who returns to her hometown and marries simple fisherman Jerry (Paul Douglas). She believes she requires the security of a home and a family. Mae seems to be out of Jerry's league, as she is very worldly and well-travelled. After Mae and Jerry marry, they live together with Jerry's father and their baby. Mae's eventual domestic dissatisfaction leads to an affair with Earl (Robert Ryan), Jerry's best friend. When Jerry finds out about Mae and Earl, Mae defends her actions with an attack on her containment in the house. The affair results in a wrecked home, until Mae decides to go back to Jerry and their child. She cannot give up her identity as a mother, even if it means living with a man she does not love. Parallel to this runs a plot line in which Mae's younger brother Joe (Keith Andes) tries to dominate his girlfriend Peggy (Marilyn Monroe), and which shows Peggy's adulation of the sophisticated Mae. Peggy seems a younger version of Mae before she left the small fishing town: yearning for excitement and unwilling to be bossed around by any man.

Clash by Night ultimately upholds the dominant social values of marriage and motherhood, but only after the alternatives have been explored (May 1999: 183; Bodnar 2003: 146). Mae is worldly, but searches for security (or so she believes), while at the same time she is unable to submit to domesticity. That Mae is considered worldly and sophisticated results from her absence from the small town, which has few options for her as a woman, as it is dominated by a fish-canning industry. The film questions the imperative to serve traditional roles by divulging the difficulties of marriage and challenging patriarchal idealisations of American life. The role provides a mature Stanwyck with a meaty but familiar role: a woman who cannot submit to domesticity and challenges the boundaries of patriarchy and gender. However, Mae's return to her hometown after years of absence, and the contrast between the domestic, older couple (Jerry and Mae) and the free, younger couple (Joe and Peggy), draw significant attention to Stanwyck/Mae's maturity.

Films with a mature all-star cast reminded audiences about the glory days of the Hollywood studio system. Increasing teenage and adolescent audiences, however, were less familiar with the stars of Stanwyck's generation. Films particularly aimed at this audience demographic starred new stars such as Marilyn Monroe, James Dean and Marlon Brando (Unauthored 1956: 3). *Roustabout* (John Rich, 1964) is Stanwyck's only youth film. The film used its star – Elvis Presley – to appeal to teenagers and adolescents; it was part of a cycle of Elvis musicals in the 1960s. Presley was under contract to Hal Wallis – who had produced a number of Stanwyck's films in the 1940s – from 1956, and made four films before being drafted for army duty in 1958 (Rose 1996: 267). In his post-1960 films, Presley's popularity as a patriotic hero was used by putting him in formulaic travelogue musicals that exploited his looks and his singing ability – for example, *Blue Hawaii* (Norman Taurog, 1961) and *Viva Las Vegas* (George Sidney, 1964). These films consisted of a recurring set of characteristics including exciting jobs – for example, a race-car driver in *Viva Las Vegas* or a trapeze artist turned lifeguard in *Fun in Acapulco* (Richard Thorpe, 1963) – as well as music, exotic or well-known locations such as Las Vegas, Mexico, a carnival, a ranch and an Indian reservation, and romance.

Roustabout is an example of such a travelogue. Here, Stanwyck plays Maggie Morgan, the determined owner of a travelling carnival who hires wandering tough guy Charlie Rogers (Presley). When Charlie learns that Maggie's carnival is in financial trouble, he displays his singing talent, which attracts large crowds. He leaves the carnival, however, after a fight with Maggie's foreman Joe (Leif Erickson), which leads to Maggie's financial ruin. When Charlie realises he is in love with Joe's daughter Cathy (Joan Freeman), he returns, and his singing saves Maggie's carnival from bankruptcy. Maggie shares certain characteristics with Stanwyck's previous characters, providing a continuation of her earlier image. Maggie is a woman in charge (in this case of a carnival), tough (she carries the burden of the carnival alone) and independent. Even though the carnival is on its last legs, Maggie seems calm and relaxed, particularly compared to Joe and Charlie's frantic behaviour. As in *Clash by Night*, Stanwyck's role is that of an advisor to a younger person. In *Clash by Night* Stanwyck's character gives advice about life and love to a younger sister-in-law; in *Roustabout* Maggie teaches Charlie to be loyal and unselfish. Stanwyck's characters' maturity is in both films connected to wisdom and authority, as opposed to the more unstable and immature younger characters/actors.

For the role of Maggie, Wallis wanted 'someone with stature' who could stand up against Presley's character (Rose 1996: 270). Stanwyck was not the first choice for the role, which was Mae West. Because West declined and Bette Davis was too expensive, Stanwyck was signed; Wallis knew her and had used her services before. Like Presley, she was a client of the William Morris Agency, and her asking price was only $30,000.[6] Stanwyck was also 'intrigued [. . .] because it would bring [her] into a younger audience than [she was] accustomed to' (Hahn 1965). Costume designer Edith Head told the press that teaming Stanwyck with Presley was 'a stroke of genius' because it 'gave him credence as an actor' (Head and Calistro 1983: 195). Head costumed Stanwyck in jeans, an unusual style for a woman in her late fifties as jeans were usually associated with youth, but the jeans made Stanwyck look younger and tougher than some of her matronly costumes as in the films *There's Always Tomorrow* and *These Wilder Years* (Roy Rowland, 1956).

The publicity for the film obviously focused on Presley. A film poster depicts Presley on his motorbike, with smaller images of Stanwyck and Freeman on either side of him. The image of Stanwyck is slightly smaller than Freeman's, but because of the colouring (Stanwyck is wearing a bright yellow shirt), Stanwyck stands out more. Freeman's image shows her running (youthful), with flaring skirts and an anxious face, while Stanwyck's pose is relaxed and confident (mature). She has her jacket thrown over one shoulder, her other hand in her trouser pocket, and one foot in front of the other, thereby suggesting self-confidence and authority. Other publicity materials show Stanwyck and Presley together in various ways: enjoying carnival rides, riding a motorbike and waiting for a scene to be set up. These photos seem to promote a bond between the younger Presley and the older Stanwyck, as well as between Charlie and Maggie; the photographs suggest a mother/son or teacher/pupil relationship, which is also evident in the film. However, David Bret's biography of Joan Crawford notes that Stanwyck and Presley could not 'stand the sight of [each] other', although it does not disclose any sources that confirm this (2006: 242). As such, Stanwyck's appearance as a mature and wise(r) woman is opposed to Presley's 'roving, restless, reckless roustabout'.

While it was inevitable that films drew attention to her ageing, and although her ageing limited the sort of roles she could play, Stanwyck still performed in various films for different audience demographics. This meant that she received more exposure than many of her contemporaries who made fewer and generally less varied films. Nonetheless, Stanwyck's ageing was overshadowed in the mid-1950s by her performances in Westerns.

Westerns played an important part in Stanwyck's image: a large proportion of her final feature films were Westerns, and she continuously stated her interest in the genre. She was 'crazy about Westerns, that's why [she] made so many of them', and she believed that the Western was 'our [American] royalty, our aristocracy' (Drew 1981: 43, 45). It seems rather surprising that a mature female star would want to work in the Western, where women were generally relegated to the margins of the plot. Stanwyck's fascination with the Western, however, fitted with her unfeminine image: refusing to dye her hair, not caring about beauty aids, and so on.

The increase in Stanwyck's Western performances in the 1950s and 1960s was an effect of a change in output in the Hollywood film industry in the post-war era. The number of Westerns increased to replace the masculine genre of the combat film, production of which had been cut back at the end of the war (Schatz 1999: 371). Many of the Westerns produced in this period were small-scale or 'B' Westerns, produced by small studios. Here, female characters had more opportunities to be tough, independent and villainous. Changes to the Western's narrative in the post-war era had influential consequences for Stanwyck's (and other female stars') performances in the genre. According to an article in the *New York Times* in 1947, in the post-war era the Western attempted 'to tell an adult story of the development of the characters', which was 'based on the idea that a clash of guns is not necessarily a replacement for a clash of emotions' (Spinrad 1947: X4). In short: more drama, fewer gunfights.

According to David Thomson, women in the classical Western 'are there as stooges or excuses' (quoted in Pye 1996: 13). However, this does not fit many of Stanwyck's roles in Westerns where the plot focuses, or gives much room to, a female perspective – for example, *The Maverick Queen* (Joe Kane, 1956) and *Cattle Queen of Montana*. Until the 1950s, Stanwyck had appeared in only four Westerns: *Annie Oakley* (George Stevens, 1935), *Union Pacific* (Cecil B. DeMille, 1939), *The Great Man's Lady* (William A. Wellman, 1942) and *California* (John Farrow, 1947). In the 1950s she made eight Westerns, and in the 1960s guest-starred in television Westerns such as *Zane Grey Theater* (CBS, 1956–61) and *Rawhide* (CBS, 1959–66). In the post-war era Westerns, Stanwyck usually plays wise-cracking, cynical and aggressive women who demand respect and elicit fear from the men they are fighting.

Stanwyck's unfeminine Western female protagonists are often positioned as the hero: they wear masculine clothing (slacks, boots, spurs), ride and shoot as well as any male hero, and are regularly involved in vigorous physical activity. Stanwyck's characters are often shot from a low angle, which emphasises their power. Unlike, for example, Joan Crawford in *Johnny Guitar* (Nicholas Ray, 1954), Stanwyck's Western characters are always up against male protagonists and hardly ever seem artificial or out of place in the films. Changes in gender roles in American post-war society legitimised the appearance of tough, masculine female protagonists in Westerns – for example, *Duel in the Sun* (King Vidor, 1947) and *Rancho Notorious* (Fritz Lang, 1952) – at least until they succumbed to heterosexual romance or until they were punished for their

Figure 7.2   Stanwyck shot from a low angle in *Forty Guns* (1957, Twentieth Century Fox Film Corporation), suggesting power.

transgression (Pumphrey 1996: 57). Pam Cook argues that 'it's unusual for the woman who starts out wearing pants, carrying a gun and riding a horse to still be doing so at the end of the movie' (1998: 294).

This is most obvious in *Forty Guns* (Samuel Fuller, 1957) (see Figure 7.2). Here, Jessica Drummond (Stanwyck) is a landowner and leader of a posse of forty men, who takes the law into her own hands. She is dressed in black, wears pants, and carries a gun. Jessica falls in love with US Marshal Griff Bonnell and bit by bit gives up her power, pride and control. However, when Griff tracks down Jessica's brother Brockie (John Ericson) to revenge Brockie's murder of his own brother Wes Bonnell, Griff deliberately shoots through Jessica in order to kill Brockie who is using her as a shield. By shooting Jessica, Griff 'kills' the unfeminine woman. In the final sequence of the film, Jessica, recovered from her gunshot wound and realising her love for Griff, is forced to run after him as he rides out of town; she now wears a white dress rather than her customary black slacks. The high-angle crane shot makes Jessica look particularly small as she runs after Griff on the broad main street and jumps on the back of his wagon. The ending is in stark contrast to Jessica's first appearance in the film when she leads – clad in black on a white horse – her forty men down a hill.

Stanwyck's characters are different from other women in Westerns. In *Forty Guns*, Jessica has her ranch far away from town, and she and her male posse only come into town to cause trouble. *Forty Guns'* theme song *Woman with a Whip* (the film's original title) underscores Jessica's image:

> She's a high-riding woman, with a whip
> She's a woman that all men desire
> But as no man can tame her
> [. . .]
> She commands and men obey
> They're just putty in her hands, so they say

However, the song also foreshadows the film's ending, which returns the woman to her proper place:

> But if someone could break her and take her whip away
> [. . .]
> You may find that the woman with a whip
> Is only a woman after all.

Another aspect that differentiated Stanwyck's characters from other women in Westerns was their physicality. Women in Westerns often stayed away from physical activity. In contrast, studio biographies and articles regularly stated that Stanwyck was an 'enthusiastic sportswoman' who loved 'being physically active' both on- and offscreen.[7] Stanwyck was also known for doing most of her own stunts in these films. As early as 1946, an article in *Movieland* stated that using a stunt double was 'not in line with Barbara's philosophy that you really have to put your heart and soul into a part' (Shallin 1946: 57). Stanwyck's ability and willingness to be physically active in her roles made her a suitable actress for the Western. Similarly, her onscreen unfeminine image was reinforced by her offscreen unfeminine image. The emphasis in her star image on her career rather than her family life suggested a resistance to conventional femininity. Similarly, although Stanwyck was married to matinee idol Robert Taylor during the 1940s, the glamorisation of their marriage was not as durable as Stanwyck's status as a film star because from the mid-1940s onwards publicity focused predominantly on her career.[8] Articles and biographies emphasised that Stanwyck's 'whole field of interest [...] lies in her career' and that she was 'interested solely in her acting job and in doing that well' (Unauthored 1951: 25).[9] This unfeminine theme is an element that can be found all through Stanwyck's career, particularly in her onscreen image but also in her offscreen image.

CONCLUSION

By examining Stanwyck as part of the industrial film process as well as the roles she played through original archival material, I have explained her fashionability in the 1950s and 1960s. This was a period in Stanwyck's career during which one would have expected her star to fade, but through her freelancing and the attractive model of womanhood she portrayed, Stanwyck managed to extend her career. As a freelance star, Stanwyck was aware of her image and managed to maintain the important elements of her image from the 1930s and 1940s (natural and unfeminine), but adapted these to the fashions of the 1950s and 1960s. Audiences therefore knew what to expect when watching Stanwyck onscreen, and her fashionability could be maintained.

Moreover, Stanwyck was promoted as a role model for mature women. She demonstrated that being over forty did not mean that women could not be attractive. The model of womanhood she offered fans fitted with her image: women should be natural. Nonetheless, the model of womanhood Stanwyck offered did not fit conventional models of femininity, but it matched her unfeminine film roles. Because Stanwyck was seen as natural and authentic, she was therefore allowed to age on the screen and this was used in various production trends. Although many films did draw attention to Stanwyck's maturity (either through her character, through other characters, through the narrative, or through the use of wigs in colour films while the audience knew that her hair was grey), they used Stanwyck's ageing as a sign of wisdom, and rarely turned her into a harridan. Admitting to her age set her apart from other stars and this benefited her chances of work.

Stanwyck's performances in Westerns played an integral part in her image at the end of her career. She was one of the few regular leading female stars of Westerns. Her characters in this genre fitted her earlier performances and her on- and offscreen image: they were tough, no-nonsense, wise-cracking women who could hold their own in a masculine world. They fitted in the world of the Western, but, like other Stanwyck characters that transgressed gender boundaries, they were always reduced to a conventional feminine role, or punished with death in the end. Nonetheless, she enacted transgression through much of the narrative, as for instance in *Forty Guns*. Although Stanwyck was considered a role model for mature women, she was not a conventional feminine role model, and this transgressive, independent angle is a likely reason for her popularity as a mature female star in the post-war era. Stanwyck's independent characters mirrored her independence in her career.

In this chapter I have tried to provide an understanding of the fashionability of Stanwyck through original archival research and an analysis of some of her less-discussed roles and films. Because Stanwyck was a freelance star, she was able to adapt her on- and offscreen image to fit production trends as well as key aspects that featured in American society. This meant she could prolong her career while other female stars from her cohort who were contract stars often replayed the same roles until the films they performed in were no longer popular and their careers diminished rapidly. Stanwyck was known for her versatility from the beginning of her career and this meant she could play most roles and remained popular at the box office (Berkvens 2011: 176). Stanwyck's onscreen pliability mirrored her offscreen pliability; her image could be reconfigured, up to a certain extent, to connect her image to popular images of women. However, her image also simultaneously seemed to challenge these dominant images, for example in connotations of the unfeminine in the Western versus the femininity of her ageing. As a freelance star, Stanwyck, together with her agents, was responsible for her career and image. Unlike many of her contemporaries – most of whom were contract stars – Stanwyck and her agent used her image as a bargaining tool. This meant that, to remain fashionable, her image had to be pliable. Examining Stanwyck's fashionability reveals that shifts in a star's image must occur so that a star can maintain his or her popularity. In Stanwyck's case, her image in the 1950s and 1960s had to be subtly reshuffled to meet popular images of women in this period, while the image also remained connected to her earlier on- and offscreen image. Stars are objects of fashion, and questions about what makes a star popular at a particular time need to be carefully researched, especially when discussing a star with a long and varied career such as Barbara Stanwyck.

NOTES

1. Hopper, Hedda (1951), 'Stanwyck Honesty and Loyalty Score High for "Fighting Lady"', in Barbara Stanwyck Scrapbook, Constance McCormick Collection (CMC), University of Southern California (USC), Los Angeles; Barbara Stanwyck Biography by Helen Ferguson Publicity c. 1948, Barbara Stanwyck Biography file at the Margaret Herrick Library, Academy of Motion Picture Arts and Sciences (AMPAS), Los Angeles.
2. Barbara Stanwyck Biography by Helen Ferguson Publicity c.1948, Barbara Stanwyck Biography file, AMPAS.
3. Articles 1949-174 and 1949–183, Jack Hirschberg Papers (JHP), AMPAS.
4. More articles and resources about Stanwyck's refusal to dye her hair: Barbara Stanwyck Biography by Helen Ferguson PR, 8 October 1958, Barbara Stanwyck Biography file, Los Angeles Examiner Collection, USC; Barbara Stanwyck Biography by Helen Ferguson PR, November 1964, JHP, AMPAS; Paramount Biography, February 1949; RKO Biography, c. 1952, Barbara Stanwyck clipping file, USC.
5. For a more detailed analysis of Stanwyck's image and her career, see Berkvens 2011.
6. Contract summary, 14 February 1964, Paramount production files, AMPAS.
7. 'Stanwyck at Home', c. 1938–9, Barbara Stanwyck Scrapbook, CMC, USC; Block, Maxime, 'Frankly 42!'.
8. Examiner Collection, USC. Various articles, Barbara Stanwyck Scrapbook vols I and II, CMC, USC.
9. Barbara Stanwyck Biography by Helen Ferguson PR, 8 October 1958, Barbara Stanwyck Biography file, Los Angeles Examiner Collection, USC.

BIBLIOGRAPHY

Anderson, Christopher (1994), Hollywood TV: The Studio System in the Fifties, Austin: University of Texas Press.
Belton, John (1990), 'Glorious Technicolor, Breathtaking CinemaScope, and Stereophonic Sound', in Tino Balio (ed.), Hollywood in the Age of Television, Boston: Unwin Hyman, pp. 185–211.
Berkvens, Linda (2011), No Crinoline-Covered Lady: Stardom, Agency, and the Career of Barbara Stanwyck, DPhil thesis, Falmer: University of Sussex.
Biggs, Simon (2004), 'Age, Gender, Narratives, and Masquerades', Journal of Aging Studies 18, 45–58.
Block, Maxime, 'Frankly 42!', Barbara Stanwyck Biography file, Margaret Herrick Library, Academy of Motion Picture Arts and Sciences (AMPAS), Los Angeles.
Bodnar, John (2003), Blue-Collar Hollywood: Liberalism, Democracy, and Working People in American Film, Baltimore: Johns Hopkins University Press.
Bret, David (2006), Joan Crawford: Hollywood Martyr, London: Robson.
Carman, Emily (2012), '"Women Rule Hollywood": Ageing and Freelance Stardom in the Studio System', Celebrity Studies 3:1, 13–24.
Cattle Queen of Montana, advertisement, Variety, 15 December 1954, p. 29.
Cook, Pam (1998), 'Women and the Western', in Jim Kitses and Gregg Rickman (eds), The Western Reader, New York: Limelight, pp. 293–300.
Drew, Bernard (1981), 'Stanwyck Speaks', Film Comment, March/April 1981, pp. 43–6.
Graham, Sheila (1966), 'Stanwyck: Film Queen's "Dead" at 50, Offered Nothing but Horror Roles', Chicago Tribune, 15 April 1966.
Hahn, Bill (1965), radio interview, Barbara Stanwyck, Boston: WNAC.
Head, Edith and Paddy Calistro (1983), Edith Head's Hollywood, New York: Dutton.
Holland, Jack (1948), 'I Want to Remember', Movieland, July 1948, pp. 61, 76–8.

Jermyn, Deborah (2012), '"Get a Life, Ladies. Your Old One is Not Coming Back":
Ageing, Ageism and the Life Span of Female Celebrity', *Celebrity Studies* 3:1,
pp. 1–12.
Lane, Lydia (1951), 'Barbara Stanwyck Unveils Mysteries of Skin Beauty', *Los Angeles
Times*, 4 March 1951.
Lincoln, Anne E. and Michael Patrick Allen (2004), 'Double Jeopardy in Hollywood:
Age and Gender in the Career of Film Actors, 1926–1999', *Sociological Forum* 19:4,
611–31.
May, Elaine Tyler (1999), *Homeward Bound: American Families in the Cold War Era*,
New York: Basic.
McCarthy, John (1994), *The Fearmakers: The Screen's Directorial Masters of Suspense*,
New York: St Martin's Press.
Parsons, Louella and Harriet Parsons, 'Barbara Stanwyck: Lots of Friends', Barbara
Stanwyck Biography file, AMPAS.
Pumphrey, Martin (1996), 'Why do Cowboys Wear Hats in the Bath?', in Ian Cameron
and Douglas Pye (eds), *The Movie Book of the Western*, London: Vista, pp. 50–62.
Pye, Douglas (1996), 'Introduction', in Ian Cameron and Douglas Pye (eds), *The Movie
Book of the Western*, London: Vista, pp. 9–21.
Rogers St Johns, Adela, 'The Hollywood Story', *American Weekly*, Barbara Stanwyck
clipping file; Barbara Stanwyck scrapbooks, Constance McCormick Collection
(CMC), University of Southern California (USC), Los Angeles.
Rose, Frank (1996), *The Agency: William Morris and the Hidden History of Show
Business*, New York: Harper.
Schatz, Thomas (1999), *Boom and Bust: American Cinema in the 1940s*, Berkeley:
University of California Press.
Shallin, G. B. (1946), 'Missy is no Sissy', *Movieland*, September 1946, pp. 56–7, 66.
Sontag, Susan (1972), 'The Double Standard of Aging', *Saturday Review of The Society*,
23 September 1972, pp. 29–38.
Spinrad, Leonard (1947), 'Boots and Saddles: Noting Changing Styles in the Western
Picture', *The New York Times*, 8 June 1947, p. X4.
Stacey, Jackie (1994), *Star Gazing: Hollywood Cinema and Female Spectatorship*,
London: Routledge.
Stanwyck, Barbara, 'Look Ahead!', *Photoplay*, CMC.
Stokes, Melvyn (1999), 'Female Audiences of the 1920s and early 1930s', in Richard
Maltby and Melvyn Stokes (eds), *Identifying Hollywood's Audiences*, London: BFI,
pp. 42–60.
Unauthored (1951), 'The Story behind the Stanwyck–Taylor Split', *Movieland*, April
1951, pp. 24–6.
Unauthored (1956), 'Hollywood's "Age of the Teens"', *Variety*, 22 August 1956, pp. 3,
14.
Weaver, William R. (1946), 'The Money-Making Stars of 1946', *Motion Picture Herald*,
28 December 1946, pp. 13–16.

8. CONFRONTING THE IMPOSSIBILITY OF IMPOSSIBLE BODIES: TOM CRUISE AND THE AGEING MALE ACTION HERO MOVIE

Lisa Purse

Since the mid-2000s, there has been a marked proliferation of veteran heroes in the action genre, exemplified by the success of franchises like *The Expendables* (2010, 2012, 2014, with a fourth in development) and *Taken* (2008, 2012, 2014), producing a growing collection of films to which *Vanity Fair* magazine was moved to apply the moniker 'Dadcore' (Taylor 2014).[1] This chapter will examine the factors that have contributed to this proliferation, but also the ways in which contemporary ageing action stars' bodies produce meaning in relation to their immediate narrative contexts, and to wider cultural narratives of ageing. The now well-established methodological emphasis on paying close attention to the details of performance (see, for example, Affron 1977, King 1991 [1985], Naremore 1988 and Klevan 2005) has historically tended to neglect the stars of action cinema. In the few studies of ageing male action stars that exist, the physical appearance of figures such as Clint Eastwood and Sylvester Stallone is analysed to highly productive ends, but the texture of their ageing star bodies' performance-*in-motion* is generalised rather than parsed in detail.[2] This may be because physical stature and the static postures of mastery that express it are such an important component of the male action hero's construction and the paratextual marketing of his action body that there is less perceived imperative to consider movement closely; or perhaps the force of normative presumptions of ageing as an inevitable slowing or stiffening of movement unwittingly situates movement as a lesser object of study (and I will return to questions of stature, slowing and stiffening in due course). Either way, there remains a need to extend existing scholarship in this area by analysing the ageing action star body not just as 'a sign of meaning' but as 'a body in action', as Paul McDonald puts it (1998: 182). This chapter will therefore use close analysis of physical performance to understand the epistemic and phenomenological consequences of real-world ageing – visible or simply known – on the construction of the ageing action star in recent action cinema. Considering the performance-in-motion of a range of ageing male action stars, and ending with an examination of the extent to which the allegedly 'ever-young' Tom Cruise might represent a productive anomaly in this context, this chapter reveals similarities and differences across star bodies, roles and narratives that suggest that this cycle of films represents a site of intense cultural negotiation over the lived experience of the ageing male body.

LOOKING BACK

The figure of the ageing hero has always had a place in action cinema's many iterations: the veteran nearing the end of his career or pressed back into active 'service' to solve a developing crisis, whose life experience and strategic expertise is crucial to the overcoming of steep odds or key to the pathos of failing at that attempt. Across the twentieth century, various male stars have achieved longevity with such roles, such as John Wayne, Burt Lancaster, Clint Eastwood and Harrison Ford.[3] As these stars aged, the markers of ageing visible on the body – from facial lines to changes in posture, musculature, fat distribution and motility – and extra-textual knowledge of the fact of the star's ageing, drove narratives which 'take the aging of these stars as their narrative focus', as Chris Holmlund has pointed out (2002: 143). The ageing star body provides a heightened embodiment of competing qualities – the strength and tenacity implied by 'still being here' as an active, influential protagonist, co-present with the observable diminutions of the aged body – that is narratively and thematically productive.[4] And while the exploration of the vicissitudes of power (physical and metaphorical) and the relationship to the past that the ageing process can engender provided rich material for character and action in, for example, Wayne's films *El Dorado* (Howard Hawks, 1966), *Rio Lobo* (John Ford, 1970) and *The Shootist* (Don Siegel, 1976), the body of the ageing action star could also resonate beyond the narrative, speaking to wider social or cultural concerns. Garry Wills suggests, for example, that in Wayne's final films, 'there was a *social* dimension to his aging, a sense that a period in *history* was slipping away, not just one man's natural powers' (1997: 281, original emphasis). We might say the same for the deployment of the ageing Wayne and the ageing Burt Lancaster in *The Green Berets* (Ray Kellogg, John Wayne, Mervyn LeRoy, 1968) and *Go Tell The Spartans* (Ted Post, 1978) respectively. While serving different ideological agendas, in both these Vietnam-set films the ageing action star's slowed motility functions to emblematise the passing of an older era of combat and the difficulty of understanding how to be effective in a new and unfamiliar theatre of war. The affective shock of seeing Burt Lancaster's aged body lying naked, exposed, inert in a field of dead bodies after a failed defensive mission at the end of *Go Tell The Spartans* dramatically reinforces the film's anti-war message. These examples suggest Richard Dyer's conceptualisation of stars' function, to 'enact ways of making sense of the experience of being a person in a particular kind of social production' (1987: 17) not just, in these cases, in allowing a making sense of the process of ageing, but in deploying the ageing star body to think through a particular socio-cultural issue or context. These examples also illustrate the extent to which nostalgia seems integral to the ageing star body's connotative power and affective impact: as Ginette Vincendeau points out, 'ageing stars carry the memory of their younger glory' (2000: 181) in narratively and thematically highly productive ways, and we should note that this memory is not just of the detail of narrative action and characteristics in previous roles, but of the phenomenological force of the star body's past performances in comparison to their present iteration (see Sternagel 2012). To what extent do these characteristics still apply in the contemporary ageing action hero film? How does the phenomenology of the action star body resonate in this new context?

A NEW ERA

We must begin by asking why recent action cinema has become such a fertile ground for performers, not just for established action stars like Sylvester Stallone or Arnold Schwarzenegger attempting to extend their careers, but also for those who have made (or are making) forays into the action film later in their careers, such as Liam Neeson (*The Grey* (2011), *Non-Stop* (2014), *A Walk Among the Tombstones* (2014), *Run All Night* (2015)), Nicolas Cage (*Drive Angry* (2011), *Seeking Justice* (2011), *Stolen* (2012), *Rage* (2014)) and Denzel Washington (*The Book of Eli* (2010), *Safe House* (2012), *2 Guns* (2013), *The Equalizer* (2014)). In part, this has been made possible by actors in both camps becoming actor-producers to help fund their own vehicles. Like Eastwood, Lancaster, Ford, Wayne and others before them, Cage, Clooney, Cruise, Washington, Stallone, Schwarzenegger and latterly Bruce Willis and Dolph Lundgren have stepped into producer roles in this way.[5] A further factor was the emergence in the 2000s of a new archetype, the uncertain teenaged male action hero, in films like the *Transformers* franchise (2007, 2009), *Jumper* (2008), *Eagle Eye* (2008), *Zombieland* (2009) and *Scott Pilgrim vs the World* (2010). Counter-intuitively, these teenage action hero films often consolidated older male heroes' persistence onscreen because, in their bid to maximise demographic appeal, they frequently co-opted an ageing action hero into the role of 'buddy' or mentor for the teenaged protagonist, such as

Schwarzenegger in *Terminator 3: Rise of the Machines* (2003), Kevin Costner in *The Guardian* (2006), or Willis in *Live Free or Die Hard* (2007) and (with his twenty-something onscreen son) in *A Good Day to Die Hard* (2013) (Purse 2011: 106–9).

However, the central factor is the extent to which a growing cultural nostalgia for the 1980s has taken hold in the last ten years or so, and the extent to which one action star in particular broadened the field of opportunity through his own attempts to capitalise on this trend. Since the early 2000s, the 1980s have become a persistent nostalgic reference point for everything from vintage band T-shirts to electronic music (for example, Chromatics, Daft Punk) to video games like *Far Cry 3: Blood Dragon* (Ubisoft, 2013). This has prompted Hollywood to stage a number of different returns to the period, narratively or stylistically (*Be Kind Rewind* (2008), *Hot Tub Time Machine* (2010), *Drive* (2011), *Wreck-It Ralph* (2012), *The Wolf of Wall Street* (2013)), or through reboots and sequels of cult '80s movies and TV shows, like *The A-Team* (2010), *TRON: Legacy* (2010), *Fright Night* (2011) and *Evil Dead* (2013). Sylvester Stallone's action stardom is indelibly linked to the 1980s: he shot to fame with his turn as small-time boxer Rocky Balboa in *Rocky* (1976), but it was his muscled incarnation as Vietnam vet John Rambo in *First Blood* (1982) and its sequels (1985, 1988), along with the *Rocky* sequels (1979, 1982, 1985, 1990), that cemented his reputation as a key 'hard-body' action star of that decade (Jeffords 1994: 24). In an era of 1980s revivals, Stallone struck early, writing and directing his own iconic characters' returns in the well-received *Rocky Balboa* (2006) and *Rambo* (2008) respectively. In doing so, Stallone achieved a significant career revival, consolidated with the ensemble piece *The Expendables*, which he wrote, directed and produced, and which teamed a roster of ageing action stars such as Stallone, Lundgren, Jet Li, Willis and Schwarzenegger with 2000s action star Jason Statham, and famous former sportsmen like NFL stars-turned-actors Terry Crews and Jim Brown and ex-wrestler Randy Couture. The film's self-ironising celebration of the former action stardom of people like Stallone, Schwarzenegger, Willis and Lundgren, combined with the casting of celebrity athletes like Crews and Couture, proved popular with cinema-goers, thus paving the way, alongside Stallone's earlier efforts, for a range of other films to be green-lit that featured older actors in ensembles, single-hero movies or buddy pairings.[6]

NARRATIVES OF AGEING

The ageing-past-youth of Sylvester Stallone's character in comparison to his younger colleague is registered explicitly in the dialogue of the very first action sequence of *The Expendables*. African pirates have demanded a ransom for a ship's crew they are holding, and the 'Expendables' team of mercenaries

infiltrate the ship covertly and attempt to prevent the pirates from killing the
hostages. Negotiations fail, prompting an initial flurry of gunfire that kills
most but not all of the pirates. The remaining few force a stand-off by threat-
ening to kill the hostages nearest to them, prompting Expendables team chief
Barney Ross (Sylvester Stallone) and his right-hand man Lee Christmas (Jason
Statham) to discuss their strategy for taking out all the pirates simultaneously:

> Lee: I'll take the four on the left.
> Barney: Why don't you take the two on the right and leave the rest alone?
> Lee: You should take the two on the right, you're not that fast anymore.
> Barney: The only thing faster is light.
> Lee: We'll see.
> Barney: Bullets go faster than blades.

Here the film acknowledges the age differential between Lee and Barney, and
frames it in terms of capacity for speed. Barney's more advanced age, it is
implied, means he will be slower than he used to be, less able to be the most
effective team member. This kind of open acknowledgement of ageing in
dialogue is a common feature of ageing male action hero films, a feature that
seems to perpetuate the 'ideology of midlife decline' that critical gerontologist
Margaret Gullette suggests is dominant in North American culture, and which
is defined by notions of loss – of youthfulness, vitality, health and social status
(1998: 5). Gullette argues that the prevalence of this idea produces a 'life-
course opposition of progress and decline [that] constrains narrative options
in our culture' (2004: 19), and the explicit suggestion that ageing heroes are
likely to be slower than their younger colleagues bears this out. The athletic
competencies – physical strength, speed, agility, stamina – that are demanded
of the action hero and the actor that plays him/her would seem to tie the
character and the actor more tightly to the midlife decline narrative, since, as
Cassandra Phoenix and Andrew Sparkes point out, ageing athletic bodies are
normatively understood in terms of an even more sharply defined 'trajectory of
progress, peak and decline' (2008: 219). One of the questions I want to explore
in this chapter is, to what extent this culturally entrenched 'midlife decline'
narrative might be perpetuated or problematised by the ageing action hero
film, and the ways in which the phenomenology of real-world ageing maps
onto the construction of the ageing action body.

In her seminal essay, 'Youthfulness as Masquerade', Kathleen Woodward
reminds us that cultural representations of the ageing body 'are constructed
primarily in terms of visual appearance. Other aspects of the body-in-age are
seldom explored, including the phenomenology and phantasies of motility,
proprioception, and the interior of the body' (1988–9: 121). In visual terms,
ageing action stars' younger selves precede them: spectators who are familiar

with an actor's earlier performances and his younger action body are, as a result, primed to scrutinise visual appearance and register any changes that have resulted from the ageing process. A crucial element of cultural depictions of ageing is the contrast between present age and past youth: ageing is constructed as an alienation from a supposedly authentic, youthful self, creating an uncanny 'cohabitation of tenses, memories of a familiar past rubbing up against the strange newness of the present', as Amelia DeFalco notes (2010: 9). In action cinema, this cohabitation of tenses necessarily relates not just to visual appearance but to the physical dimensions of lived experience, because the action hero must be capable, or become capable, of overcoming extreme physical demands in order to succeed. Central to action cinema are fantasies of empowerment, trajectories towards spatial and physical mastery enacted by the action body working at the limits of physical resistance, but also central is action stardom, and the pleasures that flow from seeing particular performers displaying their physical skills – agility, stamina, strength – across a number of films. In these generic and historical contexts, the ageing action star is likely to register with the spectator as an uncanny body because it constitutes a familiar, remembered corporeality and a strange new corporeality simultaneously. Remembered and present performances of active physicality compete in the viewing experience, the disjunction between them embodied in the biological markers of real-world added years that cannot be fully elided: not just visual cues such as increased facial lines or cosmetic changes designed to resist biological ageing, but changes in weight distribution, muscle and skin structures, and in physical mobility and expressivity.

This uncanny body can produce strong cultural responses, which seems to cluster particularly intensely around the most prominent 1980s 'hardbodies'. Yvonne Tasker notes the 'caustic media attention' which has greeted the onscreen ageing of these actors, rightly situating it in the broader context of a celebrity culture in which ageing is 'frequently a source of humour, a comedy of the inappropriate' in which trying too hard or not hard enough leads to vilification (2014: 253–4). Sylvester Stallone in particular is, as Tasker reveals, regularly located in the former category, coverage of his appearance and fitness regime dogged by derisive rumours of plastic surgery and performance–enhancing drugs (2014: 254). Arnold Schwarzenegger has avoided some of this treatment because of his stepping back from acting during his tenure as Governor of California (2003–11), but it will be interesting to see if his recent return to acting will begin to generate similar negative celebrity-media scrutiny. Julia Hallam and Margaret Marshment point out that ageing actors have generally 'secured their positions as older stars through their acting abilities rather than their physical image' (2000: 83), and this is a difficult route for stars like Stallone and Schwarzenegger to take, not least because the films in which they made their mark prioritised the display of brawn over cerebral scenes, but also because, as a result, their star personas are focused around their bodies rather than their acting skill. It is testament to the force of normative narratives of ageing and dominant conceptions of masculinity as an embodiment of phallic power that the ageing onscreen action body can call up a lost younger, more vigorous physicality across *both* the ageing 1980s action stars *and* those ageing male actors who have come late to action cinema and were not 'hardbody stars' in their youth. In the following section, I want to explore the spectacles of action these ageing action bodies generate, and the ideas they mobilise about what an ageing action body can be and do.

THE AGEING BODY IN ACTION

If the ageing action body is an uncanny body for the spectator (and for the celebrity press), it is also uncanny for the character that this body fleshes out. Like the ageing hero narratives of the past, most contemporary ageing action hero movies stage the protagonist's own encounter with, to use DeFalco's words, 'memories of a familiar past rubbing up against the strange newness of the present'. This can be an emotional past, or the unsettling blunting of familiar physical capacities. Like the retired cop or war veteran, the ageing action hero suffers because he carries the weight of difficult memories of personal and professional loss. About halfway through *The Expendables*, as Barney Ross tries to decide whether to rescue the woman he has left on a South American island, 'Vilena', who is being terrorised by a local dictator, his friend, Tool (Mickey Rourke), volunteers a painful memory. While a mercenary in Bosnia, after a firefight with Serb forces that he wasn't sure he would survive, Tool spots a woman about to commit suicide, but does nothing. 'If I'd saved that woman I might have saved what was left of my soul', he says, voice catching. The opening of *Non-Stop* (Jaume Collet-Serra, 2014) shows air marshal Bill Marks (Neeson) in his rain-drenched car in the midst of an alcoholic pre-work ritual, the sloshing of whisky into his morning coffee cup visually juxtaposed with a thumbed photograph from his past – of a daughter now lost. In both examples, the ageing action hero's elongated personal history is shown to provoke traumatic memories and destructive habits that have their own corporeal effects: pulling down the shoulders, slowing movements, altering bodily reactions. Most frequently, however, it is the distance between past and present physical capacities that is explicitly registered in dialogue, by either the protagonist or those around him, and, as the *Expendables* example attests, such moments can be useful indicators of the way the character is oriented towards his own ageing (resistant, accepting, and so on). There is, then, a productive pathos to this uncanny body, nostalgia for what is lost combining with the recognition of the increased labour of action that might be experienced by a physically depleted hero. And this pathos has a rather overdetermined quality, since it attaches both to the fictional protagonist's aged state and the performer's: both actor and character are witnessed in the moment of their negotiation of the present in relation to the past, and more specifically both must complete some version of the same stretching physical feats. As older performers act out those tasks that the spectator remembers being performed by their younger selves, and as characters exert themselves in the awareness that they used to be more physically able than they are now, the phenomenology of the ageing action body is front and centre, but to what ends?

Cultural narratives of ageing that focus on decline and loss would seem to have a particular valence in action cinema, where any action hero must suffer before they succeed. Peter Lehman has suggested that all visual representations of masculinity are poised between the assertion of phallic power and its corresponding collapse (1993: 31), and the action film reflects this in its archetypal construction of the male action hero as, to use Yvonne Tasker's phrase, both 'powerful and suffering' (1993: 127). In a recent essay, Tasker usefully sets out the ways in which suffering is narratively productive in this context:

> Physical vulnerability and themes of struggle serve at least two purposes in terms of hard-boiled action's narrative logic. First, they allow a delay to the ultimate resolution, much as obstacles are placed between the lovers in tales of romance. Second, they enhance motivation such that the hero acts to secure revenge; his violence is thus retributive and effectively justified. (2014: 248–9)

The increased labour – which these films suggest arises from the age-related physical diminution of the character – serves as another way in which the hero can struggle and suffer, and another way in which the certainty of the final outcome can be delayed to produce suspense. The comparative motility and proprioception of the ageing action performer's physically stretched body here works to intensify the affective force of spectacles of physical action and their impression of bodily risk, labour and success, as an example sequence from *The Expendables* will illustrate. Barney's reconnaissance trip to Vilena ends with him and Lee being chased off the island by the dictator's army. Lee has run ahead to the seaplane that is their escape vehicle, and fired up the engines; Barney must run along the jetty to catch the plane, which is about to take flight (see Figure 8.1). After a couple of brief shots which show him making his way towards the pier, and a shot of Lee leaning out of the plane shouting 'Come on!', we see Barney break into a run in a medium long shot. In a slightly longer but more frontal shot, Barney makes the three-foot jump down from a concrete pier to the wooden jetty and runs towards the camera (and the plane). As Lee starts to push the plane into forward motion, the camera frames Barney/Stallone running at full tilt in closer views from the

Figure 8.1   Stallone-as-Barney runs down the jetty in *The Expendables* (2010).

side, the front and from behind, before Barney throws himself at the plane door, securing his escape in a hail of enemy bullets as the plane, too, lifts into the air.

In his 1980s iterations as John Rambo, Stallone's running movement was nimble and fluid despite his heavily muscular frame: he ran with his head up, body directed forwards, his movement spare and efficient. Here, Stallone's motion has a different quality and phenomenological force. He seems to bear the weight of his physical structure less stably, moving forwards with a slightly rolling running gait and an attenuated stride length that creates a staccato, rather than smooth, stride rhythm. He swings his arms in wide arcs and thrusts the neck forwards and down, gestures that are likely motivated by the need to take extra measures to ensure forward momentum and stability are maintained at pace, but which in their form refer us to the opposite: falling forwards, swinging out of control. And this despite the fragmented nature of the physical feat's editing, showing the running in snatched, fairly brief shots which signal the production reality that the actor was able to take breaks between perfor-mances of physical exertion. Stallone's ageing-past-youth emerges particularly sharply in the fleeting hesitations that Stallone-as-Barney momentarily betrays at two points in this sequence: just before the jump, and in the transition from landing the jump to breaking back into a run. Both are physically impact-ful transition points where balance is crucial but challenging, and at both points Stallone-as-Barney seems to need to steel himself physically, altering his posture and adjusting muscular tension to make the transitions less challeng-ing and destabilising. In this scene we are confronted by the contingency of Stallone's physical capacities as well as the character's, but this neatly serves to intensify the dramatic tension of the scene, with its trope of will-he-won't-he make it. Musculature and heft, the very ingredients of the 1980s hardbody, here signal instability, the possibility of losing control. The work of the body, which the memory of the younger Stallone's motility resituates as additional work, drives an intensified release of tension as Stallone-as-Barney manages to reach the plane just in time, hangs on to the door frame, and finally manages to drag the bulk of his own body into the cabin. In this way, *The Expendables* and other similar films make the most of the dramatic potential inherent in the ageing action body's physical contingency.

The basis of this physical contingency – rigid musculature and significant corporeal heft – can, however, produce other connotative possibilities, feeding into a different reading of the ageing body's capacities and the significance of its ageing-past-youth. The action hero's suffering is often figured as a monolithic stoicism, a toleration of extremes, and the capacity, eventually, to endure. In relation to this genre commonplace, the heft of the ageing action hero can productively connote a stoicism not just of the mind, but of the body. In the opening scenes of *The Last Stand* (Jee-woon Kim, 2013),

Arnold Schwarzenegger walks around Sommerton, the border town that his sheriff character Ray Owens polices, as most of the town loads into school buses to head to an American Football away game for their local team. As Schwarzenegger-as-Owens exits his vehicle, he shuts the door behind him with a push-back of the arm, giving the opportunity to view shoulder and arm motions which clearly lack a full range of movement – that is, the motion appears stiff and awkward. There is a carnival spirit in the town but despite a cheery demeanour Owens walks slowly, his gait lumbering, his weight shifting significantly from side to side, indicating an age-related tightening of the hip or knee flexors, all of which produces a phenomenologically dense contrast with the supple and efficient running and walking styles of the younger 'Arnie' in films like *Commando* (Mark L. Lester, 1985), *Predator* (John McTiernan, 1987) and *The Running Man* (Paul Michael Glaser, 1987). *Sans* speed and agility, Owens' successful overcoming of the drug cartel is, in part, rooted in the tactical insight that an extended policing and combat career can gift, and his willingness to collaborate (points I will return to later), but he finally prevails because of the same musculature and heft that seems to weigh him down when he moves. The film culminates in a face-off between Owens and the escaped drug cartel boss, Gabriel Cortez (Eduardo Noriega, thirty-eight at the time of filming), who is trying to cross the border into Mexico. It begins with Cortez launching into the air to deliver a flying punch, but Owens blocks the punch with his entire body, which simply absorbs the impact without moving, allowing Owens to slam Cortez's body into the floor. The confrontation proceeds as an extended endgame of brutal punches, kicks and bodily struggle, Cortez placing Owens in various wrestling locks and holds to subject his body to huge strain. While Cortez requires extended breaks to recover from each debilitating body slam, even losing consciousness at one point, Owens seems able to absorb each impact without pause. Here stoicism is made flesh in the rigid body of the ageing action hero, and muscular stiffness, which contributes to a decline narrative in other moments, in these moments counters that narrative, by contributing to the visual impression of an immovable, monolithic presence that is more, rather than less, capable, and less, rather than more, vulnerable.

CONTINGENCY AND ADAPTABILITY

The phenomenological force of the age-slowed but resilient body can also mislead other characters about the ageing hero's capabilities, permitting the multiplication of tactical advantage while taking advantage of others' propensity for underestimation. Underestimation is a recurrent pattern in the ageing action hero narrative, from the condescension directed towards Sheriff Owens by the drugs cartel in *The Last Stand*, to the Russian gangsters who misrecognise former assassin Robert McCall (Denzel Washington) as a naive john when he tries to buy a young prostitute her freedom in *The Equalizer* (Antoine Fuqua, 2014), jokingly asking him whether he can 'still get it up, *dedushka* [grandfather]'. Underestimation of this kind redoubles the spectator's attentiveness to the risks and narrative stakes of the scene by reminding him/her of the physical contingency of the ageing body, and also sets the scene for the ageing action hero to pleasurably transcend limits – both the physical limits designated as credible by the ageing hero's opponents within the fictional world, and the physical limits that elsewhere the movie has suggested constrain ageing bodies in the real world. If the ageing male action hero cannot sustain heightened agility and speed over extended durations, he can deploy it in short bursts, and his experience means he knows when to unleash this power, and in what ways. *The Equalizer* takes this principle to an extreme, the Russian gangsters' bemusement turning to horror, then silence, as McCall proceeds to kill all six armed men in 28 seconds (slower than his 16-second prediction, but still fast).

The scene is also a good example of multiplying tactical advantage through adaptability: McCall uses a corkscrew and drinks glasses to enhance the force of his own punches, and times his counter-attacks and blocks to put opponents off balance or use their own momentum against them. Similarly, in *Taken 2* (Olivier Megaton, 2012), when hero Bryan Mills (Liam Neeson) gets cornered by several thugs in a small Istanbul courtyard, he uses abrupt blocking movements (immovable heft as a weapon, unexpected speed and careful timing) to divest one of the attackers of his metal baton, and then uses the baton to multiply the force of his own attacks in order to incapacitate the younger assailants. This is why Barney and Lee's discussion about whether Barney is slower than he used to be is also a discussion about the relative merits of guns and knives as weapons (Barney justifies his claim that he is 'faster than light' by pointing out that bullets 'go faster than blades'); the ageing action hero models ways in which the physical diminutions of the ageing process can be strategically compensated for by the right choice of weapon or tactic. One of the 'weapons' ageing action heroes often draw upon is other people: while the loner heroes of films like *The Equalizer* and the George Clooney-starring *The American* (Anton Corbijn, 2010) depict adaptability as a 'go-it-alone' brand of tactical ingenuity, others demonstrate an appetite for collaboration. Mills in *Taken 2* uses a mobile phone to remotely enlist his daughter to help him rescue himself and his wife from captivity, *The Last Stand* gives us a sheriff who brings together a whole team of locals to help him fight the drugs cartel, and *Escape Plan* (Mikael Håfström, 2013) focuses on the collaboration between a whole network of prisoners, who combine their different skill sets to escape from a brutal ship prison. In this context, the ensemble casts of *The Expendables* franchise make sense not just in terms of nostalgia or creative collaboration between ageing action stars, but in terms of the positive strategies the ageing action hero develops to compensate for any age-related weaknesses.

Attending to the phenomenology of the ageing action body reveals that the relationships between dominant cultural conceptions of ageing and the ageing action hero movie are complex. The possibility of age-related vulnerability actually fits well the generic framework in which any hero must physically struggle and ingeniously problem-solve in order to succeed, but the phenomenological force of such labour and the bodies that undertake it can generate competing connotations. Ageing action films are challenging the assumptions that flow from the decline narrative – that is, that ageing bodies are perpetually weaker, slower and less agile than younger bodies, and that as a result they will be less potent – because the ageing male action hero persistently demonstrates that the physical depletions of age do not need to deplete his effectiveness. Nevertheless, this does not mean that these films challenge the decline narrative itself. The ageing action star's visible facial lines and constrained motility in comparison to his younger self, combined with self-aware dialogue and other narrative references about the limits and losses associated with age, replay familiar cultural associations of ageing with physiological decline. It is precisely because ageing is being figured in these terms that the hero's recourse to collaboration, surprise and other tactical strategies is positioned as necessary, rather than optional. The extra-textual narratives that circulate around these ageing action stars similarly confirm the decline narrative: media commentators routinely speculate on the reasons why these films succeed despite their stars' advanced ages,[7] while celebrity journalism perpetuates the decline narrative through the prurient examination of film stars' attempts to sustain their youthful appearance, clustering particularly fiercely around the cosmetic and fitness regimes of established action stars like Stallone, whose 1980s hardbody offers a highly specific visual comparator (see Tasker 2014).

Tom Cruise

One action star who appears anomalous in this context is Tom Cruise. Although he achieved stardom in the 1980s, he did so with a mixed portfolio of genre films, and did not share the pumped-up musculature of stars like Schwarzenegger and Stallone. He made his first physically demanding action film in 1996 with *Mission: Impossible* (Brian De Palma), and the proportion of action films he has taken on has increased gradually over his career, particularly since the mid-2000s. What really marks him out from the recent-to-action and established action stars discussed above is his relationship to cultural narratives of youth and ageing. Cruise has historically fascinated the popular press due to his apparent ability not to age, frequently starring in films which do not overtly acknowledge his lived age (for example, *Oblivion*

(2013), *Edge of Tomorrow* (2014)). Such fascination has reached new levels of intensity as he has entered his fifth decade, his recent public appearances occasioning increasingly lively and often elaborately illustrated analyses of his alleged endless youth in print and online media, such as the *Daily Mail*'s splash feature 'Tom Cruise: 25 years on – and not a day older', accompanied by no fewer than twenty-six photographs of his face at different points between 1986 and 2011 (Boshoff and Cisotti 2011), and the *Huffington Post*'s variation on the theme, 'Tom Cruise Turns 52 Years Old But He Hasn't Aged A Day', featuring a twenty-one-image online photo slideshow (2014). Just as Woodward described, evidence of age is sought through the scrutiny of visual appearance alone, and based on this criteria Cruise seems to exemplify a cultural conception of 'successful ageing' which is the contemporary corollary of the decline narrative.

The notion of 'successful ageing' emerged in the last thirty years in the context of ageing populations and the socio-economic consequences for governmental, health and social infrastructures. In 'successful ageing', the responsibility for resisting 'midlife decline' and retaining independence in later life is emphatically individualised (Martinson and Minkler 2006: 322–3), and individuals are encouraged to attempt to achieve 'optimal lifestyles, constant activity, and successful anti-ageing' through, among other things, consumerism and physical exercise (Katz and Marshall 2003: 5). Judged by his visual appearance, Cruise stands in for these optimal lifestyle choices, his youthful appearance embodying the significant consumption of dentistry, skin care, hair care and cosmetic products and procedures that construct it, in what Woodward has called 'the proliferation of techniques for disciplining the aging body', which are 'used to evade (even while conforming to) the dominant ideology of youth – by joining it or infiltrating it' (1988–9: 132). Yet the flexible relationship that Tom Cruise seems to have to the biological reality of his own ageing also frequently generates incredulity, derision or anxious attempts to reimpose the ageing-as-decline narrative directly onto his body. For example, with their tweet, 'Tom Cruise is totally Benjamin Buttoning #Oscars', and accompanying photograph, online entertainment site *BuzzFeed* framed Cruise's youthful appearance at the 2012 Oscars as an unnatural reversal of the ageing process. Two years prior, the *Mail Online* published photographs of Tom Cruise naked from the waist up on the set of *Mission: Impossible – Ghost Protocol* (Brad Bird, 2011) with a punning headline that pointed to the middle-aged spread the photographs supposedly revealed: 'Action man Tom Cruise shows how he stays in shape at 48 (albeit an odd one)' (*Daily Mail* reporter, 2010, see Figure 8.2). And in reviews of the most recent *Mission: Impossible* outing, *Mission: Impossible – Rogue Nation* (Christopher McQuarrie, 2015), Cruise's youthful looks again prompt comment, with not one but two reviewers referencing the fantastical in their labelling of Cruise as the 'Dorian Gray' of action cinema (Hornaday 2015,

Figure 8.2   A celebrity press shot of Tom Cruise on the set of *Mission: Impossible – Ghost Protocol* (2011) © WENN.

Lane 2015). These reactions suggest the extent of cultural investment in normative conceptions of ageing, in which the decline narrative and the successful ageing narrative have socio-cultural expediency because they allow generational relations to be policed, and aged bodies to be situated and constrained in socio-economic and cultural terms (see Gullette 2004). Tom Cruise, based on these press reactions, is marked as too successful in his attempts to age successfully. But how does this supposedly 'forever young' body register outside of the discourse of celebrity takedowns, in the action cinema?

Early Cruise action melodramas like *Top Gun* (Tony Scott, 1986) and *Days of Thunder* (Tony Scott, 1990) staged what Gaylyn Studlar has called Cruise's 'male exhibitionism' (2001: 175, 181) as a movement between a vehicular form of highly mobile spatial penetration in which the body itself was mostly obscured, and the display of a fairly static, fetishised Cruise body in the scenes outside the vehicle (the beach volleyball scene in *Top Gun* in comparison to the aerial dogfight sequences, for example). This changed with the first *Mission: Impossible* film, in which Cruise starred as secret agent Ethan Hunt. The film is declarative in its construction of a new Cruise action body, and what would become Cruise's signature mode of action exhibitionism. There are two key facets of this action exhibitionism: acrobatic physical extension, and running at pace and at length, both forms of spatial extension that are emphatically rooted in the body. In the most famous scene in *Mission: Impossible*, Ethan is lowered into a vault whose security features include alarms which can be triggered by sound, floor pressure, and changes in room temperature. Ethan must access the vault terminal, download data and avoid detection, all while suspended by a cable that is being held in place by his colleague Franz Krieger (Jean Reno) in the ceiling air vent. Lowered in upside down, Ethan silently spins himself 180 degrees in order to set up a temperature gauge, and then flattens his body into a 'plank' to operate the vault computer terminal. Even as Cruise's blood-flushed face and neck signal the effort to sustain these acrobatics, the nimbleness and smoothness of the adjustments in orientation are striking, generating an appreciation for the actor's, as well as the character's, ability to retain precise physical control under duress. This appreciation is intensified when Krieger, distracted by a rat, lets go of the cable, plunging Ethan towards the floor until he is only centimetres away from the floor's pressure sensors. Cruise performs the fictional character's desperation to maintain balance without touching the floor by moving his arms around slightly manically, movements that are necessary to the performance of the character's predicament but which risk destabilising the actor's body in the process. This legible commitment to the physical dimensions of action performance is much-publicised in marketing paratexts, but is also phenomenologically tangible and impactful in the viewing experience.

It is the same commitment we see Cruise applying to his running scenes, in which he is often depicted running at pace for significantly extended periods. An emphatic example is the scene in *Mission: Impossible III* (J. J. Abrams, 2006), in which Ethan must sprint across the roofs and walkways of Xitang river town to reach his fiancée (Michelle Monaghan) before she is killed by villain Davian (Philip Seymour Hoffman). Key to the scene is a ten-second extended take which foregrounds in real time the actor's maintenance of an intense rate of physical exertion over duration. In a series of long shots, Cruise sustains a rigidly demarcated upright physical form including contained, efficient arm swings, and an intensity of speed and direction, despite the onward approach of obstacles and changes in running surface and terrain layout. The affective 'punch' of this almost-real-time spectacle of continuous running is further anchored by Cruise's vocal performance as he shouts 'Get out of the way' in Mandarin, his voice wobbling and straining awkwardly. Likely to have been re-recorded in the studio via the Automatic Dialogue Replacement (ADR) process, this performance is a convincing aural depiction of how timbre and vocal phrasing can be distorted by physical exertion. The control of vocal and facial performance is sacrificed, then, in the service of communicating physical control and intensity, a prioritisation that distinguishes Cruise from other action stars, young or old. It is this much-publicised commitment to the physical intensity of his action roles (even if he might look and sound less composed in the process) that generates regular acknowledgement and admiration of Cruise's physical aptitude from film reviewers. It has even spawned an internet meme, 'Tom Cruise Running', which includes various compilations of his running scenes on YouTube and Tumblr.[8] As Taffy Brodesser-Akner enthuses in a recent *New York Times* piece, 'the aspect that sometimes seemed to dog his other acting – that famous Cruise intensity, that overwhelming desire to keep you entertained – actually becomes an asset in an action film. He would be this thing with every fiber [sic] of his being. He would become the action hero' (2013, paragraph 15). But how do these qualities resonate as Cruise ages?

THE AGEING CRUISE

The *Mission: Impossible* franchise has spanned almost two decades, and therefore inevitably marks out milestones in the ageing of the biological entity Tom Cruise: we know rationally that he is getting older, even if the visual evidence is not always forthcoming. Writing just at the point – in 2001 – that Cruise was attempting the transition from 'All-American boy' roles to more mature protagonists, Studlar was intrigued by the possible consequences of Cruise's future ageing on his status as a film star, ending her essay with the question: 'If the mature body of Tom Cruise becomes "unseen" [that is, no longer offered as an object of the gaze] will we remain interested?' (2001: 172, 182). But this isn't quite what has happened. Rather than covering up, in several of his most recent films, including *Mission: Impossible – Ghost Protocol* and *Jack Reacher* (Christopher McQuarry, 2012), Cruise strips to his torso, a tendency rather derided by the celebrity press, and one that has mostly been interpreted as a denial of ageing through an attempted assertion of continued virility (a response that is itself structured by ageist discourse). *Jack Reacher* debunks this motivation from within the fictional world of the film in the scene in which Helen (Rosamund Pike) misreads the motivation for Jack (Cruise) stripping to the waist during a discussion of the case they are working. They are in Jack's motel room, and Jack has taken off his jumper and shirt to wash them ready for the following day (he has limited clothing as he has been on the run), but Helen misunderstands, thinking he is propositioning her, an impression she begins to articulate before realising her mistake. Aside from the rather unnecessary humiliation of Pike's character, the inclusion of the scene in the film, without obvious narrative motivation, suggests that there is something more to Cruise's bodily display in these recent movies. Studlar assumed that Cruise would want to hide those changes in muscle mass and structure that often occur in midlife ageing, but instead Cruise, in films he also produces and therefore has some control over, insists on displaying those changes, so that a series of movies are now mapping the visibly changing structure of his ageing torso.[9] The effect is to acknowledge and foreground his own ageing process over time, and to acknowledge its dialogic relation over time to the fitness regimes through which he attempts to stay lean and fit and the spectacles they still make possible.

Cruise's evolving visible body is matched by an evolution in this ageing action hero's physical performances and their narrative framing. *Mission: Impossible – Ghost Protocol* provides a useful example. It begins with a confident, even cocky, physical performance from Cruise, as Ethan breaks out of a Russian prison, a friend in tow. The sequence showcases his trademarks, as Ethan propels his body over a walkway fence bar and drops silently down onto the walkway level below, in a chain of smoothly executed gymnastic moves, and then proceeds to fight and run with a droll efficiency. Yet the film draws back from this certainty almost immediately, enacting a narrative swing between mission success and mission failure that will structure the entirety of the remaining running time, and which is frequently mapped directly onto the capacities of Cruise's body. When Ethan escapes from a Russian hospital, where he has been taken after being unexpectedly caught up in a bomb attack on the Kremlin for which he is being framed, he flees through a hospital window and out onto a ledge four storeys up. Based on the frequency with which Cruise performs acrobatic feats in the *Mission: Impossible* franchise, and based on the ease with which he executed the move between walkways at the start of the film, the audience might reasonably expect Ethan to make short work of this escape. Yet the Russian policeman who he slipped by discovers him hesitating on the ledge, Cruise's body performing the clenched muscles, push forward and definitive recoil as Ethan repeatedly steels himself to go through with the jump to a waste-disposal skip below, and repeatedly fails to initiate it. The policeman who watches from a nearby window is so sure he won't jump that he lights a cigarette to enjoy the show, but as a van approaches Ethan uses an electricity supply line as a zip wire to launch himself at the van so that its momentum can break his fall to the pavement. What is significant is not just the hesitation before the jump, but Ethan's surprised expression at the end of the jump as he realises he has made it: the implication is that he was fully expecting not to be successful in the endeavour, but tried anyway. Later Ethan is uncharacteristically happy to verbalise his reluctance to risk life and limb in an operation to climb the outside of the world's tallest building, the Burj Khalifa in Dubai. No longer the stoic, confident agent, he asks, 'How am I supposed to do this?' before his attempt, and there is a long pause at the window's edge before initiating the task that speaks of genuine trepidation. It is a trepidation that is borne out by malfunctioning equipment: falls threaten after one of the magnetised gloves that hold him to the building surface short-circuits, when the glass cutter he is using to breach the target window explodes, and when he must use a length of canvas rope which is too short to try to swing back into the window from which he started. Moreover, the resulting final giant jump misfires, so that he bounces off the top of the window frame and is only saved by his colleagues who grab his legs to stop his fall. Yet at the same time, when the solution to the problem of the too-short rope presents itself, he does not hesitate to attempt the giant jump, assertively throwing his body into it.

As in this example, Cruise frequently now plays characters within whom a tension exists between a hesitating uncertainty about whether the body can still match its younger capacities, and an openness to trying anyway. Such characters are, in a sense, a response to the phenomenological force of Cruise's own body-in-motion, which increasingly pulls in two directions: between the normative implications of visible ageing on the one hand, and the achievement of the same levels of stretching acrobatic agility that we are familiar with from earlier in his action career on the other. Cruise retains a flexible relation to ageing that marks him out from other ageing action stars, but not because he is still 'forever young'. Where the 'uncanny' of the other ageing action bodies we have considered was generated by the clear difference between present and younger selves, a difference that serves to unproblematically reinforce the decline narrative, the 'Tom Cruise uncanny' depends on eroding that difference – and by extension eroding culturally imposed generational boundaries – through a dynamic and shifting confusion of (normatively speaking) ageing and youthful attributes and attitudes. In contrast to other ageing action hero films, where hesitation to act speaks of a hero's stable relation to normatively defined and supposedly irreversible forms of age-related diminution, hesitation in a Cruise-in-age film represents a liminal state of possibility that may be triggered by ageing but is certainly not bound by it. Cruise's increasingly open acknowledgement that he performs his action exhibitionism with a body that is starting to visually evidence signs of age productively moves Cruise's ageing action star body outside of the frame of decline and attempted disavowal that structures other ageing action hero movies. Cruise's famous corporeal intensity and form, sustained in an openly midlife Cruise body, reminds us that the middle-aged body has the capacity to be physically powerful outside of narratives of lost youthfulness and evocations of past glories. As a result, while Cruise's real-world access to highly expensive and bespoke forms of cosmetic expertise and physical and nutritional regimes does not trouble decline narratives, I suggest that the affective qualities of his action stardom as it is performed and showcased in action might.

NOTES

1. 'Dadcore' can refer to music that one's father listened to, or, according to Taylor, 1980s and '90s 'macho' movies. See Patches 2013, Singer 2014 and Tucker 2014 on the modern ageing action star.
2. Christine Holmlund (on Clint Eastwood) and Yvonne Tasker (on Sylvester Stallone) offer eloquent descriptions of their subjects' physiological appearances, but are less specific about the detail of their performances-in-motion (for example, Holmlund's comment that Eastwood's movements are 'not as "catlike" as Leone originally found them' (2002: 148) seems ripe for further elaboration).
3. Wayne in *The Green Berets* (1968), *Rio Lobo* (1970), *Cahill U.S. Marshall* (1973), *McQ* (1974) and *Brannigan* (1975); Lancaster in *Ulzana's Raid* (1972), *Go Tell The Spartans* (1978) and *Zulu Dawn* (1979); Eastwood in *In the Line of Fire* (1993), *Blood Work* (2002) and *Gran Torino* (2008); Ford in *Firewall* (2006), *Indiana Jones and the Kingdom of the Crystal Skull* (2008), *Cowboys and Aliens* (2011) and *Star Wars: The Force Awakens* (2015).
4. See Ford 1976 [1971], Holmlund 2002 and Tasker 2014.
5. Some (Clooney, Cruise) are prolific producers beyond their own vehicles; others (Cage, Washington, Lundgren, Willis) produce to ensure a variety of starring roles or to extend their career, or both. The disparity with 1980s female action stars (Cynthia Rothrock with five extant producer credits, Sigourney Weaver with two, Brigitte Nielsen with one) reflects disparities in gender and race shaping the 'occupational life-course' more generally in the US, and in Hollywood (Lincoln and Allen 2004: 611–12).
6. See Boyle and Brayton 2012 on the casting of celebrity athletes in *The Expendables*.
7. See Patches 2013, Singer 2014, Tucker 2014 and Lee 2015.
8. For example: 'Tom Cruise Running', https://www.youtube.com/watch?v=NJd MDvjfyQ0; 'Run Tom Run – Ultimate Tom Cruise Running Mashup' (2015) HD; https://www.youtube.com/watch?v=qicaxJLxuOI; 'Tom Cruise Running', http://tomcruiserunning.tumblr.com/; and 'Why Is Tom Cruise Running?', http://whyis tomcruiserunning.tumblr.com/.
9. In *Mission: Impossible – Rogue Nation* (2015), *Oblivion* (Joseph Kosinski, 2013), *Jack Reacher*, *Rock of Ages* (Adam Shankman, 2012), *Mission: Impossible – Ghost Protocol*, *Knight and Day* (James Mangold, 2010).

BIBLIOGRAPHY

Affron, Charles (1977), *Star Acting: Gish, Garbo, Davis*, New York: Dutton.

Boshoff, Alison and Claire Cisotti (2011), 'Tom Cruise: 25 years on – and not a day older', *Daily Mail*, 15 December, http://www.dailymail.co.uk/femail/article-2074366/Tom-Cruise-25-years--day-older.html.

Boyle, Ellexis and Sean Brayton (2012), 'Ageing Masculinities and "Muscle work" in Hollywood Action Film: An Analysis of *The Expendables*', *Men and Masculinities* 15:5, 468–85.

Brodesser-Akner, Taffy (2013), 'Learning to (Re)Love Tom Cruise', *The New York Times Magazine*, 19 April, http://www.nytimes.com/2013/04/21/magazine/learning-to-re-love-tom-cruise.html.

Dahistrom, Linda (2012), 'How Tom Cruise has turned into Benjamin Button', *Today*, 27 February, http://www.today.com/health/how-tom-cruise-has-turned-benjamin-button-222133.

Daily Mail reporter (2010), 'Action man Tom Cruise shows how he stays in shape at 48 (albeit an odd one)', *Mail Online*, 7 October, http://www.dailymail.co.uk/tvshowbiz/article-1318522/Even-Tom-Cruise-action-man-fight-onset-middle-aged-spread.html.

DeFalco, Amelia (2010), *Uncanny Subjects: Aging in Contemporary Narrative*, Columbus: Ohio State University Press.

Dyer, Richard (1987), *Heavenly Bodies: Film Stars and Society*, London: Macmillan.

Ford, Greg (1976 [1971]), 'Mostly on *Rio Lobo*', in Bill Nichols (ed.), *Movies and Methods*, London: University of California Press, pp. 344–54.

Gullette, Margaret Morganroth (1998), 'Midlife Discourses in the Twentieth-Century United States: An Essay on the Sexuality, Ideology, and Politics of "Middle-Ageism"', in Richard A. Shweder (ed.), *Welcome to Middle Age! (And Other Cultural Fictions)*, Chicago: University of Chicago Press, pp. 3–44.

Gullette, Margaret Morganroth (2004), *Aged by Culture*, London: University of Chicago Press.

Hallam, Julia and Margaret Marshment (2000), *Realism and Popular Cinema*, Manchester: Manchester University Press.

Holmlund, Chris (2002), *Impossible Bodies: Femininity and Masculinity at the Movies*, London: Routledge.

Hornaday, Ann (2015), 'The fifth "Mission: Impossible" injects wit and energy into the franchise', *The Washington Post*, 30 July, http://www.washingtonpost.com/goingoutguide/movies/the-fifth-mission-impossible-injects-new-wit-and-energy-into-the-franchise/2015/07/30/d8564b6c-3606-11e5-9739-170df8af8eb9_story.html.

Huffington Post staff writer (2014), 'Tom Cruise Turns 52 Years Old But He Hasn't Aged A Day', *The Huffington Post Canada*, 7 March, http://www.huffingtonpost.ca/2014/07/03/tom-cruise_n_5554919.html.

Jeffers, Susan (1994), *Hard Bodies: Hollywood Masculinity in the Reagan Era*, New Brunswick, NJ: Rutgers University Press.

Katz, Stephen and Barbara L. Marshall (2003), 'New sex for old: Lifestyle, consumption and the ethics of aging well', *Journal of Aging Studies* 17:1, 3–16.

King, Barry (1991 [1985]), 'Articulating Stardom', in Christine Gledhill (ed.), *Stardom: Industry of Desire*, London: Routledge, pp. 167–82.

King, Barry (2014), *Taking Fame to Market: On the Pre-History and Post-History of Hollywood Stardom*, Basingstoke: Palgrave Macmillan.

Klevan, Andrew (2005), *Film Performance: From Achievement to Appreciation*, London: Wallflower Press.

Lane, Anthony (2015), 'Long Runs: "Mission: Impossible – Rogue Nation," "The End of the Tour," and "Best of Enemies"', *The New Yorker*, 10 August, http://www.new yorker.com/magazine/2015/08/10/long-runs.

Lee, Benjamin (2015), 'Liam Neeson's special set of skills has forced other ageing actors into training', *The Guardian*, 26 February, http://www.theguardian.com/film/ filmblog/2015/feb/26/liam-neeson-taken-3-sean-penn-the-gunman.

Lehman, Peter (1993), *Running Scared: Masculinity and the Representation of the Male Body*, Philadelphia: Temple University Press.

Lincoln, Anne E. and Michael Patrick Allen (2004), 'Double Jeopardy in Hollywood: Age and Gender in the Careers of Film Actors, 1926–1999', *Sociological Forum* 19:4, 611–31.

Martinson, Marty and Meredith Minkler (2006), 'Civic Engagement and Older Adults: A Critical Perspective', *The Gerontologist* 46:3, 318–23.

McDonald, Paul (1998), 'Reconceptualising Stardom', in Richard Dyer, *Stars*, 2nd edn, London: BFI, pp. 175–211.

Naremore, James (1988), *Acting in the Cinema*, London: University of California Press.

Patches, Matt (2013), 'On the Rise of the Geri-Action Movies', *Vulture*, 19 July, http:// www.vulture.com/2013/07/on-the-rise-of-the-geri-action-movie.html.

Phoenix, Cassandra and Andrew C. Sparkes (2008), 'Athletic bodies and aging in context: The narrative construction of experienced and anticipated selves in time', *Journal of Aging Studies* 22:3, 211–21.

Purse, Lisa (2011), *Contemporary Action Cinema*, Edinburgh: Edinburgh University Press.

Singer, Matt (2014), 'Op-ed: The slow and slightly creaky rise of the old-man action movie', *The Dissolve*, 4 March, https://thedissolve.com/news/1635-op-ed-the-very-slow-and-slightly-creaky-rise-of-th/.

Sternagel, Jörg (2012), '"Look at Me!" A Phenomenology of Heath Ledger in *The Dark Knight*', in Aaron Taylor (ed.), *Theorizing Film Acting*, London: Routledge, pp. 93–106.

Studlar, Gaylyn (2001), 'Cruise-ing into the Millennium: Performative Masculinity Stardom, and the All-American Boy's Body', in Murray Pomerance (ed.), *Ladies and Gentlemen, Boys and Girls: Gender in film at the End of the Millennium*, Albany: State University of New York Press, pp. 171–83.

Tasker, Yvonne (1993), *Spectacular Bodies: Gender, Genre and the Action Cinema*, London and New York: Routledge.

Tasker, Yvonne (2014), 'Stallone, Ageing and Action Authenticity', in Chris Holmlund (ed.), *The Ultimate Stallone Reader: Sylvester Stallone as Star, Icon, Auteur*, London: Wallflower Press, pp. 241–62.

Taylor, Drew (2014), 'From *Die Hard* to *Non-Stop*: The Beginner's Guide to "Dadcore"', *Vanity Fair*, 24 February, http://www.vanityfair.com/hollywood/2014/02/guide-to-dadcore.

Tucker, Reed (2014), 'Hollywood loves its ageing action heroes', *New York Post*, 16 February, http://nypost.com/2014/02/16/ready-aim-retired/.

Vincendeau, Ginette (2000), *Stars and Stardom in French Cinema*, London: Continuum.

Wills, Garry (1997), *John Wayne: The Politics of Celebrity*, London: Faber & Faber.

Woodward, Kathleen (1988–89), 'Youthfulness as Masquerade', *Discourse* 11:1 (Fall–Winter), 119–42.

PART 5

STARS AND AUDIENCES

9. HEROINES AT THE OUTSKIRTS OF CULTURE: HOLLYWOOD STARDOM IN INTRA- AND TRANSCULTURAL PRACTICES OF *CAMP*

Anna Malinowska

INTRODUCTION

Studies in star phenomena have paid considerable attention to the working of stardom in intra- and transcultural appropriations of stars' images (Dyer 1986, Jenkins 1992, McDonald 2000, Hills 2002, Chin and Hitchcock-Morimoto 2013). A great part of this attention has been dedicated to Hollywood stardom – an unquestionable blueprint for star/celebrity systems and the image-making process in both mainstream and oppositional practices of cultural production. As a vast term of a significant importance for most cultural development, Hollywood, although measured by its achievements in cinema, extends far beyond the filmic context, and when talking about it today, we talk less about a filmic phenomenon than about a cultural concept representative of various levels of cultural manufacture from filming aesthetics, working styles and presentation codes to manners and modes of artistic expression (Neale 1998, Schatz 2004). The change in theorising Hollywood is perhaps due to the impact its forms and styles had exerted on the culture industry for almost half a century of its monopoly over American film. During its golden period from 1927 to 1963, Hollywood created star iconographies: images, lifestyles, behavioural patterns and archetypes that did, and still do, appeal to Western and non-Western systems of culture. Becoming a potent fantasy-making arena, Hollywood has operated within a complex network of cultural and economic markets that partake in the deployment and management as well as recycling and exploitation of fantasy. Many of them do it in ways that exceed the fantasy's filmic environment.

A system that perhaps best reflects on the non-cinematic uses of filmic utopias is *fandom*. Represented by a variety of audience phenomena, it plays a crucial role for the distribution and maintenance of film images. Fandom performs an interpretative function used for transcoding imagined worlds onto discourses of reality. Being 'associated with the cultural tastes of subordinated formations of people, particularly those disempowered by any combination of gender, age, class, and race' (Fisk 1992: 30 in Gray et al. 2007: 2), fandom is a space in which *the imaginary* turns into *the real* through the transposition of film fiction onto realities of everyday life. Although it interplays with various levels of cinematic creation, fandom predominantly engages with characters, embodiments and impersonations encoded through star images and vice versa. It responds to the *manufacture of image* (Dyer 2013) and *production of desire* (Gledhill 2003), attributed to the making of screen fantasy and, as such, becomes a platform for practices that exploit both stars' 'on-screen performances' and the 'meanings about human identity' they represent (McDonald 2000: 1).

The importance of audience activities for Hollywood lies in the willingness with which fans engage with its images for reliving film fantasy through the incorporation of what stars become (privately and professionally) to their lives. As Dyer has observed, audiences transform a star's images to serve their needs, and even if '[they] cannot make media images mean anything they want to, [. . .] they can select from the complexity of the image the meanings and feelings, the variations, inflections and contradictions, that work for them' (2013: 218). Contemporary fandom is characterised by a varying degree of commitment to stars. The commitment may range from passive admiration to an engaged cult, the latter manifesting itself through ultra-exploitative worship (for example, lookalikes, star impersonators) that appropriates star images for non-cinematic (ab)uses. Being probably the most radical, and therefore most interesting, form of audiences' response to film fantasy, exploitative fandom opens a star's images to external contexts: artistic, aesthetic, social, cultural. Practised outside a filmic setting yet in connection with film fantasy, it informs us about the possibilities of stardom beyond their cinematic narratives; it also shows what stardom can become when taken away from circumstances specified by the policies of showbiz, as well as what it transforms into when entangled with the meshes of fans' personal lives and social issues those lives relate to.

The interest of this chapter is in exploitative fandom, and specifically in the practice of *camp*, whose connection with stardom has been identified through the subversive uses of stars' images (Dyer 2013, Tinkcom 2002). *Camp* has contributed to stardom processes from the beginning of the Hollywood system and falls into a large mimicry tradition of gay and lesbian subcultures that, as Dyer observes, 'have used Hollywood stars as important figures in their discourse' (138). Being probably the first example of a subcultural audience movement, and a practice to exploit stars' images outside the cinematic context, *camp* has been a way of showing how a star's image can be re-read through a subversive encoding. Under the guise of cross-dressing strategies, it has engaged in the adoption of Hollywood images to access signification codes of dominant culture for the reproduction of the social significance of the marginalised by transforming the culture's most significant symbols and tropes. It has explored stardom for its transgressive potential and enjoyed stars' images 'not for any supposed inner essence revealed but for the way they jump through the hoops of social convention' (Dyer 2013: 14), using the glamour of Hollywood stardom to produce visibility and acceptance but also to reform the *cultural* norms that *glamour* originates from.

To reflect on the complexity of *camp*'s engagement with stardom, this chapter analyses the exploitative rendition of star images – specifically of female icons – *camp* has offered in personal (private) and professional (public) performances in Western and non-Western cultural contexts. The analysis proceeds in two parts. Part one presents the cultural background of *camp*'s engagement with star images as well as concentrating on perspectives that identify *camp* star impersonation as exploitative fandom, whose 'textual poaching' leads to the production of alternative systems of stardom based on the borrowing of stars' screen images and their relocation to real life for exploitative purposes. Part two studies examples of *camp* mimicry as practised outside the cultural environment of Hollywood, drawing on Michał Witkowski's documentary novel *Lubiewo*. It provides an insight into transcultural adaptations of star images reported in stories about the life of queers in early post-communist Poland, and analyses *camp*'s interpretations of stardom made in socio-cultural circumstances foreign to the American system of stardom and outside its cultural-geographical location. This part specifically explores three aspects of *camp*'s engagement with Western stardom: (1) the working of an imagined participation with the realities of American culture and the employment of signifying codes the culture confers on the figure of star; (2) the construction of cultural homologies for reliving the utopia of glamour offered in star images to other cultural backgrounds; and (3), most importantly, the abuse of star images by adapting them to an environment that, being incompatible with their texts, violates its sublime and de-romanticises the fantasy the sublime creates.

The chapter explores *camp* in terms of exploitative fandom, understood as abusive worship disconnected from 'gay and lesbian middle-class assimilationism' (Meyer 1994: 2) whose imitative practices alienate stars from their images. It shows how, by taking stars' mainstream images to the margins of culture, *camp* exploits the glamorous and the sublime of a star and destabilises the idea of stardom itself.

CAMP AND FILM STARDOM

Camp is a cultural system of pose-making invented for the (re)construction of a 'homosexual sign' (Meyer 1994) and the production of queer presence in the straight cultural landscape of Western societies. Despite its indifference to political issues (Sontag 2013; Britton 1999; Booth 1984), *camp* has been considered an important link between art, culture and public gender policy formation, with a role of merging peripheral preferences and central aesthetics. Being both a quality in art (Sontag 2013) and a performative practice developed from eighteenth-century transvestite rituals, *camp* is 'the ensemble of strategies used to enact a queer recognition of the incongruities arising from the cultural regulation of gender and sexuality' (Cohan 2005: 1). It is a style that, by glamorising sexual difference, counterbalances the homonormative system of representation.

Camp's connection with Hollywood has manifested itself in two main ways: through the work of queer artists within the mainstream entertainment industry, and through the trans-semiotic re-readings of Hollywood narratives, specifically star images, that queer audiences have engaged with for the purpose of altering the social perception of queerness. The first is linked with the invention and spread of *gay sensibility* – 'a creative energy reflecting a consciousness that is different from the mainstream' (Babuscio 1999: 118) – which, by turning itself into a form of oppositional labour, has allowed gay people to contribute to culture and produce some social visibility (Meyer 1994; Tinkcom 2002). The latter manifestation refers to the representational technique of *camping* and the ways in which *camp* approaches dominant systems of signification. With regard to stardom, the technique relies on manipulating stars' cultural codes and transforming stars' images into alternative standards of sophistication. *Camp* is a recycler of popular texts and a ground for intertextual practices. By bringing together the mainstream and the marginal, the normative and the queer, *camp* reverses the dominant hierarchy of meaning and, as such, it elicits new senses from texts that have seemed semantically stable, rigid, reserved and irreversible.

In terms of style, *camp* is 'a great jewel, 22 carats' (Williams in Cleto 1999: 1) – too heavy, too shiny, and aesthetically vulgar. Its performances are characterised by 'representational excess, heterogeneity, and *gratuitousness* of references' (Cleto 1999: 3, italics in original), which makes it one of the most eclectic styles in the history of postmodern culture. Representations in *camp* are bricolages of textual solutions, images and tropes formed along tacky humour and excessive theatrical manner. Surplus forms that *camp* combines in its pose produce histrionic flamboyance, which, as Steven Cohan (2005) observes, is 'a fundamental component of [*camp*'s] joke' (1), which has allowed *camp* to detach itself from common aesthetic standards:

> *Camp* strategies for achieving ironic distance from the normative have always exploited the slippery space between 'posture' and 'imposture', between 'resembling' and 'dissembling' – in one way or another *camp* signals the queer eye for a straight guise. (1)

Stars' images became part of *camp* strategic acts in the early 1920s, following the emergence of film celebrities and the transition of the Hollywood style to female-impersonation shows. Early cultural descriptions of *camping* reflected the shift by marking the lean towards filmic props and people in *camp*'s generic definitions. Only at the beginning of the twentieth century, *camp* was described as 'actions and gestures of exaggerated emphasis [. . .] used chiefly by persons of exceptional want of character' (Ware 1909: 61). Forty years later, *camp* carried a strong cinematic connotation and meant 'a swishy little boy with peroxided hair in a picture hat and a feather boa, pretending to be Marlene Dietrich' (Isherwood 1966: 114).

Camp's inclination for stardom results from the discovery on the part of *camp* that star images are equipped with a certain 'magical' superpower. The superpower, or *charisma* as Max Weber has called it, is what has 'set [stars] apart from ordinary men and [made them] treated as endowed with super-natural, superhuman or at least superficially exceptional qualities' (Weber in Tinkcom 2002: 83). Charisma works as a form of agency for mediating a star's social position. When incorporated into the ground of *camp*'s closet culture, it spreads the mediating power onto queer subjects, allowing them to negotiate their presence in the mainstream through the use of the appeal associated with an image of a star or her characters. In other words, *camp* employs a star's images to aestheticise social difference and bridge it with the use of the normative canon of sophistication. Although aware of how wide and irreversible the gap actually is, *camp* engages with stardom through image manufacture, and expresses an ambition of a queer to possess those aspects of a star's charisma (outstanding beauty, exceptional wit, notable talent) that would help a queering subject reconstruct his or her socio-cultural space.

Camp's interest in Hollywood stardom has been inspired by the new possibilities of image-making that stars have introduced to cultural practice with their 'spectacles of glamour' (Tinkcom 2002). As a modality of pleasure and variant of reality, glamour 'is the sense that an image achieves what could never be made to happen in our own everyday efforts' (83). Despite that seeming unattainability, audiences – normative or subcultural – have re-created glamour in their daily existence, even if only through consuming the imagined realities of film narratives, for the purpose of overcoming the plainness of life's mundane scenarios. But whereas for normative audiences, glamour is a source of temporary distraction located in the sphere of the unreal, for *camp* it is a fantasy-making arena whose patterns of perfection can be transferred to and used in a real life. As such, *camp* is a practice aimed at reproducing the fantastic of glamour outside a cinematic world, in spectacles that, by a stylistic appropriation of the cultural idea of chic and excellence, allow for reliving or, actually, re-experiencing the Hollywood utopia in everyday life.

The recycling of glamour in *camp*, although it is common to many sub-cultural uses of stardom, meets criteria that make some forms of star imper-sonation so very much *camp*'s. First, *camp* concentrates on those aspects of an image that enable a travesty of dominant socio-cultural standards: 'the undulating contours of Mae West, the lumbering gait and drawling voice of John Wayne, the thin, spiky smile of Joan Fontaine – each can be taken as an emblem of social mores' (Dyer 2013: 14). *Camp* undertakes them and trans-lates them into non-cinematic planes to be used in reality for the production of countercultural, that is, anti-normative, spaces within the mainstream.

Second, despite occasional involvement with male images, *camp* inclines towards female forms (Tinkcom 2002). The passion for *the feminine* has been formative for the entire tradition of *camp* performance – especially its modern history, associated with drag queenism, and reflected in the cross-dressing careers of most influential *camp* practitioners such as Charles Pierce, Jim Bailey, Candy Darling or Divine, whose send-ups of Hollywood divas (Judy Garland, Marilyn Monroe, Elizabeth Taylor, Bette Davis, Joan Crawford, and so on) linked iconic femininity/femininities with postmodern forms of representational recycling, as well as rendered gender traits and mannerisms in ways transcending the already excessive cultural images of femaleness (see Figure 9.1). The role of female stardom for *camp*'s performative tradition reminds us also that *camping* is not about any type of femininity but about a

Figure 9.1   Charles Pierce's impersonation of Bette Davis.

particular female image, constructed via a capitalist market economy, social recognition and cultural modes of appreciation. *Camp* engages with femininity that comes from the heart of dominant gender codes and stereotypical gender representations; it is femininity that corresponds with the earliest examples of the Hollywood male gaze formed along a set of dramatic effects, which brings back pre-feminist, overly eroticised images of a female body.

The relationship between *camp* and a female star is in fact the relationship between the perfection of a female image that a star is able to conjure up, and a performative potential born from the perfection's representational power. Even if *camp does* rely on the attributes of a female image resulting from the objectifying work of a camera, props, screenplay and other aspects of image-making, its performances do not re-create objectification. Rather they re-create the power of what comes out from objectifying – the star's exposed sex appeal, wit and general divinity – and use them as a force against the limiting work of objectification. An illustrative case for understanding this mechanism is the use of Marlene Dietrich's image from *The Blue Angel* (1930) in Visconti's *The Damned* (1969). I am specifically referring to Helmut Berger's drag rendition of Dietrich's Lola, which, since the movie's release, has worked as a blueprint for the modern practice of *camp*, and become one of the most iconic and cult moments in cinema history. Visconti employs Dietrich's image to counterbalance the patterns of power which in the movie are represented by the deviant patriarchy of the Essenbecks and their Nazi connections; he puts the image in drag to mock the Essenbeck men's butch masculinity together with gender hierarchies they profess and believe in. Of course, the scene works on two levels and can be read as Martin von Essenbeck's manifestation of his sexual deviancy and defiance of his family values; but also as Helmut Berger's projection of his sexual identity, acknowledged by means of Dietrich's filmic persona. On both levels, however, the scene admits the possibility of creating alternative identity through an image that, although coming from dominant culture, reverses the culture's standards and systems of value.

Most of *camp* criticism, notably Moe Meyer (1994) and Steven Cohan (2005), concentrates on the politics of *camp*'s engagement with star images, forgetting about motivations behind *camp*'s leaning towards stardom. Very few scholars theorise *camp* in terms of audience activities and fandom cultures, which is, in fact, a primary perspective for understanding the complexity of *camp*–stardom symbiotic relations. *Camp* is an interesting material for fandom studies mainly due to the contradictory nature of its fan activities. Although it is seen as a progressive and oppositional practice of culture, *camp* confirms the majority of popular stereotypes of fans which portrays them as 'cultural dupes, social misfits, and mindless consumers' (Jenkins 1994: 23). On the other hand, however, *camp* practitioners contradict those short-sighted accusations by engaging themselves in activities that challenge the dominant status of cultural products and acting 'as readers who appropriate popular texts and reread them in a fashion that serves different interests, as spectators who transform the experience of watching television into a rich and complex participatory culture' (23).

Although the notion of participatory culture in *camp* gets a specific tone – *camping* is, after all, a marginal practice devoid of assimilative aspirations – the processes that *camp* undergoes in relation to stars' images and film fantasies prove it a valuable contributor to the expansion of reading possibilities of popular images and texts. Like other fandom phenomena, *camp* reaches beyond the constraints of images and text imposed on them by their original framing; it extends the text's meanings by stimulating them to further and broader circulation within the area of cultural consumption. Being a cross-textual and cross-stylistic translation of cultural content, *camp* is a form of 'textual poaching', as it manifests the possessive, if not predatory, attitude to cultural texts that Jenkins defines as an 'ongoing struggle between [media producers and audiences] for possession of the text and for control over its meanings' (1994: 24–5). This struggle, Jenkins contends, results from an imbalance between consumers' expectation about the texts and satisfaction the texts provide in the consumption process. Whereas most fan activities result from insufficient satisfaction with texts they nevertheless admire, in *camp* the incentive for re-reading stars' images (or an element of film fantasy) comes not from an utter admiration of the image or fantasy but a dissatisfaction with the limitedness of its cultural dimension. In other words, *camp* enters in a relationship with an image not only due to the unlimited admiration it bestows on it, but due to the limitedness the image carries as encoded in a dominant aesthetics.

<h2 style="text-align:center">WESTERN STARDOM IN TRANSNATIONAL CAMPING</h2>

Camp's engagement with Western star images becomes far more complex for the study of stardom when analysed from the perspective of transnational uses. When re-created beyond their original settings, stars' images undergo re-readings that open them to new semantic possibilities and even further redefine the images' consumerist programming. As a frame for those re-readings, *camp* partakes in the formation of reception processes responsible for conditioning the adoption of cultural products in international environments, and, along with other forms of fandom, it informs us about 'how and why different border-crossing media capture the imaginations of fans, as well as how fans incorporate cross-border media into their own popular cultural contexts and what meanings they attribute to them' (Chin, Hitchcock-Morimoto 2013: 93).

Except perhaps for Quiroga's study on Latino queer (2000), *camp* hardly appears in the discussion of transnational audience phenomena that has continued in fan studies for the last two decades (for example, Jenkins 1992 [2013]; Kreutzner and Seiter 1995; Larkin 1997, 2008; Stokes and Maltby 2001; Austin 2002; Hills 2002; Burnett 2007; Chin and Hitchcock-Morimoto 2013). This omission may result from some tendencies within *camp* theory, especially its preoccupation with Western manifestations of *camping* (mainly British and American), and the focus on *camp*'s political role. Quiroga's description of *camping* in terms of 'an imported aesthetics' (154) returns to thinking of *camp* as a cross-cultural interpreter of styles, one through which international media-facilitated images can be transferred to local grounds. It also inspires an analysis of *camp*'s engagement with stardom from the perspective of transcultural fandom processes responsible for mediating cultural gaps by creating space for cultures to 'participate in the imagined realities of other cultures as part of their daily lives' (Larkin 1997: 409).

An example of this participation I wish to discuss is the use of American star images – specifically, the image of Joan Collins' Alexis from *Dynasty* – by Polish queers in early post-communist Poland. I borrow this example from Michał Witkowski's documentary novel *Lubiewo* (Eng. *Lovetown*, 2004) and present it as reflective of a trend in stars' exploration and a method indicative of *camp* transcultural renditions of Western stardom. My reliance on Witkowski's novel stems from its sociological reliability as a realistic presentation of the life of Poland's queer minorities after communism. Although published as a literary work, the book is a useful source for academic exploration and compensates insufficient scholarly description of queering cultures in Poland. Based on interviews with elderly queers Patricia and Lucretia, two 'filthy' gentlemen whose stories intertwine with profile descriptions of leading 'queens' of the 1970s, '80s and '90s – Paula, Jessica, von Schretke the Countess, Cora, Joanna the Priest's Girl, Giselle, Madame d'Aubergine, La Belle Hélène and others – the book provides an insight into a homosexual ghetto-life in Poland, revealing details of the large-scale cultural transformations Poland underwent after the collapse of the Iron Curtain. Interestingly, the novel reports on new consumption patterns which, previously hindered by the regime, exploded with the arrival of Western commodities, products and contents. It portrays the emergence of new audiences' phenomena formed in the cultural peripheries of a homosexual minority of a non-Western state. Most importantly, it sheds some light on the processes responsible for the change of cultural landscapes in Eastern Europe in the 1990s.

The growing inflow of cultural content from 'the West' after the collapse of the communist bloc opened post-soviet societies to new realities and, consequently, to new cultural developments. Popular culture played a great part in those developments, since its texts resonated with mainstream desires, offering narratives which, although foreign to the experiences of Eastern audiences, stimulated cultural change. The working of Western texts during the transition period was usually twofold: firstly, they exposed the difference between 'the East' and 'the West', promoting an idealistic, if not utopian, vision of the latter shown as a promise of success and prosperity for all; secondly, they inspired a variety of processes that allowed Eastern societies to participate in the new cultural realities, either by passive consumption or by an attempted implementation of their ideas and contents to their lives (suddenly possible due to the change to a market economy). The images of Western stars stimulated that participation by epitomising the ideal of a Western lifestyle. In this sense, they extended the role of an entertainer they had in their home environments. Stars have been texts responsible for conjuring up narratives of compensation and distraction – ones that provide 'liberation from the chaffing bonds of the official world of factory, school or office, or from the worries of running the home', as well as from 'the prohibitions and demands of society' (Ang 1984: 362). When consumed in foreign settings, however, that is, from the perspective of an incompatible cultural position, they additionally become the ambassadors of realities that are either completely unknown to the new audiences or lost from their cultural landscape; in the case of Poland, the reappearance of Western stardom in national media meant a return of the idea of the movie star to a culture that had been for long denied involvement in world heritage.

The awareness of a status of the world movie star – of what a movie star has been in the Western sense – was very strong in Poland during the interwar period. *Piętro wyżej* (*One Floor Above*), a 1937 movie directed by Leon Trystan, expresses the awareness quite directly by re-creating an image of Mae West for a scene that intends to render the idea of stardom via the glamour of the female sex. The scene is announced in the following manner: 'Ladies and gentlemen, and now the attraction of this evening! Our charming and home-made Mae West!', and makes a tribute to Mae West as an enactment of 'the experience of being a person in a particular kind of social production (capitalism), with its particular organisation of life into public and private spheres', a person who 'represent[s] how we think the experience is or how it would be lovely to feel that it is' (Dyer 2013: 15). The re-creation of the image of Mae West in *Piętro wyżej* is also probably the first *camp* moment in Polish cinema, as her impersonation is of a transvestite character and points to the high affinity of Polish homosexual culture with the tradition of *camping* in the West.

The idea of stardom was back in the repertoires of Polish queers with the advent of TV series, serials and soap operas in the 1990s. Star images emerging from those televisual forms were, however, different from their Hollywood predecessors as they organised stardom around generic demands: 'exaggerated plots', 'melodramatic effect' and 'penchant for the sensational' (Ang 2013: 1945–9) rather than a star's persona. They have, nevertheless, provided narrative intensity able to beget new cultural myths, eagerly adapted to everyday life and re-created in identity performances.

Witkowski's *Lubiewo* has registered the working of those myths in an environment marked with double marginality; as I mention earlier in this chapter, Polish queerdom of the 1990s was a subculture stigmatised with a local and global exclusion, and might be characterised as a group alienated from social processes in a society that had itself developed away from major cultural narratives and representational trends. Adaptation practices the group opened itself to with the use of Western texts aimed at minimising this double exclusion and bridging conflicting cultural territories. They also enhanced oppositional readings of popular texts to test them outside their cultural contexts, producing concurring realities which would allow Polish queers to participate in normative trends of Western culture but at the same time exist outside of them. A case which illustrates this strategy in Witkowski's *Lubiewo* is the use of the image of Alexis Carrington-Colby of *Dynasty* by middle-aged pansy Jessica, who adopts the actress' filmic persona for a daily struggle against the oppressing hetero-norm at the beginning of the transition period in Poland. Jessica's impressions of Alexis might be considered as an advanced form of interaction with a star's image for re-creating the image contexts through a personal performance into a local setting. As such it may be seen as an attempt to transfer the exotic cultural texts (and textures) that Alexis' image entails to a cultural context irrevocably incompatible with the image and situated away from the image's 'natural' environment.

The choice of the image of Alexis is in itself interesting here, mainly due to the importance of *Dynasty* as a media event. The series has been considered a vital international televisual phenomenon distinguished by its role for shaping new transgressive social patterns, especially with regard to women's position, gender roles and patriarchal oppression (Press 1990, 1991; Kreutzner and Seiter 1995; Gripsrud 1995). The Alexis character is considered a major actor in this process, and most critical studies on *Dynasty* describe her as a major force behind the series' popularity, its social reception and audiences' engaged responses. Played by the British actress Joan Collins, Alexis has been seen as a heroine that 'linked *Dynasty* to a particular line of Hollywood melodrama, namely to those films in which a female character is granted narrative functions usually reserved for a male protagonist' (Kreutzner and Seiter 1995: 246). Her image of an 'aggressive, power hungry and enormously successful career woman' makes her represent 'everything our culture tells us that good women are not' (Press 1990: 164). Alexis became for modern popular television what the characters of Bette Davis, Mae West or Marlene Dietrich were for the silver screen. Constructed along representation patterns of 1950s Hollywood melodrama, she mixes the attributes of feminine charm with a feminist performance. Drawing on Joan Collins' previous infamous roles (*The Stud* 1978, *The Bitch* 1979 and others), Alexis turned into a matrix for catty, coarse womanhood. Although the show has been blamed for its lack of

Figure 9.2   Morgan McMichaels as *Dynasty*'s Alexis.

realistic references (too fantastic to be real), its characters, especially Alexis, resonated with a need for social change, begetting a variety of involvement of both normative and queer audiences (see Figure 9.2).

The cult of Alexis, based on both admiration and hate, is an example of an image fandom (one constructed around a filmic character/role), which, although extended onto a star's private persona, feeds on the filmic reality she belongs to due to her role rather than her real life. The power of the Alexis character stems mainly from her bold and subversive performance she owes to the 'combination of melodramatic fantasy' – appealing to all, and '*camp irony*' – detectable by more sophisticated or homosexual viewers (Gripsrud 1995: 40, Robertson 1996). While for queer American-British audiences, fan uses of her image seem 'natural', its transnational reception, even if marked with dedication and love, reveals cultural frictions that lead to rather abusive fan activities. Witkowski's description of Jessica's engagement with the image of Alexis, which I employ for a case study, points to several 'misuses' of star images in *camp* transnational practices. One of them is 'misused identity', that is, an attempted possession of a transferred star image by the impersonator who treats it as their own and detaches it from its original context. Witkowski writes:

> Jessica had a job as an orderly at the hospital [. . .]. Her [his] life was dominated by television shows. First, it was *Dallas*, then *Return to Eden*, then *North and South*, and at the end, before she died, *Dynasty*, which she watched in the emergency ward. Jessica would wash the dirty

windows in the hospital corridors and see herself reflected in the glass as Alexis. Perhaps it was due to the distance, or the dim light, or something else entirely, but in the glass Jessica's grubby apron, plastered with ID tags and purple stamps, looked just like the white dress worn by Alexis in the last episode. She was speechless with delight, bursting with pride. (Witkowski 2011: 28)

The Polish success of *Dynasty* was connected with the series' appeal to the economic and cultural aspirations Poles manifested after the fall of communism. Whereas for normative audiences it signified endless possibilities and opportunities to pursue, post-communist queers used its images as role-play models to communicate with mainstream society by re-creating the fictitious world's prosperity and sophistication. They did it, however, by oppressing the impersonated image with degrading standards of their home environment, where shabby outfits replaced exquisite garments, and scraped interiors of the lowest workplaces or dwellings worked as luxurious mansions, expensive yachts or modern apartments.

Jessica was filled with joy; she gushed; she was the very picture of a respectable lady! She put on airs and let the patients light her cigarettes and refused to thank them. She held her hair high, put her hair in curling papers, smeared lip balm on her lips and pretended it was lipstick. Often she would go over to the other orderlies and cleaning ladies, take a seat in their cubicles, and fall into the role of a star. (Witkowski 2011: 29)

As I mentioned before, the popularity of Alexis's image, especially among female and queer audiences, has been due to the tint of 'Britishness and bitchiness' she brought to the show – the qualities that have set a new model for subverting 'the practice of feminine exposition within masculine cinema' (Finch 1999: 155, 145). For Polish female audiences, Alexis signified the emancipatory processes of second- and third-wave feminism missing from Poland's cultural experience; she introduced new standards for women's social and professional functioning, making vulgarity a mode of elegance, which appealed to the post-soviet generation of women appropriated by propaganda. Alexis enacted female power which echoed the need for an alteration of gender systems. Polish queers borrowed the image, or as I argue, hijacked it, to empower their position in a society deprived of, but at the same time thirsty for, anything that would separate them from socialist pragmatism: 'Zdzisio just sits there like an empress with his legs crossed, and refuses to eat bread and butter left over from lunch! He uses a glass cigarette holder to smoke his cigarettes! Oh, how he smokes!' (Witkowski 2011: 29–30).

The cross-cultural appropriations of star images in *camp* may be considered a strategy for the formation of 'parallel modernities' – a space and an experience emerging from the exposure to, and consumption of, different cultural content, possible thanks to the new media models and an enhanced cultural flow. The term first appeared through Larkin's study of the reception of Hindu films in Northern Nigeria, which analyses the uses and adaptations of Indian realities to African grounds, showing '"how Indian films that migrate into Northern Nigeria allow local viewers to imaginatively engage with Hindu culture and thus to experience and envision models of fashion, beauty, music, art forms, love and romance originating in India' (Wuaku 2013: 5). 'Parallel modernities' is a category of cultural transfer that informs the existence and development of culturally parallel but different realities, marked by a varying developmental pace and cultural progression. When confronted with one another, cultural systems verify their own practices and appropriate their standards by contesting local cultural models. I am using the category of 'parallel modernities' to analyse the types of appropriations *camp* fandom makes in the process of merging cultural experiences. In my view, those appropriations – unlike in normative fandom – create realities that, although parallel and participatory, are nevertheless oppositional.

This oppositionality of *camp* adaptive practices results from the peripheral status of *camp* sensibilities. This in turn results from the character of *camp*'s narrative solutions and aesthetic intentions. They are both vastly disturbing and disturbingly different, and, when applied to normative texts (of any sort), produce alienating renditions that uproot the texts from their original grounds. *Camp*'s adaptations of cultural realities are never mere intertexts; rather, they are subversive transformations of dominant culture, which, in the course of its adaptive activities, relocate the culture's images, realities and texts to the outskirts where *camp* belongs and where it practises them as their own.

> Alexis had provided her with a long and effective apprenticeship in the tricky art of intrigue. She'd stand freezing at pay phones and waste her small change ringing up girlfriends, dishing out dirt, dialling wrong numbers, making crank calls, masking her voice with a handkerchief. In a word, she was a right bitch, and that's exactly what she wanted to be! (Witkowski 2011: 33)

An important aspect of *camp*'s oppositionality is its reliance on fictional thinking. Unlike other forms of fandom, which operate by a clear distinction between the real and the fictitious, the original and the copy, the text and the imitation, *camp* mixes reality and fiction, using created worlds for life performances with the purpose of producing identities, which, being essentially queer, do not serve the production of group identification – as it is in the case of regular fandom – but produce identifications with which a *camping* subject can position itself against dominant realities with the parodic use of the markers coming from the dominant code (popular stardom). *Camp*'s participation in cultural realities (as represented in the realities' imagined depictions) should, therefore, be read as sabotaging the fictitious or imagined worlds for the construction of fake realities that are, nevertheless, intended as real.

> At least, Jessica realised, to some degree, that it was all a fantasy, that those dirty gloves from the flea market weren't the lambskin finery she pretended they were, and that the vodka she drank at night down at the tram depot wasn't champagne. It was just a bit of make-believe, something to make it easier to knock back the goblet of her life, which tasted nothing like champagne. 'Fine. On closer inspection, it isn't entirely true,' she'd say to herself while cleaning a clogged urinal or emptying a bed pan. 'I'm still a far cry from Alexis, but maybe we can just pretend, like children do.' And she winked at the mirror as if she were lobbing a sardonic joke at Blake Carrington or, better yet, his wife Krystle. So just for today let's pretend I'm her. (Witkowski 2011: 28–9)

Based on a deliberate misuse of actors' identity, the oppositional impersonations of stars' images in *camp* show serious abusiveness when practised away from the images' cultural settings. Alterations the images undergo in a foreign environment change their artistic DNA, depriving those images of their original meaning and contexts as well as their proper cultural potential. Represented by various detaching acts and conditions, such as a lack of social infrastructure, different cultural heritage, and so on, a non-reciprocal/symbiotic approach to a star persona and non-Western *camp* renditions of stardom, although they arise from fan culture, rely on the exploitative use of stars' status. They concentrate mainly on the construction of a fan's own identity and use the image of a star for glamorising a fan's personal performance. This is what Anthony Elliott defines as 'projective identification'. He claims that '[i]n the process of identifying with a celebrity, the fan unleashes a range of fantasies and desires and [. . .] transfers personal hopes and dreams onto the celebrity' (Elliott in Hills 2002a: 110). Projective identification will be, therefore, a state in which, by borrowing a star's persona or image, a fan is able to 'experience desired qualities of the self as being contained by the other, the celebrity' (Elliott in Hills 2002a: 110). In *camp*, however, the 'splitting' is replaced by communion, in which a *camp* performing subject unites with a star image in the ritual of adaptive identification.

CONCLUSION

What *camp* adaptations of stars' images bring to the notion of stardom and its conceptualisation via the development of fan cultures is the insistence that the images of dominant culture are never stable texts. Rather, they make a set of patterns which, when transferred into another cultural dimension, allow for producing parallel but alternative and often oppositional systems of 'stardom' – even if only for personal use. This becomes particularly interesting when analysed on the transnational level, that is, on the examples that show the working of adaptive travesties in conditions other than those inherent or original to the travestied image. Transnational *camp* appropriations of star images can be seen as a transcultural homology to Western stardom. As shown in Witkowski's description of queer adaptations of Alexis to the grounds of Polish reality, those adaptations do not intend to homogenise cultural experience but reinvent it through the uses of texts in forms unexpected/unintended by the texts' design.

The subversive quality of *camp*, although it has been widely explored in *camp* studies, gains a new dimension when analysed in the fandom context. Abusive adaptations of star images make *camp* a form of textual modality able to impact and shape the existing texts of culture, as well as rewrite them for the production of new meanings: for culture, for stardom and for fan activities. The working of this modality manifests itself through *camp*'s peculiar narrative/aesthetic means. Those means violate stars' cultural sovereignty and eliminate the distance that naturally exists between stars and their audiences. By doing so, they re-evaluate stars' cultural status but also re-evaluate 'the central–peripheral position of a practice or product, its canonicity, its dominance and its primary or secondary function' (Cattrysse 2014: 243).

BIBLIOGRAPHY

Ang, I. ([1985] 2013), *Watching Dallas: Soap Opera and the Melodramatic Imagination*, London and New York: Routledge. Kindle edition.
Austin, T. (2002), *Hollywood, Hype and Audiences: Selling and Watching Popular Film in the 1990s*, Manchester: Manchester University Press.
Babuscio, J. ([1977] 1999), 'The cinema of camp (aka camp and the gay sensibility)', in F. Cleto (ed.), *Camp. Queer Aesthetics and The Performing Subject: A Reader*, Edinburgh: Edinburgh University Press, pp. 117–35.
Booth, M. (1984), *Camp*, London: Quartet.
Britton, A. ([1978] 1999), 'For interpretation: notes against camp', in F. Cleto (ed.), *Camp. Queer Aesthetics and The Performing Subject: A Reader*, Edinburgh: Edinburgh University Press, pp. 136–42.
Burnett, M. T. (2007), *Filming Shakespeare in the Global Marketplace*, New York: Palgrave Macmillan.
Cattrysse, P. (2014), *Descriptive Adaptation Studies: Epistemological and Methodological Issues*, Antwerp: Garant.

Chin, B. and L. Hitchcock Morimoto (2013), 'Towards a theory of transcultural fandom', *Participation. Journal of Audience and Reception Studies* 10:1 (May), 92–108.

Cleto, F. (1999), 'Introduction: queering the camp', in F. Cleto (ed.), *Camp. Queer Aesthetics and The Performing Subject: A Reader*, Edinburgh: Edinburgh University Press, pp. 1–42.

Cohan, S. (2005), *Incongruous Entertainment. Camp, Cultural Value, and The MGM Musical*, Durham, NC and London: Duke University Press.

Dyer, R. ([1986] 2013), *Heavenly Bodies. Film Stars and Society*, London and New York: Routledge.

Gledhill, C. ([1991] 2003), 'Introduction', in C. Gledhill (ed.), *Stardom. Industry of Desire*, London and New York: Routledge, pp. xi–xxx.

Gray, J., C. Sandvoss and C. Lee Harrington (2007), 'Introduction: Why study fans?', in J. Gray, C. Sandvoss and C. Lee Harrington (eds), *Fandom. Identities and Communities in a Mediated World*, New York: New York University Press. Kindle edition.

Grisprud, J. (1995), *The Dynasty Year: Hollywood Television and Critical Media Studies*, London: Routledge.

Hills, M. (2002), *Fan Cultures*, London: Routledge.

Isherwood, C. ([1954] 1966), *The World in the Evening*, Harmondsworth: Penguin Books.

Jenkins, H. ([1992] 2013), *Textual Poachers. Television Fans and Participatory Culture*, London and New York: Routledge.

Kreutzner, G. and E. Seiter (1995), 'Not all "soaps" are created equal: towards a cross cultural criticism of television serials', in R. C. Allen (ed.), *To Be Continued: Soap Operas Around the World*, London and New York: Routledge, pp. 234–55.

Larkin, B. (1997), 'Indian films and Nigerian lovers: media and the creation of *parallel modernities*', *Africa* 67:3 (July), 406–40.

Larkin, B. (2008), *Signal and Noise: Media, Infrastructure and Urban Culture in Nigeria*, Durham, NC: Duke University Press.

McDonald, P. (2000), *The Star System. Popular Production of Star Identities*, London: Wallflower Press.

Meyer, M. (1994), 'Introduction. Reclaiming the discourse of camp', in M. Meyer (ed.), *The Politics and Poetics of Camp*, London and New York: Routledge, pp. 1–22.

Neale, S. (ed.) (1998), *Contemporary Hollywood Cinema*, London and New York: Routledge.

Press, A. L. (1990), 'Class, gender and the female viewer: women's responses to *Dynasty*', in M. E. Brown (ed.), *Television and Women's Culture: The Politics of the Popular*, London and Newbury Park: Sage Publications, pp. 158–82.

Press, A. L. (1991), *Women Watching Television: Gender, Class and Generation in the American Television Experience*, Philadelphia: Philadelphia University Press.

Robertson, P. (1996), *Guilty Pleasures: Feminist Camp from Mae West to Madonna*, London: I. B. Tauris.

Quiroga, J. (2000), *Tropics of Desire: Inventions from Queer Latino America*, New York: New York University Press.

Schatz, T. (ed.) (2004), *Hollywood: Critical Concepts in Media and Cultural Studies*, vols 1–4, London and New York.

Sontag, S. ([1964] 2013), 'Notes on camp', in S. Sontag, *Against Interpretation And Other Essays*, London: Penguin. Kindle edition.

Stokes, M. and R. Maltby (eds) (2001), *Hollywood Spectatorship: Changing Perceptions of Cinema Audiences*, London: BFI Publishing.

Tinkcom, M (2002), *Working Like a Homosexual. Camp, Capital, Cinema*, Durham, NC and London: Duke University Press.

Ware, J. R. (1909), *Passing English of the Victorian Era*, New York: Dutton.

Witkowski, M. (2011), *Lovetown*, London: Granta Books.

Wuaku, A. (2013), *Hindu Gods in West Africa: Ghanaian Devotees of Shiva and Krishna*, Boston: Brill.

10. YOUTUBE AS ARCHIVE: FANS, GENDER AND MEXICAN FILM STARS ONLINE

Niamh Thornton

Distance from valuable archives can be frustrating when studying stars whose primary output is at a considerable geographic remove, and where there is little distribution, sharing or coverage of materials beyond a specific location. Lacking the resources to travel annually to Mexico, I frequently find myself unable to source material that is physically stored in libraries and archives or, sometimes, readily available on corner street stalls in Mexico City, but impossible to access where I am. Early twenty-first-century technology has brought about some changes to this in ways that go beyond the conventional means of research and allow for a new and, at times, dialogic understanding of the star text. YouTube has become an unexpected resource and functions as an informal and chaotic digital archive and (re)creator of star texts in ways that deserve more sustained attention.

Heretofore, the study of digital archives has largely focused on how institutions catalogue and share material in a sustainable fashion. For example, in the Fall 2014 issue of the *Cinema Journal* Rielle Navitski details some of the online resources made available by Latin American institutions and the many complicating factors surrounding access, the dissemination of materials, selectivity of the process, and uneven approaches to digital archiving (122–3). Researching YouTube content shares some of the 'tensions inherent to archiving [that] are foregrounded by digital obsolescence and the imperative of access' (Navitski 2014: 122). Where there are limitations to institutional management of archives, the apparently ad hoc manner of material uploaded, the evolving regulatory framework, and the amateur nature of much star-related content makes YouTube a dynamic, sometimes frustrating, yet invaluable resource for researchers that is often overlooked in these surveys. Through an analysis of three Mexican stars, Pedro Infante, Jorge Negrete and Emilio Fernández, this chapter will focus on their YouTube star texts, and draw out what these mean for the nascent field of online remediated star studies. It will also consider the ways in which a star's gender determines how fans produce an online star text and how YouTube can be understood to function as a precarious archive.

REMEDIATION, CONVERGENCE, DIVERGENCE

On YouTube, fans upload content that is derived from existing work. They may simply share a complete piece or an edited sequence by altering its length or by creating something new from an edited compilation of material using music to determine duration. Jay David Butler and Richard Grusin describe this act as remediation, which for them is a feature integral to contemporary media in the ways content is both interpreted and created:

> at this extended historical moment, all current media functions as remediators and that remediation offers us a means of interpreting the work of earlier media as well. Our culture conceives of each medium or constellation of media as it responds to, redeploys, competes with, and reforms other media. (2000: 55)

In their much-cited text on the nature of remediation, they suggest that it is 'the way in which one medium is seen by our culture as reforming or improving upon another' (Butler and Grusin 2000: 59). Where YouTube content is concerned, this may not necessarily involve reforming if it includes the entire interview, advertisement, and so on, nor improvement, where there might be a degradation in quality or a lesser reproduction in some form. Butler and Grusin were writing before the advent of YouTube and were very enthusiastic about the potential of digital media as an upward evolutionary trajectory in the cultural landscape.

Grusin (2009) returned to the concept of remediation in the light of what this platform offers, and suggested an addendum to their earlier definition. In the context of YouTube, remediation should be read as 'the translation of media forms and practices, the extension and complexification of media networks' (Grusin 2009: 61). Grusin's language (translation, extension, complexification) suggests a hierarchical reading of what the new platforms provide. The old form subsumed into and adapted and distributed by the new, for him, leads to a superior end product. This value-laden way of assessing work can lead scholars into ignoring content that falls short of such measures.

Where the term remediation allows ways of thinking through how one form adapts older forms, another term useful to the study of fan and amateur content is convergence culture theorised by Henry Jenkins, which he describes as when 'old and new media collide' (2006: 2). As someone who labels himself as an acafan (see Jenkins n.d.) – a portmanteau of academic and fan – he sympathetically describes fans as 'poachers' who 'take and use their plundered goods' (1992: 223); Jenkins deliberately uses language that is designed to provoke and be messy, unlike the precision of Butler and Grusin. It is Jenkins' joyous celebration of the plundering fan and the haphazard imprecision of this term that is both helpful for the researcher and gets to the heterogeneity of content that can be ascribed to a star on YouTube.

In addition to remediation and convergence, there is a third term that is useful for mapping out the traces of star content that can be found on YouTube: divergence. Put forward by Grusin, it gets to the granularity of much online content which is 'fragmented, niche-oriented, fluid and individuated' (2009: 66). This variation in content is why it is useful to gather all of those YouTubers who upload star content as fans. This still acknowledges the slipperiness and looseness of this categorisation and signals some of the difficulties that arise when studying this material. Other matrices could be employed for the exploration of these videos because the star fan online convergence culture brings together different disciplines and opens up new opportunities for readings of both the star text and their reception.

YouTube is a platform that allows for sharing, commenting on and repurposing content. There are a variety of ways that YouTubers who focus their attention on particular stars can be labelled, such as content creators, archivists or curators. These individuals' identities could also be broken down further according to subcategories based on their self-descriptions online, how they engage with their viewers, and the content of their videos. This allows for too many variables that makes cataloguing and discussion impossible. For the purposes of this chapter I shall label them all as fans. Some are fans of the musical performances of the stars and may not be fans of their onscreen performances; others may have a particular interest in performances of two or more of the stars together; there may be individuals for whom the word fan carries negative connotations and devalues what they see as their primary desire to preserve material relating to Mexican cinema. The discomfort felt by some and the very looseness of the category can be countered by the growth in the field of fan studies and the reclamation of fan activities that has taken place in academia and online. YouTube functions as a transient fan archive that reveals much about the present and how the past is configured by amateur creators.

TIME, FANDOM AND THE ARCHIVE

The temporality, contingency and transience of this fan output needs some reflection. Lev Manovich (2001: 6–8), a theorist who has traced out connections between film and other newer media, advances the need to record a history of the present. Writing in 2001, he draws parallels between the evolutionary moment of what he reads as the nascent stage of digital media production and the early days of cinema, lamenting the loss of a cataloguing of that present among producers and consumers of what was then a new form. Where there may be a limited database of writing about early cinema and some loss of copies of films due to the difficulties in preservation or a patchy sense of the need to preserve such artefacts, temporality and transience is even more pronounced in digitally produced work. Where with early cinema there is a physical object, such as film stock, to preserve, digital content is made up of code that can be deleted, altered or even inaccessible because of formatting or for geopolitical reasons, such as copyright control. Therefore, the content I discuss here may not be what you will find if you go online in the indeterminate time in the future when you may read this chapter. This chapter should, then, be read as a historiography of the present moments in which my research took place in a media landscape that is ever-evolving and that is highly location-bound.

When examining online video, that is, content on a platform that is ever-changing as is the case with YouTube, research can only ever capture a snapshot bound by temporality. Geopolitics and national boundaries also determine access: content is removed, limited or banned in certain territories dependent upon national laws and how they are implemented at a particular time and place. I documented my first search for materials in June 2013 while based in Northern Ireland and the second between November 2014 and January 2015 in England and Ireland. This is to be understood as an exploration of the now and the recent past as a UK (and occasionally Irish)-based scholar looking at Mexican stardom and the content that has emerged from my searches.

In a previous study I considered two prominent female stars, Dolores del Rio and María Félix, and how their star texts have continued to evolve online through fan vids on YouTube (Thornton 2010). Del Rio and Félix were the two most high-profile Mexican female stars of their time, and have continued to have a long afterlife online through fan vids and clips. The three male stars I consider were their contemporaries from the so-called Golden Age of Mexican film, a period that lasted from the mid-1930s to the 1950s, and during which there was a high output of genre films by a state-supported studio system. Infante, Negrete and Fernández also have high profiles online that show some variation with those of del Rio and Félix. Gender differences have resulted in distinct star texts on YouTube. Unlike the numerous creative remixes and mash-ups by fans of female star content, what can be found of male star content is predominantly less creative and includes clips from films, interviews, and song sequences. In that earlier work, I considered a range of outputs by fans from around the world who manipulated and changed the female star texts that reorder, restyle and change its meaning in ways that are highly individual for the YouTuber. They provided a personal interpretation of Félix and del Rio's filmic output and what these stars mean to the fans, thus often entering into dialogue with their viewers. With male star texts there is a sense that the fan is intervening in the preservation of an archive faithfully, for which they get praise from the viewers.

INFANTE, NEGRETE AND FERNÁNDEZ

Infante, Negrete and Fernández were high-profile stars with distinct and at times overlapping trajectories. Infante (1917–57) starred in sixty-three films and released more than 350 songs, many of which he performed onscreen. He died in a plane crash, an event that is subject to much speculation on YouTube, with some fans suggesting that his death was faked (see, in particular, Cuco Leyva, n.d.). His most iconic roles were in the trilogy of sentimental urban musical melodramas: *Nosotros los pobres* [We the Poor] (Ismael Rodríguez, 1948) and its subsequent sequels, *Ustedes los ricos* [You the Rich] (Ismael Rodríguez, 1948) and *Pepe el toro* (Ismael Rodríguez, 1952). In these he played the role of the happy but impoverished man who does well, but in reaching beyond the limits of class he is duly punished, only to reconcile himself with his lot. Just as is the case with Félix and del Rio, Infante is identified with a particular song, 'Amorcito corazón', that recurs in fan vids. A vid by omrobleto 1 (2012) that mixes archive footage compiled for a television documentary of Infante's death set to this song is a good example of music edited with visuals with little alteration to either. For Alejandro L. Madrid, 'Amorcito corazón' 'marked the beginning of the bolero ranchero' (2013: 54), a hybrid musical genre which blended the Cuban *bolero*, popularised and localised in Mexico since the 1930s, with Mexican folk music motifs originating in the countryside implied in the '*ranchero*' [ranch-style]. The *bolero ranchero* became identified with a form of nationalism that was nostalgic for an imagined distant locale founded in conservative traditionalism. Alongside Javier Solís, Infante and Negrete were nicknamed the 'Tres gallos mexicanos' [Three Mexican Roosters] because of the ways they embodied a particular type of posturing Mexican masculinity in their film roles (de la Mora 2006: ix–xiii). Frequently, fans upload videos of Infante and Negrete together. There is a small number with Solís, but his presence is negligible.

Negrete (1911–53), also known as the *Charro cantor* [singing cowboy], starred in forty-four films, released fifteen albums and was married to Félix for the final year of his life (1952–3). As well as a high-profile acting and musical career, he was one of the founding members of the actors' union and its president for a period (1944–7 and 1949–53). He died of hepatitis while on a trip to Los Angeles and his body was returned to Mexico for burial. Juan Carlos Ramírez-Pimienta describes Infante and Negrete as stars who 'personifica la galanura mexicana del llamado cine de la época de oro' [personify the Mexican leading man of the so-called Golden Age of cinema], and he asserts that Negrete's funeral was the first to be treated as a high-profile mediated event because of Negrete and Félix's fame (2010: 32). Negrete's most famous song is 'México lindo y querido' [beautiful and beloved Mexico]. Composed by Chucho Monge, it is a patriotic *ranchera* whose lyrics speak to the immigrant as much as the Mexican resident, and allude to a desire to be repatriated after death 'si muero lejos de ti' [if I die far from you] that resonates with Negrete's own death (Ramírez-Pimienta 2010: 32). This song, therefore, contains love of country and uncannily evokes biographical detail about its most famous performer. It is the most popular song used to accompany fan vids featuring Negrete.

Infante and Negrete worked closely together and were associated with a rural musical film genre which shares its name with the song genre, the *ranchera*. These films, tinged with nostalgia and sentimentality, were popular among the newly urban Mexicans displaced from the countryside (Pilcher 2012: 215). Set in large cattle farms in the state of Jalisco, the narratives are centred on struggles with changes in social hierarchies. Usually, the lowly yet skilled son of the ranch labourer endeavours to prove his worth by acting as 'protector to the peons against the powerful hacendado' (Hershfield 1999: 90) and to earn the hand of the ranch-owner's beautiful daughter. The films had extended musical numbers and led to the popularisation of the *ranchera* style of music and clothing that is probably best known internationally through the mariachi bands. These nationalist films were very popular with audiences, and musical numbers from them are often put up as videos associated with both Infante and Negrete. As genre films aimed at a mass audience, they had a different audience appeal to the more aestheticised art films directed by Fernández.

While Infante and Negrete died at the peak of their careers, Fernández (1904–86) would continue long after he became a respectable figure. He has left behind a considerable body of work. He performed in eighty-nine roles, some of these in the US, Europe and Latin America, but most were in Mexico, and he also directed forty-three films that varied considerably in quality and reception. He started his career in Hollywood as a dancer and, notoriously, is purported to have been the model for the Oscar statuette (see Tierney 2007). His womanising, heavy drinking and violent temper meant that he was infamous offscreen, and stories about him frequently appeared in news media and gossip magazines. This includes extensive coverage of his committal to jail when he was accused of murder. Fernández's 1940s and 1950s collaborations with the cinematographer Gabriel Figueroa are his most studied work, and have a similar nationalist intent as those aforementioned films starring Infante and Negrete, albeit differently realised. Where these award-winning films are often marked as a high point in Mexican cinema, his salacious 1970s and 1980s films, as well as his occasional turn as the lowlife Mexican in US Westerns, are read as low points (see, for example, Mora 1989 and Hershfield and Maciel 1999).

VIDS, CLIPS AND FOOTAGE

Despite the sizeable film output and the continued consumption of their work, content uploaded on Infante, Negrete and Fernández is not extensive and can be broken into four main types: fan vids; edited clips from films or television appearances; documentary footage which includes television interviews with the star, a family member or acquaintance; and amateur sequences of the star or a space associated with them captured on camera. As stars with considerable renown onscreen and off, whose films are repeatedly shown on television and easily available in a variety of formats, they could be expected to have an online presence similar to that of their female contemporaries. But this is not always the case. Different patterns can be traced in how fans take and circulate star content.

Creators of fan content have varying skills and follow different criteria, therefore any study must draw on a multiplicity of theoretical fields and cannot impose the same measures as upon professional output by conventional filmmakers. The selection and uploading of content is not inherently amateur and, frequently, the content is sourced from professional media works. They are usually remediated texts: a pre-recorded song used as the framing for footage, screenshots from films, shots of publicity material, and so on. The creators of remediated content that is broadcast on a variety of platforms are called vidders, but, more specifically on YouTube, they are YouTubers. The latter term describes all of those who upload content onto YouTube, while vidders suggests creative manipulation of the original source material. For Tisha Turk, vidders

> position themselves simultaneously as fans, filmmakers, and critics. Vids express what vidders find important in the source narrative, which characters, relationships, stories and subtexts they find most interesting and rewarding to examine. A vid represents a close reading, and like any close reading it is selective. (2010: 88–9)

Therefore, I shall use the term vid to refer to clips that are made up of edited material from more than one original source accompanied by music, and vidders to refer to their creators. As a broad umbrella term, YouTubers have multiple roles in helping create the star text. They are editors, critics, content creators, researchers and archivists.

Up to 9 December 2010 YouTube had a time limit of fifteen minutes on all videos (Cain Miller 2010: n.p.). This was first lifted for a select number of YouTubers who had never violated copyright rules and had special designations, and has now been lifted for all users. This means that the content associated with a particular star has grown exponentially. In particular, this is because films are now being uploaded as well as the growth in content from creators or amateur archivists. For example, out of the 209,000 results that appear under Infante's name in January 2015, of the first forty results, sixteen are films he starred in. This compares to 179,000 in 2013 which were mostly musical numbers, fan slideshow-style vids, film and television appearances, and news headlines (either shots of newspapers or edited clips of television reports) from the day he died. In that same time period, videos of Negrete have increased from 53,300 to 127,000 results. In the principal search returns, again, this is as a result of films he starred in being uploaded. For Fernández his results have gone the other direction from 121,000 to 65,200. Few full feature films starring him or directed by him are available. The copyright holders of Fernández's films are obviously more vigilant of YouTube content.

These figures and their ever-changing nature make exhaustive trawling through the content a difficult, if not impossible, task. This 'overabundance of information of all kinds' (Manovich 2001: 35) means that there is a need for a methodology, which I shall detail here. Firstly, I search YouTube and scan what comes up over a large number of pages. Each page presents twenty results. This shows patterns and trends as well as results that are extraneous. For example, in the case of Fernández, he shares his name with a skater from Guadalajara, Mexico and a Mexican progressive house and trance musician. These results are difficult to filter out as the YouTubers do not follow a standard method of tagging the videos; this can lead to missing out on content. Negrete and Infante do not share names with any identifiable figures. Then, I take a sampling of videos to watch more closely from the patterns I observe; this leads to observations on generic tropes and repetitions. With exemplary texts I download and save them, particularly with fan-produced original content, because none of this content is stable nor will I be assured that it will be there in the future. Frequently, I take screenshots that include comments. Again, these may be removed over time even if they are not offensive and the video remains in place. In this way, the researcher becomes archivist of an archive that is highly personalised, in some ways accidental, and traces an academic self which, in turn, produces its own potential for self-auditing and study.

This leads to another issue when studying new media: its modularity or, more precisely, 'the fractal structure of new media' (Manovich 2001: 30). For Manovich this is about the individual components that make up media.

He uses the term 'elements' to refer to 'images, sounds, shapes, or behaviors [which] are represented as collections of discrete samples (pixels, polygons, voxels, characters, scripts)' (Manovich 2001: 30). He continues, '[t]hese elements are assembled into larger-scale objects but continue to maintain their separate identities' (Manovich 2001: 30). This is because the technology allows for 'individual customization, rather than mass standardization' (Manovich 2001: 30). Manovich in his observations and definitions mixes consuming practices and technological scope. It is a combination of the filter bubble that determines what is seen (due to past searches, account settings, YouTube policies and practices, IP address, and so on) and how the elements that make up the content can be manipulated at a particular point in time by the creators. In practice, for the study of fan culture on YouTube, the researcher is examining a partial view that will reveal biases and inflections based on his or her own prior online habits.

There is fan-generated content which requires the curation, collation and manipulation of original material usually accompanied by music. In Jenkins' words, 'fan aesthetic centers on the selection, inflection, juxtaposition, and recirculation of ready-made images and discourses' (Jenkins 1992: 224). These are vids: 'fan-made song videos' where 'footage from television series or films is edited in conjunction with carefully chosen music to celebrate, interpret, critique, or subvert mass media narratives' (Turk 2010: 88). The ephemera, such as old advertisements, edited clips from television or film appearances (see Pedro Infante 2009 and edward fuente 2014), and home movies of visits to key locations associated with the star (see akasairg 2007 and EstacionesMusicales 2011) could also be ascribed to fans but cannot be described as vids.

Two examples of fan vids that select, inflect, juxtapose and recirculate original content are 'pedro infante y jorge negrete super mix' by Juan Pablo Rosas García (2011) and 'Emilio Fernández' by MoviePosterMM (2011) (see Figure 10.1). These vids are examples of the audiovisual curatorship by fans on YouTube. The 'About' section of Rosas García's channel declares that it is dedicated to compiling traditional music from the southern Mexican state of Oaxaca. The video reflects his particular focus on music, although what is used in this vid is not specifically Oaxacan in origin. Lasting fifteen minutes and thirty seconds, the vid is a medley of well-known songs, largely from films, performed by Infante and Negrete, while the visual element is made up of alternating still images taken from publicity photos and screenshots of the two stars. The images change as each new song plays, thus the imagery's primary function is to inform the viewer who is singing. The songs include numbers that were linked to popular films, such as 'Allá en el Rancho Grande' from the eponymous 1949 version of the film by Fernando de Fuentes, which Negrete starred in, and the aforementioned 'Amorcito corazón' and 'México lindo y querido'. This richly layered medley juxtaposed with the lack of variation in

Emilio Fernández
MoviePosterMM
Subscribe 915
14,537 views
Add to   Share   ••• More
16   0

Figure 10.1   Photograph of Fernández at the end of the compilation video.

the editing of the vid is a privileging of voice over image. The greater attention to voice and performance is typical of vids of male stars.

This mix of the well-known songs from film performances serves to prompt the memory of those familiar with Infante and Negrete's oeuvre. Given that the only song given credits below the video is 'Amorcito corazón', alongside the paucity of images employed, this is a video primarily for those already familiar with the stars and not aimed at a broader audience. By January 2015 it had garnered a healthy audience of 54,707, and received consistently positive feedback.

The choice of performers alternates in this video, no song is played in its entirety and each track is mixed into the next without any break or obvious transition, which leads to an elision of the two stars by the YouTuber as almost interchangeable signifiers for a filmic past. This is reinforced visually as the limited number of images fade in over each other. The YouTuber is recalling the association between Infante and Negrete and the songs all the while he is merging the two stars. This video is an example of the slideshow-style videos that are prevalent on YouTube and have their own generic markers. Most viewers who comment on the vid celebrate the stars, share their memories of when they first saw them on screen, and either lament their absence or bemoan the fact that there are no stars like them now. The vid functions as a prompt for those familiar with the stars and, also, a carefully curated archive of their performances.

MoviePosterMM's 'Emilio Fernández' is also slideshow-style. However, in this case imagery and a focus on output and career trajectory are privileged over the musical accompaniment. The choice of music is 'Train Montage/All Fall Down' performed by The City of Prague Philharmonic Orchestra from the soundtrack of *The Wild Bunch* (Sam Peckinpah, 1969), a film Fernández performed in as a brutal, corrupt, drunken and lascivious military leader in the Mexican Revolution (see Thornton 2012). Unlike the choice of music from Infante and Negrete's iconic roles by Rosas García, this is not a starring role for Fernández. It is a stirring piece that uses the full range of the orchestral performers with a staccato rhythm and has motifs recognisable from the Western genre. As a choice of music it builds on an association between Fernández and the Western for the audience, and with the idea of masculine prowess and lament for a glorious past that the 1960s Westerns harnessed.

The visuals are composed of hard cuts between still images of posters, screenshots or titles alone (for those which have no accompanying images) to films directed by or featuring Fernández. The edit does not follow the beat of the music slavishly, which makes it more sophisticated than many other slideshow-style videos to be found on YouTube. As Fernández does not feature on all of the posters, and given that this is an extensive range of films featuring and directed by him, it functions as an actor-director star text. The chronological approach is a visual catalogue that gives a sense of Fernández's career trajectory and is an overview of the evolution of Mexican and US posters for genre films.

The vid ends with four images that are worth remarking upon. After a screenshot from *Arriba Michoacán* (Francisco Guerrero, 1987), the last film Fernández acted in, there is a cut to black. This is followed by a photograph of Fernández in later life, another of his gravestone, a screenshot of his most iconic role as Colonel Antonio Zeta in *La Cucaracha* [*The Soldiers of Pancho Villa*] (Ismael Rodríguez, 1959), and a final screenshot from *The Wild Bunch*. This sequence acts as a form of coda and reminder of the star as a man. It is a type of summing-up of a career that is now over and signposts his legacy. Despite the many awards for direction as well as the academic attention his other films have received, and the fact that he was not the star of either film, these are the images that have had greatest traction and are repeated in most fan vids of Fernández.

Even though it has greater visual finesse and has a more completist approach, this vid has received fewer views than that of Rosas García. In part, this can be attributed to the lack of interaction with comments by MoviePosterMM. There are two comments beneath the video and one of these is a question that the vidder has left unanswered. There is a paucity of vids associated with Fernández, and thus there is also a lack of a community of viewers and fans who go from vid to vid. There is also another observable trend. Stars – and this is particularly the case with male stars – who do build a following are those who have an audio repertoire familiar to fans. Once there is a pattern of vids made using the star's song (or songs), the vidders then create variations based on their own preferences. There is, therefore, a double draw for the audience: the music and the star. Those stars who do not have this hook, such as Fernández, are often overlooked on YouTube. While each of these vids have distinct variants, they reveal generic patterns. That is, they are examples of the music- and performance-oriented vids in the case of Rosas García, and the archival survey in MoviePosterMM's vid. Both serve as useful approaches to the star text and provide audiovisual summaries of their careers and indicators of its contemporary consumption.

As well as fan vids, other videos are uploaded without significant alteration and are of a more recognisably conventional archival nature. These can include ephemera, but are more likely extended interviews and television programmes about the stars. It is not always clear what impulses are served through sharing material. But there is a further complicating factor that must be taken into account: amateurism.

AMATEUR PROFESSIONAL/PROFESSIONAL AMATEUR

Describing these videos as amateur is not so much about aesthetics as catego-rising intention, dissemination, consumption and reception. For YouTube as a business motivated by profit, consumption is where the difference lies between professional and amateur. After a high number of views, the producer is paid through advertising that is placed before or around the video (Cheshire 201: n.p.). For the creator, there can be ambitions of achieving high viewing figures that may or may not be realised, or only attained over a long time. For the media scholar, labelling the content as amateur can be a productive approach because the videos bear comparison with home movies and the theoretical debates around these. Furthermore, of interest are the ways the discourse around amateur film and its consumption shares common ground with fan theory and the concept of the star text.

Ian Craven draws on leisure studies in his discussion of amateur video, proposing that, '[f]rom this perspective, creative outcomes are understood as symptomatic of multiple-determinations and contradictory needs, played out across a "social world"' (2009: 6) that are reliant on a network 'which expresses devotion to the activity involved and generates forms of pleasurable gratification, rather than accountable remuneration' (2009: 7). Such networks can be accounted for on YouTube through the loose associations created through dedicated channels – YouTubers sharing their own and others' videos that they curate for their subscribers – and the titles ascribed to videos that form loose associations under named stars. The latter is more haphazard, and subject to multiple and changeable factors such as location and search bubbles mentioned previously.

An example of curation and networks can be found in YouTuber Nain DeLaCruz (2007) who uploaded the same clip from *Dos tipos de cuidado* as El Yeusy (2010). This YouTuber has 693 subscribers and has created playlists of over four hundred videos that subscribers can view. DeLaCruz has only thirteen videos uploaded, the majority of which are home movies with fewer than three hundred views. One is an edited clip of a performance by Elvis Presley, 'Elvis – If I can Dream', another is the clip mentioned above, and a vid homage to Infante commemorating his death, 'PEDRO INFANTE – Adios a mi pueblo Mexicano'. There is no sustained and well-defined pattern to the content. DeLaCruz can be contrasted with El Yeusy, who has a strong profile as a producer of vids and curator of content related to Mexican cinema and music (see Figure 10.2). He has thousands of subscribers; many of his vids have been watched by thousands, and some by millions, of viewers. El Yeusy's clear profile and YouTube persona has attracted a viewership that DeLaCruz, who mixes home movies with fan interests, does not.

The divergent archive could be the source of an income stream for these fans, which leads to a blurring of the amateur–professional divide. The question of payment and ascribing professional or amateur status to a YouTuber is complicated if we draw on Craven again. When he unpicks the question of leisure he breaks it down into two categories: serious and casual. For him, casual is a '*relational* category' (2009: 18) that functions as a kind of 'echo cinema' (2009: 18) which is assessed against commercial television and cinema as its 'alter ego' (2009: 19). There are elements of echo aesthetics which can be found in YouTube videos, such as those which employ

Figure 10.2　Infante and Negrete by El Yeusy, plus links to other clips and vids.

MTV-style editing using music as a structuring and narrative device. Yet the videos that contain just a single image for the duration of a song, those that use repetitive images cut to the beat, or others that are partial sequences cut to no obvious logic, are more difficult to parse as echoing other cinematic and televisual forms.

Rather than being simply dismissed, these less aestheticised videos require alternative methodologies that draw on the discussions by theorists of amateur film. In her analysis of amateur cinema, Patricia R. Zimmermann suggests that '[a]mateur film disrupts historiographic explanatory models of linearity, casuality, and deductive evidentiary claims' (2008: 275), and adds that the 'films do not deploy any systematic cinematic language' (2008: 276) but are 'often viewed as cinematic failures' (2008: 277). Zimmermann is specifically discussing home movies, but parallels can be made with YouTube videos. There may be apparently negligible aesthetic or archival value in such individual pieces; however, it is in the patterns that emerge from the YouTube star text that the strengths lie for scholars. Where Craven writes about echoes, Zimmermann uses the term 'traces rather than evidence' (2008: 276). Both discuss home movies that feature the individuals, their families or their lived experiences, such as travel, while Craven also examines fiction narratives by amateurs. These uses of narrative structuring devices (whether fact or fiction) are read by Craven and Zimmermann as extensions of the private self and the public cultural context that prove useful to an understanding of subject and object of the films. The fan's relationship to the star in the YouTube vids is an extension of a self. However hidden behind an avatar or carefully crafted single designation aspect of this self it may be, it also functions as an expression of a more generalised understanding around a star text.

Conclusions

In this voluminous and extensive fan archive, the question of repetition and reiteration becomes resonant and meaningful in ways that go beyond what Martin Shingler has identified as the usual means whereby the star text can be surveyed (2012: 111). In some respects the YouTubers are producing a crowdsourced continuation of the stars' oeuvre repurposed, relocated and reinterpreted. The stars are no longer producing work, therefore the fans are digging up little-known or ephemeral material and disseminating it, or creating new content from the old. Just as the function of the star vehicle was 'to exploit the popularity of a particular performer by accommodating their established "type" and both reworking and advancing aspects of their previous work', so too is the YouTube content (Shingler 2012: 111). It is not a fixed type, whose only change is in the interpretation of the material; its reformulation and compilation in an unstable format and ever-changing archive becomes a more slippery and challenging archive in flux than the material normally exploited for research.

The material to be found on Infante, Negrete and Fernández is evidence of how the Internet 'serves as an infrastructure for distributing data, and through accumulating resources of collectively amassed texts, it simultaneously creates an archive for cultural heritage' (Shäfer 2011: 71–2). The two separate types of content form part of this larger database and can have different functions. The remixed and mashed-up fan vids allow for critical readings of the process of creativity as part of the fan producing a self that involves 'leaving as many traces of yourself on as many media [as] a culturally desirable goal' (Grusin 2009: 66). Unaltered content is about building up a database and the forma-tion of a community of fans interested in sharing and disseminating knowledge, however ad hoc and loosely catalogued this may be. Tours around Fernández's Mexico City house (IMCINE 2013), extracts from the documentary *La histo-ria detrás del mito* (2012), and interviews such as the silent portrait by Gerard Courant (2012), another with Fernández while he was in jail for murder (Perez Verduzco 2012), and those with his daughter, Adela (Canal de laverdadentiem-poreal 2013), who wrote a well-known biography of her father, all contribute to this database and build an ever-evolving posthumous online star text.

My previous research on the female Mexican film stars Félix and del Rio resulted in a rich understanding of fans as content creators of variable skills and it opened up opportunities for transnational dialogue with fans. This led me to conclude that the stars' audiences and reception, usually considered to be culturally bound to a fixed geopolitical and linguistic set of locales, can be much more varied than previously assumed. In contrast, when looking at Infante, Negrete and Fernández, and the less varied YouTube content attached to their names, different conclusions need to be drawn. There are few vids that suggest ownership over the male stars and the media texts associated with them (music, film, television). There are no mash-ups or memes attached to male stars. There is a respect for the male star which results in a more faithful database of material. Where vids are created they use music closely associ-ated with the male stars, that is, either songs they had performed or taken from soundtracks of films they had appeared in. All of these practices suggest a gender-inflected fan practice. There is much more variation in the creative manipulation of sound and image with female star content on YouTube. The data on male stars reveals an absence of the irreverent and playful poaching of fan vids suggested by Jenkins (1992) that can be found on female stars, and in its place can be found a partial archive signalling seriousness in fan intentional-ity and their respectful collation of male star texts.

Part of the value of this content is the difficulty in finding much of the source material through conventional means for the researcher (libraries, archives, online databases), and for the non-academic in sharing and learning about the star through non-hierarchical means that are not governed by paywalls or institutional controls. As the Internet and specifically YouTube is currently constituted, it is to be understood as an unstable archive, one that is subject to possible changes in intellectual property laws and their implementation by the owners. It is an unstable and dynamic archive because the curators and content creators are amateur, it is subject to regulatory changes, and there can be arbitrary decisions to alter or remove content. As research into digital archives is still at the early stages of development and it is an ever-evolving resource, the snapshot I have provided must be understood to capture a present that is already past.

Often treated as a way of guiltily whiling away time on trivial or ephemeral content, or as merely a source of film clips for presentations, YouTube should also be understood as a digital archive with fans as curators of a star text with its own developing aesthetic forms. It requires a new set of tools and approaches and should not be presumed to be of lesser value because it is largely amateur. Although not a replacement for sustained research into the considerable holdings on stars in physical libraries and film archives, there is much online that helps to inform, shape and colour readings of the star text that means YouTube should be taken seriously as an archive. The result is that YouTube becomes a supplementary archive and invaluable resource for researchers, and a fan space with its own generic conventions, audiences and codes. Star studies as a discipline needs to pay greater critical attention to what is available, how it is curated and the aesthetic choices made by these diverse, transnational and highly engaged fans. Through fan activity on YouTube, the star lives on and has a differentiated star text that is variable among contemporaries within the same industrial context. Therefore, there is exciting potential for comparative studies with stars from other places and times.

BIBLIOGRAPHY

Butler, Jay David and Richard Grusin (2000), *Remediation: Understanding New Media*, Cambridge, MA and London: The MIT Press.

Cain Miller, Claire (2010), 'YouTube Lifts Time Limit for Some Videos', *The New York Times*, http://bits.blogs.nytimes.com/2010/12/09/youtube-lifts-time-limit-for-some-videos/?_r=0

Cheshire, Tom (2013), 'Talent Tube: how Britain's new YouTube superstars built a global fanbase', *Wired*, 7 February, http://www.wired.co.uk/magazine/archive/2013/02/features/talent-tube, last accessed 1 February 2015.

Craven, Ian (2009), 'A Very Fishy Tale: The Curious Case of Amateur Subjectivity', in *Movies on Home Ground. Explorations in Amateur Cinema*, Newcastle-upon-Tyne: Cambridge Scholars Press, pp. 1–35.

De la Mora, Sergio (2006), *Cinemachismo: Masculinities and Sexuality in Mexican Film*, Austin: University of Texas Press.

Grusin, Richard (2009), 'YouTube at the End of New Media', in Pelle Snickars and Patrick Vonderau (eds.), *The YouTube Reader*, Stockholm: Mediehistoriskt Archiv12.

Hershfield, Joanne and David R. Maciel (eds) (1999), *Mexico's Cinema: A Century of Film and Filmmakers*, Wilmington, DE: SR Books.

Hershfield, Joanne (1999), 'Race and Ethnicity in the Classical Cinema', in Joanne Hershfield Hershfield and David R. Maciel (eds), *Mexico's Cinema: A Century of Film and Filmmakers*, Wilmington, DE: SR Books.

Jenkins, Henry (1992), *Textual Poachers: Television Fans and Participatory Culture*, New York and London: Routledge.

— (2006), *Convergence Culture: Where Old and New Media Collide*, New York and London: New York University Press.

— (n.d.), *Confessions of an Aca-Fan: The Official Weblog of Henry Jenkins*, http:// henryjenkins.org/, last accessed 28 January 2015.

Madrid, Alejandro L. (2013), *Music in Mexico: Experiencing Music, Expressing Culture*, New York and Oxford: Oxford University Press.

Mora, Carl J. (1989), *Mexican Cinema: Reflections of a Society, 1896–1988*, Berkeley: University of California Press.

Navitski, Rielle (2014), 'Reconsidering the Archive: Digitization and Latin American Film Historiography', *Cinema Journal* 54:1 (Fall), 121–8.

Pilcher, Jeffrey M. (2012), 'The Gay Caballero: Machismo, Homosexuality and the Nation in Golden Age Film', in Victor M. Macías González and Anne Rubenstein (eds), *Masculinity and Sexuality in Modern Mexico*, Albuquerque: University of New Mexico Press.

Ramírez-Pimienta, Juan Carlos (2010), '*Chicago lindo y querido si muero lejos de ti*: el pasito duranguense, la onda grupera y las nuevas geografías de la identidad popular mexicana', *Mexican Studies/Estudios mexicanos*, 26:1 (Winter), 31–45.

Shäfer, Mirko Tobias (2011), *Bastard Culture!: How user Participation Transforms Cultural Production*, Amsterdam: Amsterdam University Press.

Shingler, Martin (2012), *Star Studies: A Critical Guide*, London: BFI/Palgrave Macmillan.

Thornton, Niamh (2012), '"It just looks like more of Texas": Journeys and Travel Narratives in the Western', in Wilfried Raussert and Graciela Martínez-Zalce (eds), *(Re)Discovering 'America' Road Movies and Other Travel Narratives in North America/(Re)Descubriendo 'América' Road movie y otras narrativas de viaje en América del Norte*, Trier and Arizona: Wissenschaftlicher Verlag Trier and Bilingual Press/Editorial Bilingüe.

— (2010), 'YouTube: Transnational Fandom and Mexican Divas', *Transnational Cinemas* 1:1, 53–67.

Tierney, Dolores (2007), *Emilio Fernández: Pictures in the Margins*, Manchester: Manchester University Press.

Turk, Tisha (2010), '"Your Own Imagination": Vidding and Vidwatching as Collaborative Interpretation', *Film and Film Culture* 5, 88–111.

Zimmermann, Patricia R. (2008), 'Morphing History into Histories: From Amateur Film to the Archive of the Future', in Karen L. Izhizuka and Patricia R. Zimmerman (eds), *Mining the Home Movie: Excavations in Histories and Memories*, Berkeley: University of California Press, pp. 275–88.

FILMOGRAPHY

Akshairg (2007), 'casa de Pedro Infante', https://www.youtube.com/watch?v=3sa MES0MsDA, last accessed 25 June 2015.

Canal de laverdadentiemporeal (2013), 'ENTREVISTA A ADELA FERNÁNDEZ, HIJA DE EMILIO 'EL INDIO' FERNÁNDEZ. Parte II', https://www.youtube.com/ watch?v=jGA3yvo9aww, last accessed 30 January 2015.

Courant, Gérard (2012), 'Emilio Fernandez by Gérard Courant – Cinématon #187', https://www.youtube.com/watch?v=-lrxPHZIYSQ, last accessed 30 January 2015.

Cuco Leyva Channel, https://www.youtube.com/user/DNCUC/featured, last accessed 30 January 2015.

DeLaCruz Nain (2007), 'Pedro Infante & Jorge Negrete – Dos tipos de cuidado', https://www.youtube.com/watch?v=Ec3m2J1n5_4, last accessed 30 January 2015.

— Videos, https://www.youtube.com/user/elvis4th/videos, last accessed 30 January 2015.

edward fuente (2014), 'EMILIO 'INDIO' FERNANDEZ entrevistado por Joaquín Soler Serrano 2 de 2' https://www.youtube.com/watch?v=voaqL3MVSog, last accessed 25 June 2015.

EstacionesMusicales (2011), 'GUANAJUATO PLACA Y CASA DE JORGE NEGRETE 26 NOVIEMBRE', https://www.youtube.com/watch?v=Q6Tr8o_4z5A, last accessed 25 June 2015.

El Yeusy (2010), 'Pedro Infante y Jorge Negrete_Coplas_Couplets', https://www.youtube.com/watch?v=Nxsf58X3y7o&list=RDNxsf58X3y7o#t=104, last accessed 30 January 2015.

IMCINE (2013), 'Casa Fortaleza de Emilio "El Indio" Fernández', https://www.youtube.com/watch?v=IENlRhnakgY, last accessed 30 January 2015.

Infante, Pedro (2009), 'Pedro Infante', https://www.youtube.com/watch?v=iVhn690PND8, last accessed 25 June 2015.

MoviePosterMM (2011), 'Emilio Fernández', https://www.youtube.com/watch?v=q6rNdZD6JrA, last accessed 30 January 2015.

omrobleto 1 (2012), 'Muerte de Pedro Infante', https://www.youtube.com/watch?v=7PqHaJjcFwc, last accessed 25 June 2015.

Perez Verduzco, Guillermo (2012), 'ENTREVISTA AL INDIO FERNANDEZ EN LA CARCEL POR GUILLERMO PEREZ VERDUZCO', https://www.youtube.com/watch?v=0BuWHRWsc4k, last accessed 30 January 2015.

Rosas García, Juan Pablo (2011), 'pedro infante y jorge negrete super mix', https://www.youtube.com/watch?v=8Gwi-ucGAlk, last accessed 30 January 2015.

PART 6

ABERRANT STARDOM

11. IN YOUR FACE: MONTGOMERY CLIFT COMES OUT AS CRIP IN *THE YOUNG LIONS*

Elisabetta Girelli

Montgomery Clift was, between 1948 and 1956, one of Hollywood's most marketable stars, worshipped alike by fans and critics. A three-time Oscar nominee, Clift possessed a complex star image, where his rigorous approach to acting jostled with a heart-throb status, and with thinly veiled sexual ambiguity. Every conflicting facet, however, was subordinated to a single unifying factor: his exceptional beauty, as perfect and dazzling as to place him in a canon of his own (see Figure 11.1). On 12 May 1956, this beauty vanished forever in a horrific car accident, when Clift's face was virtually destroyed. Although painstakingly 'repaired', miraculously unscarred, and certainly not plunged into ugliness, Clift was left with permanently altered features, a semi-paralysed left cheek, and a plethora of health conditions. His long yet private history of alcoholism, multiple addictions and depressive tendencies was suddenly exposed, legible in the visible trauma of his broken face. At the age of thirty-seven, Montgomery Clift was an ailing, prematurely aged man, struggling to cope with physical and mental pain; he was also facing an increasingly hostile Hollywood, and a disoriented, ambivalent fan base. *Raintree County* (Edward Dmytryk, 1956), the film he had been shooting at the time of his car crash, was released with the two versions of his face, pre- and post-accident, often combined in the same sequence. A deeply unsettling aura surrounded his star persona. Against this fraught background, Clift chose *The Young Lions* as the film to mark his return to the screen. This chapter approaches *The Young*

Figure 11.1   Clift the heart-throb in *A Place in the Sun*.

Lions as a site of 'abnormal' stardom, and as Clift's act of subversive interven-tion in his own image; in so doing, it seeks to challenge traditional star studies, which overwhelmingly highlight notions of pleasure and attraction – however complex – in relation to film stars. By framing Clift within a set of deliberately unusual, even disturbing references, as provided by frameworks of queer and 'crip' identities, this analysis rectifies orthodox understandings of stardom, considering instead the visceral difference at the core of Clift's star persona. While issues of ageing have now started to be addressed by star scholars, there is still a notable lack of research in the more unsettling aspects of screen per-sonalities; this chapter suggests to open the field to the troubling, painful and allegedly ghastly connotations of film stars.

CLIFT'S SELF-TRANSFORMATION

Directed again by Edward Dmytryk, *The Young Lions* sees Montgomery Clift as Noah Ackerman, a heroic Jewish soldier battling discrimination in the US army in the Second World War. The film premiered in New York on 2 April 1958: as soon as Clift's image appeared on the screen, a woman in the audi-ence let out a scream, and fainted. All around, people were likewise shocked, whispering incredulously, 'Is that *him*?' After the screening Clift was besieged by reporters, asking him to comment on the audience's reaction; as he ignored them, he was bombarded with questions about his post-accident condition, the amount of pain he still felt, and whether he was able to cope (Bosworth

2007: 327). This combination of horror and pity encapsulates popular receptions of Noah, Clift's beloved among all his roles, and the one he most obsessively laboured to create. The main cause of the audience's consternation was not, however, the damage inflicted on Clift by the crash. The star's changed appearance had already been seen and amply publicised; in fact, *Raintree County* had often shown Clift at his worst, with his features still swollen in the aftermath of the crash. What spectators now saw in *The Young Lions* was not just Clift post-accident: it was a face radically altered by Clift's deliberate intervention on it, an image meticulously crafted to express alienation and pain. Clift's external inspiration for his vision of Noah had been a photo of Franz Kafka, which had so impressed him that he had started to carry it around with him. Taken shortly before his death from tuberculosis, the photo shows the writer looking gaunt and ravaged by illness, with a feverish expression in his eyes; Clift set out to emulate this look not only through his performance, but by a literal reconstruction of his own face. To replicate Kafka's features, he made his ears stick out very prominently, framing his head in an almost horizontal line; he wore a prosthetic nose that was longer than his real one, and starved himself to become even thinner, shifting his weight from 150 to 130 pounds. He thus distorted his image in a profoundly disturbing way, outdoing any physical alteration caused by the accident; though inspired by Kafka, the result was a frenziedly twisted version of himself, looking rather extraterrestrial with his odd features and wasted-looking body (see Figure 11.2). This self-transformation was an extraordinary step for Clift to take. At this time he was devastated by the loss of his beauty, hunted by a press who decried his appearance, and mourned by fans as a ruined sex-symbol; yet

Figure 11.2   Clift 'cripped' in *The Young Lions*.

he had willingly made himself not simply worse-looking, but so unsettlingly different as to seem explicitly alien. As a final touch, Clift chose to wear oversized, non-matching suits in his scenes as a civilian, thus appearing even thinner and stranger. The contrast with his co-stars Marlon Brando and Dean Martin, paragons of virile stardom and both big and beefy, was simply huge.

Clift's creation of Noah did not just rest on his attraction to Kafka; it was also a projection of his own self-perception onto the role, of his sense of affinity for a character he saw as an outcast hero. Indeed, after the film's premiere Clift broke down in convulsive sobs, telling friends 'Noah was the best performance of my life – I couldn't have given more of myself' (Bosworth 2007: 328). To the journalists he had said: 'I'm thirty-seven and Noah is twenty-five, but our characters met in this movie. Strange, isn't it? It's impossible to explain, but I couldn't have played Noah ten years ago' (Kass 1979: 171). Clift's words, in fact, may contain a key to what he himself found impossible to articulate. Ten years before *The Young Lions* he had been twenty-seven, a rising star courted by Hollywood and idolised by fans; he had also, of course, been extremely beautiful. By the time he embarked on Noah as a project, Clift had just started to emerge from the accident trauma; he carried a heavy burden of pain, and his status among Hollywood stars had suddenly declined. Constantly reminded of his lost beauty, he was often described by the press as an abnormal, messed-up individual. Clift must have approached Noah knowing the scrutiny he would be subjected to, and aware that the role was a chance to again make his presence count in Hollywood. These pressures only added to the mental distress he was already experiencing, and most likely turned *The Young Lions* into a matter of life and death for him; indeed, when shooting started in Paris in May 1957, Clift's reaction was to go missing. He disappeared and was not found for days, until he was eventually located in southern Italy, in a brothel, drunk to unconsciousness (Bosworth 2007: 319). When finally on set, Clift devoted himself to his acting with even more than his usual obsession; the notes he made on the script, extremely precise and detailed, ranging from Noah's inner feelings to his wardrobe, testify to his total commitment (Clift Papers: box 17).

He was, however, dealing with increasingly unmanageable issues: dead sober while on set, he would often drink himself to stupor after filming, and spend the early mornings vomiting and taking pills. Equally gripped by pain and a painkiller addiction, he carried on set a flask containing a mixture of bourbon, narcotic pain relievers and fruit juice (LaGuardia 1977: 172); walking became painful as he developed phlebitis in both legs, and difficult because of a balance problem which belied a thyroid condition. As a result, he began to acquire the uncertain gait and off-kilter posture which would characterise him from now on, making his appearance increasingly unsettling. Carlo Fiore, Marlon Brando's acting coach on *The Young Lions* set, said on meeting Clift there for the first time: 'I thought he was a spastic [. . .]. His movements were so unco-ordinated. He'd have a weird posture, slouched; his pelvis would be thrust forward, hands in his back pockets' (LaGuardia 1979: 170). Dean Martin nicknamed Clift 'Spider' because of the odd way he moved, and even got him a cast chair with an image of a spider on it (LaGuardia 1979: 170). It is in this context of increasing distance from his former image, and enduring physical and mental pain, that Clift took control of his own appearance by making it deliberately, sensationally different. Already marked by changes in his face and body, he did not try to counter his separation from notions of male attractive-ness, or his public perception as a disturbingly strange individual. Instead, Clift immersed himself in alienation, channelling his own experience into a deviant impersonation of Noah, and forcibly directing the audience to it; physical self-construction was matched by a performance combining remoteness with frenzy, producing a deeply troubling character. As a dramatic strategy, Clift's self-recreation onscreen challenged standards of 'normality', affirming a per-sonal identity that subverted canons of Hollywood leading men. Crucially, of course, Clift expressed a changed relation to his former status as sex symbol, de-normalising his own image as much as accepted tenets of physical norm. As Noah, Clift's disruptive presence is also informed by gender and sexual ambi-guity, enhancing his strong quality of non-alignment, and further marking his contrast with the film's other male protagonists. The result is a strikingly queer figure, upsetting the normalising plot which *The Young Lions* overtly presents; in a narrative pushing for unqualified ethnic integration, social conform-ity and the development of 'boys' into 'real men', Clift's Jewish hero resists normative identifications, facing the audience from a position of intentional difference.

Based on the novel by Irwin Shaw, *The Young Lions* starts just before the onset of the Second World War and follows the intersecting lives of three men prior to and during the conflict. Christian Diestl (Marlon Brando) is a German ski instructor turned Wehrmacht officer, who comes to question and ultimately reject the Nazi doctrine he is called to defend. Michael Whiteacre (Dean Martin) is an American showbiz star, an amiable coward reluctantly drawn into the army, who will finally mature into a selfless soldier. Montgomery Clift is Noah Ackerman, a New York Jew and a loner, without family or friends, who meets Michael at the draft office; his apparent timidity gives way to savage resistance once he is bullied by his army company. The men's personal journeys during the Second World War are traced alongside their relationships with women, each one through a vastly different narrative. Michael is linked to the glamorous Margaret (Barbara Rush), who had enjoyed a fling with Christian before the war, but whose democratic views had made her recoil from his Nazi sympathies, and later pressurise Michael into active fighting. Christian has a sexual affair with the beautiful but shallow Gretchen (May Britt), the wife of his Nazi captain, while falling in love with a spirited Frenchwoman, Françoise (Liliane Montevecchi), whom he decides to leave as he feels the guilt of his Third Reich association. Noah, terribly shy of women and sexually inexperienced, meets Hope (Hope Lange), a pretty and demure girl from Brooklyn; unlike Christian and Michael's liaisons, defined by eroticism and glamour, the love story between Noah and Hope is tender, romantic and ends in marriage, although Noah has to overcome her father's anti-Semitism. The film unravels by showing Noah's vicious bullying at the hands of the US army, where Michael is his only ally; fearless and recklessly determined, Noah fights his persecutors one by one, despite his physical frailty, and is ultimately victorious. Meantime, Christian is increasingly troubled by the reality of fighting in the German army, and is repelled by his Nazi superiors. A succession of dramatic climaxes brings the three soldiers to the same place, a concentration camp in France which the Germans are fleeing; before that, however, Noah swims through enemy lines to rescue one of his former tormentors, with Michael joining in the effort. The two friends then take part in the liberation of the camp, just hours after Christian has stumbled upon it by accident. As he grasps the meaning of the Nazis' Final Solution, Christian is overcome by horror, throws away his gun and runs into the nearby fields; a few steps away, Michael is patrolling the area with Noah, who is still greatly distressed by the sight of the camp. They spot Christian in the distance and, unaware that he is not armed, Michael shoots him dead; the war has now ended for all three men. The film's last scene sees Noah returning home to New York, to embrace Hope and their child he has still not met.

The Young Lions underwent significant changes in its screen adaptation, as the script was rewritten three times to gain the Pentagon's approval: accordingly, the film dilutes and contains the US army's anti-Semitism, and Noah's Jewishness is barely touched upon. In addition, Marlon Brando insisted on his own changes to the original text, vastly improving and humanising his German character. Despite these omissions and alterations, which greatly upset both Irwin Shaw and Montgomery Clift (Bosworth 2007: 319), the film convincingly paints a multiple account of male identity; of the three protagonists, it is Noah who offers a radical challenge to orthodox representations of masculinity. Underpinned by an ambiguous sexual persona, which disrupts the normative social trajectory of his character, Clift's creation of Noah is shaped in every frame by his alienised face and body. In a production openly capitalising on its star appeal ('Brando and Clift together at last!' announced the film's publicity), Clift's manipulation of his looks subverts notions of desirability, even of normality, constructing a powerful discourse of queer difference.

CONCEPTUALISATIONS OF QUEER AND CRIP

According to Eve Kosofsky Sedgwick, the concept of queerness functions importantly at a subjective level: it can be concretised by an affirmative act on and about oneself, by an intervention in self-articulation. 'Queer', she argues, 'never can only denote; nor even can it only connote; a part of its experimental force as a speech act is the way in which it dramatizes locutionary position itself' (Sedgwick 1993: 9). In *The Young Lions*, Clift's radical operation on his appearance can be read as an experimental act, dramatising his own position of externalised difference: performing his role by literally re-producing himself, Clift's move is the visual equivalent of a speech act, a highly eloquent statement of deviancy. In Sedgwick's view, 'queer' comes into being through 'a person's undertaking particular, performative acts of experimental self-perception and filiation [. . .] there are important senses in which "queer" can signify only *when attached to the first person*' (Sedgwick's emphasis; 1993: 9). In this light, as queer makes sense as a self-description, achieved through acts of creative self-conception, queer can then be meaningfully invoked in relation to one's history of Self. While obviously Clift did not, indeed could not, refer to Sedgwick's contemporary notion of queerness, his practice in *The Young Lions* can be fruitfully analysed in relation to it. By deliberately creating a self-representation which subverts his former image, Clift is queering his own meaning in several ways: he is first subverting external identifications, by imposing a disturbingly crafted look onto evocations of his past appearance. The stunningly beautiful Montgomery Clift, the self-displaying erotic object of multiple sexual fantasies, is now superseded by a violently different presence, at odds with both this cherished image and popular ideas of masculine appeal. At the same time, Clift is also literally queering himself: drastically intervening on his own flesh to reshape form and sign, he reveals new implications attached to his persona – indeed, *attached to the first person*.

This display of a shift in self-perception is also linked, just as in Segdwick's model of queer enunciation, to an act of filiation. Brought up by anti-Semitic parents, Clift held instead a personal mythology of Jewishness which strongly idealised the Jews, whom he saw as superior to other people (LaGuardia 1979: 75). His identification with Noah rests partly on his belief in 'the Jewish genius for survival', in his empathy for him as a hero of 'persistence' (Bosworth 2007: 135); in his script notes, Clift writes 'Tenacity – as appropriate to stubbornness/ The diff – receptivity/invaluable quality' (Clift Papers: box 17). Likewise, under an unreferenced review of *The Young Lions* which claims that Clift must be Jewish after all, as he played Noah so convincingly he deserves compliments, Clift adds: 'the greatest compliment' (Clift Papers: box 17). While it is unclear if he is correcting the quote or simply commenting on it, his preservation of it and his words show his self-connection to a specific idea of Jewishness. Clift's creation of Noah is thus an act of subversive self-reinvention, hinged on a vision of Jewish identity that is both heroic and outcast.

To better identify the queer implications of Clift's approach to his role, it is useful to consider notions of 'crip theory' and 'cripping'. Recent developments in disability studies have stressed their connections to queer theory, through their shared challenge to prescriptive tenets of normality. Established notions of able-bodiedness and heterosexuality are mutually dependent, merged in a paradigm of 'natural' functionality rooted in the denial of difference; likewise, dominant notions of 'health' and 'beauty' rest on a narrow set of ideal qualities, on the illusory stability of bodies and their associated identities. The continuity between 'queer' and 'crip' has been expanded upon in *Crip Theory*: in this seminal text, Robert McRuer argues that social hegemony is based on a system of mandatory physical and sexual conformity. Highlighting how 'the system of compulsory able-bodiedness, which in a sense produces disability, is thoroughly interwoven with the system of compulsory heterosexuality that produces queerness' (McRuer 2006: 2), McRuer posits 'crip' as indissolubly overlapping with 'queer'. He thus acknowledges a field of critique encompassing 'abnormalities' not necessarily linked to traditional signs of disability. Indeed, as a critical strategy, 'cripping' aims precisely at exposing the fantasy of physical perfection and wholeness, as much as that of a monolithic and 'natural' heterosexuality; just like 'queering', 'cripping' uncovers the myriad deviations underlying and constitutive of all identities. At the same time, there is a crucial self-reflexive function associated to notions of crip: in a parallel with the homosexual closet, the crip experience can be often hidden, masked or denied, which produces the possibility for an individual to 'come out as crip'. Both externally targeted and potentially self-affirming, the concept of crip can be meaningfully applied to Montgomery Clift in *The Young Lions*. Since his 1956 accident, Clift had been increasingly turned by the press into an object of pity and even disgust, and was now facing a vaguely hostile cinema audience; however, he was still carrying a baggage of powerful star appeal, a strong association with his former erotic allure and with Hollywood glamour. In other words, Clift straddled two sides of his own star image; he remained a good-looking man, and he might have easily chosen to emphasise this. In building himself up as Noah, he could have equally used make-up, prosthetics and body-training to improve and correct his appearance, opting to stand firmly in the realm of traditional leading men. By doing exactly the opposite – deliberately increasing the faintly alien quality of his changed looks – Clift forced spectators to deal with his self-experience in a wildly uncomfortable, in-your-face manner. Through Noah, he effectively comes out as crip, as a non-beautiful Clift, traumatised yet defiant, irremediably at odds with the requirements of the star system. It is a sensational statement, a radical self-representation which Clift will not attempt again; it is anchored to a moment of personal stocktaking, when the effects of the accident were still overwhelmingly present. After *The Young Lions*, Clift will deal with his changed condition ambivalently, holding himself in tension between past and present; while in a 1963 interview he will claim he emerged from the car crash 'exactly the same' (Hy Gardner: 1963), his last performances will rely heavily on the expression of physical and mental difference. Equally, he will continue to articulate subversion onscreen through performative and narrative means, rather than by bodily deviation. *Lonelyhearts* (Vincent Donahue, 1958) and *Suddenly, Last Summer* (Joseph Mankiewicz, 1959) see Clift play socially and sexually dissident roles: a Christ-like crusader open to casual sex with the needy in the first film, a neurosurgeon committed to the vindication of gay lifestyle in the second. He thus followed *The Young Lions* by a screen alignment with the culturally unspeakable. In *Wild River* (Elia Kazan, 1960) Clift is a possibly asexual yet loving husband, while in *The Misfits* (John Huston, 1961) he is a physically battered, constantly ailing cowboy, who strikes a semi-incestuous alliance with the beautiful Roslyn (Marilyn Monroe). *Judgment at Nuremberg* (Stanley Kramer, 1961) presents Clift's shattering performance as a man castrated by the Nazis; *Freud* (John Huston, 1962) sees a sexually ambiguous, temporally subversive Sigmund Freud challenging his own theories, through Clift in the leading role.

The Young Lions represents a unique stage in Clift's career, a deliberate and bold reaction to traumatic change and external judgement; it seems no coincidence that he felt so close to Noah, and that he held him up as a hero. As the literal embodiment of a personal self-declaration, Noah stands out among Clift's roles as the most uncompromisingly deviant. According to McRuer, crip identities are constantly facing an implied social question, even in supposedly accepting environments: 'Yes, but in the end, wouldn't you rather be more like me?' (McRuer 2006: 9). In *The Young Lions*, this external query is conspicuously hanging over Noah/Clift, who replies with a resounding 'No', despite and against the film's normalising plot. Indeed, Clift here wouldn't ever be more like himself, as far as his factual appearance is concerned: the cripping of his identity reveals it as far more alien than it would otherwise look.

AMBIGUITY AND NON-NORMATIVE SEXUALITY IN *THE YOUNG LIONS*

In an early version of *The Young Lions*' script, Noah's Jewish background is emphasised, being in fact the context through which he is introduced onscreen: his first scene sees him at his father's deathbed, performing religious rituals (Clift Papers: box 17). Clift made lots of annotations for this scene, which was evidently cut out at an early stage, as it is not present in the shooting script. However, Noah's dual characterisation as a Jew and a hero was very significant for Clift, and remains a frame through which he articulates Noah's misfit status; it is also an apt vehicle for his cripping strategy of de-normalisation. Carrie Sandahl points out that 'sexual minorities and people with disability share a history of injustice': so, of course, do the Jews, and Sandahl's crip notion of a 'critique of hegemonic norms' (Sandahl 2003: 25–56) is suitably channelled through a defiant character, marginalised by default, and further isolated by his lone position in society. When he first meets Hope's father, Noah must listen not only to the latter's self-confessed anti-Semitism, but also to his proud boast of his family's established place in Brooklyn, where they have been buried in the same plot for seven generations. Noah replies: 'I don't have a family plot – I don't have a family.' Prior to the meeting, Hope had told her father that Noah was a Jew, and that he was alone in the world; with Noah thus located twice outside a 'normal' social environment, the film lays the ground for his persecution in the army. Although none of his fellow-soldiers refer to the fact that he is Jewish, Noah is inexplicably bullied from the very beginning: he is forced to wash windows, derided for his New York origins, while the James Joyce book he is reading is confiscated and described as 'filth'. Shortly afterwards, his savings are stolen; when he reacts, he is sadistically beaten. While anti-Semitism is implicitly at work, the enmity towards Noah is chiefly externalised through a physical and verbal hatred of his body: when one of the bullies says, 'I saw someone who looked like Ackerman', another retorts, 'Nobody looks like Ackerman!', to the company's raucous approval.

While his suffering at the hands of the army is evocative of Prewitt, Clift's role in *From Here to Eternity* (Fred Zinnemann, 1953), there are huge differences between Noah and Prewitt, tough and resilient as they both are. Prewitt looked the picture of the soldier, and his sense of belonging to the army vastly shaped his identity; Noah's appearance is that of an emaciated, nervous alien, dropped into an environment he does not understand nor care for. His heroism at the front, when he risks his life to save another soldier, is proof of his courage and humanity, not of his adherence to military codes. Prewitt's posture was straight, his movements skilled and confident, his expression strained in self-control; Noah is hunched, uncoordinated, with an uncertain walk and a frenzied gaze. The impact of these physical traits is vastly dependent on Clift's manipulation of his looks; although his initial scenes take place outside the army, in situations which don't yet trigger Noah's latent wildness, there is no denying the shock of his entrance. *The Young Lions* has been running for twenty minutes by the time Clift appears onscreen; up to this moment, the audience has been shown first Brando, manly handsome as a well-built ski instructor, and then Martin, stripped to the waist while being assessed for the draft, displaying an ample chest complete with medallion. The camera then cuts to Noah/Clift in a long shot, getting progressively closer as he meets the draft committee and then Martin/Michael. In contrast with Brando's sportive attire in the snow, and with the semi-naked muscularity of Martin and the other men being drafted, Clift is fully dressed, swamped by oversized and unstylish clothes; he had personally chosen these, and his handwritten notes on that scene's wardrobe memo state 'maybe odd pants', then changed to '<u>very</u> odd pants' (Clift Papers: box 17). The effect of the extra-large jacket combines with his tense, hunched-up shoulders, giving the impression that he has no neck; more striking than anything, however, is the sight of his extremely protruding ears. Together with his wide-open eyes, at times almost unblinking, his nose changed beyond recognition, and his slightly unbalanced gait, Clift makes for very uncomfortable viewing; it is impossible to exaggerate the effect of his appearance, and its contrast with the solid virilities of Brando and Martin. As they are being assessed for their fitness to fight, Noah and Michael are automatically compared, and their shared inclusion in the army is, at this stage of the film, somewhat surprising. When Noah is later introduced to Michael's girlfriend, Margaret, she asks him whether Michael was classified as 1A, the military code for 'fit to fight': the script had Noah simply replying in the affirmative, but Clift changed it to 'we were both 1A' (Clift Papers: box 17), as if anticipating that Margaret (and perhaps the audience) may expect him not to be.

The meeting with Michael also establishes Noah's ambiguous sexual credentials; as they leave the draft office together, Michael's head turns in the direction of two passing girls, whom Noah instead ignores. Michael says: 'Sometimes I think I give off a scent or something – you know – rouses the female.' Noah's spaced-out reply is 'Huh?', making Michael insist 'Those girls!' and quickly conclude: 'You are sick.' Noah does not defend or explain himself, but when Michael next asks him if he has ever had a girl, he fumbles, nervously laughing and repeating 'Have I ever had a girl . . .?'. The result is Michael's prompt invitation to a party he is giving, where girls can be found, followed by a firm: 'Let's not discuss this topic any longer.' On one hand, this brief scene presents Noah's indifference towards the opposite sex as caused by inexperience, a solvable problem requiring simply the exposure to a roomful of girls. This is indeed the film's preferred meaning, formalised by Noah's eventual marriage and fatherhood, and reinforced by the difference in age between him and Michael: the script describes them respectively as 'in his twenties' and 'in his thirties' (Clift Papers: box 17). When Hope first tells her father about Noah, she stresses that he is 'not just a man – he's a boy'. On the other hand, Michael's impression of Noah as 'sick' seems disproportionate to his failure to spot two beauties amid the New York crowd, and contains a hint of more radical implications. As the film progresses by charting Noah's heterosexual trajectory, connotations of a queer sexuality remain, undeveloped, below the surface of the narrative. His relationship with Hope shows romantic love and tenderness, yet exhibits a distinct lack of erotic passion: an ambiguous mixture, prompting Noah to summarise their first date as 'a very confusing night – I don't think I've ever been through anything so confusing'. On hearing this odd declaration, Hope kisses him, eliciting 'I love you, I love you' from Noah, who nevertheless looks completely bewildered. As a man who 'is also a boy', Clift here expresses an ambiguity which is a constant of his star persona; this time, however, his ambiguous image is devoid of any erotic charge, maintaining a mysterious sexual identity which, before 1956, he had only possessed in *The Heiress* (William Wyler, 1949). Yet unlike his character in *The Heiress*, Morris the dandy, Noah/Clift is clearly not presented as an erotic prize, and emphatically not fashioning himself as one. In the context of *The Young Lions*, Noah's non-normative sexuality is not only expressed through performance, but also signalled by his physical appearance, and reinforced by Lange's pretty yet studiously unsexy looks: together, they make a striking contrast to the film's other main couples. The Brando–Britt and Martin–Rush pairs are not only glamorous but statuesque; Clift and Lange are small, frail and very plainly dressed, with Lange's blonde hair providing the only spark in their almost severe joint appearance. The sequence in which they meet is cut first with a shot of Martin and Rush, kissing passionately in full evening attire; the film then cuts back to Clift, looking clumsy and nervous as he takes Lange home. The action next moves to Berlin, showing Brando's seduction at the hands of Britt: a lengthy scene highlights the erotic tension between them, showcasing Brando's masculine beauty and Britt's bombshell figure. Oozing sex appeal, and dominating the frame with their powerful physical presence, they are diametrically opposed to Clift and Lange, who of course share no comparable scene. At the film's very beginning, Brando and Rush cavorting in the snow had also exuded erotic vibes; interestingly, the only exception among Brando's voluptuous lovers is Françoise, who is small and average-looking, and who remains an unsexualised fantasy of love. Their union is impossible, and while Françoise's presence emphasises Christian's redeemable side, the film leaves no doubt that Christian is Brando, a sex symbol and a magnet for glamorous women. As for Noah/Clift, his only passionate scene with Hope takes places as he leaves for the war, and it is not an erotic moment: he squeezes her face hard while kissing her mouth, visibly trying not to cry, giving an impression of frenzied yet non-sexual emotion. This very brief scene also hints at the full revelation of Noah's character, at his physical manifestation of latent feelings. Once he faces bullying in the army, he will turn into a raging figure; his deviant strength will be expressed through the resilience of his waif-like body, and the disfigurement endured by his already faintly anomalous face.

PERFORMING VIOLENCE AND FRAILTY

The scenes where Noah fights his tormentors are among the film's most disturbing sights. The notion of someone so frail engaging in a brutal punch-up is unsettling in itself; as the emaciated Clift lacks both muscles and body weight, his taking on four burly soldiers looks reckless and unnatural. Indeed, Michael tries hard to dissuade Noah from fighting, calling him crazy, asking him how much he weighs, then starting: 'If I were you . . .', but Noah interrupts him: 'You're not.' Thus changing from wallflower to wild creature, Noah seems to direct an abnormal energy to his body, and while he is viciously beaten in most fights, he credibly wins the last one. When playing Prewitt in *Eternity*, Clift had eventually required a double to do most of his punching, despite weeks of training; in *The Young Lions*, however, he refused a stand-in, and was coached by ex-boxing champion Johnny Indrisano. Even so, the fight scenes took four days to film (Bosworth 2007: 321), and are very painful to watch; retrospectively, they are only made more disturbing by the knowledge that every punch Clift gives onscreen is his own. Wearing a military uniform, more fitted and revealing than his oversized civilian suits, Clift shows most clearly the result of his deliberate self-starving: he looks virtually skeletal, with no recognisable shoulders, chest, or buttocks shaped under his clothes. A physical fraction of every other man onscreen, he lacks the obvious signs of bodily masculinity, to say nothing of a soldier's ideal appearance. Despite his un-virile looks, however, Noah/Clift displays a fearless indifference to physical harm; savagely beaten and almost whipped in the air by the others' blows, he seems oblivious to pain, his odd-looking face remaining set to feverish determination. While he appears badly hurt from the first fight, Noah's physical damage is shown in its full extent before his last round; sitting in the doctor's surgery to get his wounds cleaned, he presents his most disturbing look yet. One of his eyes is so swollen as to be virtually closed, his mouth is disfigured, and both eyelid and lip are held together with massive stitches: there is a clear resemblance to Frankenstein's monster. His appearance, already self-manipulated to express difference and pain, reaches here a higher stage of alienation; with parts of his face grotesquely emphasised, he acquires a veneer of horror which completes the unnatural feel of his presence. In a film dealing with the Second World War, it is notable that Clift in this scene, out of active combat, provides the only shocking physical sight. It is true that Maximilian Schell, playing the Nazi Captain Hardenberg, ends up entirely cast in plaster with only his eyes showing, having lost several limbs; but Schell is literally de-humanised by his plaster entombment, rendered invisible and only nominally himself. Clift, instead, is intensely alive, as well as eerily recognisable, and that is why his appearance is so unsettling. De-naturalising physical prowess as well as physical norm, the monstricised Clift is calm and unfazed while the doctor treats him, a look entirely at odds with the pain he must feel and the frenzy he shows while fighting; his only comment, or self-explanation, is 'I like to fight'. Yet when victory comes, Clift again subverts notions of virility through his behaviour and appearance. Getting hold of his opponent by encircling his waist with one arm, he furiously hammers punches into him with his free hand; when the other falls down and does not get up, Clift looks around him with a pained and vacant gaze, showing no trace of satisfaction. Framed in a close-up, Clift's thin, almost triangular face is bruised and bloody, edged by his terribly protruding ears; his mouth is ripped, his hair wildly unkempt, his expression uncertain. Staring in apparent disorientation, his eyes are big and wide open, the only beautiful feature in his disturbing image.

Noah's dual status as hero and deviant outsider is emphasised in his last spoken scene, set in the concentration camp he has helped liberate. After entering the camp, Noah is very visibly affected, and Captain Green (Arthur Franz), one of the company's former bullies, tells him to go for a walk outside with Michael. In one of the film's rare acknowledgements of Noah's Jewishness, after the two friends briefly mention the gas chambers, Noah says: 'My father's brother died in one of those', adding: 'Did I tell you about my father?' But when Michael replies that he didn't, Noah abruptly shifts the subject to the newly rehabilitated Green, who is working to restore dignity to the camp's ex-inmates. 'Once this war's over, Green's gonna be running the world', he tells Michael; suddenly, a change comes over him, and he rapidly goes from looking calm to looking beside himself. With a savage countenance on his face, that more readily suggests alienation than hope, Noah shouts: 'There are millions of him! They are human beings! They will rule the world! Millions and millions!' His voice is croaky, and his words are accompanied by a violent swinging of his arm in the air; at some point he even beats Michael in the chest with his fist. It is extremely disconcerting behaviour, pointing to an alternative system of feeling, to a painful experience that, like the story of his father, he is not expanding upon. Small and skinny next to Michael, with his conspicuous ears sticking out under the army helmet, Noah the outsider, the Jew, the hero, looks decidedly different from everyone else. His words confirm his remoteness: 'they' will rule the world, hopefully for the best, but he will not. Opting out of the mainstream, outside the masculine system of power, Noah reclaims an identity away from normative structures.

CONCLUSION

In *The Young Lions* Montgomery Clift effects a radical reconstruction of his star image, choosing to disturb and even horrify fans and audiences. Refusing to conform to established norms of male stardom, and instead emphasising his vast distance from them, he offers a version of himself that is both alien and painful. This self-defining action positions Clift in a visual and performative sphere uniquely his own, yet does not sever his ties to the star system. His intervention in a high-profile film, where he shares screen time with Marlon Brando and Dean Martin, firmly locates his own stardom in the traditional place for it: the Hollywood dream factory. But as Clift turns the dream into a nightmare, he claims an alternative form for star images. Combining difference and pain with defiance and strength, he posits a new level of inescapable star presence; through his creation of Noah, Montgomery Clift unsettles the norm of the system he himself inhabits, subverting his own image with powerful crip significations.

ACKNOWLEDGEMENT

A version of this chapter has been previously published as part of the monograph *Montgomery Clift, Queer Star* (2013), and is reproduced here with the kind permission of Wayne State University Press.

BIBLIOGRAPHY

Bosworth, Patricia (2007), *Montgomery Clift: A Biography*, New York: Limelight Editions.
LaGuardia, Robert (1977), *Monty: A Biography of Montgomery Clift*, New York: Primus.
McRuer, Robert (2006), *Crip Theory: Cultural Signs of Queerness and Disability*, New York: New York University Press.
Montgomery Clift Papers, Billy Rose Theater Division, New York Public Library.
Sandahl, Carrie (2003), 'Queering the Crip or Cripping the Queer? Intersections of Queer and Crip Identities in Solo Autobiographical Performance', *JLQ: A Journal of Lesbian and Gay Studies* 9:1–2, 23–56.
Sedgwick, Eve Kosofski (1993), *Tendencies*, Durham, NC: Duke University Press.

12. 'UNA DIVA NON COME LE ALTRE': *LE STREGHE* AND THE PARADOXICAL STARDOM OF SILVANA MANGANO

Leon Hunt

She was post-war Italy's (and Europe's) first international pin-up: one British headline described her as 'the Rage of the Continent' (Schiff 1950), while in the US she became known as 'the Atomic Italian'. Director Giuseppe De Santis characterised her breakout role as 'the Rita Hayworth of the Italian periphery' (Gundle 1996: 314), but she has also been described as 'la Greta Garbo del cinema italiano' (Cimmino and Masi 1994: 134), a reference to the enigmatic and distant persona she subsequently adopted. Her career ranged from neorealism to melodrama to *commedia all'Italiana* (forming a particularly popular partnership with Alberto Sordi) to art house (Pasolini and Visconti gave her a new international profile in the late 1960s/early '70s). She was married to arguably the most famous (and controversial) Italian film producer, Dino De Laurentiis, something that is sometimes used to dismiss her as a mediocre actress promoted beyond her abilities by a powerful husband (see Shipman 1989 and Thomson 2003, for example). Iconic and era-defining in her initial roles, Silvana Mangano is nevertheless overshadowed in accounts of Italian stardom by her contemporaries Sophia Loren and Gina Lollobrigida. As the first of the so-called *maggiorate fisiche* (voluptuous beauty contest winners turned film stars), she paved the way for their success, which unquestionably overtook her own, a scenario that appears to have held little concern for her. No account of Italian film history can overlook the cultural impact of her role in the film *Riso amaro/Bitter Rice* (Giuseppe De Santis, Italy 1948), which globalised a new and powerful image of Italian female sexuality – the *mondina* in tight shorts and torn stockings, underarm hair unshaved, chewing gum, dancing to boogie-woogie on the record player she carries with her, at one point appearing from behind the magazine *Grand Hotel* that embodies her Americanised aspirations. Mangano has been seen to have incarnated 'a new prototype of Italian womanhood' (Gundle 2007: 108), 'a creature of the earth, rich with joyous sensuality, generous in its proportions, warm and familiar: a body-landscape' (Grignaffini 1988: 123). But her subsequent career is harder to map, marked by periods of inactivity, a radical reshaping of her body (from voluptuous *maggiorata* to slender, elegant diva), a well-publicised antipathy towards filmmaking, and the later move into art house (the point at which she usually resurfaces in Italian film histories, but rarely as the centre of attention).

Martin Shingler identifies the 'expansion of fields of enquiry' – different countries, periods and genres – as one of the key contemporary developments in star studies (2012: 64). Such expansions include the study of transnational stardom (Meeuf and Raphael 2013) and cult stardom (Egan and Thomas 2013). Mangano could certainly be studied as a transnational figure, shaped by both neorealist and Hollywood models of female stardom and showcased in De Laurentiis productions that increasingly sought to move beyond the national. While cult stardom is a less than perfect fit, in some ways it brings us closer to what I am choosing to call her paradoxical stardom, the way such a fascinating star has left uneven traces on film history. Her career offers some of the pleasures associated with the cult star – the sense of sometimes having been marginalised and underrated – and yet the 'outsider' status implied by cult stardom sits awkwardly alongside her privileged position in the film industry and the canonical films that sit at either end of her career. A 'reluctant' diva, or even 'anti-diva' (Kezich and Levantesi 2004: 87), who shed the voluptuous body that made her world famous; the 'Atomic Italian' who reinvented herself as elegantly aristocratic, cultivating an offscreen persona as the perfect wife and mother (Buckley 2006: 46); a career shaped first by a powerful film-producer husband and then by two art-house auteurs – Mangano's stardom is marked by a series of paradoxes. A second concern of this chapter is how stardom works through and within a specific film format popular in (but by no means exclusive to) Italian and French cinema in the 1950s and 1960s – the episode film. Thus the latter part of the chapter focuses on *Le streghe/The Witches* (Italy/France 1967), the film that seems to mark the transition from what we might call her 'De Laurentiis career' to her 'Pasolini–Visconti career'. Of its five episodes, one is directed by Luchino Visconti ('La strega bruciata viva'/The Witch Burned Alive), one by Pier Paolo Pasolini ('La terra vista dalla luna'/The Earth Seen from the Moon) and a third by another key figure in Mangano's career (and Sophia Loren's too), Vittorio De Sica ('Una sera come le altre'/An Evening like the Others). As Pauline Small has observed, the achievements of the *maggiorate* have often been attributed to their auteur directors or shrewd producer husbands (2014: 120). Thus Loren, too, had a producer-husband figure (Carlo Ponti) and an auteur who is often perceived as having 'elevated' her (De Sica) (see Small 2009). Mangano had some awards success in Italy, if not on the same international scale as Loren's 1962 Academy Award for *La Ciociara/Two Women* (Vittorio De Sica, Italy/France 1960). Unusual as an actual star vehicle for Mangano (no longer the leading lady she had been in the late 1940s and '50s), *Le streghe* is designed to demonstrate her versatility as well as her enduring glamour.

Across her career as a whole, Mangano had a less clearly defined screen persona than Sophia Loren or Gina Lollobrigida – a Google image search might leave the viewer wondering if they are always looking at the same person, so radically did she transform her appearance. The most dramatic transformation came between *Il brigante Musolino* (Mario Camerini, Italy 1950) and *Anna* (Alberto Lattuada, Italy 1951): Mangano lost a considerable amount of weight and would subsequently be a more slender figure than the one that had first captured attention in *Riso amaro*. She remained a mutable figure subsequently, with changes in hair and make-up producing strikingly different appearances: Kezich and Levantesi describe one of her more extreme images as her 'horror movie look', hair dyed a reddish colour with 'chalky foundation, brick-red lipstick, harsh eyeliner' (2004: 146). If her earliest incarnation was compared with Rita Hayworth, later versions bore some resemblance to Ava Gardner, Ingrid Bergman, Joan Fontaine and even Monica Vitti. In more inclusive accounts of her career (as opposed to those that demonstrate little interest in her career between *Riso amaro* and the Pasolini–Visconti period), two important elements recur – *duality* and *dance*. In his book on Mangano, Federico Rocca (2008) groups together three films from the height of her popularity that literally or figuratively double her in some way: *Anna*, *Ulisse/Ulysses* (Mario Camerini, Italy 1952, in which she plays both Penelope and Circe) and *Mambo* (Robert Rossen, Italy/US 1954). But he is also one of a number of commentators to be intrigued by her mixed parentage – English mother, Sicilian father – hinting that this accounts for the tension between her reserve (*algida* – icy – is one of the words he uses) and Mediterranean sensuality (ibid.: 19). For Masi and Lancia, she was 'neither a Mediterranean nor a Nordic type, but a mixture of the two. She combined the sovereign indolence of the southern belle with a cool northern gaze' (1997: 74). Further divisions can be identified, between her De Laurentiis career and her art-house career, and between the 'neorealist cheesecake' (Bondanella 2009: 107) that initially made her a star and the ethereal Mother that seemed to fascinate both Pasolini and Visconti. While there are conflicting claims about who 'discovered' her, De Laurentiis or De Santis, the director's version of events again presents contrasting Silvanas. Dressed to look her best at her audition for *Riso amaro*,

Mangano had supposedly made little impression, but then De Santis saw her again 'raw' on Rome's Via Veneto, drenched by the rain: 'It was like a bolt of lightning to see her again like that, beautiful and unassuming, authentic in her true state of a not well-off young woman' (quoted by Gundle 2007: 143).

While Mangano never made a musical as such – *Mambo* comes closest, with its backstage narrative and the choreography of Katherine Dunham – dance occupies a key role in a number of her films and has produced some of her most iconic scenes. Dance is our introduction to her in *Riso amaro*, in a scene that seems to redirect, if not derail, the narrative. As Walter (Vittorio Gassman) and Francesca (Doris Dowling) are evading the police, boogie woogie music can be heard faintly offscreen and the camera starts to track along the train carriages as if distracted, taking in a series of couples looking out of the window at something (the music growing louder), the men paying particularly appreciative attention, until finally it brings Silvana into view, dancing, a crowd surrounding and watching her, neorealist images of labour confined to the extreme background of the frame. Some thirty minutes into *Anna*, the eponymous nun working in a Milan hospital is praying for injured Raf Vallone and we are taken into a flashback that seems to come from nowhere and yet also plays like the character's real introduction: her former self, the nightclub singer performing the song 'Negro Zumbon' (see Figure 12.1), a scene that is replayed diegetically in both *Nuovo Cinema Paradiso* (Giuseppe Tornatore, Italy/France 1988) and *Caro diario/Dear Diary* (Nanni Moretti,Italy/France 1993). These are probably Mangano's two most well-loved films in Italy (*Anna* was the first Italian film to earn over a billion lire) – one of the dance scenes in *Riso amaro* is one of the 'classic' film clips projected at Turin's Cinema Museum – but *Le streghe* includes a dance sequence in Visconti's 'La strega bruciata viva' that is every bit as striking. Mangano had dance lessons as a child, and received further training for the more challenging choreography of *Mambo*, but more importantly, dance is nearly always an expression of her character's sexuality, in films like *Anna* and *Mambo* a sexuality that she struggles to contain in some way. In *Anna*, Marcia Landy suggests:

> a double pleasure is available in contemplating two sides of Mangano's image, as sinner and as saint, as transgressor and as penitent, as physical body and as spiritual icon. (2008: 113)

While Mangano is associated with dance, she is not regarded as a movie dancer in the way that someone like Cyd Charisse is (*Mambo* suggests that she lacked the technical skill for that). More appropriate points of comparison would be Sophia Loren, who danced in several of her Italian and Hollywood films, and a slightly later (and more confrontational) European sex symbol, Brigitte Bardot. The differences between Mangano and Bardot are obvious

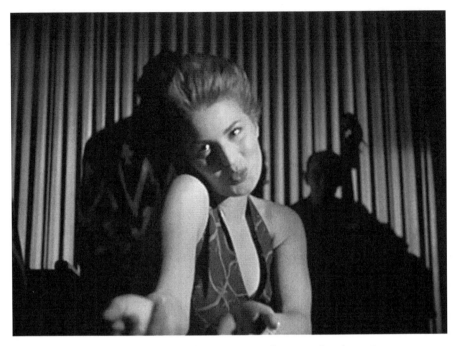

Figure 12.1   Mangano and dance: the 'Negro Zumbon' number from *Anna*.

enough and their careers followed rather different paths, but they shared a childhood training in classical dance that some of their films exploited and also a love–hate relationship with filmmaking (Vincendeau 2013: 1) – an antipathy usually linked to Bardot's rebelliousness, whereas rebellion was far from the more conservative image projected publicly by Mangano. In Loren's films, dance is an expression of her humour and vivaciousness; she invariably smiles or laughs when she is dancing. This 'innocence' sometimes serves to soften what might otherwise be seen as quite titillating performances, such as her striptease in *Ieri, oggi, domani* (Vittorio De Sica, Italy/France 1963) or the song 'Carina' in *It Started in Naples* (Melvin Shavelson, US 1960), during which she dresses in a revealing schoolgirl outfit. Bardot and Mangano, on the other hand, share an association between dance and sexual abandon, an abandonment that is sometimes given a racial dimension: black performers accompany the radiant white blondes in *Anna*, *Mambo* and *Et Dieu créa la femme* ... (Roger Vadim, France/Italy 1956). Moreover, this abandonment is sometimes pathologised, linked to despair and disturbance as much as sensual pleasure. In *Mambo*, Mangano's Giovanna loses herself at a costume ball during the Venice carnival, slightly drunk and swept along by the mambo performed by the Katherine Dunham troupe; her subsequent reaction suggests that she has found the experience more troubling than liberating. It's a short but memorable scene and makes for an interesting comparison with the more notorious mambo performed by Bardot in *Et Dieu* . . ., in which her body is displayed in a more eroticised way, her face 'flushed and sweaty, her hair dishevelled' (Austin 2003: 14), her dancing 'both more lascivious and more frantic' (Vincendeau 2013: 45), the scene culminating in violence. Contrast this with Loren's comic mambo in *Pane, amore e* . . . (Dino Risi, Italy/France 1955), where the jiggling of her breasts caused by her hip movements is offset by her combative performance, designed to see off a rival for the object of her affections. Vincendeau acknowledges that the 'natural' sexuality of post-war Italian divas paved the way for Bardot's more permissive persona – 'European eroticism was bankable' (2000: 93) – but I would suggest that it is Mangano who anticipates her most of all, from the sexual precocity of *Riso amaro* to the use of dance as an expression of her sexuality and psychology.

MAGGIORATA, DIVA AND ANTI-DIVA: MANGANO AND LOREN

In *La signora senza camelie* (Michelangelo Antonioni, Italy/France 1953), Lucia Bosé plays a *maggiorata*-type film star trying and failing to make the transition to 'serious' films, as much as anything because of the limitations of her acting talents. The film ends with her agreeing resignedly to make a tacky-looking *peplum*. Bosé's natural elegance had lost her Mangano's role in *Riso amaro* – her modest origins had already been erased, much as Silvana would subsequently erase her own – but led her to Antonioni, not quite yet the celebrated art-house auteur that he would become with the more experienced actress, Monica Vitti. Bosé, the former Miss Italia of 1947, would not achieve Mangano's level of stardom, let alone Sophia Loren's. But *La signora* is an interesting account of the difficulties faced by that generation of Italian actresses in sustaining satisfying careers, and this desire for something 'better' than being pure body onscreen was already being expressed by Mangano herself in an interview with the British press in 1950:

> All cinemagoers seem to be interested in is my shape. I had a good part in *Bitter Rice* with good lines and passionate scenes. But what do people remember about me? Merely a young girl wading around in mud in shorts and silk stockings. That's no reward for an actress. (Mosley 1950)

At that stage, Mangano's response was to be constantly announcing her retirement; she never tired of telling the press how much she hated filmmaking. This would later be modified into an aspiration to make different kinds of films: 'a good film with a good director, a good story, good dialogue – and a role, for once, that's congenial to me' (Kezich and Levantesi 2004: 146). The critical reception of the *maggiorate* was by no means an entirely positive one. De Sica famously dismissed them as 'all curves', a mere 'show of legs and eye-catching, opulent, enormous breasts' (quoted by Gundle 2007: 154), to which Mangano is reported to have responded, 'It could be that he's right'(Kezich and Levantesi 2004: 92). The former beauty queens were raw and untrained, getting by on looks and natural charisma, their voices dubbed by professional actresses – Mangano by Lidia Simoneschi (also the voice of Ingrid Bergman in Italy), not using her own voice until De Sica's *L'oro di Napoli/The Gold of Naples* (Italy 1954). When they started winning awards, their dubbed voices were a source of outrage for some critics (Small 2009: 16). Ironically, it would be De Sica who would 'elevate' both Loren and Mangano in the same film (but in different episodes), *L'oro di Napoli*. 'Pizza a credito' (Pizza on credit) is generally acknowledged as Loren's breakout role as the sexy, unfaithful pizza girl, while Mangano's performance as the scorned prostitute in 'Theresa' would win her her first acting award. Her 'extraordinary' (wordless) performance in the climactic scene would make a big impression on André Bazin in *Cahiers du Cinema*:

> Silvana Mangano's face, carefully lit by a street lamp, expresses a whole range of feelings, the final use of which is neither resignation nor envy but rather hatred, which is moreover confirmed by the way she knocks on the door to ask her husband for admittance. (2011: 161)

Loren's and Mangano's paths had crossed onscreen once before – as Sofia Lazzaro, Loren had appeared in a small role in *Anna*. If *L'oro di Napoli* did more for Loren's career than it did for Mangano's, among the likely reasons are their respective work rates and relationships with their producer-husbands (who had been partners just a few years before). There was a two-year gap between *L'oro di Napoli* and Mangano's next film, *Uomini e lupi* (Giuseppe De Santis, Italy 1957), and such gaps would characterise Mangano's stop-start career. As Masi and Lancia observe:

> Even at the peak of her popularity, she never made more than one movie a year – very few if one remembers that Loren and Lollo[brigida] were shooting three or four at the same time. (1997: 75)

In *La grande guerra* (Mario Monicelli, Italy/France 1959), Mangano received the billing 'participazione straordinario' (for her cameo, again as a prostitute) for the first but not the last time. She continued to work through the 1960s, and her performance as Mussolini's daughter Edda Ciano in *Il processo di Verona* (Carlo Lizzani, Italy/France 1963) won her further critical praise and another acting award, the David di Donatello, but it wasn't until the Pasolini–Visconti period, lasting from 1967 to 1974, that her work rate increased (at least by her own standards). It's as hard to imagine Mangano having Loren's Hollywood career – an American TV appearance on *What's My Line?* from the 1950s finds her awkward and withdrawn in public, whereas Loren's charisma seemed to be switched on twenty-four hours a day – as it is Loren having Mangano's later art-house one, even though their beginnings and career paths had many similarities. Loren was ambitious, comfortable with her stardom, and seemingly in accord with Ponti's efforts to promote her. Mangano, on the other hand, seems to have had a rather more complicated relationship with her producer-husband.

From De Laurentiis to art house

Cimmino and Masi describe Mangano's marriage to Dino De Laurentiis as a 'contratto esclusiva, a tempo indeterminato' (an exclusive contract for an indefinite period) (1994: 37). Loren and Ponti had no legally binding contract, although it was widely believed that they had (Small 2009: 21), but Ponti–De Laurentiis were one of the few Italian film companies to offer stars long- term contracts. From *Riso amaro* to *Le streghe*, De Laurentiis produced all of Mangano's films except one; a special agreement permitted her to make *Uomini e lupi* for Titanus producer Goffredo Lombardi, apparently because of her wish to work with De Santis again (Rocca 2008: 90). Whatever one might think of De Laurentiis 'controlling' Mangano's career (and those gaps in her career suggest that this control was by no means complete), it is worth observing that she gave some of her best performances during this period and worked with some of Italy's best directors, including De Santis, De Sica, Alberto Lattuada, Carlo Lizzani, Mario Camerini and Mario Monicelli. In other words, to see Pasolini and Visconti as having 'rescued' her from the vulgar commerce of De Laurentiis would be misleading. There is evidence that De Laurentiis sometimes inflated her billing; she is given second billing in the biblical epic *Barabba/Barabbas* (Richard Fleischer, Italy 1961) for a role scarcely larger than her 'extraordinary participation' in *La grande guerra*. He also seems to have been successful in making her one of the highest-paid actresses in Italy: in 1962, Loren was the highest paid (200 million lire per film), followed by Lollobrigida (150), with Mangano alongside Marcello Mastroianni and Alberto Sordi (100), ahead of Claudia Cardinale (70), Ugo Tognazzi, Totò and Monica Vitti (40) (Rocca 2008: 131). On the other hand, Cimmino and Masi relate the rumour that one of the main reasons Mangano worked so little during the 1960s was because of De Laurentiis' inflated asking price for what were often cameo roles. Kezich and Levantesi (2004) and Cimmino and Masi (1994) – inevitably, given the respective focuses of their books – present slightly different takes on the Mangano–De Laurentiis relationship, but while it probably plays an important role in shaping her pre-1967 career, such material is too anecdotal and sometimes speculative to be entirely reliable. For David Thomson, 'it was probably a good thing that Silvana Mangano was married to one of the great Italian bosses' (2003), and he presents an anecdote of De Laurentiis forcing her onto Richard Fleischer as the safe, cheap alternative to Jeanne Moreau in *Barabbas*. He observes that Loren was winning the Oscar at the same time that Mangano was being deployed as a casting consolation prize, but fails to mention that her next film was her acclaimed role in *Il processo di Verona*. But nor, as we have seen, can we cast De Laurentiis as the obstacle to Mangano making films that were worthy of her talents, which betrays as much as anything a long-term and often simplistic stereotyping of producers as the enemies of art.

De Laurentiis produced *Le streghe*, on which Mangano worked with Visconti and Pasolini for the first time. She would make three more films with Pasolini: *Edipo re/Oedipus Rex* (Italy 1967), *Teorema/Theorem* (Italy 1968) and *Il Decameron* (Italy/France/West Germany 1971), the latter a cameo as the Madonna. For Visconti, she appeared in *Morte a Venezia/Death in Venice* (Italy/France 1971), *Ludwig* (Italy/France/West Germany 1972) and *Gruppo di famiglia in un interno/Conversation Piece* (Italy/France 1974). These films form the bulk of the latter part of her original career,[1] and none of them were produced by De Laurentiis. Of the films she made between 1967 and 1974, De Laurentiis produced only two: another episode film, *Capriccio all'italiana* (Mauro Bolognini, Mario Monicelli, Pier Paolo Pasolini, Steno, Pino Zac and Franco Rossi, Italy 1968), and one of her best films, the comedy *Lo scopone scientifico* (Luigi Comencini, 1972), her final pairing with Alberto Sordi. Kezich and Levantesi interpret this shift in professional and personal circumstances as follows:[2]

> from that point on, it was almost as if a baton had been passed [. . .] the actress steadily loosened her husband's grip on her career; she began working almost exclusively with Visconti and Pasolini. (2004: 176)

These were undoubtedly more prestigious films, although Mangano evidently had misgivings about her roles in both *Teorema* (Pasolini famously wrote an 'open letter' to placate her) and *Gruppo di famiglia in un interno*. The Visconti films (*Gruppo* apart) seem more interested in her iconic presence – her performance in *Morte a Venezia* is to all intents and purposes wordless – than the actorly skills she had been allowed to display in some of the De Laurentiis films. Both were preoccupied with her maternal image (one cultivated in her society image more than in her onscreen one – she had, after all, played prostitutes in four different films). *Morte a Venezia*, the preface to *Edipo re* (where she seems to be playing Pasolini's mother) and the saintly cameo in *Il Decameron* luxuriate in this eternal Mother, while *Teorema* and *Gruppo di famiglia in un interno* seek to debase it (which was the likely source of her antipathy towards them). Landy points to a metacinematic and critical use of her in some of these films (2008: 115), and *Teorema* can be read through its star as much as its director. The camera is as besotted with Mangano's beauty as it is with that of Terence Stamp's (un)holy stranger, and she was originally billed above him. Thematically (if admittedly not stylistically), it sits quite comfortably alongside films like *Anna* and *Mambo*, in which the desire for respectability is undone by libidinous desire. Lucia picking up young men in the region of the Po valley both recalls *Riso amaro* in its setting and *Anna*'s seeking of debasement through the louche bartender played by Vittorio Gassman. The tension between reserve and sensuality runs through Mangano's screen persona, and thus *Teorema* is the film from her Pasolini–Visconti career that comes closest to forming a bridge of sorts between her two careers.

'UNA DIVA BRUCIATA VIVA': *LE STREGHE*

What little writing there is on *Le streghe* largely falls into three groups. Firstly, the film surfaces as an oddity in Clint Eastwood's career, the one film from his Italian sojourn that wasn't a Western directed by Sergio Leone. In this context, the film is generally dismissed as a vanity project for a faded diva (Cole and Williams 1983: 59), a failed attempt by De Laurentiis to 'promote his wife Sylvana [sic] Mangano to superstardom rivalling that of Sophia Loren' (Guériff 1984: 56). The second type of writing conforms to a tendency identified by both Mark Betz (2009) and David Scott Diffrient (2014) in writing about episode films, a format that was particularly popular in Italian and French cinema in the 1960s – the lifting out and isolation of episodes by auteur filmmakers:

> the episode in question is held apart from the rest of the (always unanalyzed, usually unnamed) segments as particular to its author's oeuvre and so incompatible to a grouping of works by others. In the process, the auteur's episode is shown to fit, if not clearly then arguably, into the evolutionary line of development that is a standard teleology of auteurist studies. (Betz 2009: location 2846–52)

Visconti's 'La strega bruciata viva' and Pasolini's 'La terra vista dalla luna' in *Le streghe* have been separated from *Le streghe* in this way in auteur studies – see, for example, John David Rhodes' discussion of 'La terra' in his book on Pasolini's Rome (2007: 148), which doesn't even mention that it's an episode in a feature film but treats it solely as a short film by Pasolini. But it isn't just critics and academics who do this. In the BFI's 2013 Pasolini season, episodes from various films he contributed to (including 'La terra vista dalla luna') were shown as supporting features to his feature films. Only the two Italian-language books devoted to Mangano (Cimmino and Masi 1994; Rocca 2008) approach *Le streghe* as what it clearly is – a star vehicle.

The episode film – also categorised variously as the omnibus, anthology and portmanteau film – was prevalent in both Italian and French cinema during the period of Mangano's career. Betz and Diffrient offer different and equally useful definitions of its subcategories, but for the purposes of this chapter I shall use Diffrient's definition of the umbrella category of 'episode' film: 'a feature-length motion picture composed of two or more autonomous segments that might share thematic and/or stylistic elements' (2014: 7). Mangano made several episode films throughout her career. This was not untypical for Italian stars of this period, but appearing in a single episode probably particularly suited someone who seemed not to enjoy the filmmaking process. She mostly appeared in single episodes, but the multi-director film *La mia signora* (Mauro Bolognini, Tinto Brass and Luigi Comencini, Italy 1964) pairs her with Alberto Sordi in all five episodes, their partnership the connecting element in the film: De Sica's *Ieri, oggi, domani/Yesterday, Today and Tomorrow* pairs Sophia Loren and Marcello Mastroianni across three stories (and cities) in a similar way. Episode films, Diffrient reminds us, 'are supposed to "hang together", harmoniously, around a central theme or narrative conceit' (2014: 149), while Betz points out that 'the figure of woman serves as a unifying trope for several postwar Italian and French (frequently Italo-French) omnibus films'; *Le streghe* and *La mia signora* cohere (if at all) around female sexuality as well as around their stars. One of the most notable examples of an Italian episode film that is constructed around both a loose theme and a star is Roberto Rossellini's two-part *L'amore* (Italy 1948). While the title points to the linking theme, the introduction to the second episode, 'Il miracolo', perhaps presents the film's real *raison d'être*: 'This film is an homage to the art of Anna Magnani', a dedication attributed onscreen to Rossellini himself. This is an unusual example, partly because Magnani is herself exceptional among post-war Italian female stars; she had not come out of beauty contests, was conspicuously unglamorous and 'authentic', celebrated for her craft and range. But I would suggest that Magnani was an important reference point for actresses ready to prove themselves more than spectacular bodies: Loren's role in *La ciociara* had originally been offered to Magnani (with Sophia as the daughter ultimately played by the much younger Eleonora Brown), while several of Mangano's more acclaimed roles were the sorts of parts that Magnani might have played – for example, the working-class card player from Rome's *borgate* in *Lo scopone scientifico*. Moreover, while the default version of the episode film emphasised variety and ensemble casts, it could also be used to demonstrate the versatility of stars like Loren and Mangano. If we use Barry King's distinction between impersonation (the actor 'disappearing' into a character) and 'personification' (the adherence to roles 'consonant with his or her personality') (1991: 168), the episode film potentially offers a balancing of these two things. Interestingly, in *L'oro di Napoli*, Mangano won critical plaudits for what seemed to be her first attempt at impersonation, while Loren has retrospectively been seen as inhabiting her persona for the first time as the easygoing Neapolitan pizza girl. In *Ieri, oggi, domani*, Loren plays two roles consonant with her persona – the fiery Neapolitan who avoids jail through repeated pregnancies, and the good-natured prostitute who is a rather more upbeat figure than the streetwalkers Mangano sometimes played. The middle episode presents a less characteristic Loren, a cold-hearted Milanese society girl. It might be stretching things to call it a character part exactly, but it certainly cuts against her established star persona.

When Mangano made *Le streghe*, she was inhabiting a less clearly defined persona than she once had; there had been a fair bit of 'impersonation' among her 1960s roles, most notably Mussolini's daughter in *Il processo di Verona*. But *Le streghe* also gives the impression of trying to rebuild Mangano's star aura rather than simply demonstrate her development as a character actress. The seemingly misogynist linking theme of the film – Mangano as five modern 'witches' – is more evident in some parts of the film than others. The animated opening titles by Pino Zac play on stereotypical images of dangerous women drivers as well as transforming Mangano into the archetypal (cartoon) witch, complete with broomstick and facial warts. But of the five episodes, only the two shortest – perhaps more accurately described as sketches (and positioned as interludes between the three longer episodes) – really pick up on this imagery (notwithstanding Visconti's episode title). In Mauro Bolognini's 'Senso civico', Mangano is a callous Roman society girl offering a lift to injured and delirious Alberto Sordi solely as a means to speed through the traffic (she never actually delivers him to the hospital, but dumps him near her own destination). She plays an almost identical figure in Bolognini's 'Perche?' (Why?) in *Capriccio all'italiana*. And in Franco Rossi's 'La siciliana', she manipulates susceptible Sicilian men (including her father) into a massacre and then delivers an operatic performance of grief at their funerals. It's harder to see how her characters in the three longer episodes are 'witches', except insofar as movie star Gloria 'bewitches' men and women alike in 'La strega bruciata viva' (as the subheading for this section implies, it is the figure of the diva who is 'burned alive', or stripped bare, in this episode). What I want to suggest is that just as Mangano-Sordi provide the link throughout *La mia signora*, the real subject of *Le streghe* is Silvana Mangano, but given the episode format and the rather different filmmaking sensibilities involved, her star persona is a site of contestation in the film.

Betz and Diffrient's concern regarding the over-privileging of art-house

auteurs in the episode film is well noted, and yet it has to be said that the structure of *Le streghe* invites us to recognise a hierarchy across the episodes, both
in terms of their respective directors and their positioning. Diffrient rightly
emphasises the importance of structure in the episode film: 'privileged sections tend to come *first* or *last* in the chain of miniature narratives comprising
episode films' (2014: 76).[3] *Le streghe* is bookended by the Visconti and De Sica
episodes, with Pasolini's in the middle. The stylistic separation of 'La terra vista
dalla luna' from the rest of the film is underlined by it even using a different
composer (Ennio Morricone, rather than Piero Piccioni), and Pasolini seems
less interested at this point in Mangano's star persona, the episode seemingly
more of a vehicle for Totò. But there are other reasons why 'La strega bruciata
viva' and 'Una sera come le altre' are given the most privileged positions in
the film, and why they will be my main focus in discussing the film. Both are
highly self-conscious about Mangano's stardom and 'diva' status; both strip
away and then reconstruct her glamour; and both in different ways deal with
the mutability of her image.

Kezich and Levantesi claim that Visconti was 'almost literally bewitched' by
Mangano (2004: 177), an interesting proposition given her 'burning alive' in
their first collaboration. Of Visconti's collaborations with Mangano, only 'La
strega bruciata viva' and *Gruppo di famiglia in un interno* suggest any great
interest in her as anything other than an ethereal presence. It might be going a
bit far to say that 'La strega' is solely about Mangano, as opposed to *divismo*
more broadly, and yet Kezich and Levantesi are not wrong to see barbed references to her relationship with De Laurentiis (Ibid: 176–7) – a photograph of
Mangano's producer-husband resembles Dino, while the narrative plays on the
tension between her desire to have children and his ambitions for her career. In
the critical perception of the episode film, Betz suggests, 'the vision of the director is pitted against the wallet of the producer, who is blamed for the failure
of an auteur's contribution when it has been haphazardly combined with the
others' (2009: location 2852–5). We have already seen, too, how De Laurentiis
is sometimes the elephant in the room in critical estimations of Mangano's
career. De Laurentiis and Visconti were reportedly at odds over 'La strega bruciata viva' (Kezich and Levantesi 2004: 178–9), mainly because the producer
thought it too long and cut it. But by that point, it was perhaps too late to
regard the episode as an act of revenge – it is already a sour take on the diva-
making process. Gloria arrives at a friend's house in Kitzbühel in an attempt
to escape from the pressures of stardom, but she makes the entrance of a diva
– emerging from a car dressed in black and wearing sunglasses. Gloria seems
like a combination of Mangano herself, Sophia Loren and someone a little
more fashionable such as Monica Vitti: 'You're everywhere I look', she is told,
'Every woman wants to look at you' (this was no longer true of Mangano).
Images of her proliferate in magazines (one character holds a picture of Gloria

in front of her face during an attempted seduction), and Mangano is presented in Piero Tosi's high-fashion costumes, most memorably a tight gold dress that comes with a matching helmet-like hat (one of the guests likens her to 'Nefertiti's mother-in-law', a barbed compliment that qualifies her glamour with her age). While wearing her 'Nefertiti' outfit, Gloria performs 'La canzone delle streghe' (The Witches' Song), a sensuous dance during which the camera remains tight on her body (particularly her stomach) and her hands. Cimmino and Masi claim that Mangano performed a similar dance for guests at Villa Catena, the house she shared with De Laurentiis (1994: 103). Whether this is true or not, the dance is the episode's strongest evocation of Mangano-as-diva, displaying a performative aspect of her screen persona that has recurred since *Riso amaro* and *Anna*, and here finds a form that more than matches those iconic sequences, or at least might if it were not cut short. Having placed Mangano-Gloria on a cinematic pedestal during this sequence, the 'burning alive' begins as the dance ends abruptly and prematurely. She faints during the dance (the first sign of the pregnancy that threatens her husband's plan for her career), and the jealous female guests strip away her glamour while she is unconscious – eyes artificially slanted, eyebrows made of mink. She has already been told by one male guest that she is 'a sublime product', like canned meat:

> You're a product, a sublime product – magnificently calculated for the market, though. And the product is the basis of all industry, and thus society. If a saleable product varies in quality, if it changes colour, smells different or changes shape, that means trouble for the producer. The created image must remain the same, or the competitors wake up. ('La strega bruciata viva', *Le streghe*)

If Mangano was De Laurentiis' 'product', she had not been an easy one for him to regulate and calculate for the market; not only had she altered her appearance radically, but she seems to have resisted (albeit passively) the star-making process. And yet Gloria represents a Silvana Mangano that might have been, and probably could easily have been; and her transformations within the episode in some ways resemble Mangano's own. It is at this point that the film starts to strip away the artifice of that product – a diva made out of mink and gold. By the time she is on the phone to her husband, distraught and defeated as he insists on her terminating her pregnancy, Gloria-Mangano is pale and bathed in sweat. But the episode ends with the reconstruction of her glamour as she sits semi-catatonic – even her smile is fake as the corners of her mouth are lifted before she is ready to meet the public again. In some ways, 'La strega' seeks to deny the pleasure of stardom, by interrupting what should be a showstopping set piece ('La canzone delle streghe') and stripping away Mangano's glamour to lay bare the artifice behind it.[4] But it is also part of a package designed to showcase the star's versatility and it is ultimately in the service of that project.

In his discussion of stardom as labour, Paul McDonald raises the question of agency: 'Agency does not presume that stars and moviegoers can freely determine structures of representation or power, only that they can negotiate movements within those structures' (1998: 200). How might we understand the evident paradoxes of Mangano's agency in her own career, clearly circumscribed in many ways and yet allowing a freedom of movement in others, even if only from the commercial power of the producer to the artistic 'vision' of the auteur (and this episode is retrospectively inscribed into that narrative). McDonald cites Emmanuel Levy's contention that stardom is both egalitarian and elitist (ibid.: 196). After her marriage to De Laurentiis, Mangano did not need to work and seems to have preferred not to, but was always assured of work (if sometimes seemingly pressured into it). At the same time, her origins were modest and she was part of a generation of young Italian women for whom beauty pageants and film stardom offered the possibility of celebrity and wealth (although even her early forays into filmmaking as an extra seem to have been motivated more by economic need for work than a desire for celebrity). All of the successful beauty queens turned film stars performed upward mobility in public, but while Loren, Lollobrigida and others stressed their continuing accessibility and ordinariness, Mangano sought to erase her humble origins. Later, she seems to have found other motivations to work – and work independently of De Laurentiis – the cultural capital of working with auteur directors. The Visconti episode's evident ambivalence towards Gloria (if not towards Mangano herself) – witch as monster, witch as victim of the mob – seems to arise partly out of the difficulty of separating the diva's social privilege from a gendered restriction placed on her agency. But part of the episode's fascination also lies in it, too, ultimately being seduced by the star aura.

In 'Una sera come le altre', Mangano plays Giovanna, a frustrated middle-aged housewife with a handsome but dull American husband, Carlo (Clint Eastwood). During a single evening, she tries in vain to reignite his passion while fantasy sequences cast her as a glamorous diva figure worshipped by other men. Mangano is ostensibly de-glamorised again, in horn-rimmed glasses and drab clothes (see Figure 12.2), but this time the disguise is a thinner one because the tone is lighter and her beauty is always evident in the domestic scenes, while the fantasy sequences that comprise nearly half the episode facilitate an even greater array of flamboyant hairstyles and Piero Tosi costumes than in 'La strega bruciata viva', including a comic-book dominatrix outfit with a spiky headpiece. If Visconti's episode is cynical about cinema's diva-making, De Sica's is more playful (if equally reluctant to release its female protagonist from her 'trap' – Giovanna ultimately accepts her domestic

Figure 12.2   Italian cinema's 'marriage' to Hollywood: Clint Eastwood and Mangano in *Le streghe.*

disappointment, reaffirming her love for Carlo as she falls asleep). The references to cinema include the Fellini-esque parade that Giovanna leads from Rome's Via Veneto to the Foro Italico, where she performs a climactic striptease, while Eastwood parodies the image he had only recently fashioned in Italian Westerns (in the English-language version, one of the film titles he reads out in the evening paper listings is *Per un pugno di dollari/A Fistful of Dollars* (Italy/Spain/West Germany 1964)). This relationship can also be taken to represent Italian cinema's failing 'marriage' with Hollywood; while American cinema is characterised by declining phallic potency, Italy is still characterised by fantasy and desire, even if it is fated to be unfulfilled. 'We expect so much from America, and look at this one!' she observes sourly as Carlo snores in his armchair; during her fantasy striptease, Eastwood becomes a black-clad but ineffectual cowboy, shooting into the crowd. Eastwood was a minor American performer transformed by Italian films that reinvigorated the most American of popular genres. Mangano initially emerged out of a meeting of neorealism and an American-oriented popular culture (including its star system). Giovanna's fantasy landscape is shaped by the post-war Italian popular culture that arose out of aspirations for American modernity. One of the most striking sequences has her cavort with comic-book male heroes both American (Flash Gordon, Mandrake the Magician, The Phantom) and Italian (Sadik, one of the masked anti-heroes that followed the 1962 publication of the first *fumetto* aimed at adults, *Diabolik*). Luca Barattoni sees 'Una sera come le altre' as 'a nostalgic hymn to the veterans of Neorealism' (2014: 230). But as Mangano struts along the Via Veneto (each cut finding her in a different outfit with a different hairstyle) or resembles a figure from a Guido Crepax comic book, De Sica's episode also seems nostalgic for the type of diva Mangano might have become.

The episode film format, with its abrupt shifts, tendency towards inconsistency of tone and quality, and its emphasis on 'movement and borders' (Diffrient 2014: 3), is particularly well suited to a film visibly negotiating and contesting a star persona. In the course of *Le streghe*, we witness concerted attempts to reaffirm star power alongside a savaging of the star-making process, the muting of stardom that often accompanies art-house cinema (literally so in this case: Mangano is mute in 'La terra vista dalla luna'), and an affectionate character vehicle directed by a filmmaker (De Sica) who had once dismissed the *maggiorate* as actresses but subsequently played a key role in establishing two of them as credible actors. The film sits oddly in her career, following a group of films that seemed to signal her ambitions to be a character actress and coming just before the more concerted turn to art house. Mangano's subsequent transition into her Visconti-Pasolini career is a historical fact, but *Le streghe* suggests that it was by no means an inevitable one. In this instance, the episode format seemed to mark out a number of potential points of departure for a fascinating, awkward and complex star career.

NOTES

1. After nearly ten years of inactivity, Mangano had a cameo in *Dune* (David Lynch, US 1984) – a film produced by her daughter Raffaella De Laurentiis – and a more substantial role alongside Marcello Mastroianni in *Oci ciornie/Dark Eyes* (Nikita Mikhalkov, Italy/Russia 1987). But for the purposes of this chapter, I am treating Mangano's stardom as that which began with *Riso amaro* and ended with *Gruppo di famiglia in un interno*.
2. While Mangano and De Laurentiis remained married until after the death of their son Federico in 1981, Mangano moved out of the luxurious Villa Catena during this period and took an apartment in Piazza di Spagna in Rome. This again reinforces the impression of the actress gaining her independence.
3. Although, as we have seen, the opening titles seem to privilege the themes of the 'sketches' made by the two less critically celebrated directors.
4. Visconti had stripped back the glamour of an earlier diva in his feature debut *Ossessione* (Italy 1943) in his use of Clara Calamai (who plays a supporting role in 'La strega bruciata viva').

BIBLIOGRAPHY

Austin, G. (2003), *Stars in Modern French Film*, London: Arnold.
Barattoni, L. (2014), *Italian Post-Neorealist Cinema*, Edinburgh: Edinburgh University Press.
Bazin, A. (2011), 'Cruel Naples', in B. Cardullo (ed.), *Andre Bazin and Italian Neorealism*, New York and London: Continuum, pp. 155–62.

Betz, M. (2009), *Beyond the Subtitle: Remapping European Art Cinema*, Minneapolis and London: University of Minnesota Press.

Bondanella, P. (2009), *A History of Italian Cinema*, New York and London: Continuum.

Buckley, R. (2000), 'National Body: Gina Lollobrigida and the Cult of the Star in the 1950s', *Historical Journal of Film, Radio and Television* 20:4, 527–47.

Buckley, R. (2006), 'Marriage, Motherhood, and the Italian Film Stars of the 1950s', in P. Morris (ed.), *Women in Italy 1945–1960: An Interdisciplinary Study*, New York: Palgrave Macmillan, pp. 35–49.

Buckley, R. (2008), 'Glamour and the Italian Film Stars of the 1950s', *Historical Journal of Film, Radio and Television* 28:3, 267–89.

Cimmino, G. and S. Masi (1994), *Silvana Mangano: Il Teorema della Bellezza*, Rome: Gremese Editore.

Cole, G. and P. Williams (1983) *Clint Eastwood*, London: W. H. Allen.

Diffrient, D. S. (2014), *Omnibus Films: Theorizing Transauthorial Cinema*, Edinburgh: Edinburgh University Press.

Egan, K. and R. Thomas (eds) (2013), *Cult Film Stardom: Offbeat Attractions and Processes of Cultification*, Houndmills and New York: Palgrave Macmillan.

Grignaffini, G. (1988), 'Female Identity and Italian Cinema of the 1950s', in G. Bruno and M. Nadotti (eds), *Off Screen: Women and Film in Italy*, London and New York: Routledge, pp. 111–23.

Guériff, F. (1984), *Clint Eastwood,* New York: St Martin's Press.

Gundle, S. (1996), 'Fame, Fashion and Style: The Italian Star System', in D. Forgacs and R. Lumley (eds), *Italian Cultural Studies: An Introduction*, Oxford: Oxford University Press, pp. 309–26.

Gundle, S. (2007), *Bellissima: Feminine Beauty and the Idea of Italy*, New Haven and London: Yale University Press.

Kezich, T. and A. Levantesi (2004), *Dino: The Life and Times of Dino De Laurentiis*, New York: Hyperion/Miramax Books.

King, B. (1991), 'Articulating Stardom', in C. Gledhill (ed.), *Stardom: Industry of Desire*, London and New York: Routledge, pp. 167–82.

Landy, M. (2008), *Stardom, Italian Style: Screen Performance and Personality in Italian Cinema*, Bloomington and Indianapolis: Indiana University Press.

Liehm, M. (1984), *Passion and Defiance: Film in Italy from 1942 to the Present*, London, Berkeley and Los Angeles: University of California Press.

Masi, S. and E. Lancia (1997), *Italian Movie Goddesses: Over 80 of the Greatest Women in Italian Cinema*, Rome: Gremese International s.r.l.

McDonald, P. (1998), 'Reconceptualising Stardom', in R. Dyer, *Stars* (revised edn), London: BFI, pp. 175–200.

Meeuf, R. and R. Raphael (eds) (2013), *Transnational Stardom: International Celebrity in Film and Popular Culture*, New York: Palgrave Macmillan.

Mosley, L. (1950), 'Another Baby's Cry is Heard in That Italian Film Colony', *Daily Express,* 23 February 1950.

Rhodes, J. D. (2007), *Stupendous Miserable City: Pasolini's Rome*, Minneapolis: University of Minnesota Press.

Rocca, S. (2008), *Silvana Mangano*, Palermo: L'Epos.

Schiff, V. (1950), 'Rage of the Continent Hates Acting', *Daily Herald*, 17 February 1950.

Shingler, M. (2012), *Star Studies: A Critical Guide*, London: BFI/Palgrave Macmillan.

Shipman, D. (1989), 'Obituary – Silvana Mangano', *Independent,* 18 February 1989.

Small, P. (2009), *Sophia Loren: Moulding the Star*, Bristol and Chicago: Intellect.

Small, P. (2014), 'The *Maggiorata* or Sweater Girl of the 1950s: Mangano, Lollobrigida, Loren', in P. Bondanella (ed.), *The Italian Cinema Book*, London: BFI, pp. 116–22.

Thomson, D. (2003), 'The Pin-Up of Protest', *The Guardian*, 28 March 2003, http://www.theguardian.com/culture/2003/mar/28/artsfeatures, accessed 21 July 2014.

Vincendeau, G. (2000), *Stars and Stardom in French Cinema*, London and New York: Continuum.

Vincendeau, G. (2013), *Brigitte Bardot*, London: BFI/Palgrave Macmillan.

Vitti, A. C. (2004), '*Riso Amaro/Bitter Rice*', in G. Bertellini (ed.), *The Cinema of Italy*, London: Wallflower, pp. 53–60.

Wood, M. (2005), *Italian Cinema*, Oxford and New York.

Wood, M. (2006), 'From Bust to Boom: Women and Representations of Prosperity in Italian Cinema of the Late 1940s and 1950s', in P. Morris (ed.), *Women in Italy 1945–1960: An Interdisciplinary Study*, pp. 51–63.

PART 7

AT THE MARGINS OF FILM STARDOM

13. 'I WANT JAMES DEEN TO DEEN ME WITH HIS DEEN': THE MULTI-LAYERED STARDOM OF JAMES DEEN

Clarissa Smith and Sarah Taylor-Harman

Preamble

Academic publishing can be a slow process and situations change in the period between writing a chapter and its publication; such is the case here. On 28 November 2015, the Twitter-sphere was set alight by two tweets from porn performer Stoya in which she accused her one-time boyfriend and regular professional partner, James Deen, of having raped her. More corroborating revelations from female performers surfaced over the following weeks. On Twitter and in the blogospheres – the platforms on which his stardom was staged and framed – Deen's reputation as a 'feminist porn star' and playful boy-next-door was trashed and debated. As this book goes to press, the fallout from these revelations is still not settled and the effects of the accusations on Deen, on his career and stardom, are neither clear nor inevitable. In the immediate aftermath, Deen was remarkably silent; a prolific contributor to social media (as this chapter discusses), he has yet to attempt to rehabilitate his reputation – there has been none of the 'abject contrition' that often accompanies the mainstream star/celebrity's fall from grace. Perhaps porn stardom and its commercial outcomes will not require the usual rehabilitation through confession, 'self inspection and public reparation' (Nunn and Biressi 2010: 53). All that remains to be seen and, while it is tempting to rush in with analysis and prognoses, we leave our original discussion here untouched, not least in the expectation that it will form the backdrop to subsequent analyses of the accusers, the accused, the industry and the culture of porn production.

Introduction

Most commentators insist on particular forms of 'talent' as crucial to 'stardom' and, since the physical and acting skills involved in doing sex for camera are rarely acknowledged (Smith 2012), place performers in pornography at the lowest end of the star hierarchy. Porn stars are not accorded the deference given to *real* stars – they are positioned as lacking the class, authenticity, agency and luminosity of the true *star*. While pornography studies have burgeoned in recent years, relatively little attention has been paid to individual performers, with the notable exceptions of Hoang 2004, King 2005, Mercer 2006, Nikunen and Paasonen 2007 and Shelton 2002, whose accounts bring into view the complexities of establishing a marketable persona within this uniquely stigmatised entertainment sector. That the coupling of 'porn' and 'star' precariously balances the salacious and the pejorative, the tragic and the comic, is amply demonstrated in the ways in which the figure of a porn performer such as Linda Lovelace has been constructed in autobiographical, confessional and critical literature.[1]

In thinking about porn stardom, we are, as Su Holmes puts it, 'essentially studying traces of how it is *written about*' (2007: 9). The term 'porn star' most often refers to the female performer, where her renown is understood to rest on the particularities of her bodily presentation – her stereotypically large breasts, big hair and plastic smile – and who, in much critical discourse, simply demonstrates conformity to patriarchy's hegemonic ideal of the available (and through her seeming availability, dirty) woman. In recent years, some female performers have achieved a level of mainstream acceptability, which some commentators see as an effect of 'pornification', turning the porn performer into a celebrity and thence into a role model for young women (Levy 2005; Paul 2007).

For male porn stars, the constructions are just as limited: a recognisable and easily caricatured iconography of rampant masculinity reduced to their penis size, the male performer is often placed under erasure as the faceless substitute for the male viewer (Hardy 1998; Shelton 2002), or he is discursively positioned as the 'man of action' whose place within the narrative and/or *mise-en-scène* is as the 'fucker', pile-driving orgasms out of the woman (Dines 2010). Made to come, *her* body is the primary object of the spectacle, displaying her subservience to *his* big cock. His dialogue is limited to exhortations, his body is large, pumped up and often tattooed. Traditionally paid less than his female co-star, the male performer is rarely the main attraction (at least in pornography aimed at heterosexual audiences). There are, of course, some notable exceptions such as Rocco Siffredi, the 'Italian Stallion', who is revered in his homeland having starred in French film director Catherine Breillat's *Romance* (1999) and *Anatomy of Hell* (2004), as well as coming close in 2015 to winning *L'isola dei famosi* (the Italian version of the TV reality show *Celebrity Survivor*). More generally, though, male talent rarely headlines heterosexual pornography.

In this chapter we examine the multi-layered stardom of James Deen, the straight American performer variously described as the Tom Cruise (Helmore 2012), Daniel Day-Lewis (Ayala 2013) or Ryan Gosling (ABC *Nightline* 2012) of porn. Deen has become a very visible persona in and outside of pornography, creating considerable media speculation about the causes and effects of his popularity, particularly for young women. It is in this 'crossover' that James Deen becomes particularly interesting, as the coupling of pornographic performer and celebrity persona ruptures usual understandings of relations between male stars and their fans.

With a screen name that self-consciously screams 'star', Deen is perhaps rather short at five foot seven to be considered a particularly masculine presence, and with his slim and toned boyish figure he has none of the hyper-musculature and hysterical masculinity associated with the typical male performer. Born Bryan Matthew Sevilla and brought up in Pasadena USA, Deen has been performing in pornographic films since 2004. His porn name is, apparently, a nickname given to him at school in direct homage to film legend James Dean and was earned because of his leather jacket and smoking style. Named 'Male Performer of the Year' by the porn industry magazine *Adult Video News*, he is the youngest, at twenty-two, to have won that award. He has since won many more, and has starred in more than a thousand scenes, working across a range of pornographic genres. Deen has dated at least two high-profile female co-stars; his relationship with Joanna Angel lasted almost six years and he is, at the time of writing, also linked to 'porn princess' Stoya. Deen's professional collaborations include work with WoodRocket.com, a NSFW (not safe for work) website which hosts a number of parody episodes, most notably *Game of Bones* and *SpongeKnob, Square Nuts*, and his non-porn original web series *James Deen Loves Food*, which sees Deen reviewing restaurants, and eating and cooking meals, including the world's most expensive burrito (his meal of choice).

Other high-profile projects include his pornographic scene with reality TV participant Farrah Abraham (of the MTV *Teen Mom* series), which caused controversy when its authenticity as a stolen 'celebrity sex tape' was called into question. Prior to the tape's 'leak' onto the market, Deen was rumoured to be dating Abraham, but he has since asserted this was a ploy on her side to maximise sales of the tape, observing, 'If you're going to make a celebrity sex tape and try to pass it off as an amateur home video, you don't hire a well-known porn star!' (Deen in Majeski, 2013). He also starred alongside Andy San Dimas in the first professional adult video production made with Google Glass, the soft-core and tongue-in-cheek version of which achieved more than a million views on YouTube within twenty-four hours of its release in 2013. Via his JamesDeenStore.com, he also sells his own *Baby Panda* brand of clothing and novelties, plus DVDs of his own productions and other sexual merchandise.

Not content to just take the money and run, Deen is very visible in adult industry activism. Since 2012 he has been campaigning against Measure B (legislation which would require the use of condoms on all porn shoots taking place in California) and his 'public information films' are available on YouTube. Regularly invited to college and university campuses, he has lectured to students on condom use and contraception, relationships and legislation, and frequently blogs at jamesdeen.com on rape prevention and 'sex ed'. In 2014, Deen joined the newly formed *Adult Performer Advocacy Committee* team (APAC works to protect adult film performers' rights, and provides legal representation for performers as well as promoting health and safety protocols for those in the adult industry) as treasurer and then chairperson. Deen also engages in various related charity works and gave 50 per cent of his web profits during October 2014 to breast cancer charities as part of National Breast Cancer Awareness Month.

Outside porn, Deen has produced films, raising funds for the forthcoming *Cowboys and Engines* (a steampunk Western hybrid) and is rumoured to be involved in *Novel*, a conspiracy movie written by Samuel Gonzalez, Jr. This follows his starring role in Paul Schrader's *The Canyons* (2013) alongside Lindsay Lohan. The film, written by Bret Easton Ellis, was almost universally panned by critics, but demonstrated Deen's intentions not to be constrained by his porn biography.

A prolific social media user, Deen maintains a regular blog of his exploits on set, has a highly active Twitter account and has numerous Tumblrs devoted to his work. On 25 June 2014, Deen participated in a Reddit AMA (Ask Me Anything), receiving more than four thousand questions in the course of an hour, making his Reddit appearance one of the most popular ever on the site. There is no doubt that Deen has been an astute and assiduous manager of the opportunities provided by social media, and his use of social media may be an example of what Barry King calls the production of an 'elastic persona' constructed in a 'process of constant rewriting in order to accommodate the fact that past and present personae all occupy a common discursive space' (2003: 45).

While his fan base is understood to be predominantly female, the star is also very popular with men. A favourite of the men's magazine press, Deen was featured in a huge spread in *GQ* in June 2012. The profile attempted to contain Deen within the narrative of the porn star as the stand-in for the heterosexual male, but it also drew upon the trope of the 'born-to-be-porn-star' (Nikunen, Paasonen and Saarenmaa 2007: 25). This mythical construction positions the performer as possessing an innate and natural affinity to the idea of sex, and having the natural proclivities and determination that make the enthusiastic acting of sex on camera conceivable. In a video interview for ABC's *Nightline*, Deen explains:

> [I decided to do porn in] Kindergarten. I remember I was walking home one day, and I found this magazine, I don't know, a *Hustler* or something, with people banging in it. I was enamored by it. I was like, I want to do this. I actually got in trouble in third or fourth grade. They were asking everybody what they wanted to be when they grew up, and I said I wanted to be a porn star. They didn't like that. They thought I was being a dick. I was like, 'I'm not being a dick, it's just what I want to be.'

This mythology is a discourse produced in part by the discursive construction of pornography as a coerced choice. In his description of his heeding a lifelong calling towards the career, Deen emphasises personal determination, choice and agency in direct contradiction of the popular analysis of the porn star as 'damaged' and/or 'degraded'. In the same interview, Deen insists on his choice:

> If I had to do porn, I probably wouldn't enjoy it. I get to do porn. I get to go to set. And I get to, you know, make out with girls. And I get to meet different people. And I get to, you know, experience all of this stuff. It's awesome. I can't think of anything else I would ever want to do or be. (Deen in *Nightline*)

Further, in the *GQ* article he comments, 'That's the thing. My whole life, I've never really found anything else that I've found interesting' (Deen in Tower 2012). In statements such as these, Deen constructs himself as self-actualising, driven, and as recognising the possibilities of a form of employment pursued not for the remuneration, or because he has to, or for the dream of making it into real cinema, or for the fame, but because it is 'interesting'. This is a conception of career which rests on a playful and youthful desire to be kept amused. The emphasis on Deen's work ethic, his investment in the idea of sexual exploration, liberation and/or prowess, disavows the idea of porn as hard work. Of course there are unresolved tensions in his storytelling – elsewhere he has complained about having to work with difficult co-stars, long hours and discomfort – but Deen dismisses any conception of porn as particularly onerous by drawing out its similarities to other forms of employment, for instance working at Starbucks. The narrative which emerges from this and other features is that he's 'just having fun', even if he is prepared to work hard at something other people 'just aren't cut out for'. Thus, in the *GQ* article, author Wells Tower contrasts Deen's being just like any other young man with an appetite for sex against the exceptional elements of his talents:

> we may well owe a debt of gratitude to James Deen. That just as Superman makes plain why the rest of us should not jump off buildings, the extraordinary Deen and his Kryptonian psychosexual constitution illustrate why the ordinary man should not try to peg everything with opposable thumbs. All day, every day, James Deen is fucking the planet senseless so that the rest of us don't have to try to. (Tower 2012)

In keeping with this 'psychosexual constitution' is his film roster: he has performed in 'quality porn' in edgy and hip performances for art-core directors JacktheZipper and Eon McKai, in addition to more 'mainstream' productions such as 'boy next door fucks porn star', and various compilations. His oeuvre includes, but is not limited to: anal;[2] celebrity sex tapes;[3] double penetration;[4] gangbangs;[5] MILFs;[6] oral;[7] porn parodies;[8] star vehicles;[9] and 'teen'.[10] He is also a regular performer for Kink.com in their BDSM productions at the San Francisco Armory, including *Bound Gangbangs*, *Public Disgrace* and *Sex and Submission*, where his slightly geeky, perhaps submissive persona morphs into a more demanding and in-control dominant. In addition, he has recently begun producing his own content, directing twenty-eight titles at the time of writing, including the series *James Deen Seven Sins* (2014) and *James Deen's Sex Tapes* (2013–present), and *Pornoromance* (2014). This brief overview demonstrates that, like most of his established colleagues in pornography, Deen is a prolific performer, not limited to any one genre or studio. His performances in this vast array of titles require the ability to play many differing characters as well as a flexible performance style – MILF productions, for instance, requiring a very different characterisation of 'fucker' from that in a parody of *True Blood* (*Tru: A XXX Parody*, 2010).

This abundance of titles found in a porn performer's repertoire is in direct conflict with the forms of stardom in classic Hollywood star studies. Unlike the Hollywood actor who chooses his or her vehicles carefully to maintain their profile, the porn star who seeks longevity and presence must demonstrate versatility. Yet what sets Deen apart from other performers is his ability to carry a film on his name, and in this he has made the crossover into a layer of porn stardom usually reserved for women and an elite coterie of gay stars where, as Mercer argues,

> the star is deployed as a means to ensure repeat purchase and to act as an indicator of the qualities that are considered of value within the porno-graphic text. (Mercer 2006: 147)

Deen stars in mainstream porn – although as Paasonen (2011) has cautioned, we recognise the particular limitations of such categorising – and crosses over into more esoteric productions of alt.porn and back again into fetish. He isn't simply one kind of performer, he has a sense of humour which is accessible, he has prowess and talent; his macho-ness is understated and he seems genuinely interested in the rewards of pleasure for his female co-stars. What is not to like?

At various levels James Deen is therefore interesting not simply because of his visibility and obvious popularity – he is a celebrity, a brand, and seems to have made the transition from porn to mainstream – but more than that, in the various acknowledgements of his charms Deen seems to have shattered once and for all the cliché that the male porn performer has significance only as a stand-in for the male viewer.

THE MALE PORN STAR: BEYOND THE FLABBY EVERYMAN

As one of us has observed elsewhere (Smith 2012), the popular construction of the male porn star is as a 'cock': his key accomplishment is to produce an erection – the 'prop' for the performance produced by the female star – as is clear from the following observations by legendary porn producer Seymour Butts:

> The most difficult part about being a male porn star is the hard-on. They have to get it up and off on cue essentially and all the while in between maintain [it] for two to three hours. This must be done under the most difficult of circumstances, including not being attracted to their female co-star, having sex in the most uncomfortable settings, i.e. on hard surfaces, cold/hot weather, etc., and/or having to stop frequently for direction or shot setups. They have to be in great shape in order to perform. It all adds up to being the most difficult job in porn, in my opinion. (Butts quoted in Breslin 2012)

The physicality of the male porn star is here reduced to his ability to perform erection, and it has certainly traditionally been a truism that the male in heterosexual porn is never actually *attractive*.

Emily Shelton's 2002 article 'A Star Is Porn: Corpulence, Comedy and the Homosocial Cult of Adult Film Star Ron Jeremy' offers a useful starting point for thinking about the construction of the male porn star in popular media culture. One of porn's most popular and enduring male performers, Ron Jeremy has, Shelton argues, a particular star formation and place within both the pornographic industry and the broader culture at large. With appearances on popular television, cameos in Hollywood comedies, his own brand of rum and other merchandise, Jeremy is arguably the most recognisable and prolific of all male porn performers – writing in 2002, Shelton estimated his film reel at over sixteen hundred features (115). As Shelton observes,

> Ron Jeremy [. . .] remains as popular as ever, no matter how much weight he gains or how much older he gets. He is not just a performer for hire, or even a prominent 'appendage' of the porn industry; Ron Jeremy is an institution in and of himself, a living genre that embodies the generic structure and iconographic purchase of contemporary porn. He is a star and an antistar at the same time. (117–18)

His corporeality, Shelton argues, plays into traditions of Bakhtinian grotesque comedy, reflected in the prominence of the parody genre among his filmography (125–6). Simultaneously (paradoxically?) 'everyday and outrageous', 'overweight' (118), 'unkempt' (118) and 'flamboyantly undesirable' (119), his 'disorderly body' (ibid.) means Jeremy is 'beloved *because* he is repulsive' (119, italics in original). Here desire functions as the need to recognise excess in an Other, problematizing 'the viewer's presumed erotic engagement' (122), and emphasizing 'displeasure' as much as 'pleasure'. Yet Shelton's insistence that this engagement remains 'homosocial' for his 'primary fan base as young heterosexually identified males' (122) closes down the potential for counter-readings that a broader audience theorisation might bring. In her desire to queer Jeremy's straight male fans, and referencing the opening tongue-in-cheek *Beavis and Butthead* exchange – 'Hey, that's the guy in the naked movies at your uncle's house!' [. . .] 'You were watching the *guy*?' (115) – Shelton ultimately rejects the possible *sexual* pleasures and desires female (and gay male) viewers might find in this performer and his texts. As one of the few studies to take heterosexual male porn stardom seriously, Shelton's article is important, but in its focus on Jeremy's physical 'repulsiveness' it also demonstrates a reluctance to acknowledge the specifically sexual *desirability* of the male star's body.

These assumptions draw from a range of critical tools, developed in a pre-digital media studies, which have understood women's bodies as the 'objects' of 'the gaze' (Berger 1972; Dyer 1992; Gabor 1972; Mulvey 1975). Within that research tradition the male star of popular media, television, film and pop music, is understood to offer his female fans the possibilities of romantic fantasy but not *sex*; his sex appeal is rendered safe through romantic gestures, adventurous spirit, and various forms of talent. He may be recognised as 'sexy' (Gabor 1972), but is rarely ascribed an overtly *physical* sexual appeal, partly of course because culture still prefers to believe that women have no active sexual desire and/or interests. Yet in the past two decades, we have most surely entered an era of 'sexualized masculinity' (Mercer 2013), wherein mainstream investments in the body have spilled over from the dominant paradigm of 'men look, women are to be looked at' (Berger 1972), thus exploiting both hetero and homoerotic pleasures and rendering the male body as a site of erotic investment.

This process has been uneven and, as there isn't the space here to trace the various factors which have enabled or created the 'eroticised male' or 'sexualised masculinity', we can make only the following brief observations on its incremental appearance. Cultural commentator Mark Simpson coined the term 'the metrosexual' in the early 1990s to describe the emergence of metropolitan men with developed fashion and beauty sense; he revised the concept a decade later 'as the advertiser's walking wet dream' (Simpson 2002), drawing attention to footballer David Beckham as the eroticised male body par excellence. The metrosexual has since been joined by the 'spornosexual' (Simpson 2014) – a melding of the labels 'sportsman' and 'porn actor' – who isn't just focused on grooming his body but also on presenting his developed musculature and attractiveness in a specifically sexual display. Again, Beckham is the model trope here but his sexual desirability is still, we suggest, premised on an element of disavowal. Underwear advertising lays Beckham's body out as spectacle but it is supine. In its particular stillness his physical *beauty* is eroticised but there is no projection of Beckham as an active sexual *agent* (both on- and off-scene). Unlike the fleshy, physical posing of the porn star, the mainstream male body often keeps its actual performances of sex covert.[11]

Much writing about pornography debates questions of legality, putative harms and sometimes the meanings of its texts, yet when we think about stardom significant lacunae are revealed; we have little or no understanding of porn performance and seem to be shy of understanding the specifically corporeal pleasures of those performers who have been named stars. As John Mercer observes:

> the interplay between the on/screen persona that is regarded as central to discourses surrounding the Hollywood film star is largely, if not entirely, absent in the case of the gay porn star. Unlike the film star, the gay porn star exists almost exclusively *within* the fleshy world of the pornographic text and the accompanying promotional materials that refer to the star's performance in such texts. As a result of this, the gay porn star signifies at the level of textual or 'onscreen' enunciation. (2006: 148)

In his highlighting of porn stars' restricted circulation *within* the fleshy world of porn, Mercer is specifically referring to gay performers and writing almost a decade ago. As the Internet provides more opportunities for access to and interactions with performers, there are those whose existences increasingly exceed the screen.

The porn star's body is always already saturated in sex and the ability to perform it. Where non-porn stardom is framed through the promises of desire, imagination and photographed in seductive poses, the porn star has already dispensed with decorum and revealed the absolute fleshiness of their allure. Where film (and pop) star fans are assumed to daydream of romance with their idol, the fan of the porn star has moved beyond the chaste to carnal knowledge of every inch of his skin, even if only via the screen.

'I WANT JAMES DEEN TO DEEN ME WITH HIS DEEN'

Thus, for us, it is important to recognise the very corporeality of the porn star James Deen (see Figure 13.1), and to do so is to reject any idea of him as a subcultural anti/hero among legions of male fans navigating supposedly problematic homosocial or homoerotic heterosexuality. Not least because Deen's most visible fans are female, and who seem to have no difficulty in articulating their avowedly sexual interests in Deen.[12] On discussion boards across the web, Deen's penis *is* a matter of fascination: commentators debate the size of his cock – is it really as long as 9 inches or is that measurement just another example of pornography's penchant for hyperbole and excess?[13] – and young women also express their interests in experiencing his penis (or 'Deen', as above) for themselves. Even so, he is not reduced to just his appendage. Alongside those questions, Deen's other attractions are remarked upon both by fans and more casual viewers alike:

> A big part of it is that he's actually good looking, in a way that appeals to a lot of women including myself. Handsome face, skinny but very fit, young boy-next-door thing going on. This is not too typical in straight porn.[14]

> While I may not sit around watching porn specifically because I think a particular actor is hot, many (if not most) guys I see in porn actively turn me off. They're oily and brotastic, and they say stupid, annoying things. I think a lot of women like James Deen in part because he looks like a normal (if very attractive) person that we wouldn't mind running into in a bar. He's a hot Everyman, not a glistening gym rat that can't go 2 minutes without insulting a woman.

His ordinariness, his almost mundane charms, are important to fans and are often played to full effect in his performances, especially perhaps in videos categorised as MILF (Mother I'd Like to Fuck). Deen plays the boy-next-door who gets lucky (often because his co-star's 'husband' is uncaring, has had too much to drink, can't get it up, and so on), and his youth, innocence and curious domesticity are emphasised. Central to his characterisation, his lithe and youthful body is attractive to the woman. However, these

Figure 13.1 Deen celebrated by his fans.

films also present him as an autonomous sexual adventurer: Deen may be seduced by the older woman but as the sexual play progresses he begins to orchestrate the sexual performance, aggressively fucking his paramour. In interviews, Deen also draws attention to his personal style of performance:

> My whole point is that because of the on-camera sex, I have this insane style of stunt sex. It actually is very physically strenuous. It's a good workout. All the positioning and weird things. (Deen in Bradley 2013)

His 'insane style' is recognised by commentators as mould-breaking, pushing beyond the stereotype: thus Lambert suggests that Deen challenges the 'sexual everyman, a guy who embodies the anxiety and awkwardness and fear of rejection drilled into so many American men during their teenage years' (Lambert 2012).[15]

Perhaps this is not unusual, but any idea that Deen is simply the stereotypical macho fucker is offset by his intensely intimate gazing into his partner's face, his enthusiastic kissing of her mouth and clitoris, and his inaudible whispering into her ear. Barring BDSM scenes where they are arguably de rigueur, Deen doesn't do a lot of the barked commands or obscenities that might be considered a part of mainstream pornography, and often his whispered words will result in a grin or an enthusiastic laugh from his co-star. All these elements of his performances are discussed as appealing and as 'authentic' by fans:

> He's hot, and he seems like he's really in to it. It's genuine, and I find that attractive. He makes and maintains eye contact, he can be sensual, funny, rough, he says sexy things that aren't just textbook 'porn' talk, and he kisses his partners genuinely. A lot of times watching a scene with him doesn't feel like it's porn – it's two people having sex and actually enjoying it.

We should be clear though that Deen's performances do not conform to the rather anemic porno-romance of some 'made for women' productions,[16] and his style of caress, squeezing, touching and penetration remains 'high octane'. His popularity among female fans might therefore suggest that for some women that style is distinctly pleasurable.

HIS POPULARITY MAY BE DEEPLY DISTURBING . . .

This chapter is not simply about recognising that 'star studies' have avoided engaging with porn performers. We also wish to draw attention to the ways in which the star can come to embody cultural anxieties. As pornography has become more accessible, affordable and anonymous with the rise of the net, heterosexual performers *have* made inroads into offscreen worlds, and fears about the 'influence' of the porn star have also been on the rise. In a news report for ABC, Juju Chang opined that James Deen could become a household name, while her colleague Cecilia Vega worried that

> Today the voracious unstoppable American porn industry [. . .] has now targeted and reached a new demographic [. . .] teenage girls. Evidence of that? Deen has become something of an Internet sensation with fans much younger than eighteen. A fact many parents might find disturbing. (ABC *Nightline*)

In this news report we see the anxieties writ large elsewhere that pornography is, and by implication should remain, a separate area of culture in part due to its being populated by 'bad' men and 'degraded' women who might infiltrate and contaminate 'proper' pop culture to become the wrong kind of role models for teens (see Figure 13.2). It is precisely Deen's ordinariness and lack of obvious pornographic signifiers that renders him potentially worrying for parents:

> [H]e is so *normal* and kinda doesn't look like he belongs in a world where macho is king and bigger is best. (ABC *Nightline*)

Drawing on Holmes' work on mainstream celebrity, the ABC news programme 'demonstrates precisely a celebrity dramatizing contemporary social discourses of the time, and thus having a useful discursive function in this respect' (2007: 13). The point, then, is that in news reports such as these, Deen has been used to articulate a new set of worries about the ways in which pornography and its protagonists refuse to remain in the shadows. As the reporters worry about new audiences, Deen's appeal to teenage girls and his crossover into the 'mainstream', we can observe anxieties about the control of female desire, especially as Deen's fans are utilising social media to take their interests public:

> on Tumblr, a network of teenage bloggers has emerged to turn the focus on him. The young women trade Deen videos, post candid photographs, and pluck out all the minute details that turn them on. (ABC *Nightline*)

This condemnatory mode of commentary links fan activity to broader concerns about sexualisation and particularly the young woman's embrace of '"raunch culture" wherever she finds it' (Levy 2005). Young women's appropriations of the symbols of commercial sex become therefore worrisome indications that the sex industries have commodified and debased female sexuality.

James Deen:

♈︎♀︎ 2

Yummy Mr Deen

Figure 13.2 The circulation of images of Deen includes humour.

The pessimistic views of sex being 'debased' by its contacts with 'porn sex' and 'porn culture' (Malz and Malz 2008) combine fears about addiction, child abuse, commercial sex and casual sex, as though these were all not only related but also uniformly problematic. All this is exacerbated by Deen's presence on fan sites and his enthusiastic communications with fans.

Deen has made full use of the Internet's possibilities for opening up participation in a network of like-minded sexual subjects, and it is surely this that Deenagers have begun to engage in through their online interactions, wherein fans construct communities, actions and subjectivities via message boards, blogs and Tumblrs. Not simply limited to the circulation of imagery of Deen (see Figure 13.2), their exchanges have allowed for new practices of intimacy with their chosen star and, crucially, with each other; and, as Hester, Jones and Taylor-Harman (2015) have noted, swapping expressions of desire for Deen, their fandom and its online iterations have also allowed for what Attwood termed 'new forms of [sex] which disrupt older conceptions of its status and its place in society' (Attwood 2006: 79). Such interactions clearly complicate existing concerns around youth, and in particular young *female* sexuality and desire.

To understand this phenomenon will require more research and consideration of female sexualities and their materialisation in culture beyond the scope of this chapter, but the Deenager phenomenon begins to indicate the complexities of sexualisation, commodification, objectification and, crucially, subjectification in his fans' expressions of appreciation for Deen, and their hedonistic pursuits of him via Internet exchanges and in their own sexual imaginings.

Conclusion

The porn performer has historically appeared to stand outside of other understandings of stardom but this reflects the burden of political and cultural significance still carried by the 'porn star', the ambiguities and tensions this figure inspires rather than what they mean for their own fans. In this chapter we have tried to draw out some of the ways in which James Deen as porn star embodies a mode of masculine (hetero)sexuality premised on desirability, his symbolising more than the size of his dick, and the ways in which Deen's social media presence taps into new cultures of intimacy with and through star fandom. For parents and the hyperventilating press, Deen signifies as the carrier of the dangers of sexualisation; for hipster men in *GQ* he's the priapic god who stands in 'for the poor guy who can't get it up' or 'can't get it on as often as he might like', but also a 'good-time mate' who is just like them; to the industry, Deen is a poster boy, not an elaborate joke like Ron Jeremy (though this is not all Ron Jeremy was or is).

What does he represent for teen girls, however? We'd suggest that his performances in his sex scenes offer a version of masculinity which avoids the most stereotypically macho elements understood as the sine qua non of pornography and which is desirous of female pleasure; his youth, boy-next-door good looks and social media accessibility all offer a particular articulation of the desirable male which is not premised on adulation from afar.

Notes

1. *Inside Linda Lovelace* (1974) and *Ordeal* (1987).
2. *Anal Aspirations 8* (2008) and *9* (2008), *Anal Plungers* (2012), *Elastic Assholes 7* (2008) and *8* (2009).
3. *Farrah Superstar: Backdoor Teen Mom* (2013) and *Farrah 2: Backdoor and More* (2014).
4. *DP Me Baby 3*, *4* and *5* (all 2008), *DP My Wife With Me 1* (2013), *2* (2013) and *6* (2014).
5. *Gangbang Auditions 16* (2005), *18* (2005), *19* (2006), *20* (2006), *21* (2006), *22* (2007) and *26* (2013), *Gangbanged 2* (2011), *3* (2012), *4* (2012) and *5* (2012).
6. *Cheating Housewives 4* (2007), *Cougar Club 1* (2008) and *2* (2009), *Mommy Is a Milf 2* (2007), *3* (2007), *4* (2008) and *6* (2009).
7. *Blow Jobs Gone Wild 2* and *3* (both 2005), *Swallow The Leader 3* (2006) and *Suck It* (2009).

8. *Batman XXX: A Porn Parody* (2010), *Dallas: A XXX Parody* (2012), *Death Proof: A XXX Parody* (2012), *Elvis XXX: A Porn Parody* (2011), *Family Guy: The XXX Parody* (2012), *Scrubs: A XXX Parody* (2009).
9. *Everybody Loves Sara Sloane* and *Everybody Loves Sasha Grey* (both 2013).
10. *Badass School Girls 1* (2006), *Barely 18 22* (2005) and *26* (2006).
11. See John Mercer's (2013) fascinating discussion of the enigmatic nature of sexual desire and the male body.
12. Of course, not all fans, viewers or audiences of James Deen are either female or heterosexual: research into his male and/or LGBTQI* audiences would be fascinating.
13. See, for example, the discussion on gay gossip site Datalounge, http://www. datalounge.com/cgi-bin/iowa/ajax.html?t=12407225#page:showThread,12407225, accessed 1 April 2015.
14. All fan comments here from Reddit discussion available at: http://www.reddit.com/ r/AskWomen/comments/1sgotl/for_girls_who_watch_porn_what_is_so_special_ab out/, accessed 1 April 2015.
15. Observers also suggest that Deen challenges another stereotype in his constant references to his religion, replacing the 'cliché of the sexually passive Jewish man that still pervades our popular culture, replacing it not with its anti-Semitic mirror-image, that old chestnut about insatiable Hebrew lust, but with an image of unself-conscious, upbeat, healthy male sexuality' (Lambert 2012).
16. Deen has produced and starred in two films using the title *PornoRomance*. That these are not the kind of soft-core that typifies 'made for women' porn is demonstrated in the synopsis for the sequel: 'Just how filthy can love-making be? If you think romance is all about passionate kisses and making love on a bed of roses, you haven't seen PornoRomance! James Deen orchestrates some of the roughest, hardcore, vile sex on film, shown in a highly erotic tone that complements the intense perversion. James' co-star, Dana Vespoli and supporting cast, Penny Pax, Holly Hannah, Judas, and Holly Heart learn fuck romance isn't all about flowers and chocolates. Sometimes, the passion of a good, merciless, filthy pummel says "I love you" best. The girls get throat fucked, choked and dominated, slapped, callously penetrated, and pounded in the ass. *PornoRomance 2* will have you rethinking what it means to be "romantic."'

BIBLIOGRAPHY

ABC *Nightline* (2012), 'James Deen: Wholesome-Looking, Boy-Next-Door Is Porn's Hottest Star', presented by Cecilia Vega, 2 February, http://abcnews.go.com/Entertain ment/james-deen-wholesome-boy-door-porns-hottest-star/story?id=15499092#.T1d 0vNFWo6w, last accessed 21 April 2015.
Attwood, Feona (2006), 'Sexed Up: Theorizing the Sexualization of Culture', *Sexualities* 9:1, 77–94.
Ayala, Nelson (2013), 'Zach Braff Calls James Deen the Daniel Day-Lewis of Porn', XBIZ.com, 6 March, http://newswire.xbiz.com/view.php?id=160267, last accessed 21 April 2015.
Berger, John (1972), *Ways of Seeing*, London: BBC.
Bradley, Bill (2013), 'The James Deen Workout', *GQ*, 30 April, http://www.gq.com/ how-to/rest-of-your-life/201304/james-deen-porn-star-workout-guide, last accessed 21 April 2015.
Breslin, Susannah (2012), 'The Hardest Thing About Being A Male Porn Star', *Forbes*, 23 April, http://www.forbes.com/sites/susannahbreslin/2012/04/23/the-hardest-thing-about-being-a-male-porn-star/, last accessed 21 April 2015.

Dines, Gail (2010), *Pornland: How Porn Has Hijacked Our Sexuality*, Boston, MA: Beacon Press.

Dyer, Richard (1992), *Only Entertainment*, London: Routledge.

Gabor, Mark (1972), *The Pin-Up: A Modest History*, London: Pan Books.

Hardy, Simon (1998), *The Reader, the Author, his Woman, and her Lover: Soft-core Pornography and Heterosexual Men*, London: Continuum Intl Pub.

Helmore, Edward (2012), 'James Deen: The Tom Cruise of porn', *The Guardian*, 8 March, http://www.theguardian.com/film/2012/mar/08/james-deen-porn-star-hollywood, last accessed 1 May 2015.

Hester, Helen, Bethan Jones and Sarah Taylor-Harman (2015), 'Giffing a fuck: non-narrative pleasures in participatory porn cultures and female fandom', *Porn Studies* 2:4, 356–66.

Hoang, Nguyen Tan (2004), 'The resurrection of Brandon Lee: The making of a gay Asian American porn star', in Linda Williams (ed.), *Porn studies*, Durham, NC: Duke University Press, pp. 223–70.

Holmes, Sue (2007), '"Starring . . . Dyer?": re-visiting star studies and contemporary celebrity culture', *Westminster papers in communication and culture* 2:2, 6–21.

King, Andrew (2005), 'Reconciling Nicci Lane: The "Unspeakable" Significance of Australia's First Indigenous Porn Star 1', *Continuum: Journal of Media & Cultural Studies* 19:4, 523–43.

King, Barry (2003), 'Embodying an elastic self: the parametrics of contemporary stardom', in Thomas Austin and Martin Barker (eds), *Contemporary Hollywood Stardom*, London: Arnold, pp. 29–44.

Lambert, Josh (2012), 'James Deen vs. the *Nebbishes*', *Los Angeles Review of Books*, 21 October, http://lareviewofbooks.org/essay/james-deen-vs-the-nebbishes, last accessed 21 April 2015.

Levy, Ariel (2005), *Female Chauvinist Pigs: Women and the Rise of Raunch Culture*, New York and London: Free Press.

Lovelace, Linda (1973), *Inside Linda Lovelace*, New York: Pinnacle Books.

Lovelace, Linda and Mike McGrady (1987), *Ordeal: An Autobiography*, London: Random House.

Majeski, Ashley (2013), 'James Deen: I refused to pretend to date "Teen Mom" Farrah', *Today*, 12 April, http://www.today.com/popculture/james-deen-i-refused-pretend-date-teen-mom-farrah-1C9316819, last accessed 21 April 2015.

Malz, Wendy and Larry Malz (2008), *The Porn Trap: The Essential Guide to Overcoming Problems Caused by Porn*, New York: HarperCollins.

Mercer, John (2006), 'Seeing is Believing: Constructions of Stardom and the Gay Porn Star in US Gay Video Pornography', in Sue Holmes and Sean Redmond (eds), *Framing Celebrities: New Directions in Celebrity Culture*, London: Routledge.

Mercer, John (2013), 'The enigma of the male sex symbol', *Celebrity Studies* 4:1, 81–91.

Mulvey, Laura (1975), 'Visual Pleasure and Narrative Cinema', *Screen* 16:3, 6–18.

Nikunen, Kaarina and Susanna Paasonen (2007), 'Porn star as brand: Pornification and the intermedia career of Rakel Liekki', *The Velvet Light Trap* 59:1, 30–41.

Nikunen, Karrina, Susanna Paasonen and Laura Saarenmaa (eds) (2007), *Pornification: Sex and Sexuality in Media Culture*, Oxford: Berg.

Nunn, Heather and Anita Biressi (2010), '"A trust betrayed": celebrity and the work of emotion', *Celebrity Studies* 1:1, 49–64.

Paasonen, Susanna (2011), *Carnal Resonance: Affect and Online Pornography*, London: The MIT Press.

Paul, Pamela (2007), *Pornified: How pornography is transforming our lives, our relationships, and our families*, London: Macmillan.

Shelton, Emily (2002), 'A star is porn: corpulence, comedy, and the homosocial cult of adult film star Ron Jeremy,' *Camera Obscura* 17:3, 115–46.

Simpson, Mark (2002), 'Meet the metrosexual', *Salon.com* 22, 1–6.

Simpson, Mark (2014), 'The metrosexual is dead. Long live the "spornosexual"', *The Telegraph*, 10 June, http://www.telegraph.co.uk/men/fashion-and-style/10881682/The-metrosexual-is-dead.-Long-live-the-spornosexual.html, last accessed 21 April 2015.

Smith, Clarissa (2012), 'Reel intercourse: Doing sex on camera', in Claire Hines and Darren Kerr (eds), *Hard to swallow: Hard-core pornography on screen*, New York: Columbia University Press, pp. 194–214.

Tower, Wells (2012), 'The Well-Hung Boy Next Door', *GQ*, July, http://www.gq.com/entertainment/celebrities/201207/james-deen-porn-star-gq-june-2012-interview, last accessed 21 April 2015.

14. CELEBRITY CREATURES: THE 'STARIFICATION' OF THE CINEMATIC ANIMAL

Stella Hockenhull

Uggie, who plays Jack the dog in Hazanavicius' 2011 film *The Artist*, is a constant companion to his master, George Valentin (Jean Dujardin). Frequently filmed in close-up looking out to the camera, and often playing the key protagonist motivating the plot, Jack is a significant character in the film. Throughout the narrative, the spectator is led to believe that the dog cares for the man's welfare, and that he instigates romantic encounters between George and the female love interest in the film, Peppy Miller (Bérénice Bejo). Not only does Jack appear as a loyal and devoted friend to his owner, but at one point he rescues him from a burning house, thus saving the man's life.

As expected, the success and press coverage of the film resulted in huge acclaim for its canine star: Uggie received a special mention for his performance at the Prix Lumière Awards in France, won the Palm Dog Award at the 2011 Cannes Film Festival and the golden collar award in LA. He shared the Best Animal Performance prize awarded by the *Seattle Times* with Cosmo, who performed as Arthur in Mike Mills' film *Beginners* (2011). In addition, fans mounted a campaign entitled 'Consider Uggie' to enable the dog's nomination for an Acting Academy Award in his own right, although he was not eligible – the award is only appropriate for humans. Accordingly, Uggie might be perceived as a star through his various accolades, and is indubitably afforded this status by the press and the industry. Also, arguably he produces a stellar performance through his heroic activities. While star studies has made a significant theoretical contribution to film studies over the past thirty years, and has been important in offering a variety of methods for understanding what constitutes a star, nonetheless, rarely, apart from critical reviews contemporaneous to the release of the films, has the animal been mentioned or awarded judicious attention in academic publication. Furthermore, invariably, the analysis of stardom in film is confined to the study of humans and, by extension, human performance. Using Uggie in *The Artist* as a case study, this chapter introduces the notion of animal as star, and analyses the ways in which media, publicity and the film language promote the animal to what Emmanuel Gouabault, Annik Dubied and Claudine Burton-Jeangros (2011) term 'super-individual' status.

STAR SCHOLARSHIP AND FILM STUDIES

Star studies has operated as a branch of film studies since Richard Dyer's seminal work, *Stars* (1979). Dyer constructed a comprehensive theory of stardom comprised of star power, the role of publicity, the non-desirable aspects such as scandal and gossip which the studios needed to control and, finally, stars as symbols of morality. As Martin Shingler suggests, Dyer's study 'broke new ground in providing a methodology for studying stars through a combination of semiotics and sociology' (2012: 20). While Dyer's influential work has formed the basis for humans as stars, it does not encompass the concept of non-humans, despite the fact that animals such as Trigger and Lassie are long-established screen celebrities, and animal stars have been in existence for a long period of time. As David Giles observes, '[t]he concept of animal celebrities is hardly new. As early as the 1920s Hollywood made stars of dogs such as Stubby, the American war dog promoted to the rank of sergeant during World War I, and Strongheart the German shepherd (Silverman 2001), followed later by Rin Tin Tin and Lassie' (2013:116). Although Dyer's work does not apply to animal case studies, his concepts are transferable into a framework for the analysis of animals as star constructs.

More pertinent to the notion of non-human animals as stars, however, is the work of Dyer's predecessor, French philosopher and sociologist, Edgar Morin. His work focused on the mythical aspects of venerated film individuals, and this concept is more easily translated into a framework for animal analysis. As early as 1957, in his pioneering study *Les Stars*, Morin argued that stars functioned as myths within contemporary urban society, and he perceived their role as a response to cultural change in post-war France. Morin's work, in particular, describes the notion of stars as valued public individuals, and, moreover, as *monsters sacrés* (sacred monsters). He suggests that the star film gave way to the film star, and that these new luminaries 'spring from their characters as heroes or heroines' (Morin 2005: 6). For Morin, the idols become gods and goddesses with mythic and divine status, yet they are also normal beings participating 'in the daily life of mortals: they are no longer inaccessible:

they are mediators between the screen-heaven and earth' (2005: 23). This is a reciprocal arrangement: the star infects the character and the character infects the star. As Morin suggests, the mythic quality is a tension between the actor and the role they play, and the star takes precedence over the character they are performing. As he observes, the myth occurs as

> an ensemble of imaginary situations and behaviours. These behaviours and situations may have as their protagonists superhuman beings, heroes, or gods [who] attempt to deliver mortals from their infinite misery [. . .]. The star is the actor or actress who absorbs some of the heroic – that is, divinized and mythic – substance of the hero or heroine of the movies, and who in turn enriches this substance by his or her own contribution. (Morin 2005: 29–30)

The star therefore becomes the icon of the audience, and this mythical, divine status which Morin refers to can also be conferred on animals. As he observes, 'The star is above all an actress or an actor who becomes the subject of the myth of love, to the point of instigating a veritable cult' (Morin 2005: 30).

Other desirable attributes, consistent with Morin, are 'an *adorable* [original italics] face and body' (2005: 30–1). According to Morin, the way that the star is lit, and the angle and pose adopted, contribute to their superhuman and cult status. While this description and treatment is appropriate for humans, and beauty in whatever form is deemed a necessary quality, in animals this is more difficult to define. Steve Baker approaches this by initiating a discussion on the desired appearance of an animal; he suggests that charm emanates from specific physical features. Writing in 2001, he proposes, what he terms 'the "aaah" factor . . . the preferred *look* [original italics] of the animal body' (Baker 2001: 181). Baker quotes Elizabeth Lawrence, who notes that the favoured form for an animal is youthful qualities which include a 'high and slightly bulging forehead, large brain case in proportion to the face, big eyes, rounded cheeks, and short, stubby limbs' (Baker 2001: 181). The appearance of rotund configurations, and short squat legs in an animal in its adult form, is termed neoteny, and this semblance is frequently adopted by doll and toy manufacturers, and, not surprisingly, Disney cartoonists.

It is not only looks that define the star, but, as noted, Morin suggests that the star is also idealised as heroic, and he aligns moral and corporeal beauty whereby a flawless body mirrors perfection from within. Indeed, for Morin,

> The star is profoundly good, and this cinematic goodness must be expressed in her private life as well [. . .]. The idealization of the star implies, of course, a corresponding spiritualization. Photographs often

show us the star busy painting under the inspiration of the most authentic talent, or else crouching in front of his bookshelves to consult some handsome volume whose splendid binding guarantees the spiritual value. (2005: 37–8)

Hence, for Morin, the star's personal life is public – and the star belongs to the public.

He also notes that the other side of the star phenomenon is the fans (fanatics): 'Fan clubs are the chapels in which particular passions are raised to a frenzy' (Morin 2005: 58). Further, he explains that gossip columns and journalists are more interested in the stars than the films, and these enable the fan to understand the star, thus gaining possession of some intimacy and confidence. The star is regularly photographed by the press, and this might adopt the form of official and unofficial media coverage. Such images are important in giving clues, enabling familiarity and, in more extreme cases, mimicry.

Animal as superindividual

Although Morin's assertions can be positioned in relation to animals, in a similar vein to Dyer, his contentions introduce the concept of the star as primarily a human construct. Alternatively, the notion of animal stardom has been extensively researched and mooted by media sociologists, Emmanuel Gouabault, Annik Dubied and Claudine Burton-Jeangros (2011). Using the term 'superindividuals', Gouabault et al. argue that animal figures have become increasingly personified in Euro-American information media and, moreover, are frequently described as human characters, given human names, and their feelings and thoughts described in some detail. Even in wildlife films, they suggest, the animal is usually anthropomorphised and it is this anthropomorphic treatment which permits such starification.[1]

Ranking the presentation of animals on a number of levels of intensity, Gouabault et al. commence their analysis with the image of the singular animal in the media which is bestowed little or no background information, progressing to the individualised animal with some personal history, before culminating with the superindividual, which refers to 'the most developed stage of personification, in which a process of starification is applied to the animal' (2011). Categorising elements of personification identified as human attributes further blurs the boundaries between human and animal, and this personalised centrality aids emotional connection and intimacy on the part of the spectator.

Gouabault et al. list the criteria for the most developed stage of humanisation as context, speaking, individual name (often human-like), individual history, national or territorial identity, interiority, mediatisation and starification. As

they suggest, 'In the media discourse, such an animal is attributed two qualities: on the one hand, it is like everybody (having a daily life with emotions,
difficulties, etc.), while on the other hand it is a hero, inaccessible and fascinating. The superindividual is like a model, embodying specific values'
(Gouabault et al. 2011). With each level more human attributes are associated
until the borders between human and animal are blurred. Gouabault et al.'s
research is based on an empirical analysis of Swiss media articles about Knut,
a polar bear cub. Born at Berlin Zoo, the animal received a substantial amount
of interest from the press because he was abandoned by his mother at birth,
and was subsequently reared by his keeper. Gouabault et al. afford Knut the
status of superindividual because he became 'an international narrative, and
the little bear's figure became emblematic, to be used as a trademark and a
symbol for environmental campaigns' (2011). This type of representation
is typically favoured in film to encourage sentimentality and, invariably, the
animal attains celebrity status as a result.

UGGIE AS SUPERINDIVIDUAL: PUBLICITY AND PROMOTION

To apply the above to Uggie in order for him to meet the criteria for such a
celebrity status, he must be charming, appealing and endearing, leading to the
'aaah' factor. Furthermore, to conform to Gouabault et al.'s notion of a superindividual, he must be described as a human character, given an individual
name, national or territorial identity and history (personality, biography,
preferences, desires), and his feelings and thoughts described in some detail
(remembering, understanding, believing). Nowhere is Uggie's status more
evident than in the surrounding discourse and the films in which he stars.
For example, writing in *The Independent* following the release of *The Artist*,
Rhiannon Williams headlines her article 'Canine star of "The Artist"' (2012),
accordingly verbally providing Uggie with an immediate luminary status.
Williams is not, however, commenting on the dog's performance in the film
itself, but on the launch of his autobiography, which was penned for him by
the writer Wendy Holden. Uggie's story is told from a first-person perspective
whereby he discusses his life using his real name (rarely is he referred to as
Jack). Additionally, the animal also provides an individual account of his life,
supplying background information and a personal history about his puppyhood and upbringing. As Holden in the guise of Uggie explains: 'I was born an
Aquarian in February 2002 [. . .] I can recall very little about my puppyhood.
I think I met my father once when he came to sniff dispassionately at me and
my sprawling siblings' (2012: 2). The book, therefore, endows the reader with
intimate knowledge of Uggie. He is imparted a birth sign; it is suggested that
he emanates from a deprived upbringing with an absent and neglectful father;
and to further personify him, Williams' article is illustrated with a photograph

of its canine author looking out to the camera, his paw placed over the cover in hand-like fashion to suggest that he has written it himself.

Further references to Uggie's human qualities ensue from Williams' report. Uggie is described as a lovable individual who has won 'the hearts of millions' (2012). Moreover, the article suggests that he is the creator responsible for the content of the work, but that human help is at hand to 'channel' his thoughts via his owner. Describing his humble beginnings, and his current status as one of the most recognised canines in the world, Uggie is personified, and Williams' descriptions fulfil Gouabault et al.'s criteria of the superindividual animal. Uggie also follows the ritual of undertaking a signing at Waterstones book-shop in Kensington High Street, where he 'arrived to meet his fans' (Williams 2012). To add to Uggie's endearing qualities, Williams also makes suggestion of a romance between Uggie and Reece Witherspoon, proposing that they developed a relationship when filming *Water for Elephants*:[2] as she notes, 'So enamoured was he with Witherspoon, he dedicated his book to her. "For Reece, my love, my light"' (2012). Quoting Uggie's owner, Omar von Muller, Williams notes that, 'He was crazy about Reece. One of the only people I've ever seen distract Uggie was her' (2012).

If Holden's book and Williams' comments empower Uggie with the ability to write, and an individual name and history, Sarah Anne Hughes of *The Washington Post* provides him with the gift of verbal communication. Here, Hughes discusses how Uggie makes an acceptance speech at this year's Golden Collar Awards, her review displaying an image of the dog seated on a red carpet, his mouth slightly open as though speaking. The article also mentions that 'he helped announce the nominations with his "Artist" co-star Penelope Ann Miller (And by helped, I mean he barked adorably on cue)' (Hughes 2012).

Other newspaper articles also encourage Uggie's personification. Tom Lamont, writing in *The Guardian*, entitles his article 'Uggie: "He Likes to Fly First Class"' (2012), the accompanying image depicting Uggie lying propped up on a bed covered in crisp white sheets, supported by a lacy pillow. Gazing at the camera, his face appears rounded, his eyes large, all factors which mobilise Baker's notion of the 'aaah' factor for the spectator. Accompanied in the photograph by his owner, von Muller, the animal retains centre focus, and the article confers him with human qualities and activities, ascribing him the thought processes of understanding, preferences and desires. Indeed, as the headline testifies, Uggie, in line with his human counterparts, has a predilection for the high life, enjoying first-rate treatment:

> He flies between engagements in first class – 'He's a celebrity' says trainer Omar von Muller. 'He's paid for his seat so shut up', that's what we tell [the airlines]. Travel, nonetheless, takes its toll – Uggie descends from

the mattress, stretching on to a pouffe at the foot of the bed. He flaps a forepaw feebly, like an ailing patient. Then he rolls on to his side, limp, making everybody watching sigh and coo. Uggie's a *ham*. [original italics] (Lamont 2012)

Not only does the article infer that Uggie has jetlag, it also comments on his acting ability, suggesting that he put in 'great performances' in the film. Uggie is granted superindividual status: he has a history, the capacity to write books, fall in love with humans and also watches television, favouring certain programmes (the reader is informed that Uggie watched *Loose Women* in bed after a 'draining promotional tour' (Lamont 2012).

Later, in the same article, Uggie is given the accolade of 'experienced thesp' (Lamont 2012), a sign of public recognition for his acting. He is described as having to audition for the part, but the suggestion is that in truth he possesses an innate ability which he brought to the performance: quoting Uggie's owner again, Lamont reports: 'most of the tricks in the movie, like falling backwards, or hiding his face – they were used because the director saw Uggie do them – they were not in the script. Hire Uggie and you get a performer who not only works for cheese-flavoured popcorn but who can sharpen a screenplay too' (Lamont 2012).

In a similar vein, *The Hollywood Reporter* documents Uggie as the first dog to put his paw prints in the cement at Grauman's Chinese theatre, a space usually reserved for human stars. He is also on Twitter, where he reputedly regularly retweets, and his account shows images of himself with Johnny Depp, the latter holding his hands up in paw-like fashion to imitate a dog begging, a 'selfie' with a number of other dogs superimposed in the background, and an 'Uggie The Artist app' with Judy Dench superimposed onto a dog's body. (It should be noted here that Uggie was euthanised in August 2015 after developing a prostate tumour.)

The above are only a few examples of the many articles and plethora of publicity in circulation, and the terminology used in these, accompanied by the activities reputedly undertaken by Uggie, project him as a stellar personality. Additionally, he has a charming face and popular appeal conforming to Baker's notion of neoteny. Rarely is Uggie referred to as a dog and, even when his owner discusses his predilections and activities, the inference is that he has human characteristics. Uggie has a following despite the legitimacy of some of the claims and, as Giles points out, 'it is not necessary for audiences to work through the dilemmas of authenticity/contrivance and real/false in order for them to display continued interest in following a specific celebrity' (2013: 117).

UGGIE AS HERO: ANIMAL SCREEN PERFORMANCE

If the publicity surrounding Uggie leads to his celebrity status, then, as with humans, his onscreen performance offers a further route to the cementation of his star status. As Paul McDonald (2004) notes, screen performance is a vital ingredient of understanding the unique contribution of the star to their roles, and this includes aspects such as gesture, movement, voice and facial expression. The problem that McDonald perceives, however, is 'what will count as significant in performance?' (2004: 26). He suggests that by analysing intonation and body in brief and fleeting moments it is possible to discern idiosyncrasy through 'micromeanings, the significance of which affects a film as a whole' (McDonald 2004: 32). More noteworthy for this study, however, is what McDonald argues is the irrelevance of the intentionality of the actor; as he purports, 'it does not matter how the details got there, only that they are there and seem significant' (2004: 32). Prior to McDonald's work, James Naremore, writing in *Acting in the Cinema* (1988), proposes that there is a distinction between performances which create a sense of a fictional character, termed representational, while those that eclipse the character are termed presentational. He also distinguishes between three aspects of characterisation: role in terms of the fictional character, actor as the being performing the character, and star image, which he suggests is an intertextual occurrence derived from the actor's previous roles. For Naremore, stars become associated with a gamut of performance signs recognisable by the audience (Uggie's previous roles include *What's Up Scarlett* (Caldarella, 2005), *Wassup Rockers* (Clark, 2005), *Mr Fix It* (Ferriola, 2006) and Francis Lawrence's adaptation of Sara Gruen's novel, *Water for Elephants* (2011), in the role of Queenie). Therefore, Uggie produces a performance which creates a fictional character: he is Uggie performing Jack, and he has a star image derived from his previous roles (although it is unlikely that the spectator will make these connections).

To apply performance theory to animal acting is complex, partly because the spectator cannot know what the animal thinks or feels, and interpreting animal actions requires specialist knowledge. However, despite this, it is possible to discern 'micromeanings' in Uggie's presentation and to analyse the ways in which his actions create significance in the narrative.[3] One useful example occurs towards the end of *The Artist*. As a result of his career problems, the impoverished George is forced to sell all his possessions and live in a small apartment. He has been unable to gain work acting because he cannot make the transition from silent cinema to sound (he has a foreign accent unsuited to English-speaking roles), and he subsequently falls into a depression. In a drunken rage as a result of his lowly position, he sets fire to his entire film collection and, as smoke engulfs the room, the camera cuts to a close-up shot of

Figure 14.1   Uggie as mythical and heroic character.

Uggie seated in his basket. Turning his head slightly to one side to look at the camera, the dog's eyes are bright and enquiring.

As stated by Morin, to designate Uggie as starified creature, his character should possess mythic and heroic qualities which signal dialectic between actor and role; ultimately the star takes precedence over the character they are playing. The narrative circumstances in this instance are that Uggie must save his master by attracting outside attention. As though realising the danger, Uggie races from the house and, from a rear-view shot, he is seen running speedily along a walkway, darting between various different startled onlookers. Halting at the side of a policeman, and now framed in close-up, he barks while simultaneously gazing upwards[4] (see Figure 14.1); the policeman, however, remains impassive, seemingly unable to comprehend that the dog is alerting him to George's plight. A medium shot reveals the two side-by-side, the policeman expressionless and immobile, and Uggie seated, but head directed upwards and towards the man as though listening. This creates an interaction between human and animal. At one point the policeman, becoming agitated with what appears to be the animal's strange and inexplicable behaviour, motions him to stop barking. Uggie lies down on the pavement in an act of submission. Having witnessed George's predicament, the spectator understands from this action that the dog is trying to inform the policeman of his master's danger and, urged by a bystander to pursue the animal, the man follows, finally reaching and rescuing George from the burning house. George is dragged to safety from the building, whereby the dog subsequently nuzzles his face as though to revive his master.

Narrative plausibility is constructed from the way in which this scene is shot, but arguably Uggie's performance also creates emotional identification for the spectator. The animal has clearly been instructed for the part, and Uggie's trainer explains what took place in the sequence:

> We shot the fire scene over many days in a few different locations. I worked all the exterior scenes because Omar [Uggie's owner] was out of the country during that time. To get Uggie to go to the cop and really evoke that frantic energy, I had to be super exuberant and really keep my energy at a 10 at all times. We shot the pant-leg part and the play-dead part in a few pieces, and each time, I would pattern him. When he ran into the smoky house, I was inside calling him as loud as I could and squeezing squeaky toys. I grabbed him just before the cop came charging through because the smoke was so thick that he couldn't see either. It was challenging. (Clifford 2012)

Throughout the scene the audience is asked to identify with the dog through close-ups of Uggie's face, his eyes wide open and his head turned to the camera. Here he operates to create what Naremore describes as a fictional 'representational' character and, framed in this way, he is perceived as loyal, heroic and endearing, and the spectator is mobilised to believe that he carries out courageous deeds.

Uggie's behaviour is therefore cohesive within the fictional world of the film and, while it is impossible to discern whether animals act in character (and the likelihood is that they do not), it is also reasonable to argue that he possesses individual discernible traits – a point, as above noted, reinforced by Uggie's owner.[5] If, as Naremore suggests, 'The performer, the character, and the star are joined in a single, apparently intact, image so that many viewers regard people in movies as little more than spectacular human beings like found objects or dada art, magnified by the camera' (1988: 157), then Uggie's character as hero, his brave personality and stellar performance are also intertwined. Indeed, Uggie successfully fulfils Morin's criteria by attaining heroic, mythic and divine status while remaining accessible and participating in normal life. Naremore also argues that the actor must adjust their style to perform his or herself; in other words, the actor never loses sight of the real person that they are and their presentation relates back to their own technical expertise, as well as performance abilities and star image. Uggie, aged nine at the time of making the film, has certain performance abilities and proficiencies and has achieved a signature style – an idiosyncratic set of gestures, movements and postures, along with a gamut of individual behavioural patterns, facial nuances and

Figure 14.2   Uggie has a signature style which contributes to his image.

tricks which constitute his technical capabilities and contribute to his performance and his star image[6] (see Figure 14.2).

Returning to the narrative, subsequent to the fire, George falls into a coma
and is removed to Peppy's house for nursing care. Eventually he awakens, the
dog lying by his side. A little later in the sequence the dog accompanies his
master downstairs. Stopping at the doorway of a large dining room, Uggie
appears to refuse to move. Seen from a rear view, he barks while simultaneously looking upwards to George. His posture is tense and alert, and he
displays a rigid type of pose, his ears pricked and face turned towards his
master – a repetition of his earlier behaviour with the policeman. At this junc-
ture, he turns away and trots towards the camera before disappearing from
sight offscreen. George remains in frame for some seconds before moving in
the same direction, presumably following his pet. Moving towards the camera,
the man's puzzled expression appears in close-up, before a further edit shows
Uggie facing partially away from the camera barking, while intermittently
turning his head towards his master. George subsequently opens the door to
reveal a room cluttered with his own furniture and clothing, but covered in

dustsheets, and it is revealed that Peppy has purchased all his possessions and has, in fact, been helping him all along.

In the next sequence, on making this traumatic discovery, an agitated George returns to his room and rapidly dresses before signalling to Uggie that they are leaving. The dog glances upwards to his face, before the two depart through the front entrance of the house. Eventually, after wandering the streets, they enter George's old apartment where the fire took place. Uggie remains seated while his master walks slowly around the room. Peppy, in the meantime, arrives home to find him gone and realises the mistake she has made in attempting to deceive him. The camera intercuts between Peppy's discovery of her lover's absence and George seated at an old desk in his burned-out apartment. Here, Hazanavicius displays the man and dog in the frame together, and in the ensuing last few moments of the scene the distraught George places a gun to his mouth, and images of his distressed face are intercut with shots of Uggie barking at his owner. As per script, the animal then grabs George's trousers and tugs back-wards. A further edit reveals George's distress before cutting to Uggie, who is now standing erect, his front paws on his master's knee, barking emphatically at his owner. However, George does not yield to suicide, although the sound of a gunshot is heard (presumably from outside). At this point, Uggie plays dead at the sound of the blast. This occurs as the animal, seated on his haunches, gazes at the camera, before twisting to one side and falling to the floor where he remains inert. 'Playing dead' is part of Uggie's repertoire of performance signs and this action is not scripted. Not only does this feat generally indicate canine submission, which moreover forms part of the dog's gamut of social behav-iour, it is also a component of Uggie's performance inventory.[7] Thus, spectator understanding is enabled through the demarcation of the frame, the set of nar-rative circumstances, the problem to be overcome, the actions taken by Uggie to achieve the objective, and the tactics or beats involved in the process.

While Giles argues that 'animals can never be held responsible for their celebrity status' (2013: 117), undeniably, in this sequence Uggie's individuality ascribes him cultural value. This is a point supported by Philip Drake (2004),[8] who argues that, while star routines are ostensive and associated with a reper-toire of performance signs, there might also be elements of spontaneity which are involuntary or appear to be unmotivated. Drake places more emphasis on the spectator, whose recognition of their favourite star's individual practices ascribes cultural importance to a particular performance. In other words, many stars have recognisable individual mannerisms and traits which are embraced and understood by the spectator, at least those already familiar with their specificity of style.

Arguably, in light of the above, Uggie can be classed as a superindividual. He is given heroic qualities in the film and he is personified by the press. In the numerous articles written about him, he is humanised, his opinions and thoughts expressed for him through the descriptions that abound. Also he is idealised and exalted, all his activities championed.

CONCLUSION

If indeed it is possible to ascribe star status to animals, then this raises important ethical considerations on anthropomorphism, animal celebrity ownership and welfare. Indeed, the notion of animal as star is not without its problems: this concept does not allow for anything other than personification which, historically, has a troublesome past because it doesn't permit the animal its own speciesism or positive otherness. Additionally, fandom and the creation of animal as superindividual encourage mimicry. With the animal fan in particular, possession of the same breed or animal is considered desirable, and there are associated problems with this. This concern is exemplified in an article in *The Guardian* which expressed disquiet over the surge in demand for Jack Russell terriers following the release of the film. For example, subsequent to the British Academy Film and Television Awards in 2012, this breed became the second most popular type of dog in the country to require rehousing from Battersea Dogs and Cats Home (Insley 2012). Moreover, celebrities, whether human or animal, are property. Although it seems ridiculous to suggest ownership of a person, contractual agreements between celebrities and media companies reveal that their images are constantly licensed, and decisions about who owns the rights to images are in regular debate. This type of commercial arrangement is an industry in its own right: as Graeme Turner argues,

> [t]he development of the celebrity's public profile, then, is a serious business and it is usually placed in the hands of a third party – most often a manager [. . .] Ideally, this third party has a long-term interest in the celebrity's commercial success. After all, their own income is linked to their effective management (and protection) of the celebrity's personal and commercial interests. (2012: 193)

In terms of animals, ownership is more specific, and this might be deemed more problematic in terms of ethical implications. Clearly Uggie is property yet cannot speak for himself. He was retired once because of exhaustion, brought back to work in *The Campaign* (Roach) in a cameo role in 2012, and continued to make guest appearances at public events.

Despite the above concerns, equally there are positive aspects of humanising animals. In a recent study published in the *Journal of Experimental Social Psychology*, Max Butterfield, Sarah Hill and Charles Lord argue that anthropomorphism need not necessarily be derided, and the emphasis on the human attributes of animals leads to improvements in animal welfare. As they suggest,

[t]here is little doubt that descriptive language is powerful. History is replete with examples in which dehumanizing language and animal-themed caricatures (e.g. referring to Jewish people as rats) have been used to justify genocide, subjugation and other atrocities [. . .] Given that *dehumanizing* language is often associated with the mistreatment of fellow human beings, we hypothesized that the reverse might also be true, that anthropomorphic, *humanizing* language might encourage beneficent action towards non-humans. [original italics] (2012: 957)

In sum, Uggie has proved a fruitful example to study the notion of animal as star, and these same arguments could be used in a number of other instances deploying those paradigms laid out by Morin and Dyer. Indeed, to return to Morin, the mythic quality of Uggie is the dialectic between him and his role as Jack, although, as seen through the press reviews, Uggie takes precedence over his character in the end. Not only has star theory been revisited using non-human animal in place of human, but Dyer and Morin's arguments have been taken further by including performance in the equation. This opens up debates concerning animal acting and intentionality within a framework of performance theory and critical animal studies, thereby offering a more inter-disciplinary approach to star theory.[9]

NOTES

1. Simultaneously, they note the emergence of the representation of animals in the media as threat or danger. This polarisation provides two avenues for analysis: in the case of the superindividual it gives rise to a growing anthropocentrism – the treatment of animal as personified and human construct – whereas the notion of the animal as dangerous reinforces its bestial characteristics and hence creates a desire for distance. Gouabault et al. also note another trend, which is the idealisation of certain wild and endangered species which become flagships of all threatened animals. Sometimes these are creatures previously considered pests, yet through their starification they become a cause, whereby the media focuses on their private lives.
2. Uggie played a bitch named Queenie in *Water for Elephants* (Lawrence, 2011).
3. See Brenda Austin-Smith (2012).
4. The screenplay actually suggests that the dog 'takes hold of the cop's trouser leg with his teeth and tries to pull him towards George's house' (Hazanavicius 2011).
5. See Pick (2011a; 2011b) and Weil (2012). Also, this is a perspective adopted by David Williams (2000) in his work on Théâtre Zingaro.
6. For example, in *Water for Elephants* the circus men meet after a performance and ask Queenie (Uggie) to perform tricks. Uggie falls to the floor playing dead in a similar repertoire to his actions in *The Artist*.
7. For further reading on animal behaviour, see Vicki Hearne (1986).
8. Drake is writing about the actor Jim Carrey's work, but his ideas are readily transferable to the notion of animal performance. See Drake (2004).
9. See Austin-Smith (2012) and Hockenhull (2015).

BIBLIOGRAPHY

Austin-Smith, Brenda (2012), 'Acting Matters: Noting Performance in Three Films', in Aaron Taylor (ed.), *Theorizing Film Acting*, New York and London: Routledge.

Baker, Steve (2001), *Picturing the Beast*, Urbana and Chicago: University of Illinois Press.

Butterfield, Max, Sarah Hill and Charles Lord (2012), 'Mangy Mutt or Furry Friend? Anthropomorphism Promotes Animal Welfare', *Journal of Experimental Social Psychology* 48, 957–60.

Clifford, Sarah (2012), 'For Your Consideration: Uggie', http://thebark.com/content/your-consideration-uggie, last accessed 25 September 2013.

Drake, Philip (2004), 'Jim Carrey: the cultural politics of dumbing down', in Andy Willis (ed.), *Film Stars: Hollywood and Beyond*, Manchester and New York: Manchester University Press.

Drake, Philip (2012), 'Who Owns Celebrity?: Privacy, Publicity and the Legal Regulation of Celebrity Images', in Sean Redmond and Su Holmes (eds), *Stardom and Celebrity: A Reader*, Los Angeles, London, New Delhi, Singapore and Washington, DC: Sage.

Dyer, Richard (1979), *Stars*, London: British Film Institute.

Gouabault, Emmanuel, Annik Dubied and Claudine Burton-Jeangros (2011), 'Genuine Zoocentrism or Dogged Anthropocentrism? On the Personification of Animal Figures in the News', *Animalia* 3:1, http://www.depauw.edu/site/humanalia/issue%2005/gouabault.html, last accessed 26 January 2014.

Giles, David G. (2013), 'Animal Celebrities', *Celebrity Studies* 4:2, 115–28.

Hazanavicius, Michel (2011), 'The Artist: Best Original Screenplay', www.pages.drexel.edu/~ina22/splaylib/**Screenplay-Artist,_The**.pdf, last accessed 30 June 2015.

Hearne, Vicki (1986), *Adam's Task*, New York: Vintage Books.

Hockenhull, Stella (2015), 'Horseplay: Equine Performance and Creaturely Acts in Cinema', in Barbara Creed and Maarten Reesink (eds), Special Edition 'Animals', *NECSUS: European Journal of Media Studies*, http://www.necsus-ejms.org/portfolio/spring-2015_animals/.

Hughes, Sarah Anne (2012), 'Uggie, "The Artist" Dog, Nominated for Two Golden Collar Awards', *The Washington Post*, 19 January, http://www.washingtonpost.com/blogs/celebritology/post/uggie-the-artist-dog-nominated-for-two-golden-collar-awards/2012/01/19/gIQAftG6AQ_blog.html, last accessed 29 May 2013.

Insley, Jill (2012), 'The Artist Star Uggie Unleashes Jack Russell Craze', *The Guardian*, 22 February, http://www.theguardian.com/lifeandstyle/2012/feb/22/the-artist-uggie-jack-russell-craze, last accessed 2 October 2013.

Kilday, Greg (2012), 'The Artist's Uggie to Plant His Paws in Cement at Grauman's Chinese Theatre', http://www.hollywoodreporter.com/news/artist-uggie-grauman-chinese-cement-339354, last accessed 29 May 2013.

Kirby, Michael (2011), 'On Acting and Non Acting', in Phillip Zarrilli (ed.), *Acting (Re) Considered*, Abingdon: Routledge.

Lamont, Tom (2012), 'Uggie: "He Likes to Fly First Class"', *The Observer*, 9 December, http://www.theguardian.com/film/2012/dec/09/uggie-dog-the-artist-memoirs, last accessed 29 May 2013.

McDonald, Paul (2004), 'Why Study Film Acting?', in Cynthia Baron, Diane Carson and Frank P. Tomasulo (eds), *More than a Method*, Detroit: Wayne State University Press.

Morin, Edgar (2005), *The Stars* [translated 1972 by Richard Howard], Minneapolis and London: University of Minnesota Press.

Naremore, James (1988), *Acting in the Cinema*, Berkeley, Los Angeles and London: University of California Press.

Pick, Anat (2011a), *Creaturely Poetics*, New York and Chichester: Columbia University Press.

Pick, Anat (2011b), 'Interview with Anat Pick, Author of Creaturely Poetics Columbia University Press', http://www.cup.columbia.edu/static/pick-interview, last accessed 11 May 2012.

Ridout, Nicholas (2006), *Stage Fright, Animals and Other Theatrical Problems*, Cambridge: Cambridge University Press.

Sanders, Clinton R. (1999), *Understanding Dogs: Living and Working with Canine Companions*, Philadelphia: Temple University Press.

Schechner, Richard (2002), *Performance Studies: An Introduction*, London and New York: Routledge.

Shingler, Martin (2012), *Star Studies: A Critical Guide*, London: British Film Institute.

Stacey, Jackie (1994), *Star Gazing: Hollywood Cinema and Female Spectatorship*, London and New York: Routledge.

Turner, Graeme (2012), 'The Economy of Celebrity', in Sean Redmond and Su Holmes (eds), *Stardom and Celebrity: A Reader*, Los Angeles, London, New Delhi, Singapore and Washington, DC: Sage.

Weil, Kari (2012), *Thinking Animals: Why Animal Studies Now?*, New York: Columbia University Press.

Williams, David (2000), 'The Right Horse, the Animal Eye – Bartabas and Théâtre Zingaro', *Performance Research* 5:2, 29–40.

Williams, Rhiannon (2012), 'Canine star of The Artist Uggie launches his autobiography', 26 October, *Independent Online*, http://www.independent.co.uk/arts-entertainment/books/news/canine-star-of-the-artist-uggie-launches-his-autobiography-8259770.html, last accessed 14 August 2013.

THE CONTRIBUTORS

Guy Austin is Professor of French Studies at Newcastle University. He is a specialist in contemporary French cinema – especially stardom and genre – and in Algerian cinema. He is the founding director of Newcastle's Research Centre in Film and Digital Media. Among his publications are the books *Stars in Modern French Film* (2001), *Contemporary French Cinema* (1996/2008), *Claude Chabrol* (1999) and *Algerian National Cinema* (2012). He is currently researching the representation of the Algerian civil conflict of the 1990s in Algerian documentary film.

Linda Berkvens has received a PhD in Film Studies from the University of Sussex. Her PhD focused on the creation of Hollywood's female star images, using a case study of Barbara Stanwyck's career, popularity and agency. She is currently working as an independent researcher, writing on film history, stars and the film industry. She has previously taught various courses on star studies, and film and media studies at the University of Sussex. She regularly provides introductions to film screenings in the Netherlands.

Pam Cook is Professor Emerita in Film at the University of Southampton. She is author of numerous publications on gender in cinema, and editor of *The Cinema Book* (1985), now in its third edition. Her research spans feminism and film, moving image history, national cinemas, visual design, authorship, stardom and performance. Her book-length study of Nicole Kidman as global star phenomenon was published in 2012, and she has recently extended her work into videography. Her video essays can be viewed on her website: http://profpamcook.com/video-essays-2/.

Elisabetta Girelli is Senior Lecturer in Film Studies at the University of St Andrews. Her research has recently focused on stardom and performance in silent film; her latest and forthcoming publications include essays on Rudolph Valentino, John Gilbert and Erich von Stroheim. She is currently working on issues of gendered emotions and performance in relation to the Polish/Hollywood star Pola Negri. Future projects are likely to centre on the actor Ivan Mozzhukhin, a star in czarist Russian cinema and later in France.

Stella Hockenhull is Reader in Film and Television Studies at the University of Wolverhampton. She gained a PhD in the correlation between film and painting in British wartime cinema in 2006 and has published widely in the field, including two monographs. Her more recent research focuses on animal representations in film and television, on which she has presented at a number of national and international conferences. Her publications include 'Horseplay: Equine Performance and Creaturely Acts in Cinema' in *NECSUS: Special Edition* edited by Barbara Creed and 'Horseplay: Beastly Cinematic Performances in Steven Spielberg's *War Horse*' in *Screening the Non Human Animal.*

Leon Hunt is Senior Lecturer in Film and TV Studies at Brunel University. He is the author of *British Low Culture: From Safari Suits to Sexploitation* (1998), *Kung Fu Cult Masters: From Bruce Lee to Crouching Tiger* (2003), *The League of Gentlemen* (2008) and *Cult British TV Comedy* (2013), and co-editor of *East Asian Cinemas: Exploring Transnational Connections on Film* (2008) and *Screening the Undead: Vampires and Zombies in Film and Television* (2013). He is currently writing a monograph on the film *Danger: Diabolik.*

Kiranmayi Indraganti teaches film across undergraduate and PhD programmes at Srishti Institute of Art, Design and Technology, Bangalore, India. She has authored a book for Oxford University Press on playback singing and song production (2016). Kiran has a PhD in Film Studies from the University of Nottingham and an MFA in film production from York University, Toronto. As a filmmaker, she has screened her documentaries at various forums, including Ethnografilm Festival, Paris 2014 and Mumbai International Film Festival (MIFF) 1998 and 2006.

Jaap Kooijman is Associate Professor in Media Studies and American Studies at the University of Amsterdam. His articles on American pop culture have been published in journals such as *The Velvet Light Trap, The Journal of American Culture, Post Script, Journal of International Education, GLQ, Celebrity Studies* and *[in]Transition: Journal of Videographic Film & Moving*

Image Studies. He is the author of *Fabricating the Absolute Fake: America in Contemporary Pop Culture* (revised and extended edition, 2013), editor of *European Journal of Cultural Studies* and co-founding editor of *NECSUS: European Journal of Media Studies.*

Michael Lawrence is Reader in Film Studies at the University of Sussex. He is the author of *Sabu* (2014), the editor of *Indian Film Stars* (forthcoming 2017) and the co-editor, with Laura McMahon, of *Animal Life and the Moving Image* (2015) and, with Karen Lury, of *The Zoo: Images of Exhibition and Encounter* (2016).

Anna Malinowska is Assistant Professor in Literary and Cultural Studies at the Institute of English Cultures and Literatures, University of Silesia, Poland. Her research interests embrace cultural theory, popular culture, material culture and love studies, but specifically focus on the formation of social and cultural norms, cultural narratives, and the social-aesthetic codes of cultural production. Her publications include journal papers and chapters in English and Polish, and books: *Materiality and Popular Culture. The Popular Life of Things* (with Karolina Lebek, 2016), *The Materiality of Love. Essays of Affection and Cultural Practice* (with Michael Gratzke, 2017), *The Aesthetics of Camp. Post-Queer Gender and Popular Culture* (2018).

Lisa Purse is Associate Professor of Film in the Department of Film, Theatre and Television at the University of Reading. She is the author of *Digital Imaging in Popular Cinema* (Edinburgh University Press, 2013) and *Contemporary Action Cinema* (Edinburgh University Press, 2011), and has published widely on genre cinema, digital aesthetics and the relationships between film style and the politics of representation in mainstream cinema.

Clarissa Smith is Professor of Sexual Cultures at the University of Sunderland. A founding co-editor of the Routledge journal *Porn Studies*, her research is focused on representations of sex and sexuality, their production and consumption. Publications include numerous articles and chapters exploring the specificities of pornographic imagery, forms of stardom, production and regulation. She is also particularly interested in consumption of pornography and how different audiences engage with and make sense of sexual representations.

Sarah Taylor-Harman is presently completing her PhD in Screen Media at Brunel University, London, on the subject of Female Desire, Subjectivity and Masochism and the adaptations of *Story of O*. Her research interests and publications topics include gender and sexuality, adaptation, 'bad' cultural products, queer theory, feminism, pornography and BDSM. She is also an editorial board member of the Routledge journal *Porn Studies*.

Niamh Thornton is Reader in Latin American Studies at the University of Liverpool. She is a specialist in Mexican film, literature and digital cultures with a particular focus on war stories, gendered narratives, star studies, cultures of taste and distributed content. She has published widely. Her books include *Revolution and Rebellion in Mexican Cinema* (2013), *International Perspectives on Chicana/o Studies: This World is My Place* (2013) and *Memory and Trauma in Mexican Visual Culture* (forthcoming 2017).

Yiman Wang is Associate Professor of Film and Digital Media at University of California, Santa Cruz. She is the author of *Remaking Chinese Cinema: Through the Prism of Shanghai, Hong Kong and Hollywood* (2013). Her articles/chapters have appeared in journals like *Film Quarterly, Camera Obscura, Quarterly Review of Film, Video and Literature/Film Quarterly, Positions: East Asia Cultures Critique, Journal of Chinese Cinemas* and numerous edited volumes. She is currently working on two book projects, one on Anna May Wong and the other on animality in cinema.

Sabrina Qiong Yu is Senior Lecturer in Chinese and Film Studies at Newcastle University. Her research and publications focus on stardom and performance, Chinese independent films and film festivals, and transnational Chinese-language cinema. She has published widely on stars/stardom, including her monograph *Jet Li: Chinese Masculinity and Transnational Film Stardom* (Edinburgh University Press, 2012, 2015) and articles/chapters on Chinese stardom, transnational Chinese stardom and acting/performance. She helped to launch a translation series on star studies with Peking University Press (China) in 2010 (Richard Dyer, *Stars*; Leon Hunt, *Kung Fu Cult Masters*; Rachel Moseley, *Growing Up with Audrey Hepburn*) and translated Hunt's book.

Yingjin Zhang is Distinguished Professor and Chair of Department of Literature at University of California, San Diego. His English recent books include *Cinema and Urban Culture in Shanghai* (1999), *Screening China* (2002), *Chinese National Cinema* (2004), *From Underground to Independent* (2006), *Cinema, Space, and Polylocality in a Globalizing China* (2010), *Chinese Film Stars* (2010), *A Companion to Chinese Cinema* (2012), *New Chinese-Language Documentaries* (2015), *A Companion to Modern Chinese Literature* (2016) and *Filming the Everyday* (2017).

INDEX

Note: *italic* signifies illustration

within the sex scenes in *Lust, Caution*, 54, 55, 58
local stardom, 17–18
Loren, Sophia
  dance scenes, 244, 245
  Hollywood career, 247, 248
  Ieri, oggi, domani, 244, 250, 251
  L'oro di Napoli, 246
  as maggiorate actress, 240, 243
  producer-husband, 242
Luhrmann, Baz, 30, 33, 36, 37
Lust, Caution (Ang Lee, 2007)
  Chinese film title, 55–6
  Leung's portrayal of Mr Yee, 52–5, 58–9, *59*
  liminality of dark play in, 52–3, 55, 56–7
  off screen performances, 56
  performance as protest, 57–8
  reception in China, 55, 56
  sex scenes in, 54, 55, 58
  Wang Chia-chih character, 53, 55, 56, 57

magazines
  Beyoncé on *Time* cover, 105
  black women on covers of fashion magazines, 115–16
  construction of star personas, 31–4
  Nicole Kidman's fashion shoots, 31–4
Magnani, Anna, 250
Mahogany (Berry Gordy, 1975)
  black–white dichotomy of race in, 113
  Diana Ross as Mahogany, 112–13, *114*
  Mahogany as the exotic other, 115
  montage sequence as makeover from black to white, 113–14
Majumdar, N., 2, 85
male stars
  action heroes, 162–3
  ageing and masculinity, 5–6
  fan curation of images, 12
  hero's entry, Indian cinema, 94–5
  lack of academic scholarship on, 50
  political careers of, 87, 95
  of pornography, 10, 262–3, 267–9
  roles for older men, 150

  see also action cinema; Clift, Montgomery; Cruise, Tom; Deen, James
Mangano, Silvana
  Anna, 242, *243*, 244, *244*, 246
  appearance modification, 240–1, 242
  career, 240–2, 245–7, 254
  career with Dino De Laurentiis, 240, 241, 242, 247–8, 252, 254
  as cult star, 241
  dance scenes, 243–5, *244*
  duality of, 242–3
  in *L'oro di Napoli*, 246
  as a *maggiorate*-type female star, 240, 241, 245, 246, 254
  Mambo, 242, 243, 244–5, 249
  Riso amaro, 240, 242–3, 245, 247
  Visconti films, 248–9, 252
  see also Le streghe/The Witches
Manovich, L., 208, 212–13
marginal stardom
  animal stars, 3
  camp and, 189, 190, 194
  of ethnic stars, 4, 67, 71
  of pornography stars, 10
marketing
  celebrity endorsements, 132–3
  commercials, 37–8
  commodification of stardom, 25–8
  promotional materials as texts, 26
  of star brands in Bollywood, 132
Martin, Dean, 228, 229, 234, 235, 236, 238
masquerade
  acting as, 8–10, 26, 36
  ageing as, 5–6
  appearances as, 6–7
  camp as, 10–13
  ethnicity as, 4
  notion of, 3
  stardom as, 3
mass media
  and commodification of stardom, 25
  construction of star personas, 27, 40–1
McDonald, P., 11, 163, 254, 286

YouTube (*cont.*
  conventional archive materials, 216
  convergence culture on, 207
  curation and networks, 216–17
  as digital archive, 205–6, 220
  divergence of content, 207
  music-/performance-orientated vids, 216
  patterns in star texts, 218–20
  professional-amateur divides, 217–18
  research methodology for, 212–13

  star texts of Mexican cinema stars, 208–9
  temporality of, 208
  vidders, 211
  vids on female stars, 219
YouTubers, 211–12

Zhang Ailing (Eileen Chang), 53–4, 55, 57, 58
Zimmerman, P. R., 218